PERCEPTION
—
AN APPROACH TO PERSONALITY

By

ROBERT R. BLAKE

Associate Professor of Psychology
The University of Texas

and

GLENN V. RAMSEY

Professor of Psychology
The University of Texas

in collaboration with

FRANK A. BEACH

URIE BRONFENBRENNER

JEROME S. BRUNER

NORMAN CAMERON

WAYNE DENNIS

ELSE FRENKEL-BRUNSWIK

ERNEST R. HILGARD

GEORGE S. KLEIN

ALFRED KORZYBSKI

JAMES G. MILLER

LOUIS J. MORAN

CLIFFORD T. MORGAN

CARL R. ROGERS

THE RONALD PRESS COMPANY ⁄ NEW YORK

PRINTED IN THE UNITED STATES OF AMERICA

PREFACE

This book presents the view that the study of perceptual activity provides a basic approach to an understanding of personality and interpersonal relations. Perceptual activity supplies the materials from which the individual constructs his own personally meaningful environment. This concept is employed in this volume as the frame of reference for interpreting and interrelating data from many diverse fields of personality investigation.

The advances being made in the perceptual approach to personality at a dozen different research centers are here combined in organized form. Following a general orientation to this approach, the book discusses the physical and chemical determinants of perception, the social and developmental factors which influence the individual's perceptual activities, and the role of perceptual constructs in unconscious processes, behavior pathology, and psychotherapy. So fruitful has been the impact of the perceptual approach upon the investigation of personality organization that, in the authors' view, it provides the means for constructing a comprehensive theory of personality.

In addition to the total contribution which the studies included in this book make to perceptual theory in the field of personality, each one records recent thinking and developments in the particular area which it covers. Throughout the book it is evident that the perceptual approach lends itself to the formulation of testable hypotheses in the field of personality research.

The thirteen papers comprising this volume were delivered in substance at the 1949-1950 Clinical Psychology Symposium held at the University of Texas, an undertaking which received financial support from a grant awarded by the National Institute of Mental Health of the United States Public Health Service. The book itself is an outgrowth of the Symposium, which was organized and directed by Robert R. Blake and Glenn V. Ramsey.

In the effort to achieve continuity and integration of the discussion, each author was provided with an outline of the theoretical framework of the Symposium at the start of the project. The speakers were scheduled at intervals of two or three weeks, so that each one had time to familiarize himself with the contributions of those who had preceded him. Each author likewise was given the opportunity to revise his chapter after all of the papers had been presented. This plan of operation has, we believe, produced a book with greater unity of theoretical approach than is commonly achieved in projects of multiple authorship.

The book is intended for use in upper-level courses in perception, personality, and experimental, clinical, and social psychology. Students in the neighboring disciplines of psychiatry, physiology, anthropology, sociology, social work, and semantics can profitably refer to it for information and integrative concepts which are helpful in understanding basic psychological aspects of these subjects. Clinical psychologists and psychiatrists will find a conveniently classified guide to recent perceptual research on personality in the text of the various chapters and the extensive chapter bibliographies. Comprehensive indexes of authors and subjects provide a means of rapid reference to the several hundred separate investigations cited.

The authors wish to express their appreciation of the assistance given at various points by Jacob Berg, Mrs. Wayne E. Brand, Ralph Finger, Mrs. Mary S. Ramsey, Nina L. Smelcer, James D. Vanderplas, and Glen P. Wilson. The University of Texas contributed financial assistance in the final preparation of the manuscript.

R.R.B.
G.V.R.

January, 1951

CONTENTS

ILLUSTRATIONS

PERCEPTION—AN APPROACH TO PERSONALITY

CHAPTER 1

PERCEPTUAL PROCESSES AS BASIC TO AN UNDERSTANDING OF COMPLEX BEHAVIOR

By Robert R. Blake, Ph.D.
with
Glenn V. Ramsey Ed.D., *and* Louis J. Moran, M.A.

Few branches of history reveal a story more fascinating than the one which traces man's attempt to understand the universe and himself in relation to it. How does man "know" the objects of his environment? How does one man come to know another man? Why do things look as they do? Does the world register on each person in about the same way? What are the determinants of the different ways in which individuals react to their physical and social surroundings? The present book is concerned with a systematic examination of such questions.

Ways of Knowing

Before introducing a discussion of these and other problems, it is important to state the basic issue in its clearest form. In addition to the common-sense way of knowing, there are numerous approaches to the problem of accounting for the nature of reality; the theological, philosophical, and scientific ones are included among them. And, of course, the form of approach determines the fabric of the reality which comes to be understood as a result of its application. But since the approach which is best anchored in observation and which possesses the most efficient methods for checking or verifying the adequacy or accuracy of the account of reality thus fabricated is the scientific one, it should be possible to cut to the heart of the issue by examining the techniques of knowing the world that have been developed by the most competent observer, the scientist. How does the scientist observe?

Broadly speaking, the method of science—or, as White (34) calls it, the process of "sciencing"—involves the application of a cyclical process of at least three general phases. This process is based on the desire to understand or account for some aspect of nature. It begins with an explicit statement of the problem to be explained or accounted for in the form of a conceptual system, expressed in terms of testable propositions. Such propositions, in turn, lead to planned or controlled observation designed to permit unbiased examination of the adequacy of the conceptual system in accounting for the events under observation. In the final phase, the investigator confirms, modifies, or rejects the conceptual beliefs which initiated the sequence in accordance with the yield from the planned observation, thus completing the process. The conclusions drawn from the completion of one cycle serve as the propositions to be tested in the next one, and so on (4).

An interesting change has occurred as a consequence of the application of this systematic approach to the problem of understanding. The empiricism of the prescientific era with its emphasis on "fact-finding" through reliance on raw sense perception has given way to the more adequate approach to knowing described in the preceding paragraph. "Seeing is believing" no longer serves as an adequate criterion of reality. As a consequence, what is "known" at any moment is not a fact seen from the absolute standpoint of the observer. Rather, the investigator knows only the *representation* of events or process. The reality behind such representation is inferred. Its meaning is interpreted—always with respect to the error parameters attributable to inaccuracy in observation—from an explicitly stated point of view. In other words, the conditions and operations under which the observations were made determine the interpretation of the nature of reality at any particular moment. The culmination of the application of this process in physics led Barnett in *The Universe and Dr. Einstein* to remark that, "In accepting a mathematical description of nature, physicists have been forced to abandon the ordinary world of our experience, the world of sense perceptions" (1).

Now if the scientist finds it necessary to reject as untrustworthy direct knowledge about his subject matter gained through raw perception, what are the implications of this for the behavior of the nonscientifically trained individual and for the behavior of the scientist when not dealing in his own specialized field? What is the individual to do when all that he has to guide him is sensory evidence gleaned without the benefit (and in many cases without even the possibility) of either an explicitly stated conceptual system to direct his selection of information or of controlled observation to correct his possible bias in interpretation? How can his thousands of daily choice-point actions be immediate, spontaneous, and "correct" when they can in no systematic way be based on the meticulous and time-consuming techniques of knowing used routinely in controlled inquiry? A moment's reflection suggests that, while they may be both immediate and spontaneous, they never can be correct in any absolute sense. They can be correct in terms only of degree, valid only with respect to their internal consistency, to their consistency with comparable events experienced in the past, or in terms of their agreement with what is known by others to be correct. Experiments from the psychological laboratory, for example, have demonstrated amply that no perceptual discrimination is correct, except within a margin of error—that there is no absolutely valid judgment. And sometimes, as in the Ames demonstrations (18), it is not difficult to show that the margin of interpretive error is very wide. While, in contrast with the scientist, the individual has no techniques readily available through which to assay, in an unbiased and rigorous fashion, the extent of his interpretive error, he must nevertheless act because his environment is never static.

Perceptual Basis of Behavior

In spite of its relativity, when viewed from the standpoint of other criteria, the individual cannot abandon perception as his basis for action.[1] It provides him the immediate as well as the ultimate founda-

---

[1] It should be pointed out that such terms as *organism, interaction, environment,* etc., are abstractions about behavior which have been drawn and defined in a class-theoretic tradition. In the recent literature they have been used in field-theoretic contexts. Much of the confusion in present thinking can be avoided by keeping in mind the conceptual system to which the words refer.

In a field-theoretic context, an organism can be identified as one focal aspect of *process,* the environment as another, and the moment of exchange between these *foci* as *interaction.* Interaction, then, is synonymous with the term *behavior;* and as such it is inclusive of all forms of exchange, ranging from the activity of breathing or ingesting food to waving to a neighbor or using mathematical symbols. It is not, however, the view drawn from classical mechanics, i.e., there is no implication of balanced components here. Furthermore, when seen in larger contexts, these interactions may best be thought of as transactions of a sort (7).

But since not all varieties of interaction can effectively be studied in a simultaneous and undifferentiated way, it seems desirable to restrict and group certain forms which have a common core. The interactions that are under examination in the present volume are grouped under the term *perception,* a further delineation of the implications of which is given below. (See Kantor [11, 12] in this regard.)

As the term is used here, perception refers to those interactions between an organism and its (necessary) environment in which the form of response is governed by the *signal* or *sign* significance as contrasted with the *energy strength* or *quality* or *pattern* of the stimulus configuration itself. In these cases the signal or sign significance of the stimulus comes to exist (either spontaneously or effortfully) as an emergent from certain specific previous organism-environment interactions of the individual. Responses in this restricted aspect of the total gamut of interactions, then, are always *indirect;* the reaction is not governed solely by the energy characteristics or preformed pattern of stimulus-neural configurations; it is determined by the meaning the individual's prior experiences have "given" to the stimulus configuration (i.e., the conceptual set, or assumption, or personality configuration, or schema defined as an emergent from prior perception). The reaction need not, of course, be verbal; as Boring has pointed out (3), it may be communicated to the observer in an almost infinite number of ways.

tion of experience. Unlike the scientist's reality, however, the individual's reality is not fabric composed from a systematic and orderly accumulation of verified inferences. It is only in cases of interaction with stable stimulus objects arranged in relatively fixed stimulus patterns (like tables and chairs), where sequential feed-back corrections of error can be made easily and without effort or notice, that the individual's knowledge approaches the level of correspondence with external events requisite to smooth, undisturbed adjustment.

Necessary as these kinds of adjustment are, it is becoming apparent that they do not represent the only important adjustments of the individual. The achievement of stable and accurate perceptual contact with the social events involved in interpersonal activity is also of importance for effective adjustment. In action with dynamic stimulus forms, such as a conversation with other persons, the procurement of correct knowledge is sometimes rather difficult, often impossible. Correction for error cannot easily be made in terms of sequential feed-back modifications. Rather, it must be made in terms of fairly gross trial-and-check procedures. If the norm against which a check is judged is intangible or coarse, the correction will—at best— be rough and will only crudely approximate to the stimulus situation to which it relates.[2] This is so not only because of the complexity and variability intrinsic to such stimulus forms but also because the behaviors of other persons that can be seen and heard are only signals— and sometimes very elusive and subtle ones—for the motivations or intents which they express. As with stable stimulus objects, the individual can organize his social perceptions only in terms of sensory evidence. Yet his interest is directed to inferring the intents or implications which underlie such sensory information, because, as has already been suggested, the adequacy of an individual's adjustment is dependent on the accuracy, conformity, or tolerability of his inferences about the meaning of the sensory information to which he is

---

It is recognized that this is an arbitrary distinction and that the several aspects of interaction are not actually separable in any completely satisfactory way. For example, no rigid distinctions between such terms as *perception, cognition, judgment, inference,* etc., have been drawn in the present work. Such distinctions at best are arbitrary. The behaviors collected by any one of these terms seem inevitably under critical operational examination to blend with behaviors segregated by the others. This definition of perception serves to delimit the scope of subject matter under consideration in the present book. For research purposes, of course, it is often desirable to maximize such differences in order to bring out certain significant relationships which might otherwise be obscured.

When the term is used with different implications by other contributors, modifications in the definition of perception given here are noted.

[2] But the need for correction of bias or error in interpretation is by no means always self-evident. Many times the need may even pass unrecognized. And not infrequently, as in some forms of mental illness, the person is actively resistant to the modification or correction of biased, invalid interpretations.

exposed, modified of course by the latitude in interpretive error permitted by his cultural group. Future research will undoubtedly be concerned not only with establishing empirically the determinants of valid interpretations and the degrees of latitude in error tolerable within any particular cultural group but also with identifying the manner in which an individual comes to "know" when he has transgressed these tolerance limits and with clarifying understanding of the determinants of inefficiency in detecting when such parameters have been grossly exceeded.

Viewed from this general standpoint, an individual's perceptual activity must be fabricated from his current organization of personally meaningful and significant experiences. These integrations, which achieve conceptual representation in the form of the individual's unique organization of internal sets, beliefs, attitudes, selector tendencies, or hypotheses, are derived from the ascientific techniques of knowing adapted from the past for use in achieving a stable, definite, and predictable present. While they may yield consequences appropriate to the situational demands which evoke them, there is no a priori reason to assume that they will, because with but few exceptions they are not molded on the basis of adequate inferences. On the other hand, many perceptual outcomes, because of the repetitive frequency with which they have occurred in the past, the feasibility of sequential feed-back corrections, or both, are appropriate and accurate. Except for these most carefully practiced reactions to stable stimulus situations, perceptual interactions commonly yield information which corresponds to the features of the external realities to which they apply in only a semiadequate way. Why do such discrepancies tend to develop? They tend to develop sometimes because the opportunity of checking against adequate norms is nil or because adequate norms do not exist (as far as the individual is concerned), and sometimes because the frequency of exposure is extremely limited or the range of exposure is so narrow as effectively to prevent the crystallization of functionally adequate checking techniques from developing. Nevertheless, these emergents from prior perceptual activities must enter as critical conditions determining the outcomes of present and future perceptual interactions. The important question now becomes : *What are the determinants of perception?* This question identifies a critical problem that must be answered in order to achieve new insights into the determinants of complex behavior.

The present approach to an understanding of individual personality, then, entails a significant shift in emphasis. Rather than searching for personality factors or dimensions or applying psychodiagnostic labels or identifying the traits underlying individual differences in behavior, the effort shifts to the delineation and description of the *determinants of individual differences in perceiving*. As Murphy describes it,

If we understand the differences in *perceiving* we shall go far in understanding the differences in the resulting behavior. The relation between the outer world and the individual is gravely misconstrued by the assumption that this world registers upon us all in about the same way, that the real differences between people are differences in what is *done* about this world. The contemporary point of view . . . has involved emphasis upon the basic notion that every individual lives in a more or less "private world" . . . ; there is no standard objective world except through our slow yielding to a rather painful compromise process . . . that is less coercive, less "final," than the private world (23).[3]

For the purpose, then, of clarifying the importance of various conditions that enter to determine the outcomes from perceptual interactions, the conceptual scheme described below identifies for discussion a number of determinants, categorized for convenience as structural and experiential determinants of perception.

Conceptual Framework of This Book

The most important adjustments of the individual are not the consequence of the direct effect on the organism of stimulus energies or stimulus patterns. Rather, human behavior is governed by learned *interpretations* or *implications* assigned on the basis of experience to configurations of stimulus energies.[4] Since humans know and interact only on the basis of such sensory evidence, one of the crucial tasks of psychological theory is to render perceptual activity understandable.

It is postulated at the outset that perceptual transactions are *instrumental* activities, activities that guide the reacting system within the larger aspects of nature. As Klein (13) writes, "the person is a

---

[3] From Gardner Murphy, *Personality: A Biosocial Approach to Origins and Structure,* copyright 1947 by Harper & Bros. By permission of the author and the publishers.

[4] Many of these learned interpretations or implications are undoubtedly superimposed on substructures of preformed or nativistically given stimulus-neural configurations. This would appear to be the case, for example, in space or color perception, within certain limits, and it would account for the highly accurate agreement among different observers as to characteristics within the purely physical world. But whether they are or are not superimposed on such substructures, complex sensorimotor adjustments appear necessarily to require experiential antecedents prior to their emergence as effective behavior patterns. This interpretation appears to be consistent with the implications stemming from Senden's data (28) and with those from the reports by Riesen (26). It may—at least to a degree—be at variance with Pratt's (25) analysis of the role of past experience in visual perception, however.

self-regulative system; though dynamic, this system is quasi-stable and continuous. It must continually bring into harmony needs, impulses, and wishes, and buffer these turbulences from within against limitations from without." The system is, in a word, an agency of interaction, organized to make probable its own effective spatial-temporal-social continuation. The meaning of the term *effective* for any specific individual is, of course, critical to an understanding of the manner in which he will strive for continuation through the application of the balancing techniques available to him. But the central issue of motivation and the manner in which it should be dealt with in a conceptual system have not yet been explained in any completely satisfactory or testable way.[5]

Each individual begins with certain physical structures, including the receptor, central, and effector nervous systems as well as the skeletal, respiratory, digestive, and other systems. These several part-systems in unitary organization constitute the more important structures involved in perception. The selective manner in which these part-systems are utilized in perception, however, is largely determined by the unique interaction between the individual and the cultural media which he has passed through and of which he is a part at present. Thus, the way one sees reality is contingent not only on the capacity of his given physical structure for detecting stimulus configurations and integrating information about stimuli but also on modifications in the *use* of the structure which derive from the impact of experience. The summed effects result in the individual's having more or less appropriate response patterns ready in order to cope with each of a myriad of specific stimulus configurations.

Such a formulation of the problem is not new. In various ways it is basic to the approaches founded on experimental data that have been developed by Coutu (5), Hebb (9), Krech and Crutchfield (17), Kantor (12), Masserman (22), Parsons (24), Sherif and Cantril (29), Snygg and Combs (30), Sullivan (31), and a number of others. It has elements in common with the problem as seen by several pioneers in psychology: Wundt (37), Titchener (32), and James (10) saw many of the significant problems of today very clearly before the turn of the century. But the implications in 1950 are, of course, different.

In this chapter the physical characteristics of the perceiving system are referred to as the *structural* determinants. The conditions that

---

[5] The current tendency to represent motivational problems in animistic forms stands as testimony to the inadequacy of conceptual representation in dynamic terms. This is, however, probably a necessary stage in achieving the more desirable statement.

determine the individual's instrumental utilization of these structures in specific stimulus fields are viewed as the *experiential* determinants, since they stem not only from the individual's given physical structure but also from the contributions and limitations imposed on it by experience. These two are inextricably interconnected; each experience modifies the reaction potentialities of the structure; the modified structure is then set to define the next related stimulus configuration in a characteristic way—and is in turn modified by subsequent definitions, etc. The more accurate statement then would be one in which structure and function are treated as inseparable, i.e., as structure-function.

In brief, then, the consequence is that each individual perceives a given reality in a characteristic way, and in this sense there are as many realities as there are perceivers. The particular way in which an individual interprets a stimulus configuration dictates his reaction to it. But since each individual possesses in the beginning a somewhat similar structure, the discussion of the perceptual determinants logically begins at this point.

Structural Determinants in Perceptual Activity

Basic to an understanding of complex behavior is an appreciation of its structural foundation. As has been indicated, the functional aspects are, as a matter of fact, no more than the operation of structure under given conditions. But for discussion purposes, it is necessary to deal in terms of these two levels. (See Lewin [19] in this connection.)

Seen in longitudinal perspective, the function of the sense modalities is to furnish evidence about the environment. The course of evolution has, with exceptions, been that of furnishing organisms with more adequate structures for detection, the rule being that the more complex the organism neurologically, the more adequate the equipment for perceiving the potential richness of environmental detail. But evidence that receptors—viewed from a relative standpoint —provide only a somewhat crude version of reality is suggested by the fact that science has extended the parameters of the world far beyond the dimensions known through unassisted sensory stimulation. The extensions of knowledge made possible by the microscope and telescope serve as examples of how reality expands under artificially aided sensory functioning.

The receptor systems provide information on the internal status of the organism and on the status of the environmental field in relation to the organism. Among them might be mentioned such structures as the semicircular canals, which appear to inform the organism of its position in relation to the environment, and the kinesthetic receptors, which seem to give information on the position of parts of the body with relation to its major axis. Vision and hearing, which inform the organism of events taking place outside the skin, may be placed in a second group, along with the receptors for pain, pressure, cold, warmth, etc. But it is interesting to speculate how relatively much more adequate are these distance and contact receptors for detecting objects and relationships between objects organized in space than they are for informing the organism about the state of affairs (motivation, feelings, attitudes, etc.) existing in a dynamic stimulus object like another organism.

There is little need here to go into a technical presentation of the range and acuity limits or intrinsic functioning of these receptor systems. In the effort to discover the nature of mental functioning by the process of studying the detection equipment, psychology and physiology have provided somewhat adequate descriptions of the characteristics of sensory organs. The point here is the realization that the receptor systems are able to provide the central nervous system with restricted clues or signals to events within the organism itself as well as to provide cues about the events external to it. The more important consideration in the frame of reference given here will be with the manner in which the central nervous system utilizes the clues thus furnished. It is the organization of these integrative mechanisms which constitutes the ultimate focus in the study of personality. In this regard, the works of Köhler (15) and Koffka (14) and the more recent ones that Krech (16) and Hebb (9) have provided furnish important theoretical formulations concerned with the nature of such organization.

Up to this point the discussion has been limited to the intrinsic properties of the central nervous system, that is, the inherent processes of which the human central nervous system in general is capable —although the actual total functioning of the individual is also as much a product of the unique experiential fields through which it has passed and in which it is presently located as it is of the intrinsic function or inherent capacity of the system itself.

As has been mentioned earlier, it would appear that the course of development has, broadly speaking, involved the acquisition by organisms of structures that make possible the perception and integration of more varied and potentially richer environmental detail. Along with increasingly refined receptors has come the greater capacity for central integration of stimulus cues, which is currently epitomized in the comparatively great encephalization of man. Since the reactions

of an organism to a stimulus field depend upon the way in which the
organism defines that stimulus configuration, the evolution of more
efficient equipment for differentiating and integrating the saliences in
a stimulus mosaic is accompanied by (and probably contingent upon
[33, 36]) finer differentiations and articulations of reaction. Thus
organisms may be said to be evolving in the direction of greater receptor acuity, better perceptive integration, and, hence, greater capacity for differentiation of response. In man the great evolutional
saltation in integrative capacity which has taken place makes possible
*the more effective incorporation within the nervous system of these
stimulus definitions for use in subsequent definitions and actions.*

Anatomical Factors.—This, then, is the role of the central nervous system in perception, as viewed here. Each normal individual is
endowed with a comparatively highly evolved central nervous system
having "intrinsic functions" qualitatively about the same as those of
other individuals. From birth this endowed perceptive apparatus is
slightly modified by each stimulus definition it makes. The physical
perceptive structure itself is altered and hence is set to perceive in a
slightly different way. Thus, in the language of William James,
experience is literally written into the nervous system (10). Morgan,
in Chapter 2 of the present volume, examines the basic machinery by
which "experience" is incorporated into the nervous system. Here he
addresses himself to the question of what the sense organs are like,
how the sensory systems of the body are built and function, and how
the brain works in perception. He also points to the probable fruitful lines of research at this level which will enrich future understanding of the intrinsic properties of perceiving systems.

Strongly influencing the perceptual activity of the system are the
contributing body structures mentioned earlier. Structures such as
the skeletal and muscular systems operate to place the organism in
optimal positions to perceive, and the digestive, circulatory, and respiratory systems serve to maintain the physical integrity of the perceiving system; the sympathetic nervous system and the glandular
systems appear to function to sharpen perception and to heighten
reaction in emergencies.

Chemical Factors.—The crucial contribution of these structures
to perceptual activity becomes most apparent in cases of their mal-
function. Their effect, for example, can be seen in cases of both
quantitative and qualitative dietary deficiencies, of oxygen lack, of
hormonal imbalances, and of the effects of drugs. The role of these
structures in normal perceptual activity also becomes evident in cases
of the destruction of tissue, in various forms of disease, and as a result

of injury or insult to various body structures. In discussing these relationships in Chapter 3, Beach develops a threefold approach to the problem. First, he surveys "the various types of evidence that demonstrate the existence of relationships between particular alterations in body chemistry and specific changes in behavior. The second aim is to discuss and evaluate possible explanations for these relationships. The third objective is to explore the major questions confronting specialists in the field and to determine, if possible, what procedures are most likely to provide us with solutions to these problems" (page 57).

Experiential Determinants of Perceptual Activity

The discussion to this point has been designed to draw attention to *the range and limitations of detection and integration* which are imposed on the human organism by its structure and organization. The discussion that follows attempts to show some of the ways in which experiences in the stimulus field direct the utilization of these structures in perceiving.

We have considered the structural determinants of perception as though the perceiving system were completely divorced from the unique environment and the events which are experienced by a given organism. It is necessary now to consider the interactive results from the long and continuous process of socialization which characterizes each individual organism and which results in the modifications of structure and consequently of functioning that are attributable to *experience*. To understand the perceptual characteristics that determine the definitions given by an individual, attention must be given to the contribution made by the physical-cultural media through which he has passed. Experiences within these areas determine the unique utilization of perceptive equipment and thereby produce reactive tendencies which serve as a basis for the evolution of "self."

The Role of Learning in Perception.—The problem of how the events occurring in the individual's stimulus fields are incorporated into the organism is essentially the question of the role of *learning* in perception. These matters are discussed in Chapter 4 by Hilgard, who states,

The older question about the role of learning in perception had to do with the nativism-empiricism problem. To what extent is perception natively given by way of our inherited structures and capacities, and to what extent is it the result of our experiences with the world of objects? But a new question is now being asked about the reciprocal relationship between learning and perception. This new and contemporary question is: To what extent is learning merely reorganized perception? We shall have to deal with both the older question and the contemporary one if we are to keep our thinking straight about both learning and perception (page 95).

Hilgard goes on to direct attention to what he calls the goals of perception—these two goals of perception, first, to have our perceptions keep the world about us a stable one and, second, to achieve definiteness in what we perceive, may be accepted as valid without committing ourselves as to their origin—and to discuss the ways in which perceptual achievements come about. In concluding his chapter he points out that, "The end result is, on the one hand, a world in which we feel at home because we know what to expect, and what we expect does not disagree too much with what we want. But, on the other hand, the world may be a capricious and terrifying place, where all that we do is uncertain and dangerous, where we do not learn what to expect, where what we find is never satisfying" (page 119).

A Theory of Perception.—With these remarks about the nature of learning in perception we return to a consideration of the individual and the manner in which units of knowledge about the world are gained. In an earlier section, where we discussed the way in which scientific inferences are drawn, we indicated that the understanding of "reality" thus achieved has—by comparison—rendered untrustworthy the data of experience given through raw sense perceptions. But at the same time it was pointed out that individual knowledge is knowledge achieved in consequence of the same kind of raw sense perceptions which have been abandoned by the scientist because they yield information which is too crude and too inaccurate for acceptance within the bounds of scientifically valid inference. However, in the present frame of reference we are not concerned with the manner in which the scientist comes to infer the nature of reality; rather, the central question is concerned with the manner in which the individual comes to *know* the world. The question then points to the need for a theory of perception. In Chapter 5 Bruner presents the outline of such a theory. The steps through which a perceiver translates a stimulus configuration into a perceptual unit are generalized in the following quotation from Bruner's paper:

Basically, perceiving involves a three-step cycle. Analytically, we may say that perceiving begins with an expectancy or hypothesis. In the language of Woodworth . . . , we not only see, but we look for, not only hear but listen to. In short, perceiving takes place in a "tuned organism." The assumption is that we are never randomly set or *eingestellt* but that, rather, we are always to some extent *prepared* for seeing, hearing, smelling, tasting some particular thing or class of things. What evokes an hypothesis? Any given hypothesis results from the arousal of central cognitive and motivational processes by preceding environmental states of affairs.

The second analytic step in the perceiving process is the input of information from the environment (which environment includes the stimulus complex brought to us by distance receptors and by the somatic senses). Here we purposely use the term *information* to characterize stimulus input, for we are not concerned with the energy characteristic of the stimulus as such but only with its cue or clue characteristics.

The third step in the cycle is a checking or confirmation procedure. Input information is confirmatory to or congruent with the operative hypothesis, or it is in varying degree infirming or incongruous. If confirmation does not occur, the hypothesis shifts in a direction partly determined by internal or personological or experiential factors and partly on the basis of feedback from the learning which occurred in the immediately preceding, partly unsuccessful information-checking cycle. For heuristic purposes we speak of initial and consequent hypotheses, the latter being those which follow upon an infirmed hypothesis (pages 123-24).

Having outlined this theoretical position, Bruner goes on to interpret much of the recent research in perception into these terms and to relate them to a broad conception of personality dynamics; to suggest the manner in which personality dynamics may serve to set the selection of information from the environment and, consequently, to determine important aspects of adjustment.

Cultural Determinants of Perception—With the outline of a theory of perception before us, it becomes important to consider the ingredients of culture which mold and determine the set or hypothesis of the perceiver at any moment of interaction. As L. K. Frank (8) indicates, "In every culture the individual is of necessity 'cribbed, cabinned, and confined' within the limitations of what his culture tells him to see, to believe, to do, and to feel. . . ." To understand what an individual defines into the stimulus configurations to which he reacts, then, we must first have some understanding of the residual effects from the physical and cultural media through which he has passed, and of the consequent present modifications in reactive tendencies which constitute the self.

At the outset it is desirable to provide an indication of the manner in which the term *culture* is being used here. Linton (20) has given the following definition: "A culture is the configuration of learned behavior and results of behavior whose component elements are shared and transmitted by the members of a particular society." This conception, while useful in the general study of personality, does not supply the *specificity* required for an understanding of individual behavior, since the "culture" is represented in a very different way to the different groups and, consequently, to the individuals who exist within it. A thorough study of individuals in uptown New York City will not suffice to understand the behavior of individuals in the Mormon community of Salt Lake City, or of those in the slums of Chicago, or in rural Indiana—although in a certain sense all may be said to "possess" the same culture, and all will probably participate in certain kinds of responses which have been achieved through common cultural transmission.

For the purpose of this scheme, therefore, we will make an arbitrary distinction between culture-in-general and culture-in-particular. In speaking of the experiential determinants of perceptual activity, then, we will refer to the first of these as the *general cultural determinants* and to the second as the *specific cultural determinants*. In contrast with the former, the specific cultural determinants may be defined as the unique and continuously developing stimulus configurations within the general culture to which the individual is exposed during his lifetime. That such a distinction has no counterpart in reality we fully realize. The *idea* we wish to impart by this construct is that the definitions of stimulus configurations which a specific individual makes are determined not only by the general cultural but also by the specific stimulus fields within which the individual is situated from a developmental and social standpoint. For example, the general culture of the Dobu sets parameters of acceptable (to the culture) perceptual interactions different from those of the Western culture of, say, a citizen of Boston (2). Each general culture offers a peculiarly refracted version of possible perceptual definitions and the combinations and permutations of the specific components of stimulus configurations that may be composed from it are almost infinite. But these constitute the environment for any specific individual.

In Chapter 6 Dennis develops the evidence which is of importance for an understanding of the social factors that operate to determine perceptual activity. He does this on the basis of intercultural comparisons and from the standpoint of a horizontal and developmental analysis of determinants within our own culture, as well as from the point of view of segments within it. As Dennis indicates,

Many of the approaches which have contributed most to the study of social factors in perception are usually classified under other headings. Studies of suggestion, including hypnotism, have made several contributions. Investigations of emotional expression throw light upon social influences in perception as well as upon emotion. Projective techniques, of course, must deal with perception as well as with personality. Some important lines of evidence are historical and anthropological rather than experimental. In reviewing studies of social factors in perception, the writer will feel free to draw upon sources such as these, to which our books on perception seldom make reference (pages 148-49).

Language and Perception.—Following the analysis by Dennis in a logical sequence is a survey of one of the most obvious of the cultural determinants—the *language* used by the perceiving group or individual. As Whorf (35) and other linguists have pointed out, we "cut up and organize the spread and flow of events" as we do because, through our mother tongue, we are parties to an agreement to do so, not because nature itself is thus compartmentalized for all to see. Thus, the Chukchee do not distinguish at the verbal level between blue and green (grass color) or the Trobrianders between blue and green (sea color) (21). The Eskimo, on the other hand, who has names for a dozen varieties of snow surface and formation, must "see" a landscape different from the one that meets the eye of a European traveler in the Arctic (6). In an investigation of the determinants of perception, then, it is necessary to consider macrocosmic "endowments" of culture-in-general, such as language, as well as specific institutions, mores, socioeconomic factors, etc.—the components of culture-in-particular.[6] As has been obvious for a considerable period of time, the techniques of communication, because they are structured in themselves, seem to structure the nature of experience, and consequently of perception. Korzybski analyzes the role of language in structuring perceptual activity in Chapter 7. The following quotation defines the basic issue which he develops:

Let us consider what our nervous system does when we "perceive" a happening or event. The term "event" is used here in the sense of Whitehead as an instantaneous cross-section of a process. Say we drop a box of matches. Here we have a first-order happening, which occurs on *nonverbal* or what is called the "silent" or "un-speakable" levels. The reflected light impinges on the eye, we get some sort of electro-colloidal configurations in the brain; then, since we are sentient organisms, we can react to those configurations with some sort of "feelings," some evaluations, etc., about them, on "silent" levels. Finally, on the verbal levels, we can speak about those organismal reactions. Newton may have said, about the falling matchbox, "gravitation"; Einstein

---

[6] A delightful example of the unique way in which an individual acquires language and of what effects this may have upon perception is furnished in an observation by Schlauch (27) of "a little girl who, having recently learned to read, was spelling out a political article in the newspaper. 'Father,' she asked, 'what is Tammany Hall?' And father replied in the voice usually reserved for the taboos of social communication, 'You'll understand that when you grow up, my dear.' Acceding to this adult whim of evasion, she desisted from her inquiries; but something in Daddy's tone had convinced her that Tammany Hall must be connected with illicit *amour,* and for many years she could not hear this political institution mentioned without experiencing a secret nonpolitical thrill!" Margaret Schlauch, *The Gift of Tongues,* The Viking Press, 1942. By permission of The Viking Press.

may say, "space-time curvature." Whatever we may *say* about it, the first-order happening remains on the silent levels. How we will *talk* about it may differ from day to day, or from year to year, or century to century. All our "feelings," "thinkings," our "loves," "hates," etc., *happen* on silent un-speakable levels, but may be affected by the verbal levels by a continuing interplay. We may verbalize about them, to ourselves or others, intensify, decrease them, etc., but this is a different problem (page 172).

In speaking of cultural and developmental determinants of the kind that are dealt with by Dennis and Korzybski, we refer to indirect determinants, because they influence perception only in so far as they are responsible for the peculiar modifications that characterize the perceiver at the moment of perception. The immediate objective situation supplies only a *stimulus to perception.* The selective accentuations, modifications, and deletions and, consequently, the meanings given to the situation are provided by the *perceiver.* Yet the situations within which the perceiver has interacted in the past determine how he is set in the present to define the next stimulus situation, so they in turn must be taken into consideration in the prediction of the outcome of future perceptions. Thus the description of socialization is of critical importance to an understanding of perceptual behavior.

The Individual as a Perceiver.—In an earlier section we had occasion to refer to the central nervous system in broad terms in reference to its intrinsic function as an integrator mechanism. We return to it now, not from the standpoint of inherent structure, but rather from the standpoint of the modifications of functional characteristics which are stamped into it as a result of the interactive processes constituting socialization. It is the end product of these interactions and the consequent structural modifications in the perceiving individual in which we are interested.

If one were to try to identify for discussion one of the most important aspects of interactive activities from the standpoint of the significance of their lasting effects on the perceiver, it is likely that the interpersonal actions that go on between individuals and their consequences in reference to the development of the self system or stable conceptual sets would be among those selected for analysis.

While these most important determinants are among the latest to yield to conceptual analysis and while they are only beginning to be subjected to experimental study, the development of a theoretical formulation in this connection is undertaken in Chapter 8 by Bronfenbrenner. He indicates that,

In the discussion to follow we are concerned primarily with the work of five men. In addition to Freud and Lewin, these include Otto Rank, William

McDougall, and Harry Stack Sullivan. Since it is manifestly impossible to deal with the major contributions of each in their entirety, it will be necessary to restrict discussion to those aspects which appear most significant for an attempt at theoretical integration. In this connection it appears important to note not only points that are critical for or consonant with a general theory but also those that are strikingly incompatible or leave crucial questions unanswered. Even with material thus confined, it will be necessary to resort to condensation and, in many instances, to forgo elaboration or example that might otherwise illuminate the discussion (page 210).

Having reviewed the communalties and divergencies in the writings about personality organization by these five men, Bronfenbrenner summarizes the significant and persistent ideas about the development of the self system into a series of propositions under the two heads *personality structure* and *personality development*. These ideas, which represent the rich harvest from clinical study and research analysis, constitute the basis for the future development of a systematic theory of the individual as an active and reactive perceiver.

The papers by Dennis, Korzybski, and Bronfenbrenner relate to the social and cultural, linguistic and personal determinants which contribute to the development of individual patterns of behavior and the emergence of the self and which, therefore, serve to guide the form of the reactions the individual makes to the world. The understanding of behavior variations among members of any specific culture or cultural group would be grossly inadequate if these kinds of experiential determining factors were to be ignored.

Unconscious Perceptual Processes.—But it is obvious that the individual's knowledge of the world can never be complete, that it can never achieve a universal validity, and that sometimes it does not even achieve a minimal basis of adequacy for effective action. It is also clear that, in much of the process of living, action is *mandatory;* it cannot be held in abeyance until veridical understanding of the stimulus situation has crystallized. The new question then is this: In those situations in which action is mandatory but information on which to base action is inadequate or nil, what is the course of behavior that leads to resolution? What form of determinant can be invoked to help clarify an understanding of this kind of behavior? This problem is taken up in Chapter 9 by Miller, who deals with unconscious factors in perception. He considers "the psychology of ignorance—how the individual deals with gaps in his knowledge," and he says,

Throughout our discussion we shall repeatedly refer to material presented in earlier chapters of this symposium. This is because unconscious factors in perception have already been abundantly illustrated to the reader, since a **num-**

ber of the processes which have been described are clearly unconscious. The present writer hopes to be able to organize some of these data into a pattern which will throw light on our particular problem (page 260).

Having marshaled the evidence concerned with the operation of unconscious factors in perception, Miller concludes,

Mankind, weak and limited in his power and knowledge, surrounded by ignorance, nevertheless is doing an effective job of adjusting to his environment. But our reason is beginning to show us that the chief explanation for this effectiveness, the primary principle behind our perceptual processes, conscious and unconscious, is not deductive rationality but the inductive process of irrational belief (page 279).

Behavior Pathology as Related to Perception.—While mankind may—from an over-all point of view—be doing an effective job of adjusting to his environment, it is nonetheless true that there are many glaring exceptions. The field of behavior pathology stands as testimony of the breakdown in adjustive mechanisms in modern society. But what is the relevance of considering behavior pathology in a symposium on perception? In Chapter 10 Cameron takes up this issue as his point of departure. He says,

If the writer were to attempt to relate perceptual organization to the whole field of behavior pathology in a single chapter, the reader would quickly become confused and the writer would get lost. We propose, instead, to confine the discussion to what is directly relevant in delusional development and the formation of pseudocommunities. Since the *principle of continuity* is basic to this presentation, we may begin by restating it here: *All the attitudes and responses found in behavior pathology are in some way related to and derived from normal biosocial behavior.* . . . If this is a valid principle, of course, it implies that the yield we may expect from the present resurgence of interest in perception will contribute directly or indirectly to our understanding of pathological phenomena (pages 283-84).

Building on several of the earlier formulations, Cameron relates perceptual theory to delusion formulation by examining broad correlations between the perceptual activity underlying normal behavior and that underlying behavior pathology. In this chapter are presented many testable propositions which may serve as the foundation for an essentially new and potentially rich experimental approach to the whole field of behavior deviation.

The Role of Perception in Psychotherapy.—Carrying the principle of continuity further, it follows that psychotherapy is a process which changes or reorganizes the interactions between the individual and his environment. It involves the achievement by the individual of more accurate and adequate techniques of "knowing" the environ-

ment and the self in relation to it.   Rogers introduces this conceptual
theme in Chapter 11 by indicating that:

In talking about the process and outcomes of psychotherapy, a descriptive
phrase which is frequently used by the client as well as the therapist is that
the client has come "to see things differently." Is this sort of phrase simply
a loose descriptive analogy, or is there some type of perceptual reorganization
which takes place in therapy? In this chapter, we shall endeavor to consider
the available evidence which exists in relation to this problem, touching on the
changes which come about in the perception of the environment and of the self,
and proposing a theory of psychotherapy which places heavy emphasis upon
the perceptual elements in the process (page 307).

Drawing on both clinical and experimental data and presenting the
early results from a new procedure for measuring changes in self-
evaluation, Rogers examines a broad range of evidence and securely
ties the changes that occur in conjunction with psychotherapy to perceptual theory. This reduction of superficially disparate phenomena
to a common core may prove to be important in facilitating the development of a verified body of fact about the nature of the therapeutic
experience.

The treatment by Rogers focuses attention not only on the raw
data of immediate experience but also on the significance of the learnings brought to its interpretation. This emphasis accentuates the
importance in accounting for perceptual activity of understanding the
over-all organization by the person of his techniques for handling raw
data. It points to the need for laws of perceivers, rather than for laws
of perception.

Perception and Individual Organization.—Klein develops in
Chapter 12 an approach to the problem of understanding the person's
organization through investigating his perceptual activity. He expresses his viewpoint by saying:

I think I am interpreting correctly the spirit of this symposium when I
say that our focus upon perception is secondary to an interest in persons,
that perception is for us only a convenient wedge into this larger problem.
Our target is a theory which would lead to laws of *perceivers,* not laws
of perception, a theory which would be not so much concerned with linking
generalized field conditions or states of motivation to perception in general
as with linking them to the organization of people. . . . Perception is *the*
point of reality contact, the door to reality appraisal, and there is no doubt that
here especially are the selective, adaptive controls of personality brought into
play (page 328).

Having defined the problem in this way, Klein goes on to describe
three basic perceptual attitudes, to relate a body of research findings

from studies conducted at the Menninger Foundation to them, and to develop a core outline through which to represent the idea of an ego control system.

Personality Theory and Perception.—The task of relating perceptual research to the more inclusive body of concepts and principles about the organization of personality is undertaken in Chapter 13 by Frenkel-Brunswik. She lays a foundation upon which a rapprochement between these hitherto more or less disparate areas may take place by saying:

> Instead of making perception the starting point, as has been the case in the introductory considerations by Blake, Ramsey, and Moran (Chapter 1) and in the symposium as a whole, the present writer will reverse the order and take the development of and changes within personality theory as the point of departure for this Chapter. The writer will then attempt to indicate how this development has served as a basis for bridging over into the field of perception Some attention to problems of motivation, ego structure, and reality adaptation, as well as to problems of social influences upon personality, will have to precede all this, since they define the elements upon which any personality theory must draw. Previously in this symposium, especially in the papers by Blake (Chapter 1), Bruner (Chapter 5), and Cameron (Chapter 10), these elements have been traced throughout their interweavings with perception. The general plan of procedure here will be to discuss them first in relation to the clinical level and then to apply them to the empirical findings on the interrelationship of personality with perception and cognition (page 356).

After interrelating these two bodies of data, Frenkel-Brunswik draws her conclusions by pointing to the implications of this broad development within psychology for further research. She states:

> Thus it would seem that the most promising avenue of approach should be the one which combines emphasis on general personality variables, both motivational and cognitive, with an emphasis on developmental aspects. In any event there can be little doubt that this is a most challenging period in psychology, a fact to which this symposium has given eloquent testimony (page 417).

BIBLIOGRAPHY

1. BARNETT, L. K. *The universe and Dr. Einstein.* New York: William Sloane Associates, Inc., 1949.
2. BENEDICT, RUTH. *Patterns of culture.* New York: The American Library, 1934.
3. BORING, E. G. Mind and mechanism. *Amer. J. Psychol.,* 1946, **59**, 173-92.
4. CANTRIL, H., AMES, A., JR., HASTORF, A. H., & ITTELSON, W. H. Psychology and scientific research. *Science,* 1949, **110**, 461-64, 491-97, 517-22.
5. COUTU, W. *Emergent human nature.* New York: Alfred A. Knopf, Inc., 1949.
6. DE LAGUNA, GRACE. Perception and language. In I. J. Lee (ed.), *The language of wisdom and folly.* New York: Harper & Bros., 1949.

7. DEWEY, J., & BENTLEY, A. F. *Knowing and the known.* Boston: The Beacon Press, 1949.

8. FRANK, L. K. *Society as the patient.* New Brunswick, N. J.: Rutgers University Press, 1949.

9. HEBB, D. O. *The organization of behavior.* New York: John Wiley & Sons, Inc., 1949.

10. JAMES, W. *The principles of psychology.* New York: Henry Holt & Co., Inc., 1890. Vol. II.

11. KANTOR, J. R. *A survey of the science of psychology.* Bloomington, Ind.: The Principia Press, Inc., 1933.

12. KANTOR, J. R. *Psychology and logic.* Bloomington, Ind.: The Principia Press, Inc., 1945.

13. KLEIN, G. S., & SCHLESINGER, H. Where is the perceiver in perceptual theory? *J. Personal.,* 1949, **18,** 32-47.

14. KOFFKA, K. *Principles of gestalt psychology.* New York: Harcourt, Brace & Co., Inc., 1935.

15. KÖHLER, W. *Dynamics in psychology.* New York: Liveright Publishing Corp., 1940.

16. KRECH, D. Notes toward a psychological theory. *J. Personal.,* 1949, **18,** 66-87.

17. KRECH, D., & CRUTCHFIELD, R. S. *Theory and problems of social psychology.* New York: McGraw-Hill Book Co., Inc., 1948.

18. LAWRENCE, M. *Studies in human behavior.* Princeton, N. J.: Princeton University Press, 1949.

19. LEWIN, K. *A dynamic theory of personality.* New York: McGraw-Hill Book Co., Inc., 1935.

20. LINTON, R. *The cultural background of personality.* New York: Appleton-Century-Crofts, Inc., 1945.

21. MALINOWSKI, B. The problem of meaning in primitive languages. Supplement in E. K. Ogden & I. A. Richards. *The meaning of meaning.* New York: Harcourt, Brace & Co., Inc., 1948.

22. MASSERMAN, J. H. *Principles of dynamic psychiatry.* Philadelphia: W. B. Saunders Co., 1946.

23. MURPHY, G. *Personality: a biosocial approach to origins and structure.* New York: Harper & Bros., 1947.

24. PARSONS, SIR J. H. *An introduction to the theory of perception.* New York: The Macmillan Co., 1927.

25. PRATT, C. C. The role of past experience in visual perception. *J. Psychol.,* 1950, **30,** 85-107.

26. RIESEN, A. H. The development of visual perception in man and chimpanzee. *Science,* 1947, **106,** 107-8.

27. SCHLAUCH, MARGARET. *The gift of tongues.* New York: The Viking Press, Inc., 1942.

28. SENDEN, M. V. *Raum- und Gestaltauffassung bei operierten Blindgeborenen vor und nach der Operation.* Leipzig: J. A. Barth, 1932.

29. SHERIF, M., & CANTRIL, H. *The psychology of ego involvement.* New York: John Wiley & Sons, Inc., 1947.

30. SNYGG, D., & COMBS, A. W. *Individual behavior.* New York: Harper & Bros., 1949.

31. SULLIVAN, H. S. *Conceptions of modern psychiatry.* Washington, D. C.: The William Alanson White Psychiatric Foundation, 1947.

32. TITCHENER, E. B. *A beginner's psychology.* New York: The Macmillan Co., 1917.

33. WERNER, H., & WAPNER, S. Sensory-tonic field theory of perception. *J. Personal.,* 1949, **18,** 88-107.

34. WHITE, L. A. *The science of culture.* New York: Farrar, Straus & Co., Inc., 1949.

35. WHORF, B. L. Science and linguistics. *The Technology Review,* 1940, **42,** 229-31, 247-48.
36. WOODWORTH, R. S. Reinforcement of perception. *Amer. J. Psychol.,* 1947, **60,** 119-24.
37. WUNDT, W. *Introduction to psychology.* London: George Allen & Unwin, Ltd., 1912.

CHAPTER 2

SOME STRUCTURAL FACTORS IN PERCEPTION

By CLIFFORD T. MORGAN, Ph.D.

The central purpose of this symposium is to look at personality from the point of view of perception. Most of the symposium deals with the way in which experience modifies perception, for the experiential determinants of perception are of greatest interest and importance to us in dealing with personality. Perception, however, has its substrate in structure. We can only see and feel what our sense organs and nervous system let us sense. It is natural, therefore, that this chapter—the first on determinants of perception—should deal with anatomical and structural factors in perception. Much of the chapter will say very little about perception and personality, for that is the task of later chapters. It will, however, provide a background of the facts and present conception of how physiological structures function in perception.

In setting out on this task there is obviously no point in repeating the many details of anatomy, physiology, and psychology that can be found in the various textbooks. In fact, acquaintance with the basic physics of stimuli, the anatomy of our sense organs, and the neurology of sensory systems must be assumed. Having these fundamentals in mind, however, it is possible to work toward two goals in this chapter.

One is to bring the discussion up to date on the results of recent research. Many of these results really upset our old ideas and make us take new views of the anatomy of perception.

The second goal will be to look at perceptual mechanisms as a whole. When we study some one part of a sensory system, say the retina, we often "cannot see the woods for the trees." If we stand off a bit, however, and look at all the senses together, we begin to be able to make some general rules and principles about the mechanisms of perception.

That will be attempted in this chapter—at the risk sometimes of suggesting ideas that not everyone will agree with.

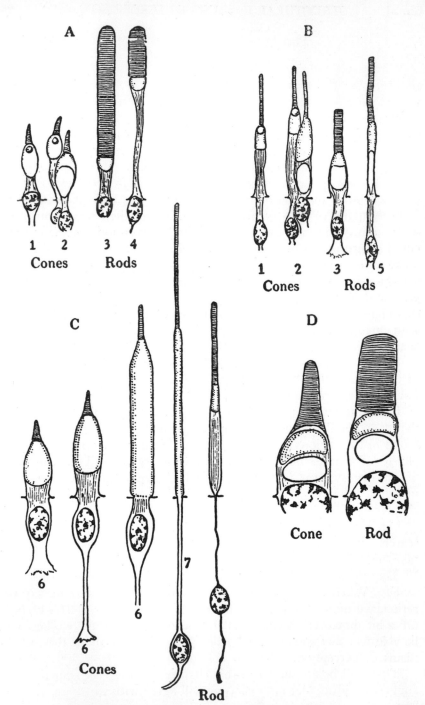

FIG. 1.—Rods and cones found in the eyes of different vertebrates. *A*, the leopard frog; *B*, the house sparrow; *C*, man; and *D*, the mud puppy. 1, typical cones; 2, so-

The Qualities of Experience

We see with our eyes, hear with our ears, and feel with our skins, and it is obvious in each case that the structure of the sense organ has a lot to do with what we perceive through it. More than a hundred years ago, however, Müller carried the anatomical approach far beyond the obvious and gave us his now famous doctrine of specific nerve energies. We see red or blue, hear high tones or low tones, feel pain or heat, he said, only because each of these perceptions involves different sensory paths. Thus he gave us an anatomical explanation for qualities of experience.

Hardly any suggestion could have been taken so seriously by so many persons for so many years. Even today some physiologists take it as an axiom, rather than a hypothesis, and try to prove other notions by it. Many specific theories of sensory functions have been based upon it, and a good many of them have been wrong. Müller's general idea, however, still looks like a good one. We have simply had to revise again and again our specific notions of how the idea works in practice.

The Shape of Receptors.—Take the question of structure of receptors. It would have been very handy not only for Müller's doctrine to prove right but for every receptor to have some unusual shape or color that would let us tell it from other receptors for other experiences. Our wishful thinking on this score has made us waste a lot of research time and peddle some bad notions. They tell us in the elementary textbooks, for example, that we have two kinds of receptors in our eyes, one for twilight vision and the other for color vision. We have been taught, too, that there are different kinds of receptors for skin perception—Meissner corpuscles for touch, Krause end-bulbs for cold, Ruffini cylinders for warmth, and free nerve endings for pain (2, pp. 489-501). It would indeed be nice if anatomy were that good to us—if each receptor had its trade-mark of experience on it—but we are gradually learning to be wary of such notions.

Visual Receptors. Take as an example the matter of visual receptors. In Figure 1 you see drawings of the photoreceptors of four different vertebrate animals (46). In *A* are those of the frog, and they divide themselves fairly well into cones and rods, just as the classical doctrine says they should. In *B* are the rods and cones of

called twin cone; 3, typical red rod; 4, green rod; 5, rod from the central area; 6, cones from different regions of the periphery of the retina; and 7, cone from the fovea. (Based on work of L. B. Arey and of G. L. Walls. From E. N. Willmer, *Retinal structure and colour vision* [Cambridge: Cambridge University Press, 1946], p. 2. By permission of the publisher.)

the house sparrow. Again they look somewhat as they are supposed to, but the rods look something like cones and the cones look like rods. In *C* we meet a disturbing situation, for these are the receptors of man. Many of the cones from the peripheral retina look like cones and the rods look like rods, but notice what is supposed to be a cone from the fovea centralis—the all-cone area of our fovea. It outdoes the rods in being long, cylindrical, and rodlike. The best excuse for calling it a cone is that our theory of duplicity says that it should be a cone. Anatomy certainly does not justify the label.

These are just a few examples of the problem. There are other animals in which it is hard to make out rods and cones. In some cases, like that of the lizard *Gecko,* the animal seems to have all rods in its eye, yet reacts to visual objects as though it had only cones (7). In other cases, histologists have a hard time deciding whether there are any cones in an animal's eye, when electrical records of the eye's behavior make it quite certain that "cones" are there (15, 46). Finally, some vision scientists have reason to believe that our perception of the color blue may rest not upon the cones, as we have so long thought, but rather upon some kind of rod (19, 46).

So the duplicity theory seems to be passing on toward its death. It gave us a kind of anatomical explanation for one aspect of perception which would have been very nice if true. Indeed, we may even go on teaching students this theory for years to come as a sort of teaching device that may be partly true. It is not true enough, however, to depend on to make correct guesses about perception. We cannot tell about the color perception of an animal by the looks of the receptors in its eyes.

Skin Receptors. We are being even more rudely disappointed by the skin senses. In Figure 2 are some of the receptors that the histologists have found in the skin (9, p. 3). The physiologists and psychologists used to assign these receptors to different experiences. Some in fact still do. The common scheme is to assign the Meissner corpuscle to the experience of touch or pressure, the Krause end-bulb to cold, the Ruffini cylinder to warmth, and the free nerve ending to pain. The reason for this kind of scheme is that one kind of receptor seems to be in greater numbers in regions of the skin where one experience may be more prominent. Other arguments can and have been made with great vigor.

The only trouble—and the big trouble—is that these receptors are not always present where they ought to be (13). It is, of course, a simple matter to make a map of the skin, marking just where we feel various experiences. When a spot seems to give one experience much more than another, we can do a biopsy on the spot, that is, cut out a piece of skin and see what receptors we have been able to trap. Such experiments have often been done in the last seventy years, and the result all too often is that the receptors our anatomical scheme calls for are missing. We do not always find Meissner corpuscles under pressure spots, Krause end-bulbs under cold spots, and so on. We can swear in fact that they very often are not there (13, 22).

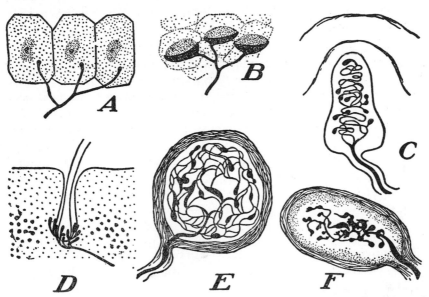

FIG. 2.—Principal cutaneous receptors. *A*, free nerve endings from the cornea of the eye; *B*, Merkel's cells from the snout of the pig; *C*, Meissner's tactile corpuscle; *D*, basket ending at the base of a hair follicle; *E*, Krause end-bulb from the human conjunctiva; *F*, Golgi-Mazzoni corpuscle from the human skin. (From J. F. Fulton, *Physiology of the nervous system* [2d ed.; New York: Oxford University Press, 1943]. Copyright 1943 by Oxford University Press, Inc. By permission of the publishers.)

What scientists always do find when they make biopsies is a network of nerve fibers and blood vessels (13). This is not strange, of course, because our skin needs blood and so do the nerve fibers. Nerve fibers are also needed to control the dilation and contraction of blood vessels. More than that, however, these networks obviously supply the skin with a good many free nerve endings. These endings, in fact, are about the only possible receptors in many areas of the skin. We can be very sure that they serve as pain receptors and as pressure receptors. The experiments leave little doubt about that. They strongly suggest, too, even if they do not prove, that we can experience cold and warmth with free nerve endings. Perhaps some of the fancier corpuscles also get involved in our experiences of touch and temperature, but they are certainly not the sole receptors.

We should not get into too many details here. The upshot of the matter is that one cannot tell much about perception from the anatomy of receptors in the skin. A free nerve ending is just as likely to give one kind of experience as another. The beautifully designed corpuscles such as the Meissner or Krause bodies do not stand for a particular experience. It would have been very nice—in fact, it would often be very helpful—if each receptor in the skin had a different function. Alas, it is not so.

The Receptors as Analyzers.—Even though the receptors do not wear uniforms that tell us their duties, Müller could still be right. Which receptor gets stimulated could still decide what we perceive. The differences in receptors might be chemical or electrical rather than anatomical. There may very well be a receptor in the eye for red, another for blue, and so on without our being able to tell it by looking at them. So, too, with the skin receptors. All the receptors have to do is respond differently to different stimuli, and then make the proper connections in the sensory pathways so that the brain can keep their identities straight. If they do that, then Müller's theory is right.

Specificity vs. Pattern. As we know, research workers have divided into two camps on this issue. Natanson, Helmholtz, Von Frey, Hecht, Stevens, and Dallenbach—to mention but a few—have stood by Müller. Lotze, Hering, Goldscheider, Wever, and Nafe are some who departed a little or a lot from the anatomical point of view (4). They have held that receptors can send in to the nervous system different kinds of messages and that these messages, and not just the receptors that sent them, affect our experiences. Wever (45) used to say, for example, that the frequency of impulses in the auditory nerve had something to do with whether we hear a high tone or a low tone. Hering believed that the same receptor could make us see red acting in one way and, sending in another kind of message, could make us see green. Nafe (33) has been saying that what receptors *do,* not just which ones they are, determines our perception.

When people argue long and loud about something, there is a fair chance that both sides are partly right, partly wrong. So it seems to be in this case. Research has been telling us enough lately to let us make some decisions about these issues, and it looks more and more as though both camps are partly right. With very small electrodes and the right electrical systems, physiologists have been finding out just what receptors do when they are stimulated (10, 11, 15). Many facts of great interest have come out of their work. Let us spend just a little time hitting their high points.

Kinds of Receptors. It looks as though we have two kinds of receptors in all the senses. One kind responds in about the same way as does the sense organ as a whole. The eye, for example, can see wave lengths of light as long as 760 mμ and as short as 380 mμ. Some of the individual receptors in the eye do exactly the same thing. Their response, in fact, when plotted on a graph looks about the same as the over-all response of the eye (15). In hearing, too, some of the

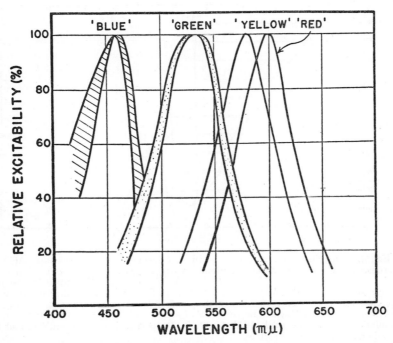

Fig. 3.—Relative excitability of four types of receptors found by Granit in different mammalian eyes. The cross-hatched and stippled portions of the "blue" and "green" receptors indicate variability in the exact forms of these curves. (From C. T. Morgan and E. Stellar, *Physiological psychology* [2d ed.; New York: McGraw-Hill Book Co., Inc., 1950]. By permission of the publisher.)

receptors of the ear are aroused by about the same range of stimuli as is the whole ear, namely, 20 cps to 20 kcps (10). In taste, too, there are receptors that give impulses to almost any kind of chemical stimulus, whether it be sour, salt, or bitter (35). Receptors such as these may be very good for telling us about the intensity of a stimulus and are thus of help in perception. They cannot tell us much, however, about the nature of a stimulus. A receptor that reacts just as does the eye as a whole, or the ear, or the tongue, is not good for quality of perception. It does not let us perceive different colors or pitches or tastes.

Besides these broad-band receptors, however, we have some narrow-band receptors—cells that pick out only some of the spectrum of stimuli that hit the receptors. Granit (15), for example, has put his electrodes in the retinas of various animals and gotten the records shown in Figure 3. Some of the nerve cells he records from have peak responses at 600 mµ, and he calls them red elements. Some have peaks at 530 mµ in the green, 580 mµ in the yellow, and 450 mµ

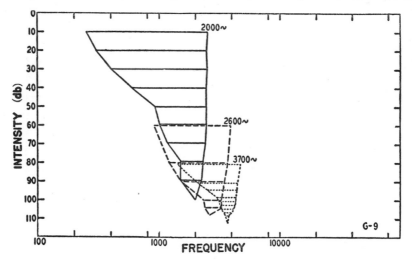

Fig. 4.—Thresholds of response at different frequencies for individual auditory neurons. Data for three different elements are shown: a 2,000-cycle element, a 2,600-cycle element, and a 3,700-cycle element. Each element is named by the frequency at which its threshold is lowest. Scale of intensity is in decibels below a reference level, and hence the larger the number the lower the threshold. (From R. Galambos and H. Davis, The response of single auditory-nerve fibers to acoustic stimulation, *J. Neurophysiol.*, 1943, **6**, 39-57. By permission of the authors and the publisher.)

in the blue. Galambos (10), making the same kind of experiments in a cat, finds nerve cells that react to a small part of the acoustic spectrum. The examples in Figure 4 are of receptors with peaks at 2,000 cps, 2,600 cps, and 3,700 cps. And from the cat's tongue, Pfaffmann (35) has picked up cells that respond more to bitter than to salt or more to salt than to bitter. Those are the only experiments we have now, but we shall probably hear before long of similar results in smell or the skin senses.

Physiology is now giving us an answer to the long debated question whether receptors are at the root of the different qualities of experience we have. Müller was at least partly right. Receptors are analyzers. One receptor picks out some stimuli to respond to more than others, and they somehow or other keep themselves identified upstream in the nervous system. We can perceive different colors, tones, tastes, and probably odors because different anatomical receptors send in messages. There is little doubt about that.

Patterns for Messages. The story, however, is not as simple as it might seem at first glance. We do not have receptor *A* sending in its private message over line *A,* and receptor *B* talking to the nervous system over line *B.* The notion of private lines from receptors to the brain is simple and attractive. Unfortunately, however, it is not true. Instead, receptors get hooked up with each other, so different receptors are talking to the nervous system at the same time. Their talk makes a complex pattern that must be uncoded by the nervous system before we can perceive their meaning.

To make this point clear, let us turn to some examples. Take first Pfaffmann's study of the taste receptors of the cat (35). What he

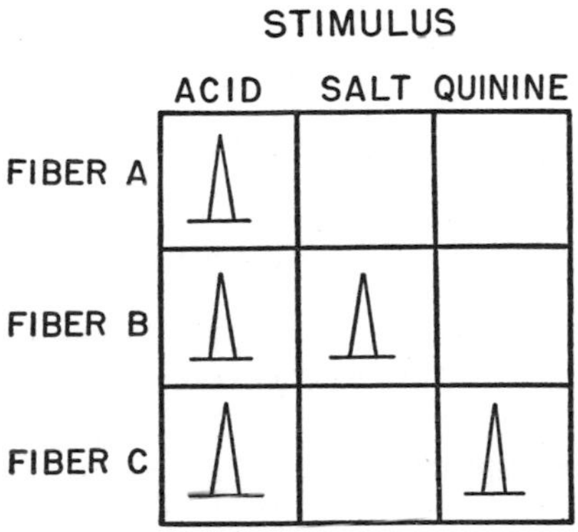

Fig. 5.—Pfaffmann's results with individual fibers from the taste nerve of the cat. *A,* type of fiber that responds only to acid; *B,* type of fiber that responds both to acid and salt; and *C,* a type of fiber that responds to acid and quinine.

found makes the pattern shown in Figure 5. All the fibers that he got under his microelectrodes would respond to acids. They were, one might say, sour receptors. Some of the fibers would respond only to acid. Another type of fiber, however, responded to both acid and bitter stimuli. Still a third class reacted to acid and salt. So there are at least three classes of taste receptors in the cat. They let the cat perceive different tastes, but not in the simple way we might expect. Instead, the cat tastes "salt" when fiber *A* is sending in messages, "bitter" when fiber *B* is signaling, but "sour" when all three fibers— *A, B,* and *C*—are firing. Thus it is a pattern of impulses that comes into the nervous system and that makes the basis for perceiving different tastes.

Coupling of Receptors. Pfaffmann's records of taste receptors come from fibers heading into the nervous system which have not yet made synapses. At the first synapse, there are a lot of possibilities for matters to get more mixed up. Perhaps the different classes of taste fibers—*A, B,* and *C*—make connections at these synapses that make the pattern much more complicated. Certainly that happens in the eye and the ear. For example, the records of Galambos (10) and of Granit (15), referred to above, probably come from nerve cells that have had synapse since the messages left the eye and ear (12). Granit's records probably come from the third order ganglion cells of the eye, and Galambos' from second order neurons of the cochlear nucleus. Both scientists report complex patterns of response in the nerve cells that gave them their records.

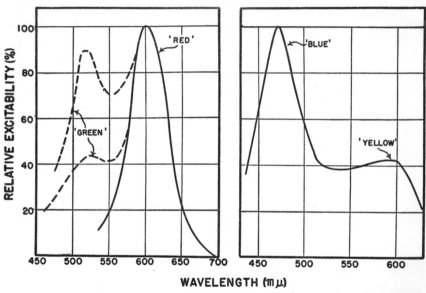

Fig. 6.—Coupling of "red" and "green" receptors in the eye of the snake (left) and coupling of "blue" and "yellow" components in the eye of the frog (right). Both graphs are based on the work of Granit with microelectrodes. (From C. T. Morgan and E. Stellar, *Physiological psychology* [2d ed.; New York: McGraw-Hill Book Co., Inc., 1950]. By permission of the publisher.)

In the eye we see receptors getting coupled together in various ways. Receptors each responding to a narrow band of the spectrum hook into the same neurons after one or two synapses are passed. Just to make this point, Figure 6 shows a few of the records that Granit got from hundreds of experiments with all sorts of animals, including the frog, snake, and cat. Sometimes a green and a blue receptor are coupled together, sometimes a blue and a yellow, and sometimes there are other combinations. There are certainly cases in which many are ganged together in different ways. That can be proved by bleaching out some receptors with one wave length of light and then seeing what records the remaining receptors give. Some day, with the right facts in hand, we may be able to say exactly how the coupling of receptors makes us see different colors. So far we know only that the receptors are coupled in many ways.

Inhibition by Receptors. Life would be simple if receptors were coupled together in only one way, so that their responses added up. Thus it would be nice if a red and a green receptor were so hooked

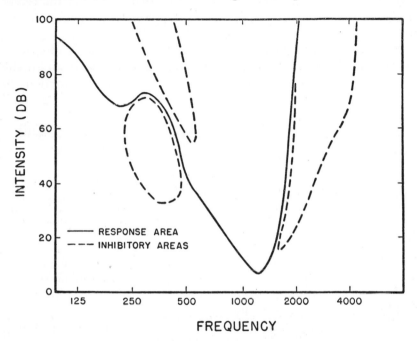

FREQUENCY

Fig. 7.—Composite schematic diagram of inhibitory and response areas of individual elements of the cat's auditory system. Probably no single element ever gives results exactly like those in the diagram. It shows, however, that inhibitory areas may occur at frequencies above, below, and the same as those involved in the response area of an element. (Based on Galambos and Davis, 1944. From C. T. Morgan and E. Stellar, *Physiological psychology* [2d ed.; New York: McGraw-Hill Book Co., Inc., 1950]. By permission of the publisher.)

onto the same bipolar or ganglion cell that their responses simply added together. Sadly enough, though, receptors not only add together, they also subtract from each other's effects. That is to say, when receptors are coupled together, one receptor sometimes inhibits or stops the effects of the other. We have examples of that in both hearing and seeing.

Figure 7, for example, is from Galambos' experiments (11). Probably no one experiment ever gave exactly the picture seen there, but it permits the right conclusion. It shows that one receptor sometimes inhibits another. In the graph, there is a nerve cell that reacts to a narrow range of frequencies and best of all to 1,200 cps. By sounding tones at the same time as one at 1,200 cps, we see that the nerve cell can be inhibited. There is a region around 300 cps, another near 500 cps, and one at 1,800 cps that will give this inhibition. We do not entirely understand this kind of picture, but we are reasonably certain that the record comes from a nerve cell upon which several fibers from the cochlea end. It seems, too, that certain of the receptors when stimulated are stopping the impulses that were set off by other receptors.

We find this sort of coupling turning up in other kinds of experiments with the eye. From electrodes in the optic nerve or in the ganglion cells of the retina, we can see several kinds of reactions to light (14, 18). As is shown in Figure 8, some nerve cells "go on,"

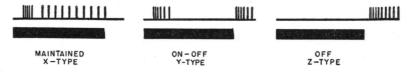

MAINTAINED   ON–OFF   OFF
X–TYPE   Y–TYPE   Z–TYPE

Fig. 8.—Activity of three types of ganglion cells distinguished in the vertebrate eye by Hartline. (From S. H. Bartley, Some factors in brightness discrimination, *Psychol. Rev.*, 1939, 46, 347. By permission of the author, the *Psychological Review*, and the American Psychological Association.)

that is, give impulses, when a light comes on. Some are in spontaneous activity while the eye is in the dark and stop firing when a light comes on. Still others go on when the light goes on, then stop while the light is on, and finally start firing again when the light goes off. The main point is that turning on a light can inhibit or stop impulses that have been started by other lights or in some other way. Thus we are led to believe that receptors are coupled not only by adding but also by subtracting, that is, by inhibiting arrangements of various sorts.

We do not understand just how the receptors add and subtract in perception. We are starting to get the general idea though, and we are making progress year by year. As matters now stand, we know this much: One cannot tell what a receptor does by the way it is built or how it looks. Receptors have different features that do not meet the eye. Some act like the sense organ as a whole, but others pick out only part of the sensory gamut of stimuli to react to. We can perceive different tones, colors, and tastes by what receptors signal that they are responding to. The signals, however, are not simple. In the synapses between the receptors and the brain, receptors get coupled to the same nerve cells. Sometimes this coupling adds up signals from different receptors. Sometimes it causes a nerve cell to be inhibited by a receptor. Our perception thus rests on very complex patterns of signals coming from receptors.

Perception of Space

We not only perceive amounts and kinds of stimuli, but we perceive the size, shape, and form of various stimuli in the world outside us. In talking about anatomy and perception, we therefore need a device of some sort for the perception of space. Offhand, of course, a mechanism like a camera might do. That is to say, if one spot on a sense organ connects with a spot up in the sensory centers of the brain, it would let the brain see, hear, or feel the picture of the world that the sense organ is getting. That is the idea that people have had about perception for a long time. Let us see what there is to it.

Overlapping of Receptors.—In Figure 9 we see an experiment that Bishop (3) has carried out fairly recently. He got a machine that let him prick the skin with an electric spark. Naturally such a spark was painful. With sparks flying, he mapped an area on the arm of a man so that he could tell where the nerve serving the skin was located. Having found nerve twigs in this way, he shot the skin with local anesthetic to deaden the nerve twigs. Then by deadening the right set of nerve fibers, he could produce an island on the skin which was still sensitive to pain. Around it, however, was a ring of skin where the subject could feel no pain. By doing this kind of experiment over and over again, Bishop managed to map the area that each nerve fiber of the skin served. This map, it turns out, is very much like that gotten in other experiments by other scientists using only anatomical methods (41, pp. 16-43).

There are three important points about the map. One is the rather large area that each nerve fiber serves. It may be a half-inch across. In some areas of the body, in fact, it is much wider than that. Another point is that nerves overlap a lot in the areas that they serve. Indeed, a prick in almost any part of the arm arouses not just one free nerve receptor but two or three. The same is true of receptors in other parts of the body. A third point, the most important of all, is that our ability to tell what point on our arm is pricked, or to tell the space between two points, is much less than the area served by any one receptor. The reason, however, is almost obvious. It is that we never perceive the signal from just one receptor but always from two or three receptors. The set of signals from two receptors—which two they are and how strongly they signal—tells us much more certainly where a prick is than we could know from just one receptor. Thus we have a sort of anatomical triangulation to help us in our perception of space.

Pricks on the skin just happen to be the method by which the map in Figure 9 was produced. We have a right to think that the same principle applies to other kinds of receptors. It certainly must work

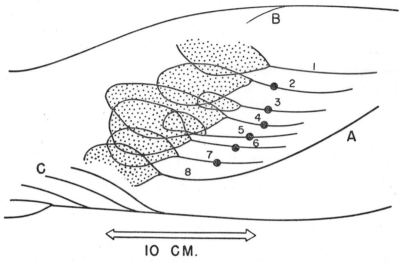

FIG. 9.—Pain units mapped in an experiment by Bishop. The dotted areas are the endings of nerve fibers 1, 2, etc., which are branches of the group of nerve fibers A. B and C are other groups. The black dots show the spots that were anesthetized. By blocking nerve twigs in different combinations and mapping the areas of remaining sensibility for pain, these maps of the areas served by each twig could be constructed. (After Bishop, 1944. From C. T. Morgan and E. Stellar, *Physiological psychology* [2d ed.; New York: McGraw-Hill Book Co., Inc., 1950]. By permission of the publisher.)

for the pressure receptors of the skin. In the eye, receptors do not sprawl about in the retina in the way that free nerve endings do in the skin, but they are coupled together with bipolar and lateral cells in a way that has about the same effect. In many regions of the retina, one ganglion cell gets impulses from several receptors, and the regions that ganglion cells serve overlap each other. So we do not have the simple mosaic we might expect, but instead we find overlapping of the areas of service of receptors.

Summation in Sensory Pathways.—Even after we leave the sense organs we do not find sensory pathways making clear tracks into the brain. At each synapse in the pathway, nerve cells connect with a good many other cells. This fact is plain in the nerve cells of almost every sense that we have observed. Thus a nice simple possibility goes by the board—that the way neurons connect with each other explains our perception of space. It does not, and the fact has been slowly dawning on physiologists for the last few years. It is something in the way neurons function, not their anatomy, that is at the root of space perception.

We have already talked about the effects of receptors in adding and subtracting. In saying that, we mean what the neurophysiologist means when he speaks of "summation" and "inhibition." Both these factors seem to be at work in the sensory pathways to let the brain see space in the world in about the same way that the sense organ does. We have no direct proof yet of the way summation and inhibition enter into spatial mechanisms, but we know that they take place in the sensory pathways, and we have enough other physiological

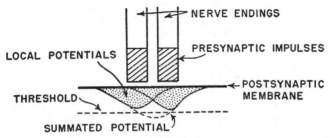

Fig. 10.—Synaptic summation. Two impulses come down nerve endings to the cell body of another neuron at about the same time. Each arouses a local potential in the cell body that is too small to evoke an impulse. The two local potentials add together, however, to make a potential above the threshold of the neuron. Thus a postsynaptic impulse gets started only through summation at the synapse. (From C. T. Morgan and E. Stellar, *Physiological psychology* [2d ed.; New York: McGraw-Hill Book Co., Inc., 1950]. By permission of the publisher.)

experiments and theories to give us a general picture of the way things must be.

Take addition or summation first. It is illustrated in Figure 10. Physiologists learned some time ago that nerve cells in the nervous system usually need more than one impulse to set them off (28, 32). When just one impulse comes to a synapse, the neuron on the other side is excited, but only locally, and it does not get an impulse started down its fibers. Much of the time what seems to be needed is two impulses arriving at just about the same time. This we call *synaptic summation.*

Figure 11 shows how such summation helps keep impulses in the right neurons of a sensory pathway to preserve the shape of the original stimulus in the picture that gets to the brain (31, p. 166). Assume that the stimulus hits only two receptors. These receptors connect with several neurons at their first synapse, and the second-order neurons in turn connect with several more. Thus impulses could get widely spread in the sensory pathway if it were not for the fact that neurons need summed impulses in order to be fired. The two receptors first aroused can add to each other's effects on two second-order neurons. The net result is as represented in Figure 11; that is to say, the pattern of the stimulus out in the world can get sent up to the brain even though neurons connect much too promiscuously.

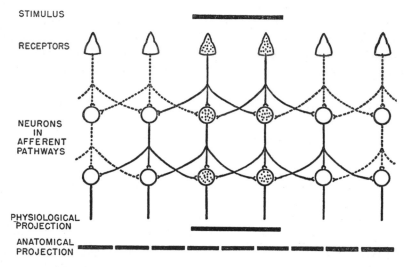

Fig. 11.—Diagram illustrating how synaptic connections at various levels of the visual system give relatively diffuse anatomical projection and how, by means of the synaptic summation required in transmission, there can be a point-to-point physiological projection of images on the cerebral cortex. (After Lorente de Nó. From C. T. Morgan and E. Stellar, *Physiological psychology* [2d ed.; New York: McGraw-Hill Book Co., Inc., 1950]. By permission of the publisher.)

In this connection, two points about the eye are interesting. Even though receptors in the eye do not ramify but are lined up like soldiers, the eye as an optic instrument spreads images on the retina so that a pin-point stimulus always excites more than one receptor. The other point is that the scientists who have taken up the question of how much energy is necessary for us to see light under the best of conditions have come out with a minimum figure of two quanta (21). They say we must have at least two quanta in order for us to see. So everything hangs together. Adding impulses is basic in the sensory pathways. We have to have it to perceive anything, and we must have it to perceive space.

Inhibition in Sensory Pathways.—As we said above, impulses must not only add but also subtract at the synapses of the sensory pathways. This means that inhibition is going on. We cannot prove just how the inhibition works, but some ideas about it occur to the present writer from seeing what physiologists are doing these days.

All through their history, physiologists have been discovering and distinguishing different types of inhibition: Wedenski inhibition, successive inhibition, spatial inhibition, reciprocal inhibition, and so on. Just a while back "direct inhibition" was added to the list (27). This is the plain and simple case where a stimulus stops impulses that otherwise would be going on. Direct inhibition, although discovered last, probably is more basic to our understanding of what goes on in normal events in the nervous system than any other sort of inhibition. Moreover, right on the heels of its discovery, physiologists had reached the point in their knowledge of how nerve cells get excited and conduct that they could give us a good theory of how and why direct inhibition occurs. It is an anatomical theory.

Figure 12 is a diagram that helps explain both the fact and the theory of direct inhibition (5). The fact is that impulses coming in over neuron E can "pass" the synapse and fire impulses off in neuron A, but impulses coming in over neuron I stop neuron A from firing. The theory is that the short neuron A is the cause of the inhibition. It is supposed to be the cause both because it is short and because it does not get enough summation of impulses from neuron I to fire. As a result, all that happens in the short neuron is that a local potential and current are set up. The current is depicted by the lines and arrows in the diagram. Currents at the bottom end of the short neuron make a loop through the neuron. They go in a focus at the foot of neuron A and come out some distance away. Physiologists now have good reason to believe that inflowing currents inhibit neurons and that outflowing currents excite them. The short neuron makes a focus of inflowing current and this inhibits neurons. That, in a nutshell, is the story. The short neuron, because it does not fire and because it is short, puts an inhibiting current on neuron A and stops it from firing.

With this notion of inhibition in mind, an anatomist—and the psychologist too—can have a heyday looking at the sensory pathways. There are lots of short neurons in the nervous system, and inhibition might be taking place wherever they are. In the retina, for example, we have long known the amacrine and horizontal cells as short lateral neurons. Now, in fact, we have good reason to believe they are there to inhibit things. Certainly many experiments, and the last of them microelectrode experiments, prove that there is inhibition in the retina. In some of the way stations too there are many short neurons, and the cerebral cortex, of course, has millions of them. It is too early to say just when and how inhibition may be at work in all these places, but we may expect the physiologists to bring us news of it in the years just ahead.

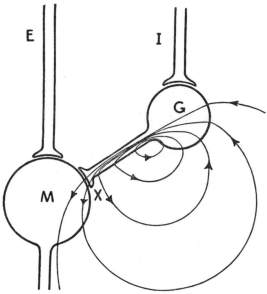

Fig. 12.—Schematic diagram of the electrical theory of direct inhibition. Impulses coming in over axon E excite neuron M, and those coming from axon I inhibit neuron M. G stands for a small internuncial neuron (Golgi type II), which is locally excited by axon I but does not get excited enough to give a propagated spike-potential. Instead, only a local flow of current, indicated by the lines with arrows on them, is set up. Because the focal currents are inflowing for the membrane of neuron M, they are inhibitory. (From C. McC. Brooks and J. C. Eccles, An electrical hypothesis of central inhibition, *Nature*, Lond., 1947, **159**, 763. By permission of the authors and the publisher.)

Spatial Projection on the Cerebral Cortex.—These comments have taken us a little off our main subject—that is, the anatomy of space perception. We have seen so far that the spatial layout of receptors and summation and inhibition all have something to do with preserving a spatial picture of the outside world in our sensory pathways. Let us come now to the projection of the sensory pathways on the cerebral cortex.

We have known for some time that there is a somewhat faithful projection of visual affairs on the occipital cortex of the brain. The spatial arrangement of the auditory and cutaneous pathways has, however, been a matter for debate and research. Fortunately, the research has been coming through with new and valuable answers. With a relatively new technique—the technique of mapping electrical potentials in the cortex during various kinds of sensory stimulation

—we have come to a new conception of how the sensory cortex is spatially arranged. This is illustrated in Figures 13 and 14.

Figure 13 is for skin perception (47). It tells what parts of the cortex give electrical waves for different parts of the body. There

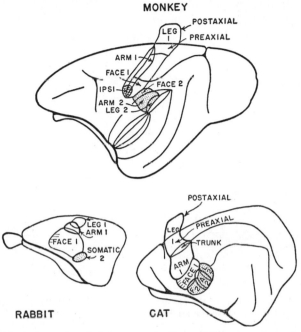

Fig. 13.—Somatic areas of the cortex in the rabbit, cat, and monkey. In each diagram, the dotted area is somatic area II. In every case, area II can be subdivided roughly into face, arm, and leg areas, but the diagram for the rabbit is too small to show that fact. There is a certain amount of overlapping of face, arm, and leg subdivisions in both areas I and II. The cross-hatched part of the face area I in each diagram is the part that has ipsilateral representation of the face. Note that somatic area II is located laterally toward the temporal lobe, not in the posterior parietal lobule. (After Woolsey, 1947. From C. T. Morgan and E. Stellar, *Physiological psychology* [2d ed.; New York: McGraw-Hill Book Co., Inc., 1950]. By permission of the publisher.)

is a clear spatial arrangement, a homunculus, so to speak, in which each part of the body has a place on the cortex. Most interesting, however, is the fact that there is not simply one area for skin perception, but rather there are two. We call them areas I and II to be neutral about them until we understand better what their jobs are. Area I, it will be noted, is about where anatomists always say the primary area for skin perception is, but area II turns up in a somewhat unexpected place on the lateral part of the cortex. It too has a spatial arrangement in which its different parts represent different parts of the body. So we have two homunculi—two little men—in our cerebral cortex.

As is indicated in Figure 14, we have also learned recently that the auditory system preserves a spatial picture up through its sensory pathways (42, 43). This picture has little to do with space in the outside world but rather makes a mechanism for telling the cortex about the frequency of auditory stimuli. In Figure 14, the letter *B* stands for the basal part of the cochlea, *M* for the middle, and *A* for the apical end of the cochlea. These letters are, therefore, crude ways of showing how the cochlea projects on the cortex. Notice,

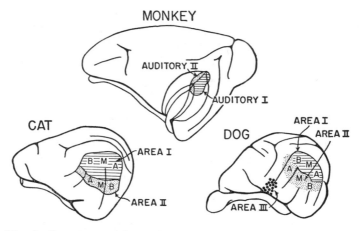

Fig. 14.—Auditory areas of the monkey, cat, and dog. All diagrams are left lateral views of the cortex. Because the auditory area of the monkey is buried partly in the lateral fissure, it is represented as it would be seen with the lateral fissure spread apart. Tonotopic organization is shown by the letters *B, M,* and *A,* which stand for the basal, middle, and apical parts of the cochlea respectively. The diagram for the dog is more approximate than the others. (After Woolsey, 1947, and Tunturi, 1945. From C. T. Morgan and E. Stellar, *Physiological psychology* [2d ed.; New York: McGraw-Hill Book Co., Inc., 1950]. By permission of the publisher.)

too, in Figure 14, that there is more than one auditory area. In all the animals so far used in this kind of experiment there are at least two areas—we call them areas I and II—and in the dog there seem to be three areas. Maybe there is a third area in other animals too and investigators just have not found it yet.

These areas of the cortex for auditory and skin perception are of interest for our purposes not because they have any obvious bearing on the anatomy of perception—we do not yet know what they mean—but because we now have a much better chance than we have had in the past to find out what the cortex has to do with perception. It is obvious now why we made so little progress for so long—we did not know what areas of the cortex to study. Now we do know, and it would not be surprising if we soon make some very great strides forward in the cortical anatomy of perception. Some members of the Hopkins laboratory, using such maps as those in Figures 13 and 14, are already at work on the psychological functions of these sensory areas.

The Embryology of Spatial Arrangements.—There is just one other point to make in connection with anatomy and space perception. It may have occurred to the reader, as we have gone along, that the sensory pathways are laid out in a very refined spatial pattern. The visual, auditory, and somatic systems—indeed, all the senses—seem to maintain a spatial projection from the surface of the body up to the cortex. Moreover, connections in each system must be very precise for the signals from the various receptors to be kept straight as they pass up the system. The precision of arrangement is remarkable.

It should be in order to ask how such an arrangement came about. What factors are at work as the organism develops to make all the connections come out right? To this question we now have an answer. First, Weiss (44), then L. S. Stone (40), and more recently Sperry (38, 39) have gone through a series of ingenious experiments to pin down the factors that control how connections are formed in the nervous system. Sperry, for example, has crossed the sensory and motor nerves in the legs of the rat, and from that has picked up some clues. He has also cut the optic nerve, rotated the eyeballs in various degrees, allowed the nerves to regenerate and then tested animals for the return of spatial vision. There are many details to his experiments, and they prove somewhat confusing, but the upshot of them all is this: *Nerve fibers grow back to make the same connections that they made in the first place.* To put the matter in another way, the nerve cells along the sensory pathways have some sort of biochemical tags that keep them straight when connections are being laid down. One might say that each nerve cell has a name and that other nerve cells know what that name is. It is still a mystery what these names are and how the cells know each other's names, and that will be a subject for future research. At any rate, nerves can be badly cut, mangled, and twisted, but somehow or other nerve fibers get back where they belong. For us, it is interesting to know that biochemical factors are at work in laying out the spatial arrangement of the nervous pathways.

Anatomy and Cognition

We have discussed so far the qualitative and spatial aspects of our experience. Both are basic, more or less unlearned features of perception. Let us turn now to cognitions, that is, to such matters as recognizing a familiar situation, knowing the names of objects, acquiring sensory discriminations, and using sensory cues in learned behavior. Both the clinician and the experimentalist have given such perceptions a good deal of attention in order to discover what anatomical features of the brain may have to do with them. The question is where we stand at present.

Arrangement of the Cortex.—The anatomists and physiologists for their part have been making good headway. As we saw just a moment ago, they have given us new facts about the primary and secondary areas of the brain. Even more than that, however, they

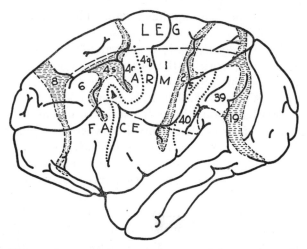

FIG. 15.—Main excitatory and suppressor areas of the sensory and motor cortex of the chimpanzee. The shaded areas are the suppressor areas. Figure 16 shows in detail how they are interrelated with excitatory areas. (From W. S. McCulloch, Cortico-cortical connections. In P. C. Bucy [ed.], *The precentral motor cortex,* 2d ed. [Urbana, Ill.: University of Illinois Press, 1949], p. 233. By permission of the publisher.)

have come forth with a wealth of information about the arrangement of the cerebral cortex. By using drugs and electrical methods of recording, they have set up a disturbance in one area of the cortex, then recorded the effects in various other areas of the cortex. From such methods they have been able to tell us in great detail how various parts of the cortex are interrelated. Moreover, to everyone's surprise, they have discovered that some areas of the cortex are inhibitory—they suppress activity in other areas—and other areas are excitatory in function (29).

First, a few words about suppressor areas. This is no place to name all the suppressor areas or to go into the details of their relations. Two of these areas, however, are in the sensory sphere of things. One of them, Brodmann's area 2, lies right alongside somatic area 1 that we were just looking at. Another is Brodmann's area 19, long known to be some sort of "visual association area." The interesting thing about both of these sensory areas is that they can suppress activity in many other areas of the cerebral cortex, both sensory and motor. The areas which they suppress are diagramed in Figure 15. The somesthetic suppressor area, for example, can suppress somatic area I and the parietal association areas 40 and 39 (Brodmann's numbers), as well as many of the motor areas in the frontal part of the cortex. The visual suppressor area, Brodmann's 19, similarly can block activity in many sensory, motor, and associative areas of the cortex.

If we continue to look at Figure 15, we see that it shows not only suppressor but also excitatory connections between different areas of the cortex. The somatic area (Brodmann's 39), for example, has connections with the motor area and with areas 5 and 39 in the parietal lobe. Motor areas have connections with the somatic and parietal areas. There are many such relations depicted in Figure 16, but we need not go into them now. In fact, we do not know what all these connections mean. We can be glad, however, that physiologists have now been able to tell us about them. With this as background information, psychologists can now devise experiments to find out more about events going on in various cortical areas in perception. That is why they are brought to the reader's attention at this time.

The Cortex and Agnosia. Although we are learning a good deal about cortical anatomy, we must admit, I think, that we have been making very little progress with the anatomy of cognitive functions. The facts stand very much as they did ten years ago (23, 24). At that time Lashley's work with animals had posed the mystery that is still with us, to wit, that the primary sensory areas of the cortex are involved in learning a sensory cognition but are not really necessary for it. We may recall his case of the rats that completely lost their memory for a brightness discrimination when he took out their striate cortical areas, yet were perfectly able to learn the discrimination again. Many a research worker has confirmed Lashley (32), not only in the matter of visual habits, but also auditory and somatic habits as well. When almost any animal, say the rat, cat, dog, or monkey, learns almost any sensory habit and then loses the appropriate sensory area of its cortex—at the hand of an experimenter—it will lose the habit. Given another chance, however, it will learn the habit again.

This problem of forgetting a sensory habit after injury to the cortex is an important problem both to the pure scientist and the practicing neurologist. Neurologists could ply their trade much better if they knew just why such things happen and could tell in advance when they would and would not happen. Those of us who are pure —that is, pure scientists—would understand learning and what goes on in the brain much better if we knew why this sort of agnosia with recovery takes place.

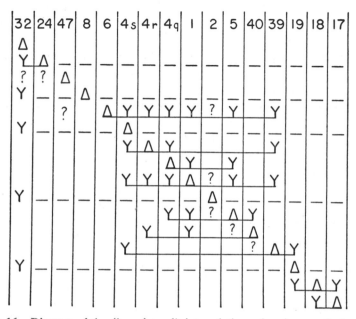

Fig. 16.—Diagram of the (homolateral) interrelations of various cortical areas of the chimpanzee as mapped by the method of strychninization. Triangles (Δ) indicate the area to which strychnine is applied. Any other areas that also show electrical activity when the strychnine is applied are indicated in the same row by the open angle (Y). Areas whose electrical activity is suppressed are represented by dashed lines. Areas whose activity is questionable have a question mark (?) in the appropriate box. Where there is no mark in a box, there is no response for that area to the strychninization of the other areas indicated in the same row. The column marked 32 refers to areas 32 and 31, which respond together as a unit. (Based on McCulloch, 1944. From C. T. Morgan and E. Stellar, *Physiological psychology* [2d ed.; New York: McGraw-Hill Book Co., Inc., 1950]. By permission of the publisher.)

Some of us think that the mystery has something to do with perception, that an animal appears to lose a habit after cortical destruction because it has lost a way of looking at its world and must learn a new one. Helping out this viewpoint a little is Harlow's experiment with monkeys (17). He took out only one side of their visual cortices after teaching them a visual discrimination. If he left them in the dark after operation, they were very disturbed and took some time to relearn. If, however, he gave them plenty of postoperative experience in the light before bringing them to the test, he found them to perform very well. Apparently they had to learn to see their world in a new way to compensate for the great change made in their visual perception by the loss of part of their brains.

We have some other recent reports that point the finger at perception, rather than memory, as the causes of the agnosia following cortical lesions. Ades (1) did a very interesting experiment with some of the visual "association" areas (Brodmann's 18 and 19). He trained some monkeys to discriminate sizes and shapes, then took the areas out. If both sides were removed, they gave the classical phenomenon of completely forgetting the habits and then relearning them anew after enough training. If, however, he took out only one side, as he did in one monkey, then gave the monkeys some practice on the habits, and finally took out the other side, there was no loss of memory. In other words, what the monkeys completely forgot when subjected to a one-stage bilateral operation they remembered without trouble when operated upon in two stages and given some training in between.

Lashley (26), for reasons we need not go into now, gives us some reason to question Ades' experiment. Perhaps there is something wrong with this particular experiment, but even if that is the case, his point is probably right. Raab (36), in fact, has done the same kind of experiment with hearing in the dog. He conditioned dogs, then took out one auditory cortex, gave them some retraining, and finally took out the other auditory cortex. His animals remembered the auditory habit all through the procedure. Other animals which had both cortices removed at once, however, gave the classical picture. Recently the present writer has been doing some work along this line with rats. In this case, the rats have learned a visual brightness discrimination and have then been subjected to removal of the striate areas in two successive unilateral stages. Between the two stages of operation, however, there has intervened a short period of "refresher" training. Animals put through this procedure do not forget the visual discrimination they have learned, as they do forget it when they have only a one-stage bilateral operation after original learning.

There must be several ways to interpret experiments like these, and the reader may already have thought of some. To this writer, however, perception looms up as the key to understanding them. In the classical, bilateral experiments in which both sensory areas are removed at the same time, we know that we make a big change in an animal's sensory capacity (32). It would seem that we make such a big change that the animal can no longer make use of the cues it has been leaning on for its discrimination. If we make the removal in stages, however, we give the animal a bridge. We let it have part of its old normal perceptual equipment, while introducing it to the new. With a little exercise in the habit and with both new and old perceptions available, it makes the switch and is able to continue when the cortical damage is made complete.

This is just a hypothesis, but the present writer is willing to make it a general one. The hypothesis is that changes in perception—that is, in the way the world looks, sounds, and feels to people and animals—account for many of the agnosias, amnesias, and apparent losses in memory that we see in both our clinical reports and animal experiments after areas of the cerebral cortex are damaged. There are many details of the hypothesis to be made specific for different kinds of habits, but it offers a challenge to research that may change our view of learning processes in the brain and put a much greater emphasis on perception.

Associative Areas of the Human Cortex. Still on this matter of anatomy and cognition, we come finally to the role of the primary and secondary sensory areas of the brain in complex perceptions. Many years ago neurologists were inclined to make elaborate, detailed maps of the brain and to stake out different functions in different areas. Many speak of these days gone by as the era of the "map makers." We gradually got away from these maps because there were many human cases of cerebral injury that did not give the symptoms that the maps called for, and also because animal experiments gave the maps no support. So the maps of cognitive areas of the cortex, and the general idea of localization of cognitive function in the cortex, have not been too popular of late.

No doubt the map makers went much too far. They certainly gave us some impossible ideas, and the present writer would not be one to uphold them. However, these maps have never been given a fair chance either in the clinic or in the laboratory, and it is worth our while to find out why. In Figure 17 is a map of the cerebral cortex of man, giving various cognitive functions for each of the many sensory areas. This map is one made up recently by the present writer (32) to represent many different opinions about localization in the human brain, but it comes rather close to what Nielson (34), the latest neurologist to make his view explicit, has to say. None of us may find it easy to take this map very seriously, yet it presents us with a hypothesis—indeed, many hypotheses—that have not been tested.

In the first place, hardly any of our experiments with animals have tested this kind of map. For that there has been good reason. We have no end of trouble, of course, devising methods that will get at some of the more complex learned perceptions implied in such a map. On the psychological side, therefore, our experiments have often been inadequate. Our anatomy, too, has been lacking. We have not, in fact, been able to tell just which areas in the rat or cat or monkey correspond to the areas you see marked out on the human brain. From the maps which were presented earlier, we know where to look in the brains of animals for the areas like these in man.

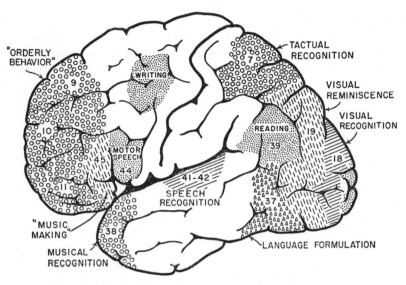

Fig. 17.—Composite diagram of the supposed "association" areas of the human cerebral cortex. Many neurologists believe that the cortex functions in some such way as is indicated here; some do not. The scheme is worth while mainly to provide hypotheses for further research and to help in thinking about the role of the cortex in learning and memory. (From C. T. Morgan and E. Stellar, *Physiological psychology* [2d ed.; New York: McGraw-Hill Book Co., Inc., 1950]. By permission of the publisher.)

Lateral dominance has also been a serious problem in getting at the anatomical basis of cognition. That one of our hands or feet or eyes is the major one and the other the minor one is a fact not easily disputed. We know, too, that in some affairs one side of the brain is dominant; that is to say, it plays a major role in perception or action, while the other side is minor. Although people have often argued about how important lateral dominance is and how many of the world's ills it accounts for, few deny altogether that it exists. We must, in fact, believe that some parts of the brain, like the speech area, show very strong one-sidedness and that, in the case of others, the sides share about equally in the functions that concern them. If that be true, how can we tell where to look for a particular function? If one kind of cognition belongs to one side of the brain and we make a lesion in the other side, we will completely miss the point. Or if a type of cognition shares equally corresponding areas on both sides, it takes a perfect bilateral lesion in the areas to make the localization known.

We ought to consider, too, the matter of individual differences. We find it natural to say that people are different in the measurements of personality, intelligence, or some other aspect of behavior, but we often seem to assume that brains are standard products turned out on an assembly line so that they look as much alike as new cars. The fact is that brains vary a lot in their size and shape. Lashley (25) has been going into that matter lately, and he assures us that there are individual differences in brain anatomy. If that be true, why are there not individual differences in which areas of the brain get involved in different functions? And how can our conventional techniques let us know beforehand which brain is which and thus tell us the answers to our questions about localization?

All these are reasons why we have not been making more progress with the question of localization of learned perceptions. There are more that we could go into in a more extended discussion. They do not answer our problem, however, and they do not tell us whether the map in Figure 17 is all right, partly right, or all wrong. There are many neurologists who would accept a good deal of it, and, if a choice were necessary, the present writer certainly would choose it before nothing at all.

If we had to end by saying *only* that we do not yet know what kinds of cognitive maps of the brain to construct, our time would be wasted; but there is a bright prospect in the progress we have made. We now know much more than we did ten years ago about the anatomical organization of the brain. We know what areas go with each sense, how they are arranged spatially, how they connect with each other, and even which areas they inhibit and excite. Moreover, we now know something of the homologues in animals, that is, what areas in animals correspond with those in man. All these, together with our previous failures and our improved techniques, let us understand clearly, probably for the first time, how we must proceed if we are to learn how the anatomy of the brain takes part in our perceptions.

Comment

The reader may wonder why some topics have received little or no discussion in this chapter on structural determinants of perception. The present writer would like in closing to make a few comments about them.

Aging.—One such topic might be age. We know that structures of the sense organs and nervous system take time to develop in the embryo and in infancy and that they may also deteriorate later in life when aging processes take their toll. There is much to be said, and also much yet to be learned, about aging and perception. In general we know that sense organs and sensory systems mature at different rates in different animals, depending upon their embryonic environment and later way of living (6). In general, however, we know that these organs and systems tend to mature about the time they are needed for the behavioral repertoire of the animal. We do not know very well, however, just how maturation affects the rate at which numerous complex perceptions develop in the young animal or child. We have anatomical evidence (32) that neural maturation goes on long after birth, certainly up to two years and perhaps much longer, but the established correlations between developing structure and perception are few.

The effect of later aging upon perception is a subject that has only recently been getting much needed attention (37). And it is probably too early to tell the general trend of conclusions from research in the area. What studies we have tend to suggest that changes in perception, at least the basic aspects of perception with which we have been dealing in this chapter, are caused by disease, injury, or retrogression of sensory structures. Visual perception fails, for example, when certain conditions develop in the retina. Apparently there are degenerative changes in the ear that cause losses and changes in auditory perception. In other words, once knowing the general structural basis of perception and knowing how structures may be affected in aging, we can piece together and predict some of the effects of aging on perception.

Brain Injury.—I have said relatively little about the numerous studies of brain injuries and their effects upon perception in clinical subjects. Freeman and Watts (8), for example, report many perceptual changes in their patients suffering frontal lobotomy. Halstead, too, has an excellent report (16) of the aspects of attention and perception that are affected in cases of brain injury. Hebb (20), in his series of research reports and in his monograph, emphasizes particularly the way in which early versus late learning is involved in the perceptual deficits found in cases of brain injury. But for a fuller discussion of these points the reader should turn to the original sources. One should also keep in mind the tentative and somewhat conflicting nature of the evidence in these clinical studies. For a thorough study that explodes many of the clinical conclusions about frontal lobotomy, for example, one may turn to the recent Columbia-Greystone study on this subject (30).

Body Chemistry.—We have been coming to realize more and more in recent years that the sense organs and the nervous system are not completely self-sufficient structures.   They function in a milieu of factors, such as circulation, enzymes, and hormones, that continually play upon them.   These factors greatly modify the perceptions which they subserve.   No attempt has been made to discuss them here, however, for Dr. Beach's chapter which follows discusses them rather fully.

BIBLIOGRAPHY

1. ADES, H. W.   Effect of extirpation of parastriate cortex on learned visual discriminations in monkeys. *J. Neuropath. exp. Neurol.*, 1946, **5**, 60-65.
2. BAZETT, H. C.   Temperature sense in man.   In American Institute of Physics, *Temperature: its measurement and control in science and industry.*   New York: Reinhold Publishing Corp., 1941.
3. BISHOP, G. H.   The peripheral unit of pain.   *J. Neurophysiol.*, 1944, **1**, 71-80.
4. BORING, E. G.   *Sensation and perception in the history of experimental psychology.*   New York: Appleton-Century-Crofts, Inc., 1942.
5. BROOKS, C. McC., & ECCLES, J. C.   An electrical hypothesis of central inhibition. *Nature*, 1947, **159**, 1-12.
6. CARMICHAEL, L.   Experimental embryology of mind. *Psychol. Bull.*, 1941, **38**, 1-28.
7. CROZIER, W. J., & WOLF, E.   The flicker response contour for the Gecko (rod retina). *J. gen. Physiol.*, 1939, **22**, 555-66.
8. FREEMAN, W., & WATTS, J. W. *Psychosurgery.*   Springfield: Charles C Thomas, Publisher, 1942.
9. FULTON, J. F. *Physiology of the nervous system* (2d ed.).   New York: Oxford University Press, 1943.
10. GALAMBOS, R., & DAVIS, H.   The response of single auditory-nerve fibers to acoustic stimulation. *J. Neurophysiol.*, 1943, **6**, 39-58.
11. GALAMBOS, R., & DAVIS, H.   Inhibition of activity in simple auditory nerve fibers by acoustic stimulation. *J. Neurophysiol.*, 1944, **7**, 287-304.
12. GALAMBOS, R., & DAVIS, H.   Action potentials from single auditory-nerve fibers? *Science,* 1943, **108**, 513.
13. GILMER, B. V. H.   The glomus body as a receptor of cutaneous pressure and vibration. *Psychol. Bull.*, 1942, **39**, 73-93.
14. GRANIT, R.   The distribution of excitation and inhibition in single-fibre responses from a polarized retina. *J. Physiol.*, 1946, **105**, 45-53.
15. GRANIT, R. *Sensory mechanisms of the retina.*   New York: Oxford University Press, 1947.
16. HALSTEAD, W. C. *Brain and intelligence.*   Chicago: University of Chicago Press, 1947.
17. HARLOW, H. F.   Recovery of pattern discrimination in monkeys following unilateral occipital lobectomy. *J. comp. Psychol.*, 1939, **27**, 467-89.
18. HARTLINE, H. K.   The response of single optic nerve fibers of the vertebrate eye to illumination of the retina. *Amer. J. Physiol.*, 1938, **121**, 400-15.
19. HARTRIDGE, H.   The visual perception of fine detail. *Phil. Trans. roy. Soc. Lond., Series B,* 1947, **232**, 519-671.
20. HEBB, D. O. *Organization of behavior.*   New York: John Wiley & Sons, Inc., 1949.
21. HECHT, S., SHLAER, S., & PIRENNE, M. H.   Energy, quanta and vision. *J. gen. Physiol.*, 1942, **25**, 819-40.

22. JENKINS, W. L., & STONE, L. J. I. Recent research in cutaneous sensitivity. II. Touch and the neural basis of the skin senses. *Psychol. Bull.*, 1941, **38**, 69-91.

23. LASHLEY, K. S. Factors limiting recovery after central nervous lesions. *J. nerv. ment. Dis.*, 1938, **88**, 733-55.

24. LASHLEY, K. S. The problem of cerebral organization in vision. In H. Klüver (ed.), Visual mechanisms. *Biol. Symp.*, 1942, **7**, 301-22.

25. LASHLEY, K. S. Structural variation in the nervous system in relation to behavior. *Psychol. Rev.*, 1947, **54**, 325-34.

26. LASHLEY, K. S. The mechanism of vision. XVIII. Effects of destroying the visual "associative areas" of the monkey. *Genet. Psychol. Monogr.*, 1948, **37**, 107-66.

27. LLOYD, D. P. C. Facilitation and inhibition of spinal motoneurons. *J. Neurophysiol.*, 1946, **9**, 421-38.

28. McCULLOCH, W. S. Irreversibility of conduction in the reflex arc. *Science*, 1938, **87**, 65-66.

29. McCULLOCH, W. S. Cortico-cortical connections. In P. C. Bucy (ed.), *The precentral motor cortex* (2d ed.). Urbana, Ill.: University of Illinois Press, 1949.

30. METTLER, F. A. (ed.). *Selective partial ablation of the frontal cortex.* New York: Harper & Bros., 1949.

31. MORGAN, C. T. *Physiological psychology.* New York: McGraw-Hill Book Co., Inc., 1943.

32. MORGAN, C. T., & STELLAR, E. *Physiological psychology* (2d ed.). New York: McGraw-Hill Book Co., Inc., 1950.

33. NAFE, J. P. Toward the quantification of psychology. *Psychol. Rev.*, 1942, **49**, 1-18.

34. NIELSON, J. M. *Agnosia, apraxia, aphasia: their value in cerebral localization.* New York: Paul B. Hoeber, Inc., Medical Book Department of Harper & Bros., 1946.

35. PFAFFMANN, C. Gustatory afferent impulses. *J. cell. comp. Physiol.*, 1941, **17**, 243-58.

36. RAAB, D. H., & ADES, H. W. Temporal and frontal contributions to an auditory conditioned response. *Amer. Psychol.*, 1948, **3**, 370.

37. SHOCK, N. W. Older people and their potentialities for gainful employment. *J. Geront.*, 1947, **2**, 93-102.

38. SPERRY, R. W. Restoration of vision after crossing of optic nerves and after contralateral transplantation of the eye. *J. Neurophysiol.*, 1945, **8**, 15-28.

39. SPERRY, R. W. The problem of central nervous reorganization after nerve regeneration and muscle transposition. *Quart. Rev. Biol.*, 1945, **20**, 311-69.

40. STONE, L. S., & ELLISON, F. S. Return of vision in eyes exchanged between adult salamanders of different species. *J. exp. Zool.*, 1946, **100**, 217-27.

41. TOWER, S. S. Pain: definition and properties of the unit for sensory reception. In Association for Research in Nervous and Mental Disease, *Pain.* Baltimore: The Williams & Wilkins Co., 1943.

42. TUNTURI, A. R. Further afferent connections to the acoustic cortex of the dog. *Amer. J. Physiol.*, 1945, **144**, 389-95.

43. WALZL, E. M., & WOOLSEY, C. N. Effects of cochlear lesions on click responses in the auditory cortex of the cat. *Bull. Johns Hopkins Hosp.*, 1946, **79**, 309-19.

44. WEISS, P. Self-differentiation of the basic patterns of coordination. *Comp. Psychol. Monogr.*, 1941, **17**, No. 88.

45. WEVER, E. G. The electrical responses of the ear. *Psychol. Bull.*, 1939, **36**, 143-87.

46. WILLMER, E. N. *Retinal structure and colour vision.* Cambridge: Cambridge University Press, 1946.

47. WOOLSEY, C. N. Patterns of sensory representation in the cerebral cortex. *Fed. Proc.*, 1947, **6**, 437-41.

CHAPTER 3

BODY CHEMISTRY AND PERCEPTION

By FRANK A. BEACH, Ph.D.

It was pointed out in Chapter 1 that behavior can be thought of as interaction between the organism and its environment; and it was further noted that perception is one name for a certain class of such interactions. In this chapter, we shall refer almost exclusively to the behavior of human beings and lower animals, and the word *perception* will rarely be used. However, much of the behavior of a mouse or a man is governed by the way in which stimuli are organized—by the way in which the individual "sees" the world about him. And complex behavior can be considered an indicator of perceptual processes. Evidence from behavioral studies often points to important inferences concerning perceptual functions.

In Chapter 2 Professor Morgan has described what might be termed "the physical machinery for behavior." This consists of the nervous system and various associated effector structures such as muscles and glands. An understanding of the structural and functional characteristics of the nervous system is most important for a physiological approach to problems of perception and behavior. It must be remembered, however, that the nervous system does not operate in a vacuum. Every cell and fiber is bathed in a medium of body fluids. The chemical constitution of this "cellular environment" profoundly affects the functional capacity of the behavioral machinery.

This chapter will be devoted to a consideration of various relations that are known to exist between behavior and certain chemical features of the body fluids. We must be careful to hold constantly in mind the fact that as yet it is rarely possible to speak of anything more than *relations* between these two classes of variables. Evidence now available reveals many correlations between body chemistry and behavior, but there are very few clear-cut examples of a direct, causal effect. For example, it is well established that increases in the amount of androgen present in the system are usually accompanied by increase in the incidence and severity of aggressive reactions in many animal species. But we have not the slightest hint as to the nature of the physiological processes responsible for this change. Therefore, it seems more appropriate to speak of relations between androgen and aggression rather than the effects of androgen upon this type of response.

The aim of the following discussion is threefold. First it aims to survey the various types of evidence that demonstrate the existence of relationships between particular alterations in body chemistry and specific changes in behavior. The second aim is to discuss and evaluate possible explanations for these relationships. The third objective is to explore the major questions confronting specialists in the field and to determine, if possible, what procedures are most likely to provide us with solutions to these problems.

Survey of the Evidence

Quantitative Dietary Deficiency.—The behavior of human beings may be profoundly altered by food deprivation, and the magnitude as well as the nature of the behavioral change is in part a function of the duration and severity of reduction in food intake. Introspective accounts of individuals forced to undergo prolonged starvation regularly include a series of complex psychological changes involving modification of sensory thresholds, increased fatigability and irritability, emotional apathy, and preoccupation with matters concerning food and eating.

Fortunately, we need not rely exclusively on such incidental evidence as has accumulated more or less by accident. Controlled studies such as that of Franklin, Schiele, Brozek, and Keys (15) provide more objective and reliable data. These workers studied thirty-six men twenty to thirty-three years of age who lived for six months under conditions of semistarvation. The subjects were first observed for three months, during which time they received an ample diet containing 3,492 calories per day. Daily food intake during the succeeding half-year was limited to 1,570 calories, a level that eventually produced an average weight loss of 24 per cent. Finally, the group was examined during a three-month rehabilitation period in which the diet was raised to the original levels.

Sensory changes during starvation were limited to a slight increase in auditory acuity. Subjective reports indicated feelings of weakness, loss of ambition to work or study, marked decrease in libido, narrowing of interests in external events, pronounced depression, and periods of extreme irritability. Depressed stages were sometimes replaced by spells of elation, but these were inevitably followed by relapse into the depressed condition. Irritability was often expressed in the form of aggression against other individuals, and particularly against those men who revealed marked social and personal deterioration as a result of inanition.

After several months of semistarvation most individuals spent a great deal of time alone. According to their own accounts, they sought solitude because they were entirely disinterested in other people and because they felt too weak to contend in any sort of social competition. Attitudes toward food and eating altered markedly. Anticipation of mealtime brought on abnormally powerful cravings for food. Men jealously guarded their place in the "chow line," and while eating they displayed very possessive attitudes toward food, hovering over the tray and even encircling it with one arm. Initial aversions toward particular kinds of food were quickly lost, and previously disliked items became highly palatable.

There seems to be no question that the "meaning" assigned to certain stimuli was radically changed. Cookbooks became preferred reading. On shopping trips men often bought kettles, frying pans, and similar utensils although there was no use for them and the purchaser was frequently at a loss to explain his new acquisitions. All the subjects felt that their general alertness had declined and that judgment and comprehension of new material was impaired. Psychological tests failed to confirm these impressions.

In a much earlier study Miles (28) investigated behavioral changes in young men whose caloric intake had been reduced from two thirds to one half of normal. Weight loss in this case did not exceed 12 per cent, and we may, therefore, judge that the degree of inanition was less severe. General vitality continued normal, and the quality and quantity of scholastic work were not impaired. Basal metabolism and pulse rate were uniformly reduced, and sexual manifestations disappeared. The subjects reported loss of interest in heterosexual social contacts, elimination of sexual dreams, and absence of nocturnal emissions. Sexual changes were also described by subjects in the experiment of Franklin, Schiele, Brozek, and Keys (15). Although they were free to have "dates," the men gradually lost interest in the company of women. Masturbation was infrequent or lacking, erotic dreams were discontinued, and little or no time was spent in sex fantasies.

Specific evidence concerning the effects of food deprivation upon thought processes is available in studies such as those of Sanford and of McClelland and Atkinson. Sanford (38) examined ten school children just before and just after a meal. They were asked to interpret ambiguous pictures and given a word-association test.

"Food responses" were names of foods or of meals and verbs meaning "to eat." In the association test the subjects gave twice as many food responses before the meal as after it. There were two and one-half times as many food responses to the pictures before eating as afterward.

McClelland and Atkinson (27) examined 108 young men who had been without food for one, four, or sixteen hours. The subjects watched a blank screen upon which, they were told, exceedingly faint images would be projected. In actuality there was no image projection, but the subjects were required to make a response each time the experimenter asked them to interpret the nonexistent picture. Increased periods of deprivation did not produce a rise in the frequency of references to food per se; but the number of food-related responses increased as a function of hours since the last meal.

Other trends in the data suggest alterations in perception. For instance, in some tests the subject was asked to count the number of objects which, he was told, were being shown on the screen. After sixteen hours of food deprivation there was a strong tendency to reply with a high number when food-related objects, such as forks or spoons, were to be counted, but no such change occurred in the counting of indifferent objects such as pencils. In other instances the subject was told that images of two different kinds of objects were being projected on the screen and he was asked to estimate the relative sizes. Men who had not eaten for sixteen hours tended to judge food objects as larger than nonfood objects.

It is beyond question that perceptual processes and the resultant behavior are altered when human beings go without eating, even for a few hours, and it is equally evident that abstinence from food is accompanied by numerous variations in body chemistry. There occurs an important increase in hydration of the body, and after prolonged semistarvation, such as occurred in the experiment of Franklin, Schiele, Brozek, and Keys (15), the extracellular fluid volume is 56 per cent above normal. Blood hemoglobin concentration decreases by about 22 per cent. Basal metabolism is greatly reduced, and the amount of O_2 used per minute is 38 per cent below normal. Lactic and pyruvic acids in the blood increase, and blood sugar levels are lowered. The question naturally arises as to which, if any, of these physiological changes are responsible for or most intimately associated with the alterations in behavior that accompany inanition. At this point, however, we are concerned only with a description of the sort of correlations that can be found between behavior and body chemistry. Explanations for these correlations are considered at a later point.

The behavior of subhuman animals is modified by relatively brief periods of starvation. Quantitative measures of running activity of rats show that this type of behavior increases as a function of length of the deprivation period. Siegel and Steinberg (41) found that within the limits of zero to forty-eight hours of starvation, the curve relating activity to food deprivation is a negatively accelerated, increasing function.

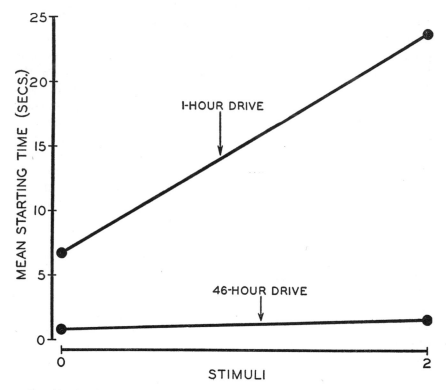

Fig. 18.—Performance of rats originally trained to approach a dim light and then tested for response to a much brighter one. Stimulus *0* is the training stimulus and Stimulus 2 is the new one. "One-hour drive" rats had eaten an hour before the test. The second group had been starved for forty-six hours. The slightly hungry animals reacted to the training stimulus after an average delay of six seconds but did not respond to the new stimulus until approximately twenty-five seconds had elapsed. The very hungry animals generalized much more rapidly. (By permission of Brown (5) and *J. comp. Psychol.*)

Learning responses are affected by inanition. Brown (5) trained one group of rats to run down a straight alleyway and approach a bright light. Animals that had learned to perform this simple task showed a tendency to generalize and make positive responses to lights of lower intensity. And the strength of the generalization tendency was directly related to the duration of the starvation period. Animals that had been without food for forty-six hours ran as fast toward medium or dim lights as toward the much brighter one of training intensity. Rats that were fed one hour before the test were slow to react to a medium light and even slower when the stimulus was dim. A second group of animals was trained to a dim light and then tested for the tendency to generalize to a brighter one. The results are shown in Figure 18.

Social behavior in animals is often altered by starvation. Nowlis (29) measured the dominance-submission relationships in pairs of chimpanzees under conditions of food satiation and after varying periods of deprivation. When both partners had been without food for the same length of time, there was rarely any change in relative dominance status. But if the normally dominant ape was satiated and its partner had not eaten for a day or so, the result was nearly always a temporary reversal of social position in which the subordinate individual assumed and maintained possession of the food source.

Many other types of behavior, including fighting, mating, and caring for the young, are influenced by food deprivation. But the data already presented suffice to indicate in general the type of results that have been obtained in experiments on animals other than man.

Qualitative Dietary Deficiencies.—Deviant behavior often appears when the body lacks or is unable to utilize a particular vitamin, amino acid, or chemical element. Complete or partial deprivation of a specific dietary factor can come about in any one of several ways. The item may be missing from the diet. It may be present in amounts that are adequate under most circumstances but insufficient for individuals in special physiological conditions such as those obtaining during pregnancy and lactation. Finally, the food item may be present in the diet in ample quantities but fail to produce its effect as a result of the individual's pathologic inability to utilize it.

Diets Lacking a Specific Item. Some of the most dramatic evidence of the effects of qualitative dietary deficiency is found in clinical descriptions of pellagrous patients before and after treatment with nicotinic acid. Some pellagrins never exhibit psychological symptoms but many of them display loss of memory, disorientation, confusion, and confabulation. Other individuals under the effect of the same deficiency exhibit excitement, mania, depression, or delirium. Paranoid delusions, which often occur, are characterized by fear of or antipathy toward relatives. That such manifestations must involve perceptual dysfunction is obvious.

Spies, Aring, Gelperin, and Bean (43) examined sixty severely psychotic pellagrous patients. Several days of hospitalization had no beneficial effects, but treatment with coramine or nicotinic acid invariably eliminated the behavioral symptoms. Unmistakable improvement became evident in some cases as shortly as ten hours after medication, and there was no recurrence as long as treatment continued. A typical case will illustrate the type of effect obtained.

A fifty-five-year-old woman was brought to the hospital with characteristic physical signs of pellagra. In addition she displayed clear-cut psychotic symptoms. Interviews with the patient's relatives, and her own account after treatment, revealed that in the pellagrous condition she suffered visual and auditory hallucinations centering around religious subjects. Paranoid tendencies were strong, and she complained about neighbors who were trying to poison her and about animals that persisted in annoying her. She saw and heard monkeys, rats, and cows running about her and felt bugs, snakes, and worms crawling over her body. Coramine, the diethyl amide of nicotinic acid, was administered, and within forty-eight hours the patient became quiet and cooperative. She had, furthermore, good insight into her previous condition, which she said had disturbed her even prior to admission to the hospital. Within twenty-four hours after treatment she began to comprehend the hallucinatory character of her symptoms.

Spies (43) and his coworkers administered coramine to twenty-six nonpellagrous patients with one of the following diagnoses: alcoholic hallucinosis, Korsakoff's psychosis, manic-depressive (depressed phase), involutional psychosis, or schizophrenia. Although treatment was continued in some cases as long as fifty days, there was no improvement in any of these individuals.

Emotional disturbances often arise in men and women whose diet is deficient in the entire B complex, and it appears that thiamine is a particularly important component. Shock (39) found that a careful examination of eleven women living on a reduced intake of the B vitamins for more than one month revealed that all individuals tended to become more irritable. Most of the women were moody and often became quarrelsome and uncooperative. They complained of vague fears, inexplicable agitation, and deeply depressive feelings. Addition to the diet of thiamine without any other B vitamin promptly eliminated these symptoms.

Brozek, Guetzkow, and Keys (6) report a series of behavior changes that occurred in eight young men whose diet contained sharply restricted amounts of thiamine, riboflavin, and niacin. Self-ratings and ratings by companions revealed that acute deficiency was accompanied by a definite increase in "neurasthenic" symptoms. Results of the Minnesota Multiphasic Personality Inventory indicated significant departure from normal in the scores on depression, hypochondriasis, and hysteria. Rorschach analyses reflected an increase in conscious control over behavior in the majority of subjects. Supplementation of the diet with thiamine occasioned rapid return to normal in all instances.

The behavior of subhuman animals may be noticeably altered when the diet lacks certain essential foodstuffs. The findings of Riess and Block (35) show that rats whose diet lacks the amino acid lysine are inferior to control animals in maze-learning, and the effect does not depend upon changes in general activity nor upon reduced motivation. The speed with which rats acquire a conditioned eyelid response is decreased by vitamin B_1 deficiency, according to Biel and Wickens (4).

In a study made by Wiesner and Bacharach (48) it was found that male rats maintained on a diet lacking vitamin E display a gradual loss of sexual responsiveness and eventually cease to copulate. Manganese deficiency interferes with reproductive behavior in female rats. Perla and Sandberg (30) demonstrated that, when this element is missing from the diet, parturient females suffer failure of lactation, rarely protect their young, and in some instances become cannibalistic. So-called "canine hysteria" appears in dogs whose rations are heated to 200°C, a procedure which apparently destroys all protein. The behavioral symptoms include functional blindness, "running fits," and continuous barking. Addition of casein to the heated diet corrects the abnormalities (2).

In many instances the eating behavior of human beings or lower animals is altered by particular types of dietary deficiencies. Rabbits respond to a diet lacking ascorbic acid by plucking and eating the fur of their cagemates, according to Rudra (36). In some cases such changes in appetite serve a compensatory function and tend to correct the physiological imbalance caused by absence of the specific dietary item. Richter (34) describes a number of instances in which this effect appears to be achieved.

Horses reared in the vicinity of Victoria, Australia, are forced to graze on grass that contains little or no lime. However, the animals do not suffer marked deficiency because they habitually chew the bark of a native tree which is exceedingly rich in this substance. In certain parts of New South Wales sheep develop marked signs of asthenia unless they are permitted to eat the earth in particular paddocks. This they will do readily, and analysis has shown that the earth at these special localities is rich in iron. South African cattle frequently display advanced symptoms of osteomalacia (softening of the bones), a condition which is associated with phosphorus deficiency in the local soil and vegetation. In regions where this condition obtains, cattle soon become confirmed bone-eaters, thus adding some amount of phosphorus to their diet. Richter (34) suggests that many examples of so-called "perverted appetites" may actually represent attempts toward balancing of a deficient diet. He found that rats that have no food except sucrose die within a relatively short time. However, if animals are allowed to eat their own feces, the average survival time is increased by approximately 50 per cent.

Richter's (34) ingenious experimental studies strongly suggest that some animals are capable of selecting for themselves a well-balanced diet. This implies, of course, that the desirability or edibility of a particular food material is governed, at least in part, by the organism's need for certain substances it contains. In some experiments rats have been allowed free access to the following purified foods: sucrose, vitamin-free casein, olive oil, sodium chloride, calcium lactate, dibasic sodium phosphate, cod liver oil, wheat germ oil, dried baker's yeast, and water. Animals that can feed only upon these substances make their choices in such a way that they grow as rapidly as other rats kept on the regular stock diet for the colony. Furthermore, the self-selection method is so efficient that the experimental animals ingest 36 per cent less food than the controls and still equal them in rate of growth. If yeast is omitted from the experimental diet and replaced by various components of the B complex, the rats alter their intake of carbohydrates or proteins in such a way as to maintain optimal metabolism.

Other domestic animals have been tested in free-choice feeding situations and found capable of selecting adequate diets. Under such conditions pigs sometimes grow more rapidly than they do on mixed diets. Weight and milk production in dairy cattle are improved by free-choice feeding. Chickens and pigeons appear able to choose the proper constituents of a balanced diet when the various items are offered in fairly pure form.

Normal Fluctuations in Dietary Requirements. It is a common observation that various long-term physiological changes are accompanied by modifications in eating behavior. The most obvious examples are found in the changes in appetite which accompany pregnancy and lactation. Naturalists and animal husbandrymen are aware of the fact that pregnant or lactating mammals of many species often seek out foods that are not eaten at other times. Carlson (7), to take but one example, observed that during pregnancy squirrels may hoard and eat old, dried bones, although they do not do so unless pregnant and although males or nongravid females of this species do not show this behavior.

Using his "cafeteria" system of feeding rats, Richter (34) was able to record the effects of pregnancy and lactation upon the voluntary intake of different food substances. The amount of sodium chloride ingested increases during the first five days of pregnancy and then rises even further in the latter half of the lactation period. A sharp drop in the sodium chloride intake occurs shortly after the litter is weaned. Pregnant females consume slightly increased amounts of calcium lactate, and lactating rats ingest from thirty to forty times as much of this substance as was eaten before impregnation. The return of calcium intake to prepregnant levels is not complete until several weeks after the young are weaned. Sodium phosphate ingestion increases slightly in pregnancy and markedly during lactation, returning to normal almost at once after lactation ceases. Olive oil as a source of fat is consumed in increasing amounts during lactation, and the same is true of casein as a protein source.

These findings indicate that during pregnancy, and particularly during lactation, the rat needs an increased amount of fat and protein as well as more sodium, calcium, phosphorus, and perhaps potassium. The results obtained with the self-selection method agree closely with biochemical studies of dietary needs during pregnancy and lactation.

Pathological Disturbance of Food Metabolism. Symptoms of a specific dietary deficiency sometimes reflect an inability on the part of the organism to utilize the food item in normal fashion. In such instances it may become necessary for the individual to alter his diet radically in order to compensate for the physiological abnormality.

A striking illustration of this type of compensatory food selection has been described by Wilkins and Richter (50). A three-and-one-half-year-old boy suffering from degeneration of the adrenal cortex kept himself alive for more than two years by devouring large quantities of table salt. In the absence of the adrenal cortex, sodium metabolism is disturbed and the body cells do not receive enough of this element. By consuming large quantities of sodium chloride, this child supplied his system with enough extra sodium to compensate for the metabolic dysfunction. Eventually he was hospitalized and placed upon the regular institutional diet, and before the nature of his pathology had been diagnosed the boy developed symptoms of sodium deficiency and died.

A second example is the case of a thirty-four-year-old man suffering from Addison's disease. This individual did not enjoy a steak unless it was covered with approximately one eighth of an inch of salt. To each glass of tomato juice he added nearly half a glass of salt. He insisted upon heavily salting oranges and grapefruit and always made his lemonade with salt instead of sugar (34).

Now it is important to note that persons who display this type of eating behavior do not do so in a calculated attempt to compensate for the failure of their systems properly to metabolize sodium. Instead they merely know that the taste of any food is profoundly improved if it is very salty. Their perception is altered as a result of the chemical changes in the body fluids and tissues.

Experimental work with animals throws some light upon this particular type of behavioral adaptation to changes in body chemistry. Adrenalectomized rats, like human patients with Addison's disease, are unable to control their metabolism of sodium, with the result that much of the sodium that they ingest is lost as salt in the urine. The only remedy is for the animals to take in much more sodium, and this they do without training. After removal of the adrenal glands rats will die in two weeks if they are kept on the usual stock diet. But if the cage contains a small can of sodium chloride in addition to the regular food the adrenalectomized rat eats enough from the supplementary source of sodium to free itself of signs of insufficiency and to keep alive indefinitely (Figure 19). There is, furthermore, an increased appetite for all sodium salts but not for other chlorides. Hence it must be the sodium in table salt that makes it attractive.

Dietary changes often accompany dysfunction of other endocrine glands. Children suffering from parathyroid deficiency frequently display an inordinate craving for chalk, plaster, and other substances rich in calcium. Destruction of the parathyroid glands in rats is followed within a few days by tetany and death. But parathyroidectomized rats allowed access to solutions containing calcium will drink sufficient amounts to prevent these results. Almost any type of calcium solution appears palatable. The acetate, gluconate, and nitrate forms are all eagerly accepted by the rat lacking parathyroid glands. If such animals are given parathyroid implants the appetite for calcium returns to normal.

Destruction of the pancreas produces diabetes in rats as in men, and in the absence of insulin both species are unable to regulate the carbohydrate metabolism. However, pancreatectomized rats drink very large amounts of water which are required for elimination of the unoxidized glucose. In addition, they avoid eating foods that are high in carbohydrates and simultaneously increase their intake of proteins. It is reported that under such conditions the behavioral change produces improvement and sometimes disappearance of the diabetic symptoms (30).

Metabolic Dysfunction and Mental Disease.—We have already seen that pathological inability to metabolize a particular food sub-

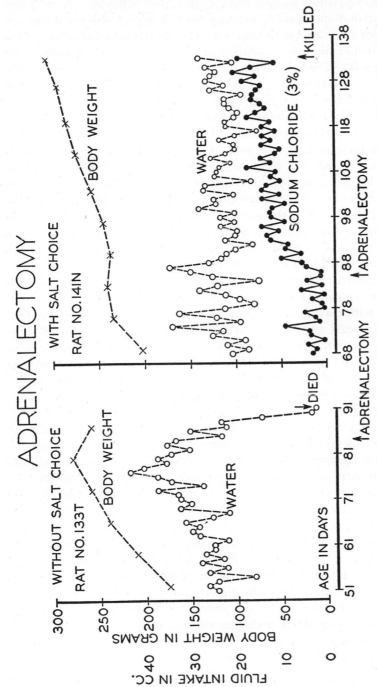

Fig. 19.—Adrenalectomized rat without opportunity to eat salt lost weight, decreased its water intake, and died. The animal provided with salt ate some before operation and then increased the amount ingested after removal of the adrenals. His body weight continued to increase, water intake was not affected, and the rat survived. (By permission of Richter (34) and *The Harvey Lectures*.)

stance may produce marked changes in eating behavior. Now it can be added that much more pronounced behavioral abnormalities are sometimes associated with failure of normal metabolic processes. One well-known example is the clinical syndrome known as phenylpyruvic oligophrenia. The behavioral picture is one of very low-grade feeble-mindedness. Jervis (20) examined 200 cases of this sort and states that two thirds of the patients were at the idiot and one third at the imbecile level. He found, furthermore, that the condition is heredi-tary, apparently being transmitted by an autosomal recessive gene.

From the physiological point of view this type of feeble-minded-ness is associated with a breakdown in the metabolism of phenylala-nine. This amino acid is not completely oxidized, but instead a block occurs at the stage of phenylpyruvic acid. The unoxidized acid is, therefore, excreted in the urine, a condition that does not occur in normal individuals nor in other types of feeble-minded patients. We have no proof of a causal relation between the metabolic and psycho-logic abnormalities, but the evidence is highly suggestive.

A somewhat more satisfactory illustration can be seen in the condition known as juvenile amaurotic family idiocy. Individuals afflicted with this disease appear to develop normally during the first five or six years after birth. At about this point the first clinical signs manifest themselves in the form of failure of vision. The progressive mental deterioration that follows is characterized by loss of interest in other persons and external events, inattentiveness, crying spells, and violent outbursts of temper involving assaultive and destructive behavior. Death occurs usually at fifteen or sixteen years.

Physiological studies made by Jervis (21) of patients suffering from juvenile amaurotic family idiocy show that they are unable to metabolize lipid properly. As one result of this defect, the nerve cells in certain parts of the brain undergo degeneration. The details of the relation between metabolism of lipids, the condition of brain cells, and the individual's behavior will be considered in greater detail in a sub-sequent section of this discussion.

More common than mental deficiency are the various psychoses, of which the condition commonly diagnosed as schizophrenia is perhaps the most ubiquitous. There is good reason to believe that schizo-phrenics suffer several serious abnormalities in body chemistry.

Hoskins (17) found that as a group they tend to be hypometabolic, consuming appreciably less oxygen than do nonschizophrenic individ-uals. According to Looney and Freeman (26), measurement of oxy-gen and carbon dioxide concentrations in the arterial and venous blood of schizophrenic patients indicates that sufficient amounts of oxygen get into the blood and are transported to the body tissues, but for some reason the cells fail to utilize oxygen in normal fashion. Reduction in the amount of oxygen used results in decreased production of carbon dioxide, and the latter change leads to increase in the chloride of the erythrocytes and heightened concentrations of lactic acid.

A focal point in the metabolic disturbance of the schizophrene seems to be the liver. The normal functions of this organ are, to a large degree, concerned with detoxification, and interference with this activity is very likely to result in autointoxication. In addition to evidence for partial loss of detoxifying powers, the symptoms of liver dysfunction in schizophrenia include slow removal of excess sugar from the blood in the glucose tolerance test, low rate of formation of cholesterol esters, and additional abnormalities in cephalin-cholesterol flocculation tests.

Evidence is available to indicate that fluctuations in the psychological or behavioral status of the schizoid individual are accompanied by alterations in metabolic process. Cholesterol is one of the phospholipins and it contributes to various important oxidative functions of the nervous system and other organs in the body. The concentration of cholesterol in the blood of schizophrenic persons varies with shifts in behavior. Stenberg (45) compared hospitalized patients who were emotionally indifferent and calm with others showing the emotionally exalted condition. He found that during the calm state the level of blood cholesterol is low and that it is raised during periods of psychotic disturbance. Confirmatory results have been reported by Randall and Cohen (33), who measured the level of total phospholipids in patients on calm and disturbed wards. The blood of individuals on disturbed wards contained significantly more phospholipid than did that of the undisturbed patients.

Oxygen Deficiency.—The effects of anoxia upon perceptual functions and associated behavior are too well known to need more than brief mention. The early stages of mild oxygen lack are sometimes characterized by exaggerated feelings of exhilaration and well-being. Continued deprivation occasions marked loss of critical ability in general, and in particular the capacity for self-criticism is greatly impaired. If the anoxic condition persists, mental confusion becomes more pronounced and emotional outbursts frequently occur.

Learning ability and memory are adversely affected by oxygen deprivation. Rats subjected to low oxygen tensions display reduced ability to distinguish between upright and inverted triangles and to master other simple tasks (40).

When the concentration of blood gases is changed, the acid-base equilibrium of the blood may be disturbed. Hyperventilation accelerates the loss of carbon dioxide from the blood and thus increases the alkalinity. The associated psychological changes include increase in sensory latencies, decreased sensory acuity, and idiosyncrasies in response to word-association tests. Minor displacements of the acid-base equilibrium in the direction of increased alkalinity often evoke subjective reports of well-being, whereas slight increases in acidity tend to create a state of mild emotional depression (39).

Drugs.—For thousands of years it has been recognized that alterations in perception and behavior can be induced by the administration of various drugs. The type of behavioral change differs according to the chemical composition of the drug, although other factors such as dosage, method of administration, and physiological and psychological peculiarities of the user are also of importance. The drug known as mescal or peyote is noted for its tendency to induce constant and vivid visual hallucinations. Klüver (23) showed that these may range from indistinct impressions of beautifully blended hues to clearly perceived scenes involving a wealth of detail and action. Marijuana or hashish markedly distorts the perception of time. The frequently reported dreams and waking fantasies produced by opium and related drugs attest the control that such substances can exert over imaginal processes.

Kubie and Margolin (25) report that hypnotic drugs are sometimes used in psychotherapy because of their tendency to decrease the strength of unconscious repression. Under mild, drug-induced narcosis, the neurotic patient may be able to remember and discuss ideas, feelings, and impulses so unacceptable to him that they cannot be recognized in normal circumstances. Somewhat analogous changes appear to occur in lower animals. Wikler and Masserman (49) have produced in cats a type of maladaptive behavior defined as an "experimental neurosis." This result is achieved by subjecting the animal to a conflict situation in which hunger and fear responses are opposed. It is reported that the "neurotic" manifestations can be temporarily eliminated by morphine. The usefulness of subhuman animals in experiments on behavioral effects of drugs is not generally realized. Spragg's (44) study of morphine addiction in apes illustrates the potential values of the method.

Morphine Addiction in Apes. The reactions of chimpanzees to morphine are remarkably similar to those of the human addict. The first effect of an injection is upon cutaneous nerves, and both apes and men experience itching of the skin. One of the animals examined by Spragg scratched himself so vigorously after each daily injection that eventually he had removed all the hair from his body.

Chimpanzees that had been on a regular schedule of morphine injections for several months gave many indications of genuine addiction. After a period of withdrawal they showed in various ways a compelling desire for their daily injection and displayed considerable ingenuity in their attempts to induce the experimenter to supply them with the drug. Before each injection the apes were put on a leash and led from their living quarters to a certain room in a different building. The hypodermic syringe was always kept in a conspicuous white box and the chimpanzees were taught to open the box, using a distinctive, white, wooden "stick-key."

After a period of drug withdrawal, all chimpanzees showed signs of distress. When the experimenter approached their living cages, the apes cried and held out their hands in the gesture that signifies desire to be picked up. If permitted to do so, the addicted animals procceded without guidance to the injection room. Once there, they searched for the white stick-key, removed the syringe from the box, and assumed the posture for injection.

Adjacent to the white box in the injection room was a black box of similar size and shape which always contained a piece of fruit. The black box could be opened with a black stick-key. When they were hungry and did not need a dose of morphine, the apes readily employed the black stick-key to obtain the food reward. But under conditions of simultaneous food and drug deprivation the white stick-key was almost always chosen. The "meaning" of the two keys had thus come to be a function of the animal's physiological condition. Drug-deprived animals were so strongly motivated to obtain morphine that they readily solved various learning problems when the drug was the reward. Multiple-choice, delayed-reaction, box-stacking, and pulling-in tests were learned more rapidly for morphine than for food.

Human morphine addicts are often sexually hyperactive under conditions of drug withdrawal and, in contrast, sexual functions tend to be depressed by administration of the drug. The chimpanzee is affected differently. Male addicts in Spragg's experiment consistently displayed sexual excitement immediately after receiving their regular injection. The behavioral signs included prompt and continued erection, frequent masturbation to the point of ejaculation, and eagerness to copulate with receptive females. As the length of time since the last injection increased, sexual responsiveness was reduced progressively.

The sexual stimulation initially aroused by injection of the drug was generalized gradually, and various objects that had been indirectly associated with the injection procedure acquired an erotic significance for the chimpanzees. After addiction had been established, the apes began to exhibit sexual responses that were directed toward the white box that contained the syringe. Males sometimes stood over the box making copulatory movements. The white stick-key also became a sexual object, and one individual employed the stick to stimulate his own genitals.

After two weeks without morphine, all signs of addiction disappeared. At the end of this period, the apes showed no particular interest in the injection room. The white box and its associated stick-key had lost their special stimulus value, were no longer an adequate source of motivation for learning, and had no power to elicit emotional responses of any sort. The behavioral significance, the "meaning," of the room and its contents had changed completely as the body chemistry returned to normal.

Alcohol. One of the most widely used drugs in our own society is ethyl alcohol, and the capacity of this substance for producing disorders of perception and behavior is familiar. Immanuel Kant once set forth a definition of the effects of alcohol which might have been written especially for this symposium that is devoted to perception. Kant described drunkenness as "the unnatural state of inability to organize sense impressions according to the laws of experience."

Clinical accounts of mild intoxication stress the exaggeration of emotional expression and the mild euphoria produced by small amounts of alcohol. Larger doses of the drug tend to impair the sensory processes, to produce flight of ideas, and often to result in paranoid reactions. Jellinek and McFarland (19) showed that laboratory experiments yield more objective and quantifiable measures of behavioral changes under moderate amounts of alcohol.

Alterations in sensory function vary according to the modality involved. Cutaneous sensation is impaired, and the two-point threshold may increase 90 per cent over normal. Absolute sensitivity to light is increased, but the discrimination of differences in intensity is impaired. The absolute auditory threshold may be lowered, with the result that sounds too faint to be detected under normal conditions now become audible. However, in audition as in vision the discrimination threshold is raised by alcohol. The increase may amount to as much as 30 per cent.

Perceptual functions have been examined by presenting words, phrases, or letters in tachistoscopic fashion and noting any changes in the accuracy of response. Alcohol markedly reduces the ability to recognize long words or word groups that are exposed for a very short time. Color-naming is less accurate and tests of letter cancellation indicate deterioration. Simple reaction time is generally increased, and motor coordination is impaired. The amount of interference is proportional to the complexity of the motor task and the degree of dexterity required.

Learning ability probably is lowered under the influence of alcohol, although well-controlled studies of this question are needed. Impairment of immediate memory, as tested in the delayed-reaction situation, is severe. Free associations decrease in number and variety in alcoholized individuals. Summing up the results of experimental work, Jellinek and McFarland (19) indicate the bearing of the results upon the general subject with which this symposium is concerned.

One of the most important findings is that, in any sensory modality, discrimination is much more impaired than acuity. The ability to relate things to each other and to grasp contents suffers greatly under the influence of alcohol (p. 364).

All the evidence presented thus far has dealt with what we may call normal reactions to alcohol. Pathological reactions to the same drug are recognized clinically to be relatively independent of the amount of alcohol ingested. They are characterized by relatively short periods of blind rage and confusion, often followed by complete amnesia for the outburst. There is none of the motor incoordination nor the slurred speech that signal ordinary intoxication. To an observer the behavior seems unreal, fantastic, and marked by complete misunderstanding of the external situation.

Certain diseases associated with chronic alcoholism present symptoms of perceptual disorganization that are not due to the immediate effects of the drug. Korsakoff's psychosis is accompanied by illusions, by disorientation in space and time, and occasionally by aphasia and agraphia. Acute alcoholic hallucinosis involves vague fears, chronic anxiety, and auditory hallucinations. The latter usually include the voices of several persons who are discussing the patient in critical fashion.

The classic syndrome of delirium tremens is particularly rich in examples of perceptual dysfunction. The attack is usually preceded by restlessness, persistent fear, nightmares, and (occasionally) hallucinations. During the acute phase visual hallucinations predominate. Objects seem to be in movement and to change in size, number, form, or color. The objects of the hallucinations are mostly fast-moving animals such as small rodents, cats and dogs, or insects. Reptiles and larger mammals may also be hallucinated. It is interesting to note that since the introduction of continuous baths in the treatment of delirium tremens the popular white mice have been replaced by fishes and lobsters as the objects of hallucination. Disorientation in space and time is common during attacks of this disease. Patients see the hospital room as a tavern or a church and "recognize" the physician and nursing attendants as old friends from an earlier life period.

Hormonal Secretions.—The subject of hormonal control of behavior was touched upon in the preceding discussion of altered eating habits consequent to glandular dysfunction. There are many other examples cited by Beach (3) of correlation between secretory activity of various endocrine organs and specific behavioral functions.

Anterior Pituitary. Several anterior pituitary hormones are directly or indirectly related to behavior. Through its control of the thyroid, the adrenal, and the sex glands, the hypophysis indirectly regulates much of the organism's behavioral activity.

More immediate effects of hypophyseal secretions upon behavior probably exist, although they have yet to be studied in detail. At menopause there occurs a pronounced increase in the amount of pituitary gonadotrophins. The rise in gonadotrophic materials is considered by some endocrinologists to be chiefly responsible for the emotional instability of many menopausal women. One anterior pituitary hormone, prolactin, is closely associated with the display of maternal reactions by lower animals. Males and virgin females injected with prolactin are reported to care for and protect newborn young of their own species.

Thyroid. The clinical effects of thyroid deficiency are known in considerable detail. Severe, congenital hypothyroidism results in the condition known as cretinism, which includes a number of physical, physiological, and behavioral abnormalities. From the psychological standpoint the cretin represents a low type of feeble-mindedness. Myxedema is caused by degeneration of the thyroid in adulthood. Individuals afflicted with this condition are slow in movement, easily exhausted by exercise, mentally dull.

Thyroid removal in experimental animals produces a marked drop in the amount of general activity. Muscular strength is decreased, and body temperature is lowered. Rats deprived of the thyroid gland show an enormous increase in nest-building behavior (34).

Abnormally high concentrations of thyroid hormone in human beings are associated with hypermetabolism, restlessness, hyperactivity, and often with emotional instability. Animals treated with thyroid substance become very active and overly reactive to sensory stimulation.

Adrenal. The adrenal is in actuality two glands. The hormone of the adrenal medulla, adrenalin, is secreted in large amounts when the organism is under conditions of intense emotional excitement. Its physiological effects include increased tone in striped muscles, redistribution of the blood supply with emphasis upon the peripheral vessels, cardiac acceleration, and release of glycogen from the liver. Human subjects injected with adrenalin usually experience vague feelings of anxiety and unrest.

The adrenal cortex secretes a number of different hormones, some of which are believed to protect the organism against stress. There is some indication that the performance of skilled tasks under stress conditions is improved by administration of adrenocortical hormone. The products of this gland are chemically related to those of the sex glands. Virilism in human females is often due to adrenal dysfunction involving oversecretion of androgen.

Loss of the adrenal cortex by disease or surgery results in an increased appetite for sodium salts, as indicated in the preceding discussion. It also produces a decrease in general activity and an increase in nest-building on the part of experimental animals.

Ovary. The relationship between ovarian hormones and behavior varies somewhat according to the species of the animal studied. The most prominent effects are exerted upon sexual activities, and the correlation between hormonal secretion and behavior is most marked in lower animals. In adult females of lower mammalian species such as mice, rats, cats, or dogs, the ovaries periodically produce and release ripe eggs. Associated with the maturation of ova is an increase in the secretion of the estrogenic ovarian hormone known as estrin. When estrogen concentrations in the blood are high, the female becomes sexually receptive to the male. At all other times she avoids sexual contact. (Progesterone, a second ovarian hormone, is also involved in the mating behavior of some mammals, but it is omitted from consideration here to simplify the discussion.) Willingness to mate is thus synchronized with capacity to conceive, and the mechanism of synchronization is alteration in the level of ovarian hormone.

At this same level of the evolutionary scale there is little or no feminine sexual activity prior to puberty; and the complete, adult copulatory pattern usually appears for the first time when the female has her initial heat, or estrus period. It is possible, however, to induce sexual behavior in immature females by treating them with ovarian hormone.

Removal of the ovaries in lower mammals is followed by total and permanent loss of female sexual responses. However, in every species that has been investigated, it has been found possible to evoke completely normal mating behavior in spayed females by the administration of the appropriate ovarian hormones. All the evidence points to the conclusion that the animal's tendency to become sexually aroused and to execute coital reactions is heavily dependent upon hormones from the ovaries.

Now, if we turn our attention to monkeys, apes, and other animals of higher evolutionary status, we find that the physiology of the ovary has not changed appreciably. The female sex glands still function in cyclical fashion. Ripe eggs are produced periodically, and their appearance coincides with the point of maximal secretion of estrogen. However, the relation between sex hormones and sexual behavior has become less precise. The full-grown female chimpanzee with constant opportunity for sexual contact displays an obvious cycle of sexual desire that correlates fairly well with the rhythm of ovarian hormone secretion. Nevertheless, she may, under certain conditions, invite or permit copulation by the male at times when she is not fertile and when the estrogen concentration is low.

In contrast to the tendencies of lower mammals, the female ape engages in sex play long before the first menstrual cycle or puberty. Her immature ovaries are no more active than those of a young dog or cat, but her behavior during infancy and childhood indicates partial independence from the supportive influence of sexual hormones. Finally, apes that have been ovariectomized for years occasionally indulge in sexual relations even though no estrogen is present in their systems. It is clear that the female primate's capacity for erotic excitement is strongly affected by ovarian secretions, and at the same time that the dependence is less complete than in the case of lower mammals.

The human ovary appears to function in much the same fashion as the reproductive glands of female monkeys and apes. It secretes the same hormones and does so with rhythmic regularity from menarche to menopause unless illness or pregnancy intervenes. One might expect, therefore, a regular rhythm of sexual need that would follow closely the rise and fall of hormonal tides. Questionnaire and interview studies have revealed that many women do experience fairly regular cycles of erotic sensitivity or sexual desire (13, 14, 47). Furthermore, these fluctuations in responsiveness are clearly related to the menstrual cycle, which of course is timed by the hormone factors.

But for the majority of women the greatest degree of sexual reactivity is experienced just before or just after the period of menstrual flow. Now this is not at all analogous to the relationship obtaining in other mammals. In women as in females of other species, the secretion of estrogen is greatest at about the time of ovulation, that is, somewhere near the midpoint between two periods of menstrual flow. Yet relatively few women feel their highest sexual drive at this time. Peaks of sexual desire that occur near the time of menstruation cannot be accounted for in terms of high estrogen levels. Factors other than hormonal ones have become maximally important in determining the level of sexual responsiveness in females of the human species.

This conclusion is substantiated by observations to the effect that surgical or natural menopause need not produce a decrease in the sexual activities of healthy, emotionally well-balanced women. Although ovarian hormones are no longer present in the system many individuals continue to experience sexual desires and to participate in sexual relations.

The behavioral effects of ovarian hormones are not limited to the strictly sexual sphere. Studies by Daniels (11) indicate that fluctuations in emotional tone or general mood often occur in specific phases of the menstrual cycle, and in some individuals the content of dreams varies at different stages in the cycle. According to Stone and Barker (46), the onset of menstruation is accompanied in many girls by a distinct shift in social interests that appears to be more or less independent of the individual's chronological age. Hormonal changes at the time of menopause include withdrawal of estrogen, and this may account in part for the impairment of emotional balance that sometimes accompanies cessation of the menses.

Nonsexual behavior is affected by sex hormones in many species other than our own. For example, female chimpanzees that are socially subordinate to their masculine partners often become temporarily dominant during the period of estrus. If two female apes are kept together in the absence of males, a fairly stable dominance pattern emerges; and this is frequently reversed when one or the other animal comes into estrus. Similar reversals can be induced in spayed apes by the injection of ovarian hormone (10).

Testis. The relations between testicular hormone and masculine sexual behavior differ from species to species. Male rats, mice, rabbits, and guinea pigs that are castrated before puberty show very little interest in receptive females after they become adult. And gonadectomy performed upon full grown males is followed within a few days or weeks by profound and permanent depression of sexual responsiveness. Occasional mating attempts may continue to occur for many months, but they are infrequent and incomplete. When castrated rodents are injected with male hormone, their sexual reactivity rises to normal, and the capacity for vigorous coital responses is restored (Figure 20).

At Yale we are at present investigating the effects of castration upon the reproductive behavior of male dogs. The study is not complete, but certain trends already are evident. The effect of male hormone withdrawal upon sexual performance is subject to wide individual differences. Some dogs evince a definite reduction in sexual interest within a few months after castration, whereas other males continue to mate with normal frequency and vigor for at least twenty months and perhaps indefinitely after removal of the sex glands. The animals that we have studied were allowed a great

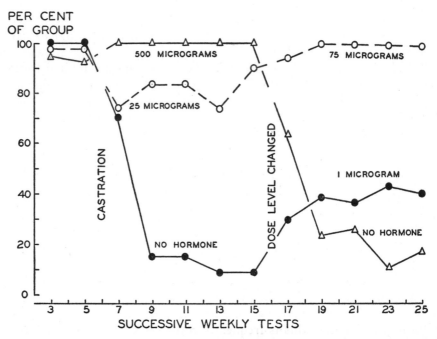

FIG. 20.—Records on three groups of male rats tested as normals, castrated, and retested while different amounts of androgen were supplied by daily injections. The function measured here was proportion of each group copulating with a receptive female.

deal of sexual experience prior to operation in adulthood. It may be that castration before acquisition of experience or before puberty would prevent sexual responses. These questions remain to be investigated. Prepuberal castration does not necessarily prevent the development of strong sexual reactions in male chimpanzees. Clark (8) reports that one ape of this type is known to have exhibited normal sex play during infancy, and in adulthood this animal copulates eagerly and vigorously with receptive females.

The effects of castration upon human sexuality are difficult to assess because of the infeasibility of direct observation and experimental control. It is obvious, however, that the operation affects different individuals variously. Some men castrated after puberty experience no reduction in sex drive nor in capacity for sexual performance. Others describe marked lowering of interest in sexual matters and varying degrees of impotence. Male patients whose sexual ability is sharply restricted as a result of androgen deficiency may react to supplementary therapy with a quick resurgence of sex drive. Spontaneous erections become frequent, and with very large androgen doses they may be partially maintained for as long as twelve hours, according to Pratt (32). Daniels and Tauber (12) report that reflexive genital response to the hormone may occur in complete absence of desire for sexual relations. The capacity for complete and satisfactory coitus is often renewed.

Effects of testis hormone upon behavior extend beyond the realm of simple sexual responses. Androgen treatment of hypogonadal men often evokes changes in the content of dreams and waking thought. Aggressive tendencies are augmented and may be expressed in social relations. A similar correlation between androgen and aggressive behavior exists in many animal species, according to Collias (9). Fighting is increased in fishes, reptiles, and birds by androgen administration. Male rats and mice fight less frequently and vigorously after castration, and normal or even hypernormal aggressiveness can be evoked in castrates by administration of large amounts of male hormone. Female mammals and birds become increasingly likely to fight with each other or with males if they are treated with male hormone.

Interpretations

Incomplete and abbreviated as it is, this survey of the evidence leaves no doubt that the behavior of men and other animals is powerfully affected by chemical changes within the body. The establishment of a correlation between a given behavioral phenomenon and a particular feature of blood chemistry is often of great practical importance. When the correlation is close enough, it is often possible to control behavior by controlling the chemical variable. The medical profession makes daily use of this type of knowledge.

General Principles.—The research scientist, however, is not content to demonstrate the sort of correlations described thus far. His goal is to discover the underlying physiological changes responsible for the correlation. If it is granted that reduction of atmospheric oxygen produces fairly predictable changes in behavior, how is this result brought about? We know, of course, that lowered oxygen tension in the inspired air is accompanied by parallel reduction of this element in all body tissues, but why and how does oxygen deficiency produce its specific behavioral consequences?

As was indicated in the introductory remarks to this Chapter, we have very few satisfactory answers to questions that are oriented toward this level of explanation. It will be fruitful to examine some of them nevertheless, but first two general principles must be mentioned.

The first can be called the *principle of multiple causation*. It states that for every behavioral act there exist not one but many physiological correlates. In no instance does one find that an organismic response is due to one and only one physiological factor. The second generalization is termed the *principle of multiple effects*. It embodies explicit recognition of the fact that no physiological process or condition has one and only one behavioral result. Instead, every physiological event that affects one type of behavior simultaneously influences other types as well. These two principles are so simple as to seem self-evident, and yet they are often overlooked. They apply to the interpretation of any and every relationship between physiology and behavior. They should be kept in mind while we evaluate some of the attempts that have been made to explain correlations between the body chemistry and the behavior of organisms.

Any behavioral response involves the nervous system, and changes in behavior are, therefore, quite properly regarded as consequences of some neural change. Unfortunately, however, too many purported explanations of chemical effects upon behavior consist of nothing more than facile reference to some presumed modification in the cortex, the hypothalamus, or some other part of the central nervous system. The following quotation by Freudenberg (16) illustrates the point.

In schizophrenia there is probably a primary disturbance in cerebral respiration, perhaps due to some lack of oxygenating substances. This disturbance leads to a collection of toxic products, probably originating from the protein metabolism. Insulin therapy induces the oxybiotic processes necessary for detoxication and also an irritation of the cell membranes, which results in an increased exchange between the cells and their surroundings.

This kind of interpretation represents little more than arm-chair speculation and is too vague and general to permit empirical verification. Much more desirable are tentative explanations that can be evaluated by actual experimentation. If we are to focus our attention upon the nervous system, we must ask questions that can be answered with facts rather than guesses. What reasonable assumptions can be made concerning the various ways whereby changes in body chemistry might influence behavior? One obvious answer is that a particular chemical change might result in the destruction of certain groups of nerve cells and thus interfere with the behavior they normally mediate.

Destruction of Nervous Tissue.—There are several instances in which degenerative changes are known to occur in the central nervous system as a result of chemical abnormalities. This appears to be the case in juvenile amaurotic family idiocy. It will be recalled that in this disease the first five or six years of life are apparently normal and the symptoms begin with failure of vision. The subsequent mental deterioration is progressive, and death occurs during adolescence. Physiological tests reveal that the behavioral change is accompanied by interference with the metabolism of lipids. The metabolic failure, in turn, has severe effects upon the nervous system.

The brains of individuals who have died of this disease are definitely pathological (21). Many nerve cells in the cerebral cortex are found to be crowded with small lipoid granules. Swollen and infiltrated cells occur not only in the cortex but also in the basal ganglia, thalamus, hypothalamus, and, to a lesser extent, in the brain stem. Neurons having this appearance cannot be expected to function normally nor to survive for long. The behavioral signs of juvenile amaurotic family idiocy undoubtedly are due in large measure to brain injury caused by inability to metabolize lipids.

Let us note, however, that this cannot be considered a complete explanation. The two principles enunciated earlier apply here. The metabolic dysfunction undoubtedly affects many organs and organ systems in addition to the brain, and extraneural changes probably exert indirect effects upon behavior. Furthermore, we do not know how the demonstrated changes in the brain produce the changes in behavior. Thus, in partially answering one question, we have raised many new ones. But this is a common event in scientific research and should not be discouraging. Although our explanation is incomplete, it pushes beyond the realm of general correlations and affords us a new starting point from which to launch the next step in the investigation of the problem.

There are other examples of chemical changes that cause permanent or temporary damage in the nervous system. For example, Shock (39) reports that brain cells may be killed in animals that are repeatedly subjected to partial anoxia. Chronic alcoholism sometimes leads to degenerative changes in the central nervous system. The condition known as alcoholic polyneuropathy involves deterioration in peripheral and central nervous structures. The means by which nervous injury is effected are not fully understood, but an important factor is known to be avitaminosis in which deficiency of B_1 is dominant.

Prolonged quantitative or qualitative dietary deficiencies are capable of producing irreversible brain changes. Irving and Richards (18) report that rats that are weaned prematurely and fed a diet that contains no vitamin A suffer degeneration of various parts of the central nervous system, particularly in the region of the medulla. Prolonged starvation produces severe effects in the brain of the mouse. Microglial cells are gradually transformed in so-called "gitter" cells. These then continue to grow at the expense of neighboring nerve cells. The neurons are slowly phagocytized by the transformed glial elements, according to Andrew (1).

The behavioral effects of certain drugs appear to depend upon physical changes in the central nervous system. It has frequently been postulated that metrazol and insulin alter the behavior of the schizophrenic patient by inducing some kind of modification in unidentified neural mechanisms. Sakel (37), to take but one example, thinks that the altered adrenal activity in psychotic patients results in a general lowering of neural thresholds. One result is said to be that nerve pathways for infantile responses become much more active than they are in the normal adult. Insulin, acting as an adrenalin antagonist, is supposed to counteract its activity.

This type of explanation has little to recommend it. The existence of "infantile" pathways for complex behavior is a pure assumption. The lowering of thresholds in these hypothetical mechanisms by adrenalin is likewise extremely hypothetical. The presumed antagonistic action of adrenalin and insulin upon nervous thresholds is established in only a few specific and restricted cases.

A more fruitful approach to the problem of convulsive drugs and their long-term effects upon behavior is suggested by the experimental work of Speidel (42), who examined the reactions of peripheral nerves to metrazol. The drug was applied directly to the tail fins of frog tadpoles. This structure is so thin and transparent that it can be studied microscopically *in vivo*. Metrazol causes visible changes in the terminal portions of nerve fibers. The tips of fine fibers are retracted and tend to swell. Sometimes the most distal portions degenerate and are completely destroyed. Slightly injured fibers recover normal appearance within a few days. When a portion of the fiber is killed, regeneration usually occurs, and the new endings that are extended often make connections different from those that existed prior to metrazol treatment.

Speidel (42) suggests that similar changes occur in the brains of the human patients who are subjected to metrazol shock. It is assumed that the drug destroys structural connections between cells and that subsequent regeneration involves the formation of new synaptic relations. This physical change is supposed to account for behavioral changes subsequent to shock. The interpretation has the disadvantage of contradicting the generally accepted belief that regeneration does not occur within the central nervous system. However, the type of regrowth or re-extension required by Speidel's hypothesis is so minute that it might well escape detection during histological examination.

Modification of Nervous Function.—It is entirely conceivable that certain chemicals might affect behavior, not by altering the structure of the nervous system, but by modifying its activities in some other way. A particular response might disappear from the behavioral repertoire simply because the neural mechanisms that mediate it have been rendered unresponsive to stimulation. Or, conversely, a given reaction pattern such as convulsions may appear because the associated nervous circuits are abnormally sensitive.

Temporary vitamin A deficiency does not, as far as is known, cause irreversible damage to nervous tissue, but it does reduce visual acuity under conditions of low illumination. The vitamin is essential for the resynthesis of visual purple in the retina, and visual purple in turn is necessary for normal function of the rod cells upon which night vision depends.

In this example it is clear that the physiological effect of the chemical change occurs in a peripheral receptor. There are undoubtedly other cases in which this is true. It has been stated that rats deprived of their adrenal glands spontaneously ingest large quantities of sodium chloride. Furthermore, such animals are able to detect the presence of salt in their drinking water in concentrations too weak to be tasted by normal rats. Richter (34) suggests that removal of the adrenals directly affects the peripheral gustatory receptors.

Adrenalectomy produces a condition of chronic sodium deficiency in all parts of the body, including the taste buds of the tongue. Therefore, salt solutions of a given concentration that are brought into contact with the taste buds will encounter a situation different from that existing in normal animals where the salt content of the receptor structures is higher. The sodium ion will diffuse through the cell membrane more readily when the internal concentration of salt is low. Thus, the taste buds will be stimulated by concentrations too weak to evoke a sensory discharge in normal animals. One difficulty with this theory is that sodium ions pass through semi-permeable membranes very slowly, if at all, and there are only minute amounts of sodium inside the body cells.

Furthermore, an unpublished study by Pfaffmann and his collaborators (31) at Brown University indicates that the sensitivity of the taste buds is not altered by adrenalectomy. These researchers measured action potentials from the taste nerves. The occurrence of afferent discharges revealed that the taste buds had been caused to fire by the stimulus solution which was dropped on the tongue. Normal and adrenalectomized rats were compared by this electrophysiological method. In each case the investigators determined the lowest concentration of salt that would produce a nervous discharge from the taste buds. There was no significant difference between the operated and normal animals. In other words, there had been no change in the sensitivity of the taste buds as a result of the glandular deficiency. But Richter has shown, and Pfaffmann produces corroborative evidence, that when thresholds are measured in terms of the animal's discriminatory drinking behavior, there is a marked change after loss of the adrenal cortex. The evidence strongly suggests that, if this modification of behavior is caused by changes in the nervous system, such changes must occur at a more central point than the peripheral receptors.

It is generally assumed that central nervous changes are primarily responsible for many of the recognized correlations between body chemistry and behavior. Many writers have proposed that the immediate effects of alcohol upon behavior are related to reduced oxidation in the cerebral cortex. There is some partially confirmatory evidence. The performance of men on various tasks has been measured when the subjects were under the influence of alcohol, when they were free from the drug, and when they were alcoholized but allowed to breathe oxygen. The deteriorating effects of alcohol were partially alleviated by oxygen (19). This does not, however, prove conclusively that either the drug or the gas exerts its principal effects upon the cortex.

Severe reduction in the blood-sugar level results in loss of consciousness, and this effect has been interpreted as the result of metabolic changes in the brain. The assumption is plausible enough, but it must be recognized as an assumption rather than an established fact. We have seen that the behavioral symptoms of schizophrenia are often referred to as disturbances of various metabolic processes and consequent abnormalities of body chemistry. It has become standard practice to conclude, as do Looney and Freeman (26), that schizophrenia is probably due to disorders of oxidative functions in the brain cells. Statements of this nature merely reveal the extent of our ignorance concerning the behavioral phenomena involved in the disease and the ways in which the brain influences any sort of complex behavior. To demonstrate a correlation between an observable change in the brain's structure or activity and a behavioral defect is a genuine scientific contribution. To hypothesize that some systemic dysfunction affects behavior because it affects the brain is merely to restate an obvious but unilluminating probability.

There is some experimental evidence to support the theory that certain chemicals influence behavior by virtue of their ability to alter the function of central nervous mechanisms. Kollros (24) implanted agar pellets containing thyroxin into the brains of larval amphibia just prior to the normal development of the cyclid reflex. The hormone produced precocious appearance of the behavioral response within a few hours after treatment. The effect was so localized that implantations to one or the other side of the midline of the brain caused the reflex to appear earlier in one eye than the other.

A recent report by Kent and Liberman (22) is another case in point. These workers investigated the effects of ovarian hormones upon mating responses in spayed hamsters. The animals were given a series of estrogen injections followed by one injection of progesterone. The estrogen alone did not elicit coital reactions. The amount of progesterone necessary to stimulate sexual behavior varied according to the site of injection. When the progesterone was injected directly into the lateral ventricle of the brain, the effective dose proved to be very small and the response rapid. In some instances sexual receptivity appeared within ten minutes after the injection. If the hormone was administered subcutaneously, larger amounts were needed and the behavioral change did not occur so quickly. These results are consistent with the theory that progesterone's behavioral effects are due at least in part to changes induced in the brain. The nature and precise locus of the change remain to be determined.

Changes Outside the Nervous System.—The effect of a chemical factor upon behavior is in some instances traceable to changes that occur outside of the nervous system but subsequently influence its function.

Male rats maintained upon a diet lacking vitamin E inevitably display gradual loss of mating reactions and eventually become completely unresponsive to receptive females. It would be easy to speculate concerning the probable effects of the dietary deficiency upon the nervous system and to formulate hypotheses to account for the behavioral change in terms of altered neural function. However, the facts indicate that no such direct relationship obtains.

Vitamin E is essential for normal activity in the anterior pituitary gland. In the absence of this vitamin, the hypophysis fails to secrete the gonadotrophic hormones that normally stimulate the testes. As a consequence, gonads cease to produce male sex hormone. And it is the disappearance of testicular androgen from the blood stream that accounts for deterioration of sexual behavior.

If rats are continued on the vitamin E-free diet but treated with pregnant mare serum their mating behavior is restored to normal (48). Gonadotrophic hormones in the serum reactivate the testes, with the result that androgen is again secreted into the blood. The original change in blood chemistry is associated with the characteristic behavioral symptoms not by virtue of any direct effect upon the nervous system but as the result of a chain of intervening physiological events.

This particular example suggests that the final relationship in the causal chain is a correlation between the presence or absence of androgen and the presence or absence of overt sexual behavior. The question then arises as to how the chemical compound, androgen, exerts its effect upon behavior, and we are back once more to the problem of possible changes in the nervous system. It is customary to refer rather vaguely to presumed influences upon "thresholds" in some as yet unidentified nervous circuits. The present author has proposed precisely such interpretations in the past, but they are of no more value than the clinician's explanation of schizophrenia as a product of altered cerebral metabolism. What is needed is more information as to the identity and normal functioning of these hypothetical mechanisms. Until they are identified, it will be impossible to do more than speculate about their response to changes in blood chemistry. Meanwhile, recalling the principles of multiple causation and multiple effects, we are well advised to search for possible androgenic effects occurring outside the nervous system. A step in this direction has recently been taken, and the results are instructive.

The effects of castration include changes in anatomy as well as in behavior. For example, in the male rat the skin that covers the glans penis is modified within a few days after removal of the testes. The changes can be retarded or completely prevented if the castrated animal is given regular injections of androgen. Figure 21 illustrates the effects of the operation and hormone therapy. The irregularity of the periphery of the glans decreases within one week after the operation, and fourteen days postoperatively the surface has become very smooth.

The deterioration can be prevented if castrated males are supplied with a sufficient amount of androgen. Five micrograms of testosterone propionate per day is not enough to prevent some atrophy in the integument of the glans, but this minute amount of androgen does exert a detectable, supportive effect and prevents total regression to the castrate condition. Large doses of the hormone maintain the gross appearance of the glans in normal condition for at least four weeks and quite probably the effect would continue as long as the androgen was supplied.

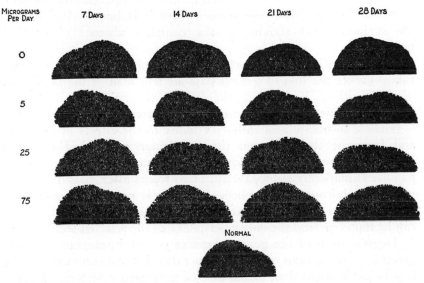

FIG. 21.—Tracings of microscopic sections through the glans penis of seventeen rats. Only one-half of the structure is shown. The organs were sectioned and stained, and a representative section was projected through a microscope onto the tracing paper. The point to be illustrated is the change which appears in the outlines from week to week after castration. The animals represented in the top line received no hormone. Castrates represented in the second horizontal line received five micrograms of androgen per day. The other two groups were given twenty-five and seventy-five micrograms respectively.

The next step in the analysis calls for a detailed study of the nature of the changes taking place, and for this it is necessary to examine the histological structure of the anatomical material. Under higher magnification the epithelium of the glans is seen to be thrown into deep folds that create fairly regular plateaus and depressions on the surface (Figure 22). Withdrawal of testis hormone as a result of castration is followed by filling-in of the valleys or depressions and consequent decrease in the irregularity of the periphery (Figure 23). It is this change that accounts for the alterations illustrated in Figure 21. However, in castrated rats that are receiving regular injections of testosterone propionate these changes do not occur and the epithelium retains its normal appearance.

Re-examination of the normal glans reveals another fact. Situated in the valleys between epithelial ridges are other structures known as genital papillae. When we are fortunate enough to find a papilla that has been cut directly through the center, we see that it consists of an epithelial "core" overlaid with a thick covering of hard, cornified material. Inspection of the glans in untreated castrates shows that the genital papillae have almost completely disappeared. Occasionally it is possible to identify vestigial fragments of a papilla, but only the core remains and it is buried deep beneath the surface. Most striking is the complete absence of cornified material.

Administration of appropriate amounts of androgen to castrated rats prevents the loss of genital papillae and insures the persistence of cornification. By counting the number of cornified papillae visible on the circumference of representative sections through the glans it is possible to obtain a quantitative index to the effects of castration and hormone therapy upon this particular anatomical character. When this procedure is followed, it is found that the number of papillae is markedly reduced within two weeks after castration unless exogenous hormone is supplied. The loss is progressive and at the end of the fourth postoperative week only two or three small papillae can be found around the entire periphery of the selected section.

Degeneration of the genital papillae occurs in castrates that are given five micrograms of androgen per day, but the extent and rate of loss is less marked than in the case of untreated castrates. Twenty-five micrograms of hormone per day are almost sufficient to maintain the normal number of papillae, and seventy-five micrograms is an ample amount to achieve this result.

It is possible to compare this index to the effects of castration with other indicators that have greater interest to the student of behavior. For this purpose we can select any feature of the rat's mating performance. After castration, the male's tendency to copulate with a receptive female is rapidly reduced unless there is some replacement therapy. Within four weeks after the operation, mating responses are infrequent and incomplete. But the coital tendency can be kept up to preoperative levels if sufficient amounts of androgen are made available to the castrated individual. Suboptimal concentrations of hormone maintain some sexual behavior but do not hold mating performance at normal frequency. Thus, by controlling the amount of androgen present in the castrated individual, it is possible to manipulate the frequency and intensity of the behavioral response.

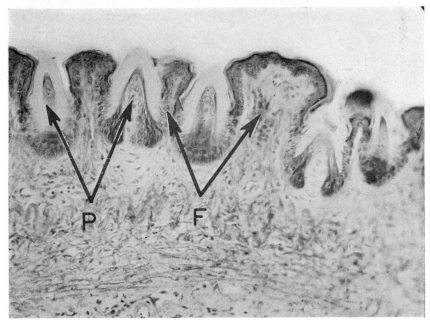

Fig. 22.—Section of epithelium of glans in a normal animal. Stained with haematoxylin and eosin. Magnification approximately 230. *P* indicates genital papillae with thick covering of cornified material. *F* indicates soft, epithelial folds.

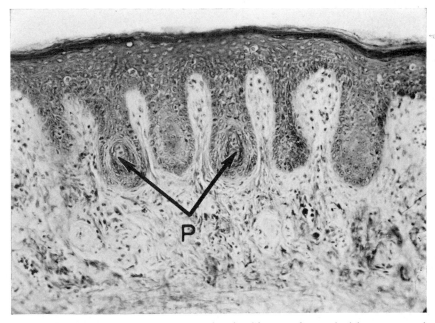

Fig. 23.—Same as Figure 22 except that in this case the rat had been castrated four weeks previously and had received no androgen treatment. *P* indicates remnants of two genital papillae, now completely devoid of cornification and deeply buried beneath the surface.

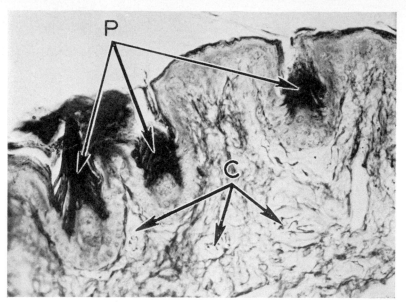

Fig. 24.—Section through the epithelium of a normal glans. Stained by the Bodian method. Magnification approximately 230. *P* indicates cornified, genital papillae, none of which has been cut precisely through the center. *C* indicates touch corpuscles.

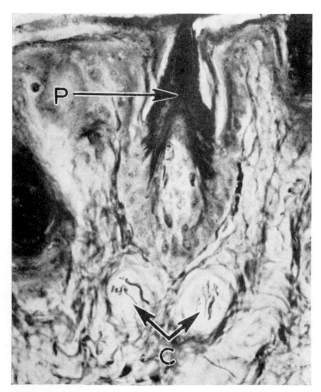

Fig. 25.—Same as Figure 24 except that the magnification is approximately 375. *P* indicates a single papilla, and *C* shows two touch corpuscles lying directly beneath it.

Now the present writer is prepared to demonstrate a close relationship between the changes in behavior and those in the genital papillae. Figure 26 illustrates the correlation. This figure shows that the injection of seventy-five micrograms of testosterone pro-

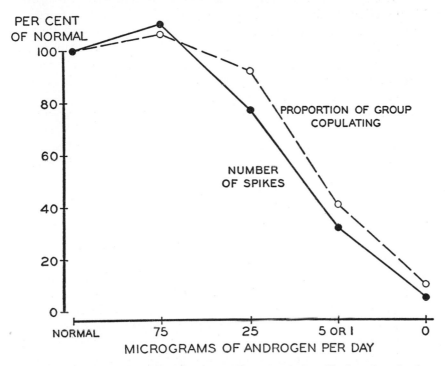

Fig. 26.—Relation between number of "spikes" (genital papillae) and mating behavior. These two sets of data do not refer to the same experimental populations. All scores are expressed as per cent of normal. After castration, if males are given seventy-five micrograms of androgen per day, they show a slight increase in the number of papillae and the proportion of the group displaying copulatory responses is raised a little. Smaller doses of hormone produce some decrease in both structural and behavioral indices. Lack of any androgen causes pronounced depression of the anatomical and behavioral characters. These values are based upon scores made one month after operation.

pionate per day into castrated male rats produces a slight increase in the mean frequency of genital papillae and also in the proportion of the group continuing to copulate. If the dosage is reduced to twenty-five micrograms, both variables fall slightly below normal. Daily injections containing from one to five micrograms of hormone have much less marked effects upon behavior and upon papillae frequency, but in both instances the character under consideration is held distinctly above the level which would be reached if no androgen were provided.

These data provide us with convincing proof of a close correlation between two variable functions, but they do not establish the existence of a causal relation. There is evidence, however, to suggest that such a relation does exist. To understand and evaluate this evidence, we must examine once more the histological structure of the glans. When sections of the tissue are stained in such a manner as to reveal the nerve fibers, one can identify numerous touch corpuscles that lie beneath the base of the genital papillae. Three such structures are evident in Figure 24. In some instances the spatial relations are more intimate, as shown in Figure 25, where one papilla is seen to rest almost directly upon a pair of large tactile receptors.

From this point on it is necessary to speculate, but the argument is reasonably straightforward. All the illustrations shown here represent the phallus in a flaccid condition. Under conditions of erection the organ becomes engorged with blood and, in consequence, its diameter is increased. It can safely be assumed that when the periphery is stretched the soft epithelial folds will increase in width and decrease in height. The papillae, being encased in a hard covering of cornified material, will not change their shape. As a result the points of papillae will project well above the tops of the foreshortened epithelial ridges.

In the act of coitus the erect phallus is moved backward and forward within the close confines of the vagina. The projecting papillae, rubbing against the vaginal walls, must be displaced laterally, first in one direction and then in the other. And when a papilla is deflected from its resting position there will follow a distortion of the tissues that lie beneath it. Any touch corpuscles in the immediate vicinity of the base of the papilla are likely to be mechanically stimulated and thus caused to discharge a nervous impulse.

When, as a result of castration, the number of papillae is materially reduced, the tactile sensitivity of the glans must be lowered. And marked reduction in this important source of sensory input might logically be expected to exert an inhibiting effect upon copulatory performance. This is the hypothesis that is proposed, and it seems to be well supported by evidence from the anatomical and the behavioral studies.

It is certain that this is only one of several ways in which androgen influences sexual behavior. We know, in fact, that although they are very important, genital sensations are not essential to mating behavior. In accordance with the principle of multiple effects, we expect that androgen will produce alterations in many organs and organ systems of the body. Some of these may not influence behavior, but numerous others certainly will do so. The task is to discover the nature of the changes induced and to establish their relations to behavioral function.

Major Needs

The evidence presented here demonstrates three things: first, that there are many correlations between the body chemistry of organisms and their behavior; second, that these correlations can be explained and interpreted if the proper research techniques are applied; and third, that thus far we have been able to interpret satisfactorily very few of the correlations that are known to exist. The question then arises, how can we increase our comprehension of the available evidence?

Two principal tasks confront research workers interested in this problem. The first is to devise and validate more objective and exact definitions and measures of the behavior under examination. As long as we continue to deal with the ambiguous, intuitively derived behavioral categories used in clinical medicine, we cannot expect to make much progress. The symptoms of schizophrenia, for example, are so complex and variable that the syndrome cannot be considered a scientifically reliable category of behavior. The vocabulary employed to describe different psychotic and neurotic states exposes the serious inadequacies of current methods of behavioral analysis. Descriptions of behavior as "depressed," "exalted," or "disoriented" are too crude and subjective to be compared and correlated with the relatively precise and refined measures employed by the physiologist.

The formulation of valid, reliable definitions and measures of behavior will depend first of all upon the methods by which data are collected. Experimental work on animals has contributed more to the development of this area of psychology than have clinical and experimental studies of human beings. This is due in part to the fact that animal material can be manipulated and controlled to a much greater degree than human beings. But this is not the full explanation. There is in most instances a significant difference in the methods with which the investigators approach their problems. Since he cannot interview or psychoanalyze his subjects, the worker who studies animals is forced to deal exclusively with their external responses. He is, furthermore, compelled to employ operational definitions and quantitative measures of the behavior with which he is concerned. His data, therefore, can be checked as to their reliability, and the validity of his interpretations can be judged directly. In contrast, most of the published work on human subjects has involved a qualitative, subjective, or introspective approach.

There are outstanding exceptions, of course, and some of them have been mentioned in this chapter; but careful, well-designed experiments on human beings are relatively scarce. They can be done, however, and must be done if we hope to answer the questions confronting us.

Laboratory methods cannot be employed in many instances, but the scientific approach is possible, nevertheless. There is much to be learned about the overt behavior of human beings in natural situations. A great deal of work has been devoted to description of the subjective aspects of normal and deviant behavior, but there has been relatively little quantitative measurement of the associated objective phenomena. More information about the observable verbal and nonverbal behavior of mental patients and less speculation concerning their inward, psychological states would be highly desirable. The changes in mood or emotional tone that some women experience during menstruation or pregnancy may be worth recording, but direct measures of overt reactions to controlled situations would be infinitely more valuable.

The second major obstacle to a more complete understanding of relations between body chemistry and behavior is our ignorance with respect to the behavioral functions of the nervous system. If we hope to interpret adequately the effects of a particular chemical upon intelligence, learning, or memory, we must learn a great deal more than is now known concerning the neural basis for these phenomena. If we wish to explain the influence of androgen upon sexual behavior, it is necessary to know what structures and processes within the nervous system mediate the individual's sexual responses.

Fortunately, the various problems listed here can be attacked simultaneously. And progress is being made toward the solution of some of them. The task is extremely complex and difficult, but the methods and tools for its accomplishment are at hand. We have, in the present writer's belief, every reason to expect that the near future will bring significant and impressive increases in the understanding of the relations between body chemistry and behavior.

BIBLIOGRAPHY

1. ANDREW, W. Neuronophagia in the brain of the mouse as a result of inanition, and in the normal ageing process. *J. comp. Neurol.,* 1939, **70,** 413-36.
2. ARNOLD, A., & ELVEHJEM, C. A. Is "running fits" a deficiency disease? *J. Amer. Vet. Med. Assn.,* 1939, **95,** 303-8.
3. BEACH, F. A. *Hormones and behavior.* New York: Paul B. Hoeber, Inc., Medical Book Department of Harper & Bros., 1948.
4. BIEL, W. C., & WICKENS, D. D. The effects of vitamin B_1 deficiency on the

conditioning of eyelid responses in the rat. *J. comp. Psychol.*, 1941, **32**, 329-40.

5. BROWN, J. S. The generalization of approach responses as a function of stimulus intensity and strength of motivation. *J. comp. Psychol.*, 1942, **33**, 209-26.

6. BROZEK, J., GUETZKOW, H., & KEYS, A. A study of personality of normal young men maintained on restricted intakes of vitamins of the B complex. *Psychosom. Med.*, 1946, **8**, 98-109.

7. CARLSON, A. J. Eating of bone by the pregnant and lactating gray squirrel. *Science*, 1940, **91**, 573.

8. CLARK, G. Prepuberal castration in the male chimpanzee with some effects of replacement therapy. *Growth*, 1945, **9**, 327-39.

9. COLLIAS, N. E. Aggressive behavior among vertebrate animals. *Physiol. Zoöl.*, 1944, **17**, 83-123.

10. CRAWFORD, M. P. The relation between social dominance and the menstrual cycle in female chimpanzees. *J. comp. Psychol.*, 1940, **30**, 483-513.

11. DANIELS, G. E. An approach to psychological control studies of urinary sex hormones. *Amer. J. Psychiat.*, 1943, **100**, 231-39.

12. DANIELS, G. E., & TAUBER, E. S. A dynamic approach to the study of replacement therapy in cases of castration. *Amer. J. Psychiat.*, 1941, **97**, 905-18.

13. DAVIS, K. B. *Factors in the sex life of twenty-two hundred women.* New York: Harper & Bros., 1929.

14. DICKINSON, R. L. *A thousand marriages: a medical study of sex adjustment.* Baltimore: The Williams & Wilkins Co., 1931.

15. FRANKLIN, J. C., SCHIELE, B. C., BROZEK, J., & KEYS, A. Observations of human behavior in experimental semistarvation and rehabilitation. *J. clin. Psychol.*, 1948, **4**, 28-45.

16. FREUDENBERG, R. Insulin therapy: a review with special reference to the mechanism of cure. *J. ment. Sci.*, 1938, **84**, 165-76.

17. HOSKINS, R. G. Schizophrenia from the physiological point of view. *Ann. Int. Med.*, 1933-34, **7**, 445-56.

18. IRVING, J. T., & RICHARDS, M. B. Early lesions of vitamin A deficiency. *J. Physiol.*, 1938, **94**, 307-21.

19. JELLINEK, E. M., & MCFARLAND, R. A. Analysis of psychological experiments on the effects of alcohol. *Quart. J. Stud. Alcohol*, 1940, **1**, 272-371.

20. JERVIS, G. A. The genetics of phenylpyruvic oligophrenia. *J. ment. Sci.*, 1939, **85**, 719-62.

21. JERVIS, G. A. Juvenile amaurotic family idiocy: six cases of its occurrence in siblings. *Amer. J. Dis. Child.*, 1941, **61**, 327-38.

22. KENT, G. C., & LIBERMAN, M. J. Induction of psychic estrus in the hamster with progesterone administered via the lateral brain ventricle. *Endocrinology*, 1949, **45**, 29-32.

23. KLÜVER, H. Mescal visions and eidetic vision. *Amer. J. Psychol.*, 1926, **37**, 502.

24. KOLLROS, J. J. Localized maturation of lid-closure reflex mechanism by thyroid implants into tadpole hindbrain. *Proc. Soc. exp. Biol. Med.*, 1942, **49**, 204-6.

25. KUBIE, L. S., & MARGOLIN, S. The therapeutic role of drugs in the process of repression, dissociation and synthesis. *Psychosom. Med.*, 1945, **7**, 147-51.

26. LOONEY, J., & FREEMAN, H. Oxygen and carbon dioxide contents of arterial and venous blood of schizophrenic patients. *Arch. Neurol. Psychiat.*, Chicago, 1938, **39**, 276-93.

27. MCCLELLAND, D. C., & ATKINSON, J. W. The projective expression of needs. I. The effect of different intensities of the hunger drive on perception. *J. Psychol.*, 1948, **25**, 205-22.

28. MILES, W. R. The sex expression of men living on a lowered nutritional level. *J. nerv. ment. Dis.*, 1919, **49**, 208-24.

29. Nowlis, V.   The relation of degree of hunger to competitive interaction in chimpanzee. *J. comp. Psychol.,* 1941, **32,** 91-115.
30. Perla, D., & Sandberg, M.   Mechanisms of action: metabolic interdependence of vitamin B and manganese; reciprocal neutralization of their toxic effects. *Proc. Soc. exp. Biol. Med.,* 1939, **41,** 522-27.
31. Pfaffmann, C.   Personal communication to Frank A. Beach, 1949.
32. Pratt, J. P.   A personal note on methyl testosterone in hypogonadism. *J. clin. Endocrinology,* 1942, **2,** 460-64.
33. Randall, L., & Cohen, L.   The serum lipids in schizophrenia. *Psychiat. Quart.,* 1939, **13,** 441-59.
34. Richter, C. P.   Total self-regulatory functions in animals and human beings. *The Harvey Lect.,* Series 38, 1942-43, 63-103.
35. Riess, B. F., & Block, R. J.   The effect of amino acid deficiency on the behavior of the white rat. I. Lysine and cystine deficiency. *J. Psychol.,* 1942, **14,** 101-13.
36. Rudra, M. N.   Manganese hunger in animals. *Nature,* London, 1944, **153,** 111-12.
37. Sakel, M.   A new treatment of schizophrenia. *Amer. J. Psychiat.,* 1937, **93,** 829-41.
38. Sanford, R. N.   The effects of abstinence from food upon imaginal processes: a preliminary experiment. *J. Psychol.,* 1936, **2,** 129-36.
39. Shock, N. W.   Physiological factors in behavior. In J. McV. Hunt (ed.), *Personality and the behavior disorders.* New York: The Ronald Press Co., 1944. Vol. 1.
40. Shock, N. W., & Scow, R. O.   The effect on learning of repeated exposures to lowered oxygen tension of the inspired air. *J. comp. Psychol.,* 1942, **34,** 55-63.
41. Siegel, P. S., & Steinberg, M.   Activity level as a function of hunger. *J. comp. physiol. Psychol.,* 1949, **42,** 413-16.
42. Speidel, C. C.   Studies of living nerves. VI. Effects of metrazol on tissues of frog tadpoles with special reference to the injury and recovery of individual nerve fibers. *Proc. Amer. phil. Soc.,* 1940, **83,** 349-478.
43. Spies, T. D., Aring, C. D., Gelperin, J., & Bean, W. B.   The mental symptoms of pellagra: their relief with nicotinic acid. *Amer. J. med. Sci.,* 1938, **196,** 461-75.
44. Spragg, S. D. S.   Morphine addiction in chimpanzees. *Comp. Psychol. Monogr.,* 1940, **15,** 1-132.
45. Stenberg, S.   Psychosis and blood lipoids: quantitative variation of total cholesterin and total fatty acids in the blood in dementia praecox. *Acta. Med. Scand.,* 1929, **72,** 1-49.
46. Stone, C. P., & Barker, R. G.   The attitudes and interest of premenarcheal and postmenarcheal girls. *J. genet. Psychol.,* 1939, **54,** 27-71.
47. Stopes, M. C.   *Married love.* London: A. C. Fifield, 1921.
48. Wiesner, B. P., & Bacharach, A. L.   Effect upon sex behavior of a diet deficient in vitamin E. *Nature,* London, 1937, **140,** 972-73.
49. Wikler, A., & Masserman, J. H.   Effects of morphine on learned adaptive responses and experimental neuroses in cats. *Arch. Neurol. Psychiat.,* Chicago, 1943, **50,** 401-4.
50. Wilkins, L., & Richter, C. P.   A great craving for salt by a child with corticoadrenal insufficiency. *J. Amer. med. Ass'n.,* 1940, **114,** 866-68.

CHAPTER 4

THE ROLE OF LEARNING IN PERCEPTION

By Ernest R. Hilgard, Ph.D.

There is a famous saying by Immanuel Kant that concepts without percepts are empty and percepts without concepts are blind. That was his way of saying that what we perceive depends upon the kind of organism we are as well as upon the kind of stimulation that the outside world provides. In some sense his statement might be taken as the text for this symposium. We are trying to discover how our perceptions may be influenced by the realities outside and by the realities within ourselves.

The older question about the role of learning in perception had to do with the nativism-empiricism problem. To what extent is perception natively given by way of our inherited structures and capacities, and to what extent is it the result of our experiences with the world of objects? But a new question is now being asked about the reciprocal relationship between learning and perception. This new and contemporary question is: To what extent is learning merely reorganized perception? We shall have to deal with both the older question and the contemporary one if we are to keep our thinking straight about both learning and perception.

Nativism in Perception

Because this chapter will have to do almost exclusively with the role of learning in perception, the present writer wishes first of all to call attention briefly to native or inborn factors in perception, so that the following discussion will not be misinterpreted as a denial of such factors.

The preceding chapters by Morgan and Beach have shown how structural, anatomical, and chemical factors modify perception. We see because we have eyes, stereoscopic vision is possible because we have two eyes located as they are, we see colors if we are not color-blind because of deficiencies in inherited capacity. Inherited structures determine both species differences in perceiving and some individual differences within the species.

Another point, not to be overlooked, is that some sensory preferences are innate. Studies of the sensory discriminations of newborn
infants show, for example, a preference for the taste of sugar over
quinine, a preference for moderate ranges of milk temperature over
extremes of hot or cold. Avoidance responses are made to noxious
stimuli by the fetal animal prior to birth. The preference for one
kind of stimulation over another places a motivational or affective
component at the very beginning of perceptual discrimination. When
we later on attempt to develop a dynamic theory of perception, we
are not assigning to perception properties that are entirely novel,

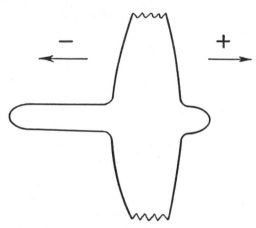

FIG. 27.—Silhouette that looks like a hawk when moved to the right and like a goose
when moved to the left. (Redrawn from Tinbergen [25].)

for there are dynamic properties to sensory discrimination as we find
it at birth.

Are there also innate preferences for some *patterns* of stimuli
over others? The answer to this question is more controversial and
resurrects some of the questions that got buried when instincts went
out of style. Perhaps we are again ready to admit that a hen raised
in isolation might, under appropriate hormonal conditions, see an egg
as a much-to-be-sat-upon object. The quality perceived may be
a patterned one, provided by an egg or a near replica thereof.

The most fascinating recent study of innate perceptual patterns is
that reported by Tinbergen (25). He prepared a silhouette of a
flying bird that looked like a hawk when moved to the right, but
resembled a harmless long-necked bird (like a goose) when moved
to the left. This figure, appropriately suspended on wires, caused
fright among a number of species of birds raised in captivity when
it moved in the hawklike direction, but it was not reacted to when

it moved in the goose-like direction. The ambiguous bird silhouette
is reproduced in Figure 27.

This is enough to show that the side of the nativists in the
argument over nativism and empiricism has a good deal of support.
If we inherit our sensory and perceptual capacities, if we inherit our
sensory preferences, possibly including some preferences for patterned stimuli, then we cannot ignore heredity as we try to understand perception.

Empiricism in Perception

The passive registration or copy theory of perception seems so
plausible that it comes as something of a jolt to find how easily it
can be exploded. That is, the analogies between the eye and a
camera, between the ear and a microphone, between the taste buds
and a chemical indicator, are so close that it is convenient to think
about perception as though the organism were merely sensitive to
its environment and were taking account of external events through
its inherited sense organs.

To psychologists the criticism of a passive registration or copy
theory is an old story. We have studied after-images, double-images,
paradoxical sensations, autokinetic phenomena, and illusions enough
to know that the organism contributes to its perceptions. Thus
perception results from an interaction between within-the-organism
factors and within-the-environment factors. Some of the discrepancies that make a copy theory of perception inadequate are innate.
Adaptation to temperature is probably as inborn as the fact of seeing
or hearing, yet it is that adaptation that can make the same pail of
water feel warm to one hand and cool to the other. Another step
is involved if we are to demonstrate that learning accounts for the
lack of correspondence between what we perceive and what is out
there.

The argument for a learned factor in perception can be illustrated
by a simple demonstration of the lack of agreement between the
image on the retina and what is seen. Consider a rectangular figure
projected upon a wall and seen from an angle, as illustrated in
Figure 28.

When the rectangle is projected as a rectangle upon the wall, it
is seen as a rectangle, even though the observer is at one side so that
his retinal image is that of an irregular trapezoid. When the
rectangle is projected from the side, so that a trapezoid is produced
on the wall, it is seen as a trapezoid, even though the eye is in line
with the projector so that the retinal image is that of a rectangle. In

this case, our perception is accurate, so far as reproducing what is projected upon the wall is concerned, but it is not faithful to the image furnished by our sense organs. A correction is made for the fact that what we see is projected upon a flat surface. Those who accept the role of learning in perception say that we have learned what rectangular figures look like when seen at an angle, so that our perception corresponds in both cases to the projected picture, not to our retinal image. This is an achievement of perception that comes about through learning.

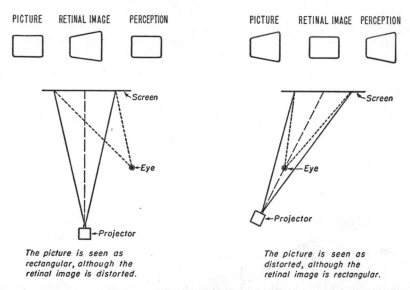

The picture is seen as rectangular, although the retinal image is distorted.

The picture is seen as distorted, although the retinal image is rectangular.

FIG. 28.—Discrepancy between retinal image and the figure that is perceived. (From Gibson [7, p. 171].)

It may be said in passing that there are those who would not accept the interpretation that these effects come about through learning. But the following discussion presents a number of additional demonstrations in support of the learning interpretation. This much of an introduction suggests that we need not take sides on the nativism-empiricism controversy, but that instead we may proceed to see what is the case, granting that both heredity and learning play their parts.

A Functional Interpretation of Perception

Before proceeding to a functional interpretation of perception, it will be of interest to consider some experiments that have helped to dramatize the problems of perception and have led, in some quarters, to a rebirth of interest in aspects of perception that have tended to fall into neglect.

The Hanover Institute Demonstrations.—The demonstrations described below were arranged by Professor Adelbert Ames, Jr., of the Hanover Institute, Hanover, New Hampshire. The fascination of these demonstrations is attested to by a book on education by Kelley (17) and one on social psychology by Cantril (3). That an educator should base his discussion of education for what is real on a series of demonstrations in visual perception and that a social psychologist should be led to ponder about man's social behavior on the basis of the same demonstrations show that perception has been given a new orientation. The Hanover Institute demonstrations are

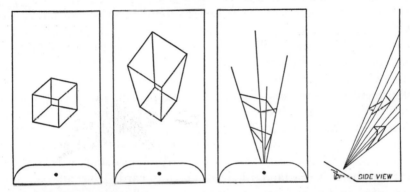

Fig. 29.—Three arrangements of wires, lines, and strings respectively, each of which is perceived monocularly as a cube. "The one at the left is a cube made of wires. The center one is a drawing on a flat surface. The third is a set of wires with strings on them . . . also shown in a side view. The second and third ones do not resemble cubes in any regard. They lack rectilinear sides, and one of them lacks three dimensions." (From E. C. Kelley, *Education for what is real* [New York: Harper & Bros., 1947], p. 27. By permission of the author and the publisher.)

now described by Lawrence (18) in a laboratory manual from Princeton, and what follows is based upon this manual and Kelley's book, plus the writer's own verification of the phenomena in the Princeton laboratory.

The first demonstration is concerned with the source of perceptions. Monocular vision reconstructs a three-dimensional cube out of strings, wires, and lines in the visual field. After having seen three cubes that look alike, one through each of three peepholes, the observer is shown what he has been looking at. The three external sources of his perceptions are shown in Figure 29.

The first of the three figures is indeed a cube made of wires, but the other two figures are quite uncubelike. One is a flat drawing, made with pen and ink. The third is a curious set of wires and strings, shown in the figure as seen from the top and also as seen from the side. The observer who saw all three as alike is ready to admit that there is something wrong with the adage that seeing is believing.

The second experiment refers to perception of distance as a function of size and brightness. For example, the larger an object is and the brighter it is, the closer it appears to be. At the same distance, a larger square looks closer than a smaller square of the same brightness. If the larger square is then made brighter, it will look still closer. Here two cues cooperate. The cues may also conflict. A large balloon looks closer than a smaller one at the same distance, but if the smaller one is made brighter, the apparent separation between them is reduced.

The third experiment of the series shows the effects of familiarity with objects upon the distance at which they are perceived. The main point is that familiar objects are usually perceived at their correct distance. Error can be introduced, however, by distorting the otherwise familiar object. For example, if three playing cards are all presented at the same distance in an apparatus in which the usual cues to distance are absent, then an oversized playing card is seen as closer than an undersized one, while a standard playing card is seen as at its correct distance. If the experiment is done with oak leaves, something else enters in, for there is no standard-sized oak leaf as there is a standard-sized playing card. But an oak leaf, presented in the ambiguous situation, is still seen as at a definite distance.

The oak-leaf demonstration is particularly instructive. An oak leaf presented in the alley experiment, with cues of size and distance ambiguous, is seen as of a given size and at a given distance. How can this be? In the case of the playing card there is a standard-sized card. But there is no standard-sized oak leaf. Oak leaves come in a distribution of sizes from very small to very large. The fact is that each person has his own standard-sized oak leaf. In the ambiguous situation he sees any oak leaf, whether large or small, according to his preconception as to how big a standard oak leaf is. Then he places it perceptually at a distance that fits this preconception. If what he looks at is a small oak leaf, he sees it as farther away, if a large oak leaf, as nearer to him.

There are further interesting variations on the theme of familiarity. A rectangular white card is more ambiguous as to size than either a playing card or an oak leaf. When such a card is exposed in the apparatus in which distance is ambiguous, the distance at which the card is seen depends upon what it is imagined to be. If it is imagined to be a calling card, it is seen as at an appropriate near distance; if it is imagined to be a business envelope, it is seen at an appropriate greater distance.

The fourth experiment is the dramatic one with a miniature distorted room. When viewed monocularly (or with special glasses that need not concern us) this distorted room seems to be the shape of an ordinary room, with the angles between the floor and ceiling right angles, windows all the same size, and so on. But things happening in the room are very strange. Faces at the windows appear to be magnified or reduced, marbles roll uphill, standard rats change size as they wander across the floor. Photographs and diagrams fail to communicate the weirdness of the effects. Some idea of what happens is given by the photograph that is used on the cover of the Lawrence manual, as reproduced in Figure 32. The actual plan of the room is shown in Figure 30.

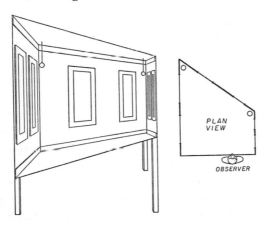

Fig. 30.—Plan of distorted room. "It does not show the distortion fully, because the back left corner does not appear to be far enough away from us. The reason for this is that there are so many things built into the room which violate the usual rules of perspective. For example, consider the two back windows. If they were the same size, the left one should look smaller than the right one, because it is farther away. It is actually larger, and when drawn larger, the left corner refuses to go back where it belongs. In order to realize how far away the back left corner is, we have to have the plan view, which is a horizontal cross section of the room. For the experiment, the observer is placed nearer the right wall than the left one." (From E. C. Kelley, *Education for what is real* [New York: Harper & Bros., 1947], p. 39. By permission of the author and the publisher.)

Note that the right rear window through which the enlarged face is seen is in fact much closer than the left rear window and is a much smaller window. But when viewed monocularly the room falls into cubical form much as do the wires and strings of the previous demonstration. Instead of looking like Figure 30, it looks like Figure 31. The explanation is not unlike that of the wire cube constructed visually out of wires and strings that were not at all like a cube in actual three-dimensional arrangements. The difference is that the room has many additional features to confirm its "normal" appearance—the windows, the pattern in the linoleum, symmetrical objects dangling from the ceiling.

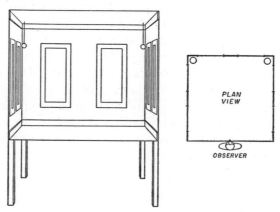

FIG. 31.—How the distorted room appears. This is the distorted room as it appears with the glasses. Note that the back left corner appears to be the same distance away as the back right one. The back windows appear to be the same size. While the observer is actually to the right of the center as he is shown in the plan view he seems to be in the center as shown here. (From E. C. Kelley, *Education for what is real* [New York: Harper & Bros., 1947], p. 41. By permission of the author and the publisher.)

The final experiment of this series is entitled "Perceptions and surety of action." When playing cards are displayed through two windows, and moved through them, contradictory cues are introduced. One window is of usual shape, but it is seen from an angle. The other is trapezoidal, but both windows appear to lie in the same plane, like two windows in a wall. Size relations are distorted, and the relative motions of portions seen as closer and as farther away are unusual. The subject immediately accepts the perceptual results gained from the window in which these contradictions are lacking, but he feels most insecure about what he sees in the window that introduces the contradictions. It is the immediacy of this security-insecurity pattern that is of interest.

The Princeton manual emphasizes how old ideas give way to new as these demonstrations are witnessed. Here are some of the new ideas said to emerge:

1. . . . your perceptions are based, not on one phenomenon, but on the statistical averages you use as presumptions.
2. . . . these statistical averages you used as presumptions are based on a great many past experiences.

3. . . . your perceptions result from an apparent weighing your
   mind makes of a very large number of indications and . . . this
   weighing of numerous factors goes on swiftly and unconsciously.
4. . . . your mind takes conflicting indications into account.

—Lawrence (18, p. 101).

A fifth point is added a little later:

. . . your perceptions serve not only as guides for action, but as
guides for purposeful action.

—Lawrence (18, p. 103).

These conclusions go ahead of the story. I believe we may accept
the demonstrations as showing, however, that there is a great deal
of learning in perception.

The Goals of Perception.—Perception is not a passive process of
registration, but, as was pointed out in Chapter 1, an active process
of interaction between organism and environment. Perception is an
achievement. As in the case of other achievements, it is regulated and
given direction by what the organism is trying to do. Let us now
turn our attention to two of the goals of perception and then consider
how these goals are determined and how perceptual dilemmas are
resolved according to these goals.

Achievement of Environmental Stability. The organism seeks
a perceptually stable environment in somewhat parallel fashion to
the way in which it seeks an internally stable environment. There is
a kind of environmental homeostasis parallel to physiological homeostasis. In both cases the stability is one of dynamic equilibrium,
not of static equilibrium. An environment that has some stable
reference points in it can still be a changing one. The organism
tolerates perceptual differences between night and day as it does
physiological differences between sleep and waking. But the organism does not like an environment that distorts too rapidly. If a
man's environment distorts too rapidly, he gets upset or seasick.

In normal perception, the goal of stability accounts for many of
our perceptual achievements. For example, were it not for this
achieved stability, the visual world would move as you move your
head from side to side. That stability is an achievement is easily
demonstrated by seeing what happens when you view the world
through reversing lenses. When the visual world is unfamiliar, as
it is through reversing lenses, the line of regard is the anchoring
point, so that when you move your head the world races by in the
direction opposite to the movement of your line of regard. The
anchorage thus involves a choice between the line of regard (used

in inverted vision) and a stable world (used in normal vision). Confronted by a familiar visual world, you prefer to have the world stay put as you look about.

This stability of the world has two features to it. One is the stability of objects, the other the stability of the world in which these objects have position. We have all sorts of object constancies. Our goal is to have both objects and the environment remain constant. But in a choice between a reference frame and an object, we will sacrifice the object to the framework. This is the basis for distortion in the miniature distorted room. It is more comfortable (hence a firmer goal reaction) to keep the room in shape than to make faces stay the sizes we know them to be. So we keep the room and let the faces at the windows enlarge or shrink. In the conflict for stability, the larger framework for stability will win over the smaller.

Definiteness. Definiteness and stability have much in common, but they are not alike. In reversible geometrical figures, definiteness is achieved at the price of stability. Stability might be better achieved if a geometrical figure were seen as only so many lines. But we prefer to see it as something, even though it is ambiguous, and so the "somethings" it represents tend to alternate.

Woodworth (27) is convinced that there is a fundamental motive to perceive clearly. As he puts it: "To see, to hear—to see clearly, to hear distinctly—to make out what it is one is seeing or hearing— moment by moment, such concrete, immediate motives dominate the life of relation with the environment" (27, p. 123).

He goes on to show how the clarity that comes as the goal of search is satisfying and hence, in terms of learning principles, reinforcing. There may, of course, be further reinforcement through the needs that the perceived objects satisfy.

The tendency to structure into figure and ground is one indication of the strain toward definiteness and thing-quality. The tendency is to construct concrete things out of the patterns we perceive, for concrete things have definiteness.. The present writer is not too sure which is the cart and which the horse. It may be that the figure-ground relation is learned as an abstract residue from our experience with objects. The real figures of our experience are those manipulable things that we see and touch, that slide over their backgrounds, that cast shadows. Because our ends are served by these real things, we tend to see ambiguous patterns as thinglike.[1]

---

[1] Hebb, (10, pp. 19-35) distinguishes three conceptions: (1) a primitive, sensorily determined unity, as that of a splash of black ink on a white card; (2) a nonsensory unity, affected by experience, as in the perception of familiar geometrical figures like

Edna Heidbreder's work on concepts (12), according to the present writer's interpretation, fits what is said above. When shown figures and asked to assign the appropriate nonsense concept name, her subjects always found it easier to name objects rather than to name the abstract relations of space or number. We want to see things clearly, and what we prefer to perceive is a concrete thing.

These two goals of perception, first, to have our perceptions keep the world about us a stable one and, second, to achieve definiteness in what we perceive, may be accepted as valid without committing ourselves as to their origin. Perhaps a little speculation is in order.

The present writer's conjecture is that perceptual goals are intimately related to the other goals of the learner. The basic reason for achieving a stable world is that such a world is the most convenient one in which to satisfy our needs. Only in such a world can we use maps and libraries and filing cabinets. We want to know where we are, where we are going, where we have put things. It is difficult even to see a problem here. Imagine, if you can, a pulsating world in which everything was as mobile as man. The cabbages you planted in rows might move across the street, your house would turn around to face the sun, you would not know whether you lived on a hill or in a valley. So accustomed are we to a predictable and orderly world that such notions are fantastic. Fortunately, the world is the kind of world in which a measure of stability can be achieved. It serves our purposes to have our perceptions correspond to such a stable world. There are, in fact, many mobile features to our world. Lights and shadows change the colors of objects; many objects, both animate and inanimate, are mobile. To keep our world of objects stable, we have to learn to take distance and motion into account, as well as light and shadow. We achieve more constancy, in fact, than is present to our senses. Were this not the case, we would not have to think of stability as an achievement. What this means is that the goal of environmental stability arises out of our need for a stable world in which to satisfy other motives. The stability of the world is not an end in itself.

The second goal, the achievement of definiteness, is likewise in the interest of other motives. The objects recognized while they are not yet too clear may be dangerous ones to be avoided or desirable ones to be pursued. It helps us to be ready for them before they are clear. Therefore, it helps us to identify things from partial cues.

squares and circles; and (3) the identity of a perceived figure, also affected by experience. A figure may be seen as unified without being identified for what it is. The paragraph to which this footnote is appended was written before Hebb's book appeared. The discussions do not appear to be in conflict, but Hebb's analysis would have permitted a more pointed interpretation.

This is enough to encourage object perception as an aid to need satisfaction.

There is another motive that supports our desire for clarity. This is related to the tendency for strange objects to invoke fear. Spitz (22) observed that infants during the first year of life show increasing responsiveness to strangeness. They smile at all faces during the first few months, but by six months they are frightened by strange faces. In another study by Bayley (1) infants in the test situation were observed to cry more frequently in response to strangeness than to other features of the test situation as they grow older. Hebb (10) reports that chimpanzees reared in captivity show marked fear of strange things and of strange people. The clinical experience of depersonalization, when everything is strange, is terrifying. It may be that the desire to find something clear and familiar in what is presented to the senses is part of feeling secure in the world, of being protected against the anxiety that strangeness engenders. It is no fun to be lost in a homogeneous environment, like a fog, the open sea, a dense forest, or even a dark corridor. We seek something familiar and identifiable, something that gives us anchorage. Possibly curiosity, a motive sufficiently important for McDougall (19) to have called it an instinct, is a defense against the anxiety that strangeness and lack of clarity produce.

These conjectures about the origin of the desire for a stable world and for definiteness of perception may or may not be correct. Whether they are or not does not prevent our accepting stability and clarity as goals of perception.

Harmonizing the Contributions of the Several Senses.—In order for the world to provide a firm and stable environment in which we may carry on our enterprises, it must be the same world that we see and hear and smell and touch. This sameness is an achievement, for our sensory givens are not in harmony except in the grossest of fashions. A hole in a tooth is not the same size to the tongue as it is to the eye; so far as our ears tell us, a cricket might be almost anywhere in the room, not only where our eyes find it.

The most plausible basis for making the world of objects one world is that of manipulation. In meeting our own needs, we have commerce with many objects. We go where they are, we carry them about, we dodge them if they are thrown at us, we place them in our pockets, and in countless other ways handle them according to their sizes, shapes, distances, and movements. We are not fooled by sizes, shapes, distances, or movements if our locomotion and manipulation are appropriate. Most of us are realists according to the way we find the world of things to exist outside ourselves and to be manageable according to stubborn and substantial characteristics.

In fact, the real world seems so real that we are persuaded, so long as we are not being fooled by recognized illusions, that our perceptions are accurate. They are, indeed, reasonably accurate, but they are not copies of real objects. Our perceptions achieve *for us* a world that is relatively stable by excluding so far as possible contradictory evidence. If a pail is to be filled with water, we soon learn its size relative to other vessels and relative to our own bodies. Its true perceived size fits with other size perceptions of things we handle. We never have to gather in the moon, so we have no way of knowing whether it is the size of a cheese or a dishpan or a silver dollar. Consequently, we see it as of some convenient size and at some convenient distance, without concern over its true size or its true distance. There is nothing to conflict with it, so the dimensions of size and distance need not conform in any precise manner to the sizes and distances of other objects.

Perceptual harmony is an achievement. It is not a given. Von Hornbostel (14) once wrote a lyrical paper on the "Unity of the Senses" in which he showed the great extent to which we do use analogies from one sense in dealing with the data from another. We can give fairly consistent answers to questions that appear silly. Students, when asked to tell how much a minute weighs, may think the question is insane, but nobody ever thinks it weighs as much as 100 pounds, and scarcely anyone thinks it weighs as much as 10 pounds. The present writer agrees that Von Hornbostel is right in postulating a kind of unity or interrelatedness to which the various senses contribute but is inclined to believe that we achieve this unity largely through experience.

The senses, when acting alone, provide different phenomenal worlds from the one yielded when they act together. The blind man gets around all right and recognizes objects by touch. His phenomenal world corresponds to reality and is satisfactory, so far as it goes. But if by removal of cataracts he is made able to see, the phenomenal world that comes to him by sight must be harmonized with the phenomenal world that comes to him through touch. Many observations show that the two worlds have to be harmonized by learning. Senden (20) reports, for example, that with restored vision the man once blind may distinguish between a ball and a block as visual objects, but he does not know which is the ball and which the block until he handles them. We are able to parallel these experiences to some extent in the laboratory. For example, a subject who has learned a maze blindfolded tends, if asked to draw the pattern that he has learned, to draw it too large.

The Stratton (23, 24) experiments with inverted lenses are appropriate in this connection. The distorted world that Stratton saw when he wore the lenses had to be harmonized with the world in which he moved about. Soon there was no problem of locating objects in the new visual space. Sounds seemed to come from the places where objects were seen. That is, after an observer had worn the glasses for a while, he heard the fire sputter audibly where the fire was seen to be. The visual scene did not swing with head movements as much as it did at first. The return to normal vision was at first bewildering; the world would again swing when the head was turned. The old habits were, of course, quickly restored.

The experiments of P. T. Young (28) with the pseudophone gave results similar to those of Stratton. With the ears reversed, the subject presently learned to see and hear things as though coming from a common source. It appears, however, that the reorganization was accomplished largely through accommodating the auditory experience to vision for, with the eyes closed, auditory localization took place as before the reversal. After the pseudophone was removed, there was no residual effect from wearing it. Had Young attempted to regulate his behavior largely by audition (say by blindfolding himself while wearing the pseudophone) his reorganization of auditory localization might have been more complete.

We coordinate the data from the various senses by manipulating objects in the environment. We can know that our sense data are "true" and "accurate" only if they lead to objects that serve our purposes. If the paper fits the envelope, if the car gets through the garage door, if the pen fits the penholder, then all the perceptions involved have been realistic. Our world is in order; whether or not it is a real world may be difficult to answer philosophically, but by pragmatic tests we know that the real and the perceived are alike, for the environment meets our expectations and suits our purposes.

Achieving Clarity from Ambiguous Cues.—When cues are ambiguous, we can accept them as such and postpone judgment pending their clarification. But perceptual mechanisms do not work that way. Instead, we are impatient, and we struggle to achieve clarity and definiteness even when the cues are insufficient to provide an objective basis.

If we do not know, then we guess. That is what we do when we recognize someone at a distance too great, when we try to anticipate who would be sending us a telegram from St. Louis, or when we

FIG. 32.—Distorted sizes of faces at the windows of a distorted room. (From M. Lawrence, *Studies in human behavior* [Princeton, N. J.: Princeton University Press, 1949]. By permission of the author and the publisher.)

FIG. 33.—Judgment of size at a distance. (Adapted from Gibson [7, opposite, p. 202].)

FIG. 34.—Distance as produced by natural gradient of texture. (Adapted from Gibson [7, opposite p. 188].)

infer that the noise is coming from an airplane rather than a motor-cycle. There is a strong tendency to jump ahead, to take a short cut, to act in accordance with a few indicators, even though more information might be forthcoming if we but waited. This is a general characteristic of behavior, based on a need to be prepared for what may be coming. Perhaps the person coming down the street is someone we would rather not meet, or someone from whom we wish to ask a favor in an auspicious manner; maybe the telegram will bring bad news, and we must guard against an undue display of emotion; possibly our son has threatened to buy himself a motor-cycle, and so we are apprehensive about noises that might confirm our fears. We not only respond to the stimuli that confront us but respond in preparatory ways to expected stimuli. Such preparatory or anticipatory response is an achievement of learning and intelligence in which perception shares.

The general tendency to reach conclusions promptly from ambiguous cues is illustrated by the constancy experiments. We have already referred to the alley experiment, where a rectangular card is presented with the usual cues for distance absent. Although neither size nor distance is defined by the information available to the senses, the perception that results is not ambiguous. On the contrary the card is seen immediately as of *a* size at *a* distance. The urge to definiteness is too great for us to wait or to tolerate ambiguity.[2] What size we make it and where we put it will differ from person to person and from time to time. But we see it as a real something at a real place. That is the first point: the goal of perception is toward definiteness, and definiteness is a prompt consequence of the perceptual process.

By shifting the "set" we can shift both size and distance. By imagining the rectangle to be either a calling card or an envelope, we adjust its distance accordingly. That shows us that the end result is an achievement, not something forced upon us by the environment. It is what is called in Chapter 1 a *transaction,* following Dewey. The transaction involves the stimulus, for if we make it a smaller object we see it as closer, and if we make it a larger object we see it as farther away. The transaction represents some sort of compromise between ambiguous external cues and our preconceptions of what those cues may signify.

When cues to distance are ambiguous, both size and distance are inferred from the known (or guessed) size of the object. Thus

---

[2] The degree to which a person can tolerate ambiguity has been considered as an aspect of personality by Frenkel-Brunswik (5). Her study provides another illustration of the intimacy between perception and personality.

playing cards are inferred to be of normal size when they are presented at ambiguous distances. In that case we suffer an illusion if the cards are actually smaller or larger than normal. It is an illusion only because the manipulable card is not the real object that we interpret it to be.

Size constancy is determined only in part by the familiarity of perceived objects at a distance. If cues are available by which distance can be judged, then the sizes of unfamiliar objects can be estimated remarkably well. Gibson (7, 8) has shown that the height of upright poles between 2 and 7 feet high can be judged with a high degree of constancy as far as they can be seen, say nearly half a mile distant on a horizontal plain. In his experiment, a single pole was planted at a distance. Subjects were asked to select from a number of poles at 14 yards distance the one that seemed to correspond to the single pole seen at a greater distance. When a 69-inch pole, for example, was planted 784 yards away, the mean size of near poles selected to correspond to it was 72 inches. Although the retinal image at that distance is but $\frac{1}{56}$th the size at 14 yards, the distant pole and the near pole appear to be of nearly constant and equal size. The experimental arrangement is illustrated in Figure 33.

The only conceivable manner according to which successful judgments of size at a distance can be made (if the distant object is of unknown or ambiguous size) is through taking into account the distance of the object. Consider the size of a toy automobile. A model can be made in any size from very small to very large. We have no trouble in judging the size of a model car because we see it close at hand. If its distance were entirely indeterminate, we would not know its size. No time will be taken here to discuss in any detail the cues of distance, most of which are treated in elementary psychology textbooks. Gibson has proposed that we supplement or correct our usual textbook discussion of these cues by giving recognition to *retinal gradients* that aid us in constructing the continuous surfaces out of which three-dimensional perceptions are made. What is meant by a gradient may be illustrated by the gradient of texture shown in Figure 34.

In the experiment with the poles, the distance of the single upright pole could be judged by such a gradient of texture in the plain and by the height of the pole's base as seen in relation to the horizon. That the cues used are monocular ones was demonstrated by Gibson through presenting the problem to subjects by means of photographs. The constancy judgments could be made about as well from photographs as from the experience in real space (7, pp. 206-7).

We have seen that size constancy depends both upon the known sizes of familiar objects and upon perception of the distances at which objects of unknown size are seen. What happens when the cues for distance are distorted? Do familiar objects remain constant, or do the sizes of objects change to conform to the faulty perception of distance?

During the dry summers of California, the grass in the valleys and on the hillsides turns a uniform brown. The rounded contours of the hills make it difficult to detect where the level plain begins to rise and become a hillside. A hillside, however, looks much closer than a level plain at the same distance. Here, then, we have a situation in which the estimate of distance is incorrect. What now happens to the sizes of the cows grazing on the hillside? Even though we are thoroughly familiar with cow sizes, the cows on the hillside look much smaller than cow size. The perception of distance, even though faulty, has won over the perception of familiar size, even though correct. Another illustration of the same kind is provided by the sizes of houses as viewed from an airplane. Because the ground looks closer than it is, houses look like doll houses. The same houses, seen at the same distance on a horizontal plain, would look house size. Again distorted distance wins in the competition with constancy as mediated by familiarity with houses.

Why does distance win over familiar size when the two conflict? The reason is that, in the long run, the goal of stability in perception is better served by a stable frame of reference than by a stable object. In most situations, objects that move about and hence change in retinal size remain stable precisely because they have been referred to a stable world. Familiarity of experienced objects and cues for distance usually cooperate. Because objects are perceptually more fickle than the world of space, preference for environmental stability usually serves our purposes well. It is not then surprising that, on those rare occasions when the cues to distance are misleading, we follow them rather than the cues from objects of familiar size.

What this means is that we achieve clarity in ambiguous situations by seeing objects as of a definite size and as at a definite distance, even though cues are ambiguous. Ambiguity is resolved through familiarity both with identifiable objects and with cues to distance. We may now turn to a consideration of how we are able to make use of the familiarity that repeated experiences provide.

Experienced Probabilities and the Resolving of Ambiguity.— A great many perceptual experiences can be understood by considering the perceiving person to be a statistical machine capable of quickly estimating probabilities. That is, each of the cues present now is related to many past experiences. Past experiences provide a kind of table of probabilities according to which estimates are made, but the perceiver has to make use at once of the experience tables corresponding to each of the cues, some of which will point in one direction, some in another. In the easier situations, past experience with men tells us that the man seen at a distance is probably man size, the playing card standard playing-card size, and so on. We have seen how such estimates may lead into error in ambiguous situations, but that is no defect in the theory. In fact, the theory is supported because it accounts so well for many illusions. A theory of perception has to take account of illusion as well as realistic perception.

An important paper by Tolman and Brunswik (26), appearing in 1935, bore the title "The organism and the causal texture of the environment." The environment has many causal strands, that is, cause-and-effect sequences, some of which are firm, consistent, and dependable, others of which are unsure, inconsistent, and contingent upon circumstances. Because these cause-and-effect sequences intertwine in complex ways, Tolman and Brunswik speak aptly of the "causal texture" of the environment. We learn that electric lights usually turn on when we throw the switch, although a fuse may be blown, the power may be off, the lamp cord may be disconnected, or the light bulb may be worn out. Clouds in the sky mean that it may rain, although there may be a wind without rain, or it may snow, or the clouds may disappear and the sun come out. We can light the fire on the hearth by striking a match on the bricks, unless the match is a safety match that must be struck on its own box, unless the wood is wet, unless there is a downdraft through the chimney. The problem of getting along in the environment involves more than a perception of the objects found in it. We need to see these objects according to their relationships and according to their uses. The organism has to find its way in an environment with many ambiguous signposts. It has to distinguish between the causal strands that are firm and those that are arbitrary and uncertain. Tolman and Brunswik deal with the organism's interpretation of cause-and-effect sequences as a matter of probability, based on experience. Because the paper represents a reconciliation of Tolman's views about learning and Brunswik's views about perception, it is particularly cogent for this discussion. It is recommended, with the warning that it will be found difficult, for it translates Brunswik's abstruse German into Tolman's abstruse English. But it is worth the effort that it costs to read.

The paper was followed up by Brunswik (2) with an experimental study of probability as a determiner of learning in the rat. It was found that the rat could learn to estimate ratios of reward, going to that side of a T-maze where it would have the higher probability of being rewarded. But both the theoretical and the experimental paper point out that factors other than simple probability determine conduct.

Two main problems arise in connection with the interpretation of probability as a factor controlling what is perceived. One problem is how appropriate probabilities are selected from among many possible ones. The second problem is how distortions occur so that a bias is introduced that goes against probabilities. These are related problems, but we may approach them separately.

How Patterns of Experienced Frequencies Determine the Interpretation of Data Present to the Senses. A simple frequency theory of perception is like a simple frequency theory of habit formation. Both say that we do in the present what we most often have done in the past. Just as in a word-association test we reply to the word "day" with the word "night" because of the frequency of day-night association, so in perception we see the object that the presented cues have most often signified. Thus in the cube demonstration, we saw a cube made of right angles even though the materials were not arranged in cubelike fashion. We saw a cube because similar sensory information in the past usually came from cubelike objects. This is a simple frequency interpretation. But such a simple interpretation is no more appropriate to perception than a simple practice-makes-perfect theory is appropriate to learning. The main criticism is that in perception, as in learning, interpretations are modified by the patterns of experienced frequencies and not solely by the totals of such frequencies.

In order to make this more concrete, let me refer to a simple but convincing experiment performed by Humphreys (15). The subject saw two lights on a board, one on the left and one on the right. His task was to guess, after the left light came on, whether or not the right light would come on. For one group of subjects, the right light invariably followed the left one. They gradually came to expect the right light every time, thus acting according to past experience with the two lights. For another group of subjects, the right light followed only half the time, in a prearranged chance order. Subjects of this group behaved according to the ambiguity of the situation and guessed half the time that the light on the right would come on, half the time that it would not. So far, nothing in the experiment contradicts a simple frequency explanation.

The next phase of the experiment makes the point that behavior is not regulated solely by the sum of prior experiences, but is affected also by the pattern of such experiences. In this second phase of the experiment, the right light never came on, so that the repeated repetition of the left light alone simulated what is called extinction in a conditioning experiment. Now the group that had regularly experienced the right light following the left quickly came to expect no more lights on the right. One or two absences of the right light were enough. But the group that had experienced the right light irregularly took much longer to decide that there would be no more lights on the right. These results contradict a simple frequency theory, for the ones who had uniformly experienced the left-right sequence had seen the right light follow the left twice as often as those who had seen the right light only half the time. Yet the ones who had seen the right light follow less often continued to expect it for more trials than those who had seen it follow more often.

This paradox is easily resolved if, instead of considering only frequency, we consider the pattern of experience. Subjects who saw the right light follow the left every time had come to expect uniformity. A single absence of the right light broke the uniform pattern, and could lead to continued uniformity only if the left light were no longer followed by the right. This new hypothesis, easily adopted by the subjects, turned out to be correct. The left light, having always been followed by the right, led plausibly to the conjecture that, when once not followed by the right light, it would never be followed by it. The experience that tells is the experience of uniformity, rather than the experience of frequency.

Those subjects who had experienced the right light irregularly continued to expect irregularity, so that, even though the left light was not followed by the right one for several consecutive trials, they continued for many trials to expect the right light to appear.

These experiments of Humphreys are of interest for our purposes because the relationships are so simple that an interpretation according to cumulative frequencies might be expected to apply. But even in such a simple situation, we see that organizational factors enter. The pattern of experiences is important as well as the frequency of experiences.[3]

---

[3] The interpretation of Humphreys' experiment according to expectancy has been objected to by several experimenters, who offer stimulus-response alternatives. A recent one of these, Sheffield (21), offers an ingenious alternative interpretation of the differences in extinction rate under the two conditions of reinforcement and supports the interpretation by confirming experiments. Her article summarizes the pertinent literature and gives a clear exposition of the issues involved. For the present purpose the precise explanation of the phenomena is not crucial. The main

Another series of experiments calling attention to the importance of experienced patterns is that of Harlow (9), with the results summarized according to his interpretation of learning "sets." Monkeys that have had enough experience in discrimination experiments can learn to reverse positive and negative stimuli very promptly. For example, if the food reward appears under a circle rather than under a square, the monkey will choose the circle time after time. If now on a single trial the food is omitted under the circle, the monkey will select the square the next time, and, having found food there, will continue thereafter to select the square. According to Harlow, the animal has learned how to learn. That is, it has learned to pay attention to significant features of the environment that go beyond the accumulation of particular experiences. These significant features are what I have been calling patterns to distinguish between them and mere sums or totals.

How does all this apply to perception? Perceptual signs lead us to expect objects as the sources of the perceptual experience exactly as learning signs lead the monkey to expect food under the circle or under the square. The expectations arise out of past experience with signs and the things or events that the signs have pointed to. But perception, especially visual perception, provides some of our most highly patterned experiences. If experienced patterns are important in the learning of simple stimulus-response sequences, they are all the more important in the learning of perceptual meanings.

In the distorted room, for example, as pictured on the cover of Lawrence's manual and reproduced as Figure 30, the faces are distorted rather than the room. Human faces furnish patterned stimuli, and there is a strong tendency to constancy, that is, to see faces as face size, no matter what their distance. Our experience has taught us that human faces are seldom found except on human beings, and human beings do not vary too much in the sizes of their faces. If the faces seen at the windows of the distorted room were spotlighted, while the room was dark, they would be seen as ordinary human faces, with the larger one seen as nearer than the smaller one. But the room also possesses patterning. Were we able to measure stability of organization or patterning, we would find the room more stably organized than the faces, so that the faces at the windows are placed at a distance in the space determined by the appearance of the room. Hence one face has to be magnified over the other in

---

point in this context is that, in her experiments, Sheffield also found results requiring explanation on grounds other than the simple frequency of reinforcement and nonreinforcement. A further contribution to the discussion has been made by Jenkins and Rigby (16).

order to resolve the dilemma of different-sized faces at the same distance.

What does it mean to say that the room has more stable organization than the faces? Two interpretations are possible. One is that the innate or inherent tendencies to symmetry are so great that, regardless of experience, the room is likely to be seen as symmetrical. In that way it becomes a good Gestalt. An explanation like this would be preferred by classical Gestalt psychologists. An alternative is that past experiences pile in a consistent way so as to lead to the same results. We have had countless experiences with walls and ceilings joining at right angles, with symmetrical windows, with uniformly patterned linoleum, with parallel lines coming together as signs of distance. Because all these many signposts from the past point in the same direction, the room looks like a normal room, and everything incoherent with that appearance is distorted. Because I favor this latter interpretation does not mean that I reject entirely the Gestalt emphasis upon contemporary organization. Gestalt-like principles may be needed to help us understand how contemporary organization draws upon past experience in achieving our perceptions.

This calls for a little further discussion. Possibly the cumulative frequency of experiences is enough to account for what happens in the distorted room, so that no new principle of contemporary organization is involved. Against the frequency interpretation is the extreme unlikelihood that we have experienced bare rooms more often than faces. If mere frequency operated, so this objection goes, we ought to see the faces as of normal size, and let the room be distorted. But we have already pointed out that we have to examine what frequencies we are talking about. Let us try some conjectures to show what may lie behind the perception of the room and the faces.

Suppose that bare rooms have been seen fifty times and faces a thousand times. It may still be true, as a matter of experience, that we will relate face size to room space rather than room space to face size. How can this be? The thousand faces that we saw in the past were at many different distances, and hence of many different retinal sizes. We were able to see all those faces harmoniously as human faces of nearly constant size by referring them to a stable spatial frame. That is, smaller faces were seen as at a greater distance, larger faces at a nearer distance, so that the faces remained the "same size" as objects in external reality. When we then compare our fifty experiences of bare rooms with our thousand experiences of faces, what are we comparing? We are comparing fifty rooms-seen-as-stable with a thousand faces-perceived-in-stable-space. So we come to the experiment with a thousand and fifty experiences of stable space with which our one thousand experiences of faces have not conflicted. Now we have a new experience where, possibly for the first time, the face and the stability of space are in conflict. If we now distort the face, we have not denied the influence of past experiences with faces in space. But note that in order to apply a past frequency interpretation to the present it is necessary to refer to the patterning of past experiences, in this case to faces-perceived-in-stable-space, as well as to perceived empty rooms.

How Set and Affective Loading Bias Perception. We have already seen how the subject's set may change the size of a visually perceived rectangular card, so that it is seen at different distances if perceived as a calling card or as an envelope. Such a set is not independent of experience with calling cards and envelopes, but something enters to regulate which of several past experiences shall be controlling in the present circumstances. There are many experienced frequencies waiting to be tapped, and, under appropriate sets, less frequent experiences may be as influential as more frequent ones. Because a person has had more experiences with envelopes than with calling cards does not mean that he is unable to use the calling-card interpretation of the ambiguous rectangle.

Affective loadings of stimuli modify perception, again distorting or contradicting what would be predicted from the simple frequencies of past experience. Some stimuli are threatening, anxiety-producing; others are reassuring, relieving of anxiety. Faced with the same external signs, subjects will perceive them differently because of the emotional experiences that these stimuli tap.

To show what is meant, let us consider an experiment now under way in the Stanford laboratory, an experiment in which the present writer has been assisted by Sylvan Kaplan and Lyle Jones (13). This is an experiment in discriminatory eyelid conditioning. There are two windows before the eyes of the subject, one on his left, one on his right. After a light appears on the right window there is a puff of air to his cornea. The right window is therefore "threatening." When the light appears on the left window, there is no air puff. The left window is therefore "safe." It was our conjecture that well-adjusted individuals, reacting to environmental probabilities, would learn to discriminate. That is, they would blink to the right window, thus avoiding the air puff, but would not blink to the left window, because it was neutral. Anxious individuals, on the other hand, who see much of the environment as threatening, might not discriminate. The left window is part of the general environment of which the right window is also a part. It costs very little in energy to play safe and blink at both windows, and no penalties are involved. Our experimental results are not yet completed, but it is possible to report some encouragement in relationship to our hypothesis. We are not satisfied with our measure of anxiety, which is based on responses to selected items on the Minnesota Multiphasic Test. These items were furnished us by Miss Taylor and Dr. Spence of the University of Iowa, who made use of them in a related experiment. We have found no correlation between frequency of simple conditioning and anxiety, a result we would have anticipated, in that the puff to the eye is threatening to those who react to the environment as well as those who react to a private world. (Miss Taylor did find some relationship, suggesting that the air puff was possibly *more* threatening to those who were anxious.) When it comes to discrimination, however, we have found a low correlation $(+.37)$ between anxiety and failure to discriminate, conforming to the hypothesis.

The point is, then, that the causal texture of the environment is perceived in one way by the well-adjusted realist and in another way by the person whose own apprehensions prevent his making simple actuarial computations. In the extension of the principles of perception to the problems of clinical psychology, distortions of perception by way of set and affectivity will undoubtedly require consideration. The paranoid person does not use his past experiences the way other persons do when he interprets what is going on in the present.

Summary Comments on the Functional Interpretation of Perception

In emphasizing the learned aspects of perception, this chapter has called attention both to the goals of perception and to the ways in which perceptual achievements come about.

The goals of perception may themselves be learned, as part of the larger background of learning how to satisfy our needs. In any case, we may count upon two goals that come to regulate the ways in which perceptual conflicts are resolved. These are: first, the goal to keep the world of space a stable one, with all the contributions of the senses in harmony; second, to achieve immediate clarity and definiteness in our apprehension of objects, even though the cues furnished are ambiguous. These goals ordinarily are not contradictory. That is, in the achieving of one we tend to achieve the other, while at the same time satisfying motives that go beyond perception. Occasionally there is conflict. Then the first of the two goals, that of stability of the spatial framework, tends to take priority over the stability of the things within this space.

In achieving these goals, we interpret what is given to the senses by what has gone before. We take into account not only the simple frequencies of prior experiences but also patterns of such experience, and we have also to recognize the distorting influences of sets and apprehensions.

The end result is, on the one hand, a world in which we feel at home because we know what to expect, and what we expect does not disagree too much with what we want. But, on the other hand, the world may be a capricious and terrifying place, where all that we do is uncertain and dangerous, where we do not learn what to expect, where what we find is never satisfying. The world out there does not treat all people equally, but the inequalities between men are determined not only by the ways in which the world treats them, but by the ways in which they perceive the world as treating them.

BIBLIOGRAPHY

1. BAYLEY, N. A study of the crying of infants during mental and physical tests. *J. genet. Psychol.*, 1932, **40**, 306-29.
2. BRUNSWIK, E. Probability as a determiner of rat behavior. *J. exp. Psychol.*, 1939, **25**, 175-97.
3. CANTRIL, H. *Understanding man's social behavior: preliminary notes.* Princeton, N. J.: Office of Public Opinion Research, 1947.
4. CARMICHAEL, L., HOGAN, H. P., & WALTER, A. A. An experimental study of the effect of language on the reproduction of visually perceived form. *J. exp. Psychol.*, 1932, **15**, 73-86.
5. FRENKEL-BRUNSWIK, ELSE. Intolerance of ambiguity as an emotional and perceptual personality variable. *J. Personal.*, 1949, **18**, 108-43.
6. GIBSON, J. J. The reproduction of visually perceived forms. *J. exp. Psychol.*, 1929, **12**, 1-39.
7. GIBSON, J. J. (ed.). *Motion picture and testing research.* Washington, D. C.: U. S. Government Printing Office, 1947.
8. GIBSON, J. J. *The perception of the visual world.* Boston: Houghton Mifflin Co., 1950.
9. HARLOW, H. F. The formation of learning sets. *Psychol. Rev.*, 1949, **56**, 51-65.
10. HEBB, D. O. On the nature of fear. *Psychol. Rev.*, 1946, **53**, 259-76.
11. HEBB, D. O. *The organization of behavior.* New York: John Wiley & Sons, Inc., 1949.
12. HEIDBREDER, EDNA. Toward a dynamic theory of cognition. *Psychol. Rev.*, 1945, **52**, 1-22.
13. HILGARD, E. R., JONES, L. V., & KAPLAN, S. J. Conditioned discrimination as related to anxiety. *J. exp. Psychol.* (To appear.)
14. HORNBOSTEL, E. M. VON. The unity of the senses. *Psyche,* Lond., 1927, **7**, 83-89.
15. HUMPHREYS, L. G. Acquisition and extinction of verbal expectations in a situation analogous to conditioning. *J. exp. Psychol.*, 1939, **25**, 294-301.
16. JENKINS, W. O., & RIGBY, MARILYN K. Partial (periodic) versus continuous reinforcement in resistance to extinction. *J. comp. physiol. Psychol.*, 1950, **43**, 30-40.
17. KELLEY, E. C. *Education for what is real.* New York: Harper & Bros., 1947.

18. LAWRENCE, M. *Studies in human behavior.* Princeton: Princeton University Press, 1949.
19. McDOUGALL, W. *An introduction to social psychology* (14th ed.). Boston: John W. Luce & Co., 1921.
20. SENDEN, M. VON. *Raum- und Gestaltauffassung bei operierten Blindgeborenen vor und nach der Operation.* Leipzig: J. A. Barth, 1932.
21. SHEFFIELD, VIRGINIA F. Extinction as a function of partial reinforcement and distribution of practice. *J. exp. Psychol.,* 1949, **39,** 511-26.
22. SPITZ, R. A. The smiling response: a contribution to the autogenesis of special relations. *Genet. Psychol. Monogr.,* 1946, **34,** 57-125.
23. STRATTON, G. M. Some preliminary experiments on vision without inversion of the retinal image. *Psychol. Rev.,* 1896, **3,** 611-17.
24. STRATTON, G. M. Vision without inversion of the retinal image. *Psychol. Rev.,* 1897, **4,** 341-60, 463-81.
25. TINBERGEN, N. Social releases and the experimental method required for their study. *Wilson Bull.,* 1948, **60,** 6-51.
26. TOLMAN, E. C., & BRUNSWIK, E. The organism and the causal texture of the environment. *Psychol. Rev.,* 1935, **42,** 43-77.
27. WOODWORTH, R. S. Reinforcement of perception. *Amer. J. Psychol.,* 1947, **60,** 119-24.
28. YOUNG, P. T. Auditory localization with acoustical transposition of the ears. *J. exp. Psychol.,* 1928, **11,** 399-429.

CHAPTER 5

PERSONALITY DYNAMICS AND THE PROCESS OF PERCEIVING [1]

By Jerome S. Bruner, Ph.D.

Our aim in these pages is to show the interdependence of the dynamics of personality and the dynamics of perceiving. A theory of personality, I shall contend, cannot be complete without a complementary theory of perception, and, by the same logic, one cannot account for the full range of perceptual phenomena without broadening perceptual theory to a point where it contains personality variables. Our intention is not to show that perception achieves objectives necessary to personality functioning, as Hilgard has done (Chapter 4) in outlining the adaptive functions performed by perceiving. This functionalist analysis has been admirably performed by Hilgard, Brunswik (13), and others. Let us, rather, examine the proposition that perceptual processes are critical intervening variables for personality theory and that personality processes are indispensable intervening variables for perceptual theory.

Else Frenkel-Brunswik (25), in a recent article, has drawn a distinction between "personality-centered" and "perception-centered" perceptual research. The perception-centered approach takes as its primary focus of interest the *variables of perception* and studies the way these are affected by various learnings, motivational states, personological structures, etc. A study of the effect of hunger on the recognition of food objects is "perception-centered," its main interest being in the *variability of recognition limens* as a function of need. In so far as "perceptionists" make forays into the theory of personality, the result is usually a projection of perception categories on to the nature of personality. Rorschach's work is typical, and we find investigators today who, in conversation if not in print,

---

[1] I am particularly grateful to my colleagues, Dr. Leo Postman and Dr. David McClelland, for the opportunity to clarify many points in the course of preparing this paper. Members of the Seminar on Perception at Harvard have also provided many valuable suggestions. The author is indebted to the Laboratory of Social Relations at Harvard for assistance in carrying out several experiments reported in these pages.

will refer to a patient as "typically a rare detail kind of personality" or "highly coarted" or "very CF."

The personality-centered approach, perhaps best represented by the work of Frenkel-Brunswik herself (25) as well as by the research of Klein and his associates (e.g., 36) at the Menninger Clinic, is characterized by a primary concern with variables of personality and their manifestation in the perceptual and other spheres. One begins, for example, with the concept of personality rigidity, inquiring whether and how it manifests itself in such areas of functioning as thinking, perceiving, remembering, and so on. A typical example is the following series of experiments carried out under the general direction of Sanford and Frenkel-Brunswik. A preliminary study (23) demonstrates first that personalities can be categorized in terms of certain basic patterns which can best be described in shorthand as the authoritarian, rigid personality and, at the opposite extreme, the flexible, tolerant personality. A variety of projective and life-history methods are used in classifying subjects. A second series of researches (24) then shows that rigid, authoritarian personalities are more prone to exhibit ethnocentric attitudes as measured by a questionnaire dealing with interracial attitudes. Rokeach (47) then carries the research one step further and shows that those high in ethnocentrism are more rigid or less flexible in performing problem-solving tasks involving basically neutral material. Another study (25) demonstrates less perceptual tolerance for ambiguity in the rigid personalities. Throughout the course of these research projects, the major emphasis is upon the representation of certain generalized personality processes in different specific spheres of mental functioning.

While the distinction has a certain heuristic value at the present stage of research, I think that in the long run it will disappear. For there cannot be one way of thinking about perception when one is interested in personality, and another way of thinking about it when one is interested in, say, size constancy. The two approaches must inevitably converge, the result being a set of personality variables useful in perceptual theory and a set of perceptual variables essential in personality theory. At that happy point of convergence, doubtless, personality theory and perceptual theory will themselves merge into a common theory of behavior.[2]

---

[2] One may briefly mention a third approach to the study of perception, one best called the "culture-centered" approach, whose aim is to study the manner in which various cultural forms operate in the modeling of both personality and its subsidiary functions, including cognition. Perhaps the best illustration of this work is to be found in a paper by Whorf (56), whose objective is to show how various linguistic structures place limits to and set the framework of the experience of members of a

Outline of a Theory of Perception

We seek a theory, then, adequate both to the laboratory and to the clinic. It is a theory which, in the words of Klein (35), makes room for the perceiver in perception. Above all, such a theory of perception should account systematically for individual differences in the perceptual process and not assign them to random error. Perhaps at its most general level, to be sure, certain perceptual laws can be stated without regard to the principles which account for individual difference. But in the main, the theory we seek must contain within it the possibility of handling the differences in perceiving which characterize different personality constellations. That much is essential if there is to be a rapprochement between the perceptual theorist and the personality theorist. Indeed, if, in the words of this symposium, perception is to be regarded as an approach to personality, we will have to come a long way from the period in which Fechner (21) enunciated the dogma that to get at the true state of perceptual affairs, one should seek to cancel out the systematic or constant errors in perception by counterbalancing them. In future research, we must, I think, seek to maximize the constant errors and, what is more, cease calling them by the old-fashioned statistical name of errors. Let the word "error" apply only to that portion of total variance which can be attributed to no source. This is *our* error, not the subject's. A personality-oriented perceptual theory precisely needs laws to account for the systematic judgmental and perceptual tendencies of different groups of people displaying different personality patterns—not just general laws of perception each embellished with a statement of variance.

My collaborator, Leo Postman and I have been drawn increasingly closer over the last few years toward an expectancy or hypothesis theory of perception as one which is adequate for dealing with both the laboratory experiment in perception and the observations of the clinician. Let me sketch briefly the general outlines of the theory on which we have been working and in terms of which we have been trying to interpret experimental results. After that we may turn to the implications of this discussion for personality-oriented perceptual research.

Basically, perceiving involves a three-step cycle. Analytically, we may say that perceiving begins with an expectancy or hypothesis. In the language of Woodworth (58), we not only see, but we look

given culture. Indeed, Dennis in his paper (Chapter 6) has treated some of the research in this field of "ethnophenomenology" and, better to illustrate some of the points which we must make, we will have recourse to other examples.

for, not only hear but listen to. In short, perceiving takes place in a "tuned organism." The assumption is that we are never randomly set or *eingestellt* but that, rather, we are always to some extent *prepared* for seeing, hearing, smelling, tasting some particular thing or class of things. What evokes an hypothesis? Any given hypothesis results from the arousal of central cognitive and motivational processes by preceding environmental states of affairs.

The second analytic step in the perceiving process is the input of information from the environment (which environment includes the stimulus complex brought to us by distance receptors and by the somatic senses). Here we purposely use the term "information" to characterize stimulus input, for we are not concerned with the energy characteristic of the stimulus as such but only with its cue or clue characteristics.

The third step in the cycle is a checking or confirmation procedure. Input information is confirmatory to or congruent with the operative hypothesis, or it is in varying degree infirming or incongruous. If confirmation does not occur, the hypothesis shifts in a direction partly determined by internal or personological or experiential factors and partly on the basis of feedback from the learning which occurred in the immediately preceding, partly unsuccessful information-checking cycle. For heuristic purposes we speak of initial and consequent hypotheses, the latter being those which follow upon an infirmed hypothesis.

The reader may object that our model of the information-confirming cycle seems too saccadic, too jumpy, that perception seems to work more smoothly than our model indicates. There are two legitimate answers to this objection. The first is that only under well-practiced conditions of perceiving is the process so smooth. Faced with a strange slide in a microscope, perceiving and recognizing are steplike processes. But this rejoinder is trivial in the light of the second one. There need be no phenomenal resemblance, we would insist, between the feeling tone of a psychic process and the conceptual model used to predict or describe it. Nobody would seriously object today, for example, that the atomic theory of matter is an inadequate theory because matter, this rock for instance, does not look or feel like an amalgam of whirling atoms.

A series of theoretical queries pose themselves about the information cycles which constitute the perceiving process. These fall into three broad categories:

1. Queries about the characteristics and dimensions of hypotheses or expectancies which characterize the first stage of perceiving and the conditions which elicit hypotheses of different kinds.

2. Queries about the nature of information that may confirm or infirm any given hypothesis.

3. Queries about the process whereby a hypothesis is confirmed or infirmed and altered.

Although the three sets of problems are analytically separable, they are difficult to keep separated in discussion. In what follows, I shall not attempt to isolate each step but only to highlight these analytic distinctions in the course of general discussion.

The Nature of Hypothesis.—The concept *hypothesis* is best likened to such terms as *determining tendency, set, Aufgabe, cognitive predisposition.* It may be regarded as a highly generalized state of readiness to respond selectively to classes of events in the environment. We may characterize it as generalized, for it is a form of tuning of the organism that may govern all cognitive activity carried out during its period of operation. The selectivity of remembering, problem solving, perceiving, imagining, in so far as they show a unity or consistency at a given time, are in this formulation assumed to be governed jointly by the intervening variable, the *hypothesis.* An operational definition of *hypothesis* can be stated by reference to the specific selectivity of a given perception at a given time. In theory an hypothesis is inferred, of course, from the presence of certain antecedent and consequent events, e.g., prior instruction and consequent reduction in threshold. If, as in the tachistoscopic experiments of Yokoyama (59) and Chapman (15), subjects are presented multi-attributive material (containing equally perceptible colors, numbers, sizes, etc.) we may infer the nature of the hypothesis by reference to prior instruction and to the attribute which is reported on most accurately, i.e., whether it was a set or hypothesis for color, number, or what not.

As postulated here, a hypothesis is in no sense limited with respect to the substantive nature of its selectivity. A hypothesis can be tuned selectively for the perception of colors of a certain hue; more often it is tuned to the perception of such environmental attributes as personal warmth or threateningness or the need-gratifyingness of objects of a certain kind. This is in no sense to imply that hypotheses about the environment are wishful in nature. They may and do tune the organism to aspects of the environment the perception of which is a guide to the most realistic behavior.

A specific hypothesis is not simply an isolated expectancy about the environment but rather relates to more integrated systems of belief or expectancy about environmental events in general. Put in terms of current systems of learning, for example, we may think of a hypothesis as dependent upon a "cognitive map" in Tolman's sense (53) or upon an established habit-family hierarchy (30).

Hypothesis Strength.—Thus far, we have been completely descriptive or taxonomic in our approach, describing the analytic steps involved in the process of perceiving. One further step is necessary before the implications of the "hypothesis-information-confirmation" cycle can be made apparent. A basic property of hypothesis is what we shall refer to as *strength*. There are three theorems that are contingent upon this concept of *strength:*

1. The stronger a hypothesis, the greater its likelihood of arousal in a given situation.
2. The greater the strength of a hypothesis, the less the amount of appropriate information necessary to confirm it.
3. The greater the strength of a hypothesis, the more the amount of inappropriate or contradictory information necessary to infirm it.

We see immediately that there is need for defining more precisely how we infer the strength of a hypothesis and how we know what amount of appropriate information has been necessary in confirming it.

I should like to propose that there are five determinants of hypothesis strength that may be used as measures of this variable in an experimental procedure. Let me describe them briefly, and then present some preliminary evidence as to their effect on the processes of hypothesis arousal, hypothesis confirmation and hypothesis rejection.

Frequency of Past Confirmation. The more frequently a hypothesis or expectancy has been confirmed in the past, the greater will be its strength. Such a frequently confirmed hypothesis will be more readily arousable, will require less environmental information to confirm it, and will, conversely, require more contradictory evidence to infirm it than would be required for a less frequently confirmed hypothesis.

Monopoly. The smaller the number of alternative hypotheses held by the person concerning his environment at a given moment, the greater their strength will be. If the person faces a perceptual situation with the hypothesis that "In this situation *A, B* and only *B* will occur," his hypothesis can be described as completely monopolistic. A monopolistic hypothesis is stronger than duopolistic hypotheses, etc. The closer to monopoly a hypothesis is, the less information will be required to confirm it and the more tenaciously will it be retained in the face of stimulus contradiction.

Cognitive Consequences. Any given hypothesis, e.g., that infants are generally smaller than grownups, can as we have noted be conceived of as imbedded in a larger system of supporting hypotheses and beliefs. The larger the number of supporting hypotheses or the more integrated the supporting system of hypotheses, the stronger the hypothesis with all that it implies for arousal, confirmation, and infirmation.

Motivational Consequences. Hypotheses have varying consequences in aiding the organism to the fulfilment of needs. The more basic the confirmation of a hypothesis is to the carrying out of goal-striving activity, the greater will be its strength. It will be more readily aroused, more easily confirmed, less readily infirmed. This must not be taken as a redefinition of autism, for many needs which operate and which are guided by perception to their fulfilment are not simple or infantile strivings for immediate gratification.

Social Consequences. Where stimulus conditions are such that information for either confirming or infirming a hypothesis is minimal, the hypothesis may be strengthened by virtue of its agreement with the hypotheses of other observers to whom the perceiver may turn.

If we may indulge our fantasies for a moment, let us assume that if a hypothesis, say "if *A* then *B*," had been frequently confirmed in the past, was the only one operative at the moment, was strongly supported by the beliefs of the perceiver, had immense consequences for the individual's adjustment, and was widely agreed on within his circle—if all these strengthening conditions prevailed, the hypothesis would be tediously evident in the behavior of the person, would be confirmed by the very least pip of confirming information, and would be obdurately resistant to rejection by contradictory evidence. If we were dealing with the kind of perception for which stimulus information was inherently poor—for example, the perception of characteristics in persons other than ourselves—we might have here a good description of the bigot, the anti-Semite, the xenophobe, or, for that matter, the starry-eyed idealist who can see no evil and/or can see only good in all men.

Although we have not yet attempted a definition of "appropriateness of information," let us turn away to some very simple supporting laboratory evidence for the series of propositions thus far presented.

Frequency of confirmation is a good one to start with, for it is a variable easily manipulated in experiment and one which yields such complex results as to stimulate a proper sense of humility in the student of perception. Miller (cited in 10) and Postman and Bruner (10) have shown that a shorter exposure is necessary for the recognition of nonsense words whose structure conforms to more probable letter linkages in the English language than for nonsense words whose letter linkages are less likely to occur in our language. In brief, the higher the "probableness" or likeness to English of our nonsense words, the less the amount of stimulus information (in terms of length of exposure) necessary for recognizing them correctly. We may assume, without too much violence to experience, that English letter linkages such as *th* and *qu* and *ty* have been more frequently confirmed than such bizarre linkages as *rw* or *tx*.

A good transition to the difficulties of the prediction of hypothesis strength from frequency alone is found in an elegantly designed experiment of Mary Henle's (29) in which she found that her subjects were better able to recognize words in printwise position when presented peripherally or tachistoscopically than when these words were presented in reverse face. However, when her subjects were told that both printwise and reverse words were being presented, the superiority of printwise letters disappeared. It would seem that a simple instruction altering the set of her subjects countervailed against a lifetime of frequency training.

Two other instances of the complex effects of frequency can be cited. In an experiment by Bruner and Postman (11), subjects were presented playing cards in a tachistoscope—some of them ordinary, some with suit and color reversed in such bizarre cards as a red six of clubs. The threshold for the full recognition of the incongruous cards was, of course, much higher than the threshold of recognition for the familiar normal cards (28 as compared with 114 milliseconds). But with respect to frequency of confirmation as a principle of expectancy learning, it is interesting that, when a subject had once perceived an incongruous card, the threshold for later incongruous cards was materially reduced. Stated in terms of hypothesis theory: *One* confirmation of the hypothesis that black suits can be red and vice versa had a very marked effect on the strength of this hypothesis. Certainly frequency does not operate by the addition of small increments of strength.

Ellson (18) has demonstrated a conditioned hallucinatory response in which, by initial pairing of a faint tone of gradual onset with a light, a subject can be brought to hear a physically nonexistent tone when the light alone is flashed on. Ellson points out that the data concerning acquisition of this conditioned hallucinatory response show no evidence "for the progressive acquisition of the response by any one subject" as a function of the repetition of training trials (18,

p. 9). In any event, frequency provides no *uniform* increments of strength to the response. Moreover, when one examines the data on the extinction of this hallucinatory response (19), again one finds that the number of extinction trials (where there is no adequate and clear-cut condition for checking on the adequacy of the expectancy that a tone will follow the light) seems to have no discernible effect on the course of extinction. If, however, the subject is told that there will be no further pairing of the two stimuli and if the subject accepts this account as true (as revealed by later questioning), then the hallucinatory responses of subjects are markedly diminished. Such instruction need be given only *once*.

Lest we be left with the feeling that frequency of confirmation is a variable too slippery to deal with, we should point out that there is a host of experiments which do underline the importance of past confirmation as a condition for strengthening expectancies and for reducing the amount of information necessary to confirm expectancies once established. Bartlett's early experiments (2), showing the readiness of his subjects to report the well-confirmed word "aeroplane" when "aeroplaxe" had been presented tachistoscopically, and many others (see 9) could be cited. We do not wish to belittle the importance of past experience *qua* past experience in determining our hypotheses but only to guard against oversimplification.

The confirming evidence on monopoly as a determinant of hypothesis strength is rather scanty, though quite unambiguous. Postman and Bruner (45) have shown, for example, that less exposure is required for recognition of words having to do with food when subjects are set with the simple instruction to find such words than when they are told to find food words *or* color words, in spite of the fact that, in the series of words, both kinds of words are equally often presented. This experiment has been repeated with other kinds of stimuli with substantially the same results.

Evidence for cognitive support at a simple level is provided in an as yet unpublished study at Harvard. Briefly, a reversed letter is imbedded in a word. The word may be either a nonsense word or a regular English word. If it is the latter, subjects have more difficulty discovering the reversed letter than if the reversed letter is in a nonsense word. The supporting context of a meaningful word is far greater in disguising the incorrect letter. An incorrect hypothesis that all letters are facing correctly is confirmed by minimal information and is consequently slow in being rejected. Indeed, this experiment, one must confess, goes little beyond what has been known to experts in camouflage for many, many years. If one sets up or arouses a context of hypotheses about the environment, it is difficult for the observer to see minor details which violate that context. I suspect, by the way, that the best method of training observers to break camouflage is to give them highly multiple hypotheses with which to face stimulus situations, thereby increasing the amount of information necessary for any expectancy to be confirmed.

Various lines of evidence—experimental, observational, and clinical—can be cited in support of the role of motivational support in strengthening hypotheses. Postman, Bruner, and McGinnies (46) and Vanderplas and Blake (55) have reported a positive relationship between an individual's hierarchy of personal values and the ease with which he recognizes words relating to his differently cherished values. And we may cite Thouless' finding (52) that artists come to depend more upon "retinal" cues of size and brightness, necessary to their occupational tasks. By the same token, microscopists become skilful in evaluating minimal cues in their preparations, and lovers, either for defense or enhancement, see only the good and the beautiful in their chosen ones.

There is also ample evidence to indicate that many complexities are involved in the relationship between hypothesis strength and motivational consequences. Thus, McClelland and Liberman (43) have shown that, where the recognition of negative achievement-related (failure) words are concerned, subjects with moderate need achievement are less quick in their recognition than those who are either high or low in this need. And experiments by McGinnies (44) and by McCleary and Lazarus (42) have indicated that response to stimulus information when one is operating with expectancies of high motivational consequence may not necessarily result in altered recognition but in lowered autonomic response thresholds as measured by galvanic skin responses.

It suffices to mention the results of Sherif's classic experiments (49) on the autokinetic effect as evidence for the effect of social validation on hypothesis strength. It is necessary to recall that in this experiment the possibility of confirming or infirming hypotheses with the kind of stimulus used was virtually nil. Under the circumstances, only social factors could operate.

The Nature of Confirming and Infirming Information.—We have tried in the preceding pages to utilize independent measures of hypothesis strength. Frequency of past confirmation could be controlled, in a typical experiment, and its effect measured by the amount of time necessary, say in tachistoscopic exposure, for the subject to perceive a stimulus. If threshold is reduced as a function of past confirmation or monopoly, we say that an alteration has occurred in our intervening variable, hypothesis strength. In our discussion, there has been one serious omission: the definition in any given experiment of what constitutes appropriate or relevant information. In a later section of this chapter we shall treat this problem in considerable detail; here we must pause to examine what is meant by information.

Let us distinguish first between relevant and nonrelevant information. Relevant information, or a relevant cue, refers to stimulus input which can be used by the subject for confirming or infirming an expectancy about the environment. The case is simplest in the area of space perception. Certain information like perspective lines, parallactic movements, etc., is clearly relevant as cues for confirming or infirming an hypothesis concerning the distance of a haystack in the valley. Other cues are obviously not relevant: the heat of the day, assorted sounds, etc. Among the cues that are relevant, one may distinguish a hierarchy of reliability. The texture of intervening terrain, particularly under circumstances where we do not recognize clearly the composition of the terrain, is a relevant but not very reliable item of stimulus information. The apparent size of a haystack in a section of the country where we do not know the characteristic sizes of haystacks is also a relevant informational cue but again, not a very reliable one. As dusk falls, the more reliable cues such as the perspective gained from parallel fences, while still relevant, also become less reliable. We have then a continuum from relevant and reliable information, through relevant and unreliable information, to nonrelevant information.

The words "relevant" and "reliable" are defined in the above example not with respect to the perceiver's experience, but with reference to the experimenter's knowledge about how people, in Brunswik's terms (13), correctly attain objects in their environment. By using what to the experimenter seem like highly unreliable cues, a subject can perceive with great subjective certainty the distance of an object. He may, to be sure, be all wrong. His hypotheses about distance may be psychotic to the point where he may even utilize conventionally nonrelevant, almost "magical" informational cues. He may see the haystack as his castle and displace it according to the grandiosity of his views about castle sizes.

We must distinguish, then, between the experimenter's *definition* of relevant and reliable information and the subject's *utilization* of information. It is of the essence in any given experiment that we define in advance what *we* as experimenters mean by relevant information and do not depend upon the subject's response to do it for us; otherwise we would be in a complete circle. In any experiment on perception, such a distinction is made implicitly or explicitly, whatever the nature of the stimulus materials dealt with. In short, we set a criterion of what is a correct perception, i.e., when the subject has used what we have defined as the relevant cues in coming to a final report about what is there before him on the screen, in the tachistoscope, in the room around him, or elsewhere.

What we study in most perceptual experiments is the extent to which the subject is able to *maximize* relevant cues (defined by the experimenter) for confirming and/or infirming hypotheses. This maximization depends upon the kind and strength of the hypotheses which he employs in his perception of a situation. Let us take a typical experiment. We have a series of pictures drawn, each depicting one of the six Spranger values: religious, economic, theoretical, social, political, and aesthetic. We choose a group of subjects showing certain scores in these value areas as defined by the Allport-Vernon test. We arbitrarily define in each picture what shall be the correct perception of the activity depicted. In each picture, there is some highly reliable relevant information, some nonrelevant information, and much rather unreliable relevant information. In the religious picture, for example, there is a man with head bowed in prayer or reverence. The outline of the man, however, is rather low grade, "ambiguous" information for, at rapid exposure, his figure can be seen as tired, dejected, stooped in work, and in many ways other than prayerful. Now if our subject has a strong religious orientation, and if he is prone to approach his perceptual environment armed with hypotheses concerning religious behavior, he will see the figure as in a religious posture and rapidly reconstruct the remainder of the stimulus in terms of his religious hypothesis. Elsewhere, we have referred to this sequence of events as "resonance" (45). Another subject, economically oriented, will perceive the stooped figure as at work. Before he will be able to perceive the picture for what it is (or what the experimenter says it is), his economic hypothesis will have to be rejected by contradictory information. Perhaps he will have to see the Gothic window behind the stooped figure.

When a hypothesis is strong, there will be a tendency for it to be confirmed by what is normally considered by the experimenter to be "unreliable" information. Likely as not, the confirmation may be "incorrect" from the experimenter's point of view. Whether it is or is not depends upon the relationship which happens to exist between the stimulus information present and the hypothesis employed by the subject.

It is primarily when we are dealing with "low grade" or unreliable stimulus-information that one gets a clear view of the differences in hypotheses which different individuals normally employ. Given high grade, reliable information, differences tend to be washed out. Yet this formulation is too facile. For it is also true that, when hypotheses are strong enough, stimulus information considered highly reliable by the experimenter is not utilized by subjects or is utilized in a manner to confirm "wrong" hypotheses. Subjects in our playing-card experiment reported incongruously colored red cards as black at exposure levels well above their normal thresholds for color discrimination. And at still higher exposure levels, after they had become uncertain of their perceptions, they were unable to tell whether the cards were black or red or any other color (11). In sum, reliable information may for some subjects confirm a "correct" hypothesis, for others an incorrect one, and for still others it may be subjectively ambiguous in the sense of neither confirming nor infirming any hypothesis.

All we can say finally, and it is not very much, is that in any given experiment the experimenter decides what is relevant information and then studies how subjects utilize this information in the course of perceiving.

As Luchins (40), Dennis (Chapter 6 below), and others have pointed out, much of the work in the field of perception and personality is done with "ambiguous" stimuli—dimly illuminated pictures or words, rapidly exposed materials, ambiguous drawings, and the like. The justification, generally, has been that by using less than optimal presentational methods the subject is thrown back on his own resources and that hypothesis arousal is more guided by motivational or experiential factors than by the characteristics of the stimulus immediately present. Another way of stating this is to say that these investigators have been interested in discovering the extent to which hypotheses varying in strength would be able to utilize substandard information, assuming that the greater the strength, the greater would be the utilization. One can name a long list of investigators who have been more or less explicitly guided by such reasoning: McClelland and Liberman (43), Sanford (48), Vanderplas and Blake (55), Sherif (49), Bruner and Postman (7), Luchins (39), and many others.

Let me cite the additional evidence of three related experiments recently completed by Bruner, Postman, and Rodrigues (12) in more specific support of this general proposition concerning the utilization of "low grade" information. The subject has the task of matching two-dimensional objects, all uniformly colored orange, to a variable color mixer. His task is to perform a simple color match. The objects differ in respect to their "normal" or everyday color : some are objects which are normally red (a cooked lobster claw and a tomato), some orange (a tangerine and a carrot), and some normally yellow (a banana and a lemon). In the first experiment, the orange color of the objects is highly unstable, being induced by color contrast (a gray object is placed on a blue-green ground, entirely covered by a ground glass). The variable color wheel and the object to be matched which lies before the subject are separated by ninety degrees of visual arc. In the second experiment the conditions are identical save that the objects to be matched are well-saturated orange paper; but as before objects are separated from the variable color wheel by ninety degrees of visual arc. In the third condition, the orange paper objects are placed immediately adjacent to the color wheel, and object and color wheel appear against a uniform gray background. The three conditions, then, represent steps in decreasing ambiguity. The first step involves highly unstable, ambiguous information. The second step contains more stable or less ambiguous information, but its appropriateness is kept ambiguous by heterogeneous background cues and by the necessity for successive comparison across ninety degrees of arc. In the third experiment, heterogeneous background is replaced by homogeneity, and simultaneous comparison is possible. Again to use communications engineering language, as we go from the first to the third experiment, the signal-to-noise ratio in our input information steadily increases.

The results can be simply stated. In the first condition, the match for the normally red objects is significantly redder and for the normally yellow objects significantly yellower than is the match for the normally orange objects. The same results hold, though to a considerably lesser degree, for the second condition. In the third condition, when high grade information is made available, the influence of past experience is wiped out altogether and no significant judgment tendency for the three kinds of objects is noticeable. In sum, the less "ambiguous" the information, the less the effect of past experience in confirming hypotheses and the greater the use of input information.[3]

Two other experiments underline the dependence of learning and motivational effects on the use of "substandard" stimulus information. Both Ellson (20) and Kelley (31) have shown that conditioned sensory hallucinations can only be obtained when the onset of the stimulus to be conditioned is gradual to the point of "ambiguity."

Does what we have been saying imply that only under conditions of "poor perception" do the effects of learning and personality show

---

[3] Incidentally, in all conditions, subjects insisted that all objects were of the same color and that their color matches were the same for all objects.

themselves? Perhaps so. It might be better to say that there are limits imposed by stimulus factors which reduce the effects of past experience and present needs almost to zero when one works with rather simple stimuli. I insist, however, that most complex perception, particularly in our social lives, is dependent upon the integration of information of a far less reliable kind than we normally provide in a tachistoscope at rapid exposure.

Implications for Personality Theory

Our first insistence was that a personality-oriented theory of perception must have systematic means whereby it can account for individual differences in perceiving. Let me mention two points in the theory outlined above at which articulation can be and is being made with personality theory and theories of social behavior.

1. Differences in the kinds of hypotheses that different individuals habitually employ, reflecting differences in past history, personality structure, etc.
2. Differences in strength of hypotheses characterizing different individuals, again reflecting divergent life histories and major personality trends.

Bearing these points in mind, we turn to material drawn from the work of social psychologists and personality theorists on the functioning of personality.

Consider first the matter of cultural differences. In the Cambridge Anthropological Expedition to the Torres Straits at the turn of the century, McDougall and Rivers (28) drew a distinction between *acuity* on the one hand and *observational powers* on the other. While there appeared to be no difference between the standardly obtained acuity test scores of Murray Islanders and white Europeans (leaving aside cases where the effects of endemic or epidemic disease were to be noted), the investigators observed a rather striking superiority of the native men over themselves in such matters as being able to spot distant horizon objects looked at from the sea against the background of the island. In like manner, the native men were superior in being able to unmask the camouflage of coral fish against the background of their matching habitat. The natives had learned to use "good" hypotheses which served to utilize maximally what appropriate information was available. Their hypotheses were strong enough to maximize relevant confirming information, but not so strong as to be confirmed by what to the uninitiated might have been confirming information.

More bizarre examples can be cited in which "powers of observation" seem to belie the evidence of acuity data. Bogoras (3), who has provided a monumental monographic study of the Chukchee, reports that it was only with the greatest of difficulty that he could force and/or teach these people to carry out anything resembling an adequate sorting of the Holmgren yarns. The Chukchee, of course, have an exceedingly impoverished color nomenclature. Yet these reindeer-herding people can and do apply more than two dozen names to the task of distinguishing the patterns of reindeer hides. Bogoras reports his own considerable difficulty in learning to make such fine distinctions in patterns, many of which at the outset looked identical to him.

One last example suffices. It has often been commented upon that perhaps for reasons deep in the nature of man's inhibitions about the excretory functions or perhaps because of their inadequacy as locomotion guides, we utilize smell cues to a very minimum in our Western society. Save in matters of high cuisine and high fashion, we are not "attentive," have few hypotheses about odors. Hence we notice them rarely, have a barren smell terminology, and are generally undiscriminating in this modality. Here again, the Chukchee provide a striking contrast. For reasons which are far from clear, but which might well be rewarding to study, they lead an intensely discriminating smell life, even to the point of greeting each other by sniffing down the back of the neck. They frequently describe the odor of things where we would use visual, gustatory, or tactual descriptions. Indeed, so strong are these odor hypotheses that certain hysterical phenomena come to be mediated by them. Bogoras reports that strangeness, for example, is translated into bad smell. On one occasion, he brought a strange box into his host's house. The mistress of the house upon spying the box almost went into a faint at its strong and malevolent odor. Bogoras himself could get no smell from the box. So strong, apparently, is this hypothesis that strange things smell badly that this Chukchee woman's hypothesis could be confirmed by the highly ambiguous and inappropriate smell atmosphere of her own house.

Part of the shock of these examples, to be sure, derives from their distance. The exquisite sensitivity of the musician, the tea taster, or the microscopist; the prodigies of observation of the veteran naval lookout, the experienced hunter, the novelists of character—all these are close at hand to challenge us. The fact that some parents see the obstreperous behavior of their children as fatigued, some as naughty, some as expressing sibling rivalry—and that these may differ by social

class—is perhaps of the same order. They indicate the utilization of
different hypotheses of different strength, depending for their confirmation on different kinds of environmental information, reflecting
different adjustmental needs in the perceiver.

Moving one step closer to the functioning of the individual personality, a good continuity is provided by historical reference. Logan
Pearsall Smith (50) writes that self-prefixes (self-esteem, self-
regard, etc.) do not appear in English usage until the seventeenth
century, their introduction coinciding with the rise of individualistic
Puritanism. The word *selfish,* for example, was introduced in 1640,
and at that date by the Scottish Presbyterians. It is interesting to
speculate about the gradual change in the perception of self which
resulted from the revolution in hypotheses during the Reformation.
We shall return to this question in the final section. One wonders
too about the changes that have occurred in our perception of abnormal or aberrant behavior as our hypotheses about mental disease
have shifted from a theory of possession to one of degeneration and
then to a theory of psychic dynamics. Zilboorg's account (60) of the
medical rebellion of Cornelius Agrippa against the possession theory
of the Middle Ages is as much an essay on social perception as on
the history of medicine. Where perceptual evidence or, in our terms,
environmental information is so ambiguous in its appropriateness for
confirming or infirming hypotheses about cause and effect in behavior, it is not surprising that the battle of diagnosis of behavior is
almost as sharply joined today as in Agrippa's day.

It is perhaps in the perception of attributes of the social environment that people vary most strikingly. For in this sphere hypotheses
are strong, information is low grade, and adjustmental consequences
are serious. We shall, in the final section, refer to a study of the
perception of causation in group behavior by extrapunitive and
intrapunitive leaders in which intrapunitive leaders more often perceived themselves as sources of causation. Intrapunitiveness may,
indeed, be considered a description of the kinds of hypotheses with
which an individual approaches frustrating situations. He is set to
evaluate normally ambiguous information as confirming his own
guilt. The more marked the degree of intrapunitiveness, the less
the appropriate information necessary to confirm self-guilt. As the
hypothesis attains greater and greater strength, intrapunitiveness
attains neurotic proportions, which is to say that self-guilt hypotheses
are confirmed by information judged by society to be grossly inappropriate or ambiguous.

Programmatic Implications for Future Research

Thus far we have been speaking rather generally about the manner in which the theory described earlier throws light on various personality processes and cultural differences. What of specific research on personality-perception interdependence, research which has as its object the introduction of personality variables into perceptual theory and perceptual variables into personality theory?

We have already made reference to studies involving the perception of more or less "ambiguous stimuli" by subjects in varying states of need, with different past experience, and so forth. These studies have been reviewed elsewhere (9, 10) and need not be dealt with in detail here. They have been in the direction of investigating the utilization of different kinds of stimulus information by subjects operating under rather haphazardly selected motivations. By and large, they have been demonstrational in nature in the sense that they represented isolated instances of the operation of needs or other states on perceptual selectivity. Few of these studies have utilized motivational states and stimulus materials, a relation between which is predicted by a coherent theory of personality. More specifically, few studies have started out with a hypothesis which stated explicitly that, according to such and such a theory of personality, we would expect people of such and such a type to handle stimuli of such and such a kind in such and such a manner. Hypotheses of this kind can be stated, but first let us examine a second type of "perception-and-personality" research.

In this kind of investigation—and here one may name studies by Thouless (52), Duncker (17), Cramer (16), Klein (33, 36), Witkin (57), Bruner and Postman (6), Tresselt (54), Ansbacher (1), and others—the focus is upon judgments of such classical attributes as size, movement, brightness, hue, etc. Characteristically, one investigates the extent to which subjects show certain systematic "errors" in judgment, the nature of which "errors" are then related to past experience, present motivation, and other more or less personal factors. One thing must certainly be said for studies of this kind. They provided an *a fortiori* demonstration of the fruitfulness of considering the contribution of behavioral or personality factors in perception. To take but a sample of findings for comment, it is an impressive challenge to classical perceptual theory to show (*a*) that the color constancy of artists shows a systematic and occupationally useful verging-away from "phenomenal regression to the real object" (52); (*b*) that dependence on the body for orientation in the gravitational field as compared with dependence on the visual framework increases with age and, in a more complex manner, with degree of adjustment (57) ; and (c) that the appearance of a color depends on one's expectancy concerning the "normal" color of an object (12, 16, 17). Has not the time passed, however, when we must continue to restrict ourselves to such experiments?

Investigations of motivational or behavioral factors as determinants of apparent size, brightness, hue, shape, and so forth have perhaps obscured a basic theoretical point. Consider, for example, the question of apparent size. Studies by Bruner and Goodman (5), Bruner and Postman (8), and Lambert, Soloman, and Watson (37) have served to support a general principle of accentuation in size judgment : apparent size is accentuated in judgments of valuable or need-relevant objects. I suspect that there is something adventitious about these results, that they are to some extent misleading because they have never been stated in a proper theoretical context. Several things lead to this conclusion. In the first place, Bruner and Postman (6) have shown that accentuation is absent when the object in question is to be manipulated—that is, when the stimulus information from the object is used in the confirmation of highly accurate manipulative hypotheses. I suspect, moreover, that if a subject is given a highly critical, accuracy-oriented set for judging, size accentuation is markedly diminished. Experiments now in progress at Harvard are designed to test this point but are not yet completed. There is reason to suspect that they will confirm our expectations. For example, Klein, Meister, and Schlesinger (34) have reported results which indicate that if the subject is given a critical judging set, a form of accentuation earlier noted by Bruner and Postman (8) fails to occur. And finally, it appears that the use of optimal viewing conditions can wipe out accentuation of simple attributes in the normal laboratory situation. Again, our own experiments on this point are in their initial stages, but certainly the results of the color-judgment experiments cited earlier in some detail show the basic importance of poor viewing conditions as a necessary condition for the operation of behavioral factors in the laboratory setting. Carter and Schooler (14), for example, achieved a considerable reduction in perceptual accentuation of valuable objects when ambiguity was reduced to a minimum, though accentuation appeared in their more ambiguous memory situation.

What is theoretically wrong about most of these studies, both those which have and those which have not found perceptual accentuation, is that there is rarely stated a specific hypothesis about why the attribute being studied should be influenced by behavioral factors. Is it that the attribute studied provides highly appropriate information for the confirmation of an unsuspected hypothesis operative in the judging situation? Take judgments of size, for example. A subject is set to judge the sizes of coins. He comes to the situation with hypotheses about the size of the object (very likely based, as we have indicated in an earlier paper [10], on principle of adaptation level) but also with hypotheses about the value of the coin. In this experiment, size information confirms both size and value hypotheses. For size increases as value increases in the objects being judged, and this linkage is widespread in our culture. There is, therefore, likely to be a maximization of size cues, such cues serving to confirm both the value and the size hypothesis. We would propose that it is this joint maximization of size cues which brings about accentuation in apparent size.

But what is crucial in this line of reasoning is that the conventional size attribute being studied here bears some confirmatory relationship to the value or need-gratification hypothesis that is operating in the situation. In short, if we are to work on the "distortion" of conventional attributes by behavioral factors or personality factors, we must be explicit in recognizing that such distortions occur because the size or shape or color of the object being studied *provides appropriate information for the confirmation of a motivational or personality-related hypothesis.* If this is not the case, I would predict that there will be no "distortion."

This brings us to the problem of adequate personality-oriented research on perception. It seems to me that the most basic point to be made is this: If we wish to work on personality factors in perceiving, then we must concentrate upon the investigation of those environmental cues which are appropriate to the confirmation of *hypotheses which reflect basic personality patterns.* By and large, these environmental cues are *not* size cues or color cues or brightness cues. They are cues which aid more directly in our interpersonal adjustment: the apparent warmth or coldness of people, the apparent threateningness of situations, the apparent intelligence or apparent sincerity of others. Let me cite a few experiments which have been concerned with such attributes. Kelley (32) has shown that the behavior of a teacher in a group situation is perceived quite differently with respect to its warmth or coldness as a function of prior information given the class about the instructor. If the prior description of the teacher contains elements which maximize the threatening character of the teacher-figure, the perceiver is predisposed or sensitized toward experiencing cues appropriate to "spotting" such behavior when it appears. Maas (41), to take another example, has shown the manner in which the perception of causation (whether the group or the leader appears to be "to blame" for an event) varies depending in combination upon (*a*) whether the leader is intrapunitive or extra-punitive on the one hand and (*b*) whether the group is informal and "open" or formalized and "closed." Environmental cues indicating social causation, however ambiguous, are the crucial perceptual attributes here. Lindsey and Rogolsky (38) have suggested, to cite another instance, that the sensitivity of the anti-Semite which results in his readier recognition of Jewish faces stems from the fact that he is more dependent upon such cues for his general adjustment—that, in short, such cues have high appropriateness to him, in confirming hypotheses which guide behavior.

Such environmental cues as "Jewishness" or "personal warmth" are, to be sure, highly composite with respect to the myriad of size, movement, color, and other cues that support them. But phenomeno-logically speaking, they are unitary and not readily reducible. They can no more be dismissed for their compositeness than one can dismiss the dimension of roughness as a tonal attribute—in spite of the fact that it depends upon an intricate temporal interaction of loudness, pitch, and other factors.

I realize at the outset that working with such complex adjust-ment-appropriate attributes of experience as we have been dis-cussing bars one from the comfort of using physical measures as reference points in his experiments. In studying size, for example, we may speak of "distortion" in terms of deviation of judgments from "actual" or physically measurable size. There is no such "base meas-urement" of apparent personal warmth. What we must do, then, is to utilize instead judgments by different groups or different individuals under different psychological conditions. Our basic metric will in-volve the comparison of group scores. And where possible we can use ratings of the stimulus by independent judges against which to com-pare the perceptions of our subjects. The task is difficult, but far from impossible.

The Selection of Personally Relevant Cues.—There are, I believe, two guides to the selection of personally relevant stimulus cues for investigation. One is theoretical. Various theories of per-sonality contain implicit or explicit statements concerning the cues in the environment which guide the individual in maintaining or advancing his personal adjustment. Thus, the psychoanalytic theory of ego defenses contains some implicit suggestions for perceptual investigation and serves well as an example. Consider the classical description of the obsessional-compulsive character structure described in such detail by Fenichel (22). It seems reasonable to pose the hypothesis that the supposedly anal-sadistic, compulsive character because of his defensive needs would be highly dependent upon or set to perceive cues to orderliness in his immediate environment. For him the attribute of orderliness (and its many translations into, say, symmetry, cleanliness, etc.) would provide highly appropriate and personally relevant information. We say of him that he "notices" pictures in a room that hang slightly askew; he has a low threshold for seeing poorly cleaned silverware; and, perhaps at a more basic dynamic level, he is either defensively blind toward, or hypervigilant to, minimally aggressive or sadistic events in his immediate environment (7). Indeed, one might suppose, and the matter can be tested, that his defense of isolation and undoing and his ritual behavior depend upon certain perceptual predispositions for their effectiveness. There are no adequate experimental studies dealing with such a problem—in spite of the fact that Freud early referred to one aspect of the ego as "perceptual consciousness" (27) and despite the title of the first chapter in Anna Freud's *The Ego and the Mechanisms of Defence* (26).[4]

Another example drawn from psychoanalytic theory relates to the theory of schizophrenia as a regression to primary narcism, a withdrawal from object relationships (22). What might follow perceptually from such a theory? Might not we predict, for example, that a withdrawal from object relations and an increasing concern for the self would lead to a breakdown in such phenomena as size and shape constancy? Might not apparent size and shape conform more toward retinal proportions than toward "real object" proportions and particularly so if the stimulus objects used were other people?

One could go on and propose perceptual hypotheses stemming from psychoanalytic concepts or from concepts embodied in other theories of personality. That is not our task here. We have simply presented these examples to suggest one approach to research on appropriate, personally relevant stimulus information.

Another approach to the selection of adjustmentally relevant cues for study is frankly phenomenological. We begin by inquiring how the world appears to us. The answer to such a naïve question would be that the world consists of many things, perhaps divisible into our perception of self, of objects and people sensed as related to us in some way, and of objects basically neutral with respect to ourselves. Along the borders of these regions of the perceptual field there might be certain ambiguities. Where the perceived self terminates and the world of objects begins is, under extraordinary conditions, a

---

4 "The Ego as the Seat of Observation."

matter of confusion; and there is also a shading off between those objects which have a self-relating characteristic and those which do not. But we need not concern ourselves here with, say, whether a phantom limb or well-practiced prosthetic aid is part of the self. We will accept simply the naïve distinction between perceived self, objects which have some personal meaning for us, and objects which have little or no personal meaning.[5]

As a highly tentative general theorem—one proposed more in the spirit of starting a discussion than of concluding it—we would propose that variations in the attributes of the perceived self provide the most highly relevant stimulus information for confirming adjustmentally relevant hypotheses, i.e., hypotheses the confirmation of which are crucial to adjustment.

What do we mean by the "attributes of the perceived self"? We mean simply a dimension of variation in terms of which experience can be described and along which judgments can be arrayed. These need not, as Boring (4) and Stevens (51) have pointed out, be independently variable or orthogonal. But will there not be an infinity of attributes characterizing the perceived self? If a pure tone can be systematically described by at least four attributes—pitch, loudness, volume, and density—will not the complex set of stimuli which evoke the experience of self be described by a bewildering array of attributes? If indeed Boring (4) is correct in remarking "that there is theoretically no limit to the number of attributes, except the nature of the nervous system" which can characterize a perception, then again we may expect that the self-experience will be multiattributive in the extreme. For in considerable measure the process of development involves learning to discriminate many different attributes of the self. Let us forget the complexity of the task for the moment. Can we suggest some possible attributes of self which provide particularly crucial information for guiding us in our adjustment?

One obvious dimension is *self-salience,* what in everyday language is probably called self-consciousness. How well aware is the person of himself, and how differentiated does he feel from his environment? Subjects should be able to rate themselves on this attribute. Again I ask a very naïve question: What kinds of situations increase or decrease self-salience in individuals with different kinds of past developmental histories? A better way of asking the question, one closer to our theoretical scheme, is: What kinds of hypotheses

---

[5] The reader will note that we are speaking here of the experience of self and *not* of the psychologist's Ego or the philosopher's Self. Self is here treated as an *object* of experience rather than as an *agent* or a knower.

depend for their confirmation on self-saliency cues, and what kinds of individuals characteristically use such hypotheses?

The sense of *self-potency* is another such attributive dimension of perceived self to be pondered. By it we mean self-confidence, the sense of being able to act effectively in a situation, to overcome obstacles, to "make out all right." We may ask the same kind of questions about it as we did about self-salience.

Take these two attributes or forms of stimulus information or cues as illustrations and let us examine them. In neither case is it clear what kinds of stimuli "evoke" the perceptions. Certainly there is still enough lingering of the James-Lange theory for us to assume that part of the stimulus is somatic in nature and that autonomic activity has no small part in mediating these somatic stimulus components. We know, too, I suspect, that "self-cues" are probably ambiguous in nature, that they rarely are very appropriate for confirming specific hypotheses, that, in short, self-information is a good deal vaguer than the highly salient information we get from the external environment. Beyond this we know little indeed about the stimulus—even less than is known about the stimulus in smell and in the vestibular senses. Here, moreover, we are working with a stimulus where it is impossible to get any independent measure, for even independent judges cannot get inside the skin. This is particularly troublesome, for it seems reasonable to suppose that the base line state of self-potency in a "resting situation" differs markedly in different individuals. We are literally limited in measuring self-attributes to the use of carefully constructed self-rating scales. But even with these there is much that can be accomplished, not only in studying differences in these attributes in groups of different past histories, but also in studying intra-individual differences as a person moves from one kind of diagnostic situation to another. Again in theoretical terms, we will find the kinds of personalities which depend upon and maximize self-cues for the confirmation of characteristic hypotheses. Such cues, we can surmise already, will be utilized and maximized more by the introvert, the intrapunitive, the person with inadequately developed object relations, the adolescent, the insecure generally, etc.

However banal such predictions may seem, we must not overlook the fact that it is far from banal to ask what kinds of situations and what kinds of therapy reduce overdependence upon self-salience cues and increase the extent to which an individual maximizes self-potency cues. You will read of this kind of problem in Rogers' Chapter below, so we need not go into the matter here save to say that the continued neglect of research on self-perception is, at least to me, a source of great puzzlement.

A second phenomenological proposition—really a tautology—is that those cues in the environment which confirm or infirm hypotheses derived from basic and enduring needs and values are also crucial in guiding adjustment. What kinds of hypotheses serve such basic needs, and what kinds of environmental information are needed to confirm or infirm them? My colleague David McClelland has remarked, half in jest, that it would not be amiss to carry out a phenomenological census to discover what things and attributes in the environment people look for and attend to in guiding their behavior. When we have found out something about the phenomenology of everyday life, perhaps we shall be in a better position to choose the stimulus materials to use in future research on the way in which personality factors affect perception.

One last point in conclusion. In looking back over this chapter, I find it hard to decide whether I have been discussing the role of personality factors in the process of perceiving or the role of perceptual factors in personality functioning. But I think this is trivial. This symposium might as easily have been called "Personality: An Approach to Perception."

BIBLIOGRAPHY

1. ANSBACHER, H. *Perception of number as affected by the monetary value of the objects.* Arch. Psychol., No. 215. New York, 1937.
2. BARTLETT, F. C. An experimental study of some problems of perceiving and imaging. *Brit. J. Psychol.,* 1916, **8,** 222-66.
3. BOGORAS, W. *The Chukchee.* New York: G. E. Stechert & Co., 1909.
4. BORING, E. G. *Sensation and perception in the history of experimental psychology.* New York: Appleton-Century-Crofts, Inc., 1942.
5. BRUNER, J. S., & GOODMAN, C. C. Value and need as organizing factors in perception. *J. abnorm. soc. Psychol.,* 1947, **42,** 33-44.
6. BRUNER, J. S., & POSTMAN, L. Tension and tension-release as organizing factors in perception. *J. Personal.,* 1947, **15,** 300-308.
7. BRUNER, J. S., & POSTMAN, L. Emotional selectivity in perception and reaction. *J. Personal.,* 1947, **16,** 69-77.
8. BRUNER, J. S., & POSTMAN, L. Symbolic value as an organizing factor in perception. *J. soc. Psychol.,* 1948, **27,** 203-8.
9. BRUNER, J. S., & POSTMAN, L. An approach to social perception. In W. Dennis (ed.), *Current trends in social psychology.* Pittsburgh: University of Pittsburgh Press, 1948.
10. BRUNER, J. S., & POSTMAN, L. Perception, cognition, and behavior. *J. Personal.,* 1949, **18,** 14-31.
11. BRUNER, J. S., & POSTMAN, L. On the perception of incongruity: a paradigm. *J. Personal.,* 1949, **18,** 206-23.
12. BRUNER, J. S., POSTMAN, L., & RODRIGUES, J. S. Stimulus appropriateness and ambiguity as factors in judgment. Presented at the annual meeting of the Eastern Psychological Association, 1950.
13. BRUNSWIK, E. *Systematic and representative design of psychological experiments.* Berkeley: University of California Press, 1947.
14. CARTER, L., & SCHOOLER, E. Value, need, and other factors in perception. *Psychol. Rev.,* 1949, **56,** 200-208.

15. CHAPMAN, D. W. Relative effects of determinate and indeterminate Aufgaben. *Amer. J. Psychol.*, 1932, **44**, 163-74.

16. CRAMER, T. Ueber die Beziehung des Zwischenmediums zu den Transformations- und Kontrasterscheinungen. *Z. Sinnesphysiol.*, 1923, **54**, 214-42.

17. DUNCKER, K. The influence of past experience upon perceptual properties. *Amer. J. Psychol.*, 1939, **52**, 255-65.

18. ELLSON, D. G. Hallucinations produced by sensory conditioning. *J. exp. Psychol.*, 1941, **28**, 1-20.

19. ELLSON, D. G. Experimental extinction of an hallucination produced by sensory conditioning. *J. exp. Psychol.*, 1941, **28**, 350-61.

20. ELLSON, D. G. Critical conditions influencing sensory conditioning. *J. exp. Psychol.*, 1942, **31**, 333-38.

21. FECHNER, G. T. *Elemente der Psychophysik.* 2 vols. Leipzig, 1869.

22. FENICHEL, O. *The psychoanalytic theory of neurosis.* New York: W. W. Norton & Co., Inc., 1945.

23. FRENKEL-BRUNSWIK, ELSE. Dynamic and cognitive categorization of qualitative material. I. General problems and the thematic apperception test. *J. Psychol.*, 1948, **25**, 253-60.

24. FRENKEL-BRUNSWIK, ELSE. Dynamic and cognitive categorization of qualitative material. II. Interviews of the ethnically prejudiced. *J. Psychol.*, 1948, **25**, 261-77.

25. FRENKEL-BRUNSWIK, ELSE. Intolerance of ambiguity as an emotional and perceptual personality variable. *J. Personal.*, 1949, **18**, 108-43.

26. FREUD, ANNA. *The ego and the mechanisms of defence.* New York: International Universities Press, Inc., 1946.

27. FREUD, S. *A general introduction to psychoanalysis.* New York: Boni & Liveright, 1920.

28. HADDON, A. C. (ed.). *Reports of the Cambridge Anthropological Expedition to Torres Straits. Physiology and psychology.* Cambridge: Cambridge University Press, 1901. Vol. II.

29. HENLE, MARY. An experimental investigation of past experience as a determinant of visual form perception. *J. exp. Psychol.*, 1942, **30**, 1-21.

30. HULL, C. L. *Principals of behavior.* New York: Appleton-Century-Crofts, Inc., 1943.

31. KELLEY, E. L. An experimental attempt to produce artificial chromesthesia by the technique of the conditioned response. *J. exp. Psychol.*, 1934, **17**, 315-41.

32. KELLEY, H. H. The effects of expectations upon first impressions of persons. *Amer. Psychologist,* 1949, **4**, 252.

33. KLEIN, G. S., & HOLZMAN, P. S. The "schematizing process": perceptual attitudes and personality qualities in sensitivity to change. *Amer. Psychologist,* 1950, **5**.

34. KLEIN, G. S., MEISTER, D., & SCHLESINGER, H. J. The effect of personal values on perception: an experimental critique. *Amer. Psychologist,* 1949, **4**, 252-53.

35. KLEIN, G. S., & SCHLESINGER, H. J. Where is the perceiver in perceptual theory? *J. Personal.*, 1949, **18**, 32-47.

36. KLEIN, G. S., & SCHLESINGER, H. J. Studies of the schematizing process: shifting behavior in "paranoid" and "non-paranoid" individuals. (In preparation.)

37. LAMBERT, W. W., SOLOMAN, R. L., & WATSON, P. D. Reinforcement and extinction as factors in size estimation. *J. exp. Psychol.*, 1949, **39**, 637-41.

38. LINDSEY, G., & ROGOLSKY, S. Prejudice and identification of minority group membership. *J. abnorm. soc. Psychol.*, 1950, **45**, 37-53.

39. LUCHINS, A. S. Social influences on perception of complex drawings. *J. soc. Psychol.*, 1945, **21**, 257-73.

40. LUCHINS, A. S. A critique of current research on perception. *J. Personal.* (To be published.)

41. Maas, H. S. Personal and group factors in leaders' social perception. *J. abnorm. soc. Psychol.,* 1950, **45,** 54-63.
42. McCleary, R. A., & Lazarus, R. S. Autonomic discrimination without awareness. *J. Personal.,* 1949, **18,** 171-79.
43. McClelland, D. C., & Liberman, A. M. The effect of need for achievement on recognition of need-related words. *J. Personal.,* 1949, **18,** 236-51.
44. McGinnies, E. Emotionality and perceptual defense. *Psychol. Rev.,* 1949, **56,** 244-51.
45. Postman, L., & Bruner, J. S. Multiplicity of set as a determinant of perceptual organization. *J. exp. Psychol.,* 1949, **39,** 369-77.
46. Postman, L., Bruner, J. S., & McGinnies, E. Personal values as selective factors in perception. *J. abnorm. soc. Psychol.,* 1948, **43,** 142-54.
47. Rokeach, M. Generalized mental rigidity as a factor in ethnocentrism. *J. abnorm. soc. Psychol.,* 1943, **48,** 259-78.
48. Sanford, R. N. The effect of abstinence from food upon imaginal processes: a further experiment. *J. Psychol.,* 1947, **3,** 145-59.
49. Sherif, M. A study in some social factors in perception. *Arch. Psychol.,* No. 187. New York, 1935.
50. Smith, L. P. *The English language.* New York: Henry Holt & Co., Inc., 1912.
51. Stevens, S. S. The attributes of tone. *Proc. nat. Acad. Sci.,* Washington, D.C., 1934, **20,** 457-59.
52. Thouless, R. H. Individual differences in phenomenal regression. *Brit. J. Psychol.,* 1932, **22,** 216-41.
53. Tolman, E. C. Cognitive maps in rats and men. *Psychol. Rev.,* 1948, **55,** 189-208.
54. Tresselt, M. E. The shift of a scale of judgment and a personality correlate. *Amer. Psychologist,* 1949, **4,** 251-52.
55. Vanderplas, J. M., & Blake, R. R. Selective sensitization in auditory perception. *J. Personal.,* 1949, **18,** 252-66.
56. Whorf, B. L. Science and linguistics. In E. L. Hartley & T. M. Newcomb (eds.), *Readings in social psychology.* New York: Henry Holt & Co., Inc., 1947.
57. Witkin, H. A. The nature and importance of individual differences in perception. *J. Personal.,* 1949, **18,** 145-70.
58. Woodworth, R. S. Reinforcement of perception. *Amer. J. Psychol.,* 1947, **60,** 119-24.
59. Yokoyama, M., as reported by Boring, E. G. Attribute and sensation. *Amer. J. Psychol.,* 1924, **35,** 301-4.
60. Zilboorg, G. *The medical men and the witch during the Renaissance.* Noguchi Lecture in the History of Medicine. Baltimore: Johns Hopkins Press, 1935.

CHAPTER 6

CULTURAL AND DEVELOPMENTAL FACTORS IN PERCEPTION

By WAYNE DENNIS, Ph.D.

In the research literature on perception, one finds that the majority of investigators in this field have been interested in perception as it occurs in dark rooms and at exposure times of fractions of a second. The stimuli perceived usually are geometrical figures, numbers, letters, or words. The subjects, of course, are university students. The factors studied most commonly are stimulus factors. Psychologists in the past have been more interested in spatial relations than in social relations, more concerned with sensory interaction than with interaction between persons. If one wishes evidence on this point he may turn to reviews of the experimental literature, such as Vernon's book *Visual Perception* (78) or Woodworth's appropriate chapters in his *Experimental Psychology* (81) or Boring's in his *Sensation and Perception in the History of Experimental Psychology* (13).

Even in a considerable proportion of the instances in which psychological research has been concerned with social factors in perception, the traditional subject matters and procedures of the laboratory have been used (6, 65, 72). Sherif (74), who deserves considerable credit for demonstrating the influence of frames of reference, employed the autokinetic phenomenon. Bruner (15, 16, 17, 18) and his associates continue the laboratory tradition by using a tachistoscope, even though their research is concerned with social relations rather than with experimental psychology. Tradition dies slowly; the invention of new approaches is an arduous process.

Many of the approaches which have contributed most to the study of social factors in perception are usually classified under other headings. Studies of suggestion, including hypnotism, have made several contributions. Investigations of emotional expression throw light upon social influences in perception as well as upon emotion. Projective techniques, of course, must deal with perception as well as with personality. Some important lines of evidence are historical and anthropological rather than experimental. In reviewing studies of social factors in perception, the writer will feel free to draw upon sources such as these, to which our books on perception seldom make reference.

It should be understood that, in developing his own topic, the present writer recognizes that he is dealing with only one of the factors which influence the perceptual processes. Structural determinants, chemical determinants, linguistic determinants all are present, but these topics are covered in other Chapters. While convinced of the importance of his topic, the present writer does not wish to be understood as championing a cause. If this Chapter neglects other factors, it is because that is expected. An adequate approach to problems in perception will require that all factors be considered in proper proportion. The plan of this symposium shows that the persons responsible for its organization were fully aware that a many-sided attack upon perceptual processes is demanded and that scientific partisanship is to be avoided.

Definition of "Perception"

To prevent misunderstanding, it is necessary to indicate first in what sense the word *perception* is used in this Chapter. It will be used to refer to an experience which is occasioned by the stimulation of sense organs. That is, perceptions are to be distinguished from memory images, reveries, trains of association, and hallucinations because these are not directly caused by stimulation. A perception requires the presence of a stimulus. However, it is generally agreed that an experience which is occasioned by a stimulus is influenced not only by the immediate stimulus but also by the reinstatement of the effects of previous stimuli. If this were not so, we would speak of sensation rather than of perception. A stimulus not only elicits direct sensory effects but also arouses images and feelings which are fused with the more direct effects of the stimulus. The direct sensory effects are followed not only by immediate supplements to the stimulus but also by a whole chain of associations, memories, daydreams, reasoning, etc. The more distant of these, as indicated above, are not called perceptions. Ordinarily only the interpretation of the stimulus is called perception. The present writer believes, however, that the demarcation between perception and subsequent experiences must be an arbitrary one, and a precise distinction will not be attempted.

It should not be inferred from the preceding discussion that a stimulus appears as if out of the blue. That, of course, is erroneous. A stimulus breaks in upon a pre-existing experience which acts in part to determine whether or not the stimulus will be perceived and, if so, how it will be perceived. Thus, perception is not the result of a succession of discrete impingements from the outside world, but rather it is a continuous tuning-in, amplification, suppression, and interpretation.

Cultural Factors in Perception

Historical and Anthropological Evidence.—As indicated previously, the experimental evidence for social influence in perception is slight, but the historical and anthropological evidence is great. Let us first take some instances from the recent past of our own society. Not many decades ago the use of lipstick and of cigarettes by the feminine sex was restricted to a certain group of professional women. Today no such restriction exists. It is almost certain that a woman wearing lipstick and smoking a cigarette not only arouses attitudes different today from formerly but that she is perceived differently. Within the same era of change, to choose a different example, the qualities perceived in a man with a full beard have doubtless altered considerably. We know that Wundt, William James, and G. Stanley Hall, bearded as they were, were perceived as unaffected, whereas it does not seem at all likely that these traits would be attributed to a psychologist of today who appeared in the same type of facial adornment.

Such simple examples of the influence of the social milieu upon the perception of personality traits could be multiplied endlessly. In certain Far Eastern areas, the woman who appears with a veil is perceived as conventional and modest; here the woman who appears with one may be judged to be alluring, probably intentionally alluring. What is heard in the South as normal speech is diagnosed as dialect in the North and vice versa. What is understood in Texas as a simple statement of fact is often interpreted elsewhere as unconscionable exaggeration. Turning to anthropological literature, we note that an illness which is seen in one society as a sign of supernatural favor is seen in another group as proof of sorcery. What is an omen of good luck in one culture forebodes ill in another. Old people are endowed with wisdom and power in the minds of one tribe, but by a second group they are despised and shunned. The sun itself is perceived variously as baleful and beneficent, moonlight may be eerie or romantic, and the same shooting star may have different significances, depending upon him who sees it.

Malinowski (42, 43) has shown that even the perception of resemblance in facial features is affected by culture, the Trobriand Islanders steadfastly refusing to see resemblances among maternal kinsmen but noting and perhaps exaggerating resemblances in the paternal line.

Among the few instances of traditional psychological research conducted among primitive groups, there is one (73) which is concerned with the Müller-Lyer illusion. The staff of the Torres Straits expedition in 1898 found that certain native groups were much less subject to the illusion than were European subjects. One hypothesis which was advanced to account for this relative immunity to the illusion was that the natives' use of spears, the heads of which resembled part of the Müller-Lyer figure, might have had some effect upon their responses to the test figure. Whatever the interpretation of this observation, the Torres Straits expedition deserves mention for including not only this illusion, but also many other perceptual tests in their research schedule, an inclusion which has not been duplicated by modern anthropological field workers.

Experimental Evidence.—*Studies of Set and Suggestion.* As indicated previously, some of the experimental evidence regarding the effects of another person or of a group of persons upon an individual's perception comes from studies of set and of suggestion (9, 10). Thus there is experimental evidence that what a person sees in a complex situation are the aspects of it to which he has been instructed to attend. For instance, if told to observe what follows certain stimuli, he does not perceive nearly as well what it is that precedes them. The control of experience by another person extends even to perceiving objects which are not present. This may seem to be a self-contradiction in the terms in which we have defined perception, but let us, nevertheless, discuss such extreme cases.

We are familiar with the warmth illusion (14, 37), in which the subject reports an experience of warmth even though no heat has been applied to the apparatus, and a similar phenomenon in which an electric shock is reported in connection with a piece of equipment which has been disconnected from the electric circuit. A group suggestion demonstration has been reported by Slosson (76), who opened a vial of distilled water before a college chemistry class, telling the class that the vial contained a powerful odor. He asked the members of the class to hold up their hands as they smelled the odor. A wave of hands went up, starting with the foremost rows and spreading to the back. At least three fourths of the class perceived odor. The experiment had to be discontinued at the end of a minute because some of those in the front seats were being unpleasantly affected and were about to leave the room.

If it is objected that the subjects mentioned in the preceding experiments did not really have the experiences which they claimed but were giving reports merely to please the experimenter or to avoid punishment, more convincing evidence is provided by the study of Perky (48), which was done in Titchener's laboratory. Perky's subjects, several of whom were psychologists experienced in introspection, were, under certain conditions, unable to distinguish between visual stimuli and subjective visual images which were aroused by the instructions.

As an area intermediate between anthropological evidence and experimental evidence, the studies of Bartlett (7) may be mentioned. He investigated the reproduction by subjects of stories and pictures alien to their own culture. Bartlett found that reproduction was characteristically modified toward the familiar. Unfortunately for our purposes, Bartlett did not determine how much of this distortion occurred in perception and how much took place in the interval between perception and reproduction. Still other studies could be cited relevant to our present topic, but they would serve merely as further illustrations of an already evident point.

Among the recent writers who have stressed the social factors in perception is Ichheiser (39). He has proposed several types of false perception of the qualities of other persons. For instance, he proposes that what is true of a small segment of an individual's behavior is frequently assumed to be a general trait of that person. Again he proposes that a situational factor, such as unemployment, is often seen as due to personal qualities, a type of figure-and-ground effect in social perception. His monograph is full of fruitful hypotheses, although to be sure they are presented as obvious facts rather than as theories. Ichheiser presents no data; he scarcely suggests that data are needed to prove his views.

Thus in regard to social factors in perception we are at this point: no one seems to doubt that our perception of objects in the inanimate world, and particularly the meaning of these objects, is determined by culture. Our interpretation of persons likewise is admittedly influenced by our own group membership. While we recognize these influences when they are pointed out to us, they seem to play little part in our systematic accounts of personality. We assume that the general citizen's perception of the world is affected by his church, his vocation, his party, his lodge, and his newspaper, but we have not taken the trouble to study these influences. We assume that we as psychologists are somewhat more "scientific" and impartial in our perceptions than is the average man, but evidence on this point is similarly lacking.

Perceptual Errors in Psychologists. It is difficult to know where to begin in considering a topic in which the chief principle seems so obvious and yet for which there are so few adequate supporting investigations. However, it seems best to begin at home. So long as we as psychologists assume that we are relatively free of errors, prejudices, or preconceptions, we are less likely to develop effective demonstrations of the fallibility of perception. Let us see, therefore, whether there is evidence that we have not yet attained the objectivity and sophistication which we desire. In pursuing this aim, we shall review some instances in which psychologists have failed to recognize the role of social influences upon perception in their own professional subject matter.

Hypnosis. In this area, the field of hypnosis (38) provides some pretty examples of the fact that an observer's beliefs concerning psychological phenomena will determine what he perceives and, even further, what phenomena are actually produced.

Hypnotic phenomena were first believed to be due to a special form of energy, animal magnetism. This belief resulted in a person's experiencing magnetism and in exhibiting the expected behavior. When hypnosis was believed by Mesmer (45) to lead to crises, the crises were produced. For hypnotists who believed otherwise, the crises did not occur. When hypnosis was believed by Charcot to go through certain stages, the appropriate stages were exhibited by his subjects. When subjects knew nothing of these stages, they behaved differently. When conceptions changed, the phenomena changed. Gradually the hypnotists found that they had been under the control of their own suggestions no less than had their subjects. Today it is very generally agreed that hypnotism is scarcely to be distinguished from any other control of one person by another in situations in which no resistance, suspicion, or antagonism is aroused in the subject. One could cite experiments showing that results comparable to hypnosis can be obtained without any use of the concepts or the patter of hypnosis. In general, Hull's extensive experiments (38) show little difference between so-called hypnotic and waking suggestion.

Infant Emotions. For a second example of the fallibility of perceptions, let us consider a study by a behaviorist, who might be expected to perceive data with little admixture of cultural influences. All of us are familiar with the views of Watson on emotions in infancy. Watson (79), in part on the basis of general observation and no doubt in part on other bases, became convinced that certain stimuli elicited distinctive results in the infant. Specifically, he proposed that loud sounds and falling elicited a pattern called fear and that restraint of movements was followed by a pattern called anger. Both of these were alleged to be distinguishable from the effects of hunger and of pain. These views were published by Watson not as theories but as facts based upon observation, and this was the beginning of a sub-culture in American psychology. The views were very widely disseminated and were accepted uncritically.

Sherman (75) took movies of infants stimulated in the ways indicated above and exhibited them to graduate students in psychology, to medical students, and to nurses. Apparently all these students had been indoctrinated with Watson's views, for their judgments concerning the response patterns which followed each stimulus corresponded closely to those of Watson. When, however, Sherman removed from the movie the frames which revealed the stimuli which were used, there was little agreement as to the patterns of response. In other words, Watson and the student subjects had been seeing what they expected to see. A better demonstration of social influences in the interpretation of human behavior could scarcely be devised. It should be especially important for us to know that the supposedly "hardboiled" behaviorists were subject to distortion in their observation of behavior. One would expect persons engaged in psychological research to be particularly aware of the extent to which their "objective" data may be of their own creation.

The Rorschach Test: Cultural Influences upon Responses. Let us turn next to the Rorschach test. One cannot deny the present importance of this test. Since clinical psychologists make up approximately half of the membership of the American Psychological Association and since nearly all clinical psychologists use the Rorschach to some extent, we are concerned with a major professional problem. Typically the interpretation of this test assumes that variations in Rorschach responses are reflections primarily of personality structure. Variations in the cultural experiences of the subject are assumed to be relatively unimportant, except as they produce changes in personality structure. Those employing the Rorschach have largely ignored the possibility that there may be direct influences upon perception which are not necessarily accompanied by changes in anxiety, emotionality, etc. With this in mind, let us review briefly some cultural data on the Rorschach.

While the data are not ideal, they are numerous. No other set of standard stimuli has been presented to so many persons as have the ink blots prepared by Rorschach. The Müller-Lyer figure, the hollow square, the outline of a staircase, all introduced into psychology much earlier, have been outstripped by these relative newcomers to the psychological field.

Let us turn first to results from groups showing the greatest cultural variation, the preliterate societies (4). Rorschach responses have been recorded for members of several primitive groups. The earliest study was done by the Bleulers (12), who in 1935 published an investigation of twenty-nine peasants of Morocco. The Henrys (36, 71) obtained results from ten Pilaga Indian children living in the Gran Chaco in Argentina. Hallowell (33, 34, 35) has reported Rorschach results on 151 Salteaux Indians from Manitoba. Du Bois (46) recorded the responses of thirty-five Alorese in the East Indies. The records of forty Samoan boys and men have been presented by Cook (22). Partial reports have been made of Rorschach testing of the Hopi (77), Zuñi, Navaho, Papago, and Sioux, conducted jointly by the University of Chicago and the United States Office of Indian Affairs.

It cannot be argued that the samples obtained in these societies were either random or describable. Societies differ in regard to the willingness of their members to take the Rorschach; the samples from different societies differ in age, sex, status, and many unknown respects. Nevertheless, some of the group differences reported are such that it seems likely that these differences would exist even if complete or representative populations could be tested. The Moroccans, for instance, gave a remarkably high proportion of small details and many anatomy responses. The Pilaga children gave many details and many sex responses. Among the Samoans, on the other hand, wholes were predominant and space responses were unusually frequent. In the Salteaux groups, dream material was frequently seen in the blots and some of the most frequent contents were figures which in American subjects would be originals. The Alorese gave fewer movement responses and many more achromatic color responses than do American and European groups. The group differences just mentioned are merely illustrative; a comprehensive résumé has not been attempted in the present circumstances.

If we ask why these primitive groups differ so greatly among themselves and why each of them deviates from our American and European standards in what they perceive in the Rorschach cards, we must answer in a general way that these differences are due to experience, although we do not know definitely what factors are operative. Certain of the investigators have given hints as to what some of the experiential determinants of group differences in perception may be. Moroccan art and religion give importance to details. The frequency of sex responses by Pilaga children seems to be directly related to the sexual experience and sexual freedom permitted them. In Samoa, the frequency of space responses seems to be tied up with the fact that white is a favorite and a symbolic color. The recognition, on the part of the Salteaux, of Rorschach cards as figures previously seen only in dreams is in line with the importance given to dream experiences among these people. To the Salteaux dreams are a means of communication used by supernatural beings, and direct experiences with the supernatural are likely to be vivid. In other words, it seems probable that many of the Rorschach peculiarities of a given group could be accounted for in terms of the visual experiences common to that group.

Rorschach research has not been oriented toward discovering what in experience influences perception on the Rorschach. Investigation has not been concerned with what sort of experience leads to the seeing of wholes, of details, of movement, of color, of space, etc. Instead, it has been assumed that there is some sort of inherent connection between perception and personality which requires no explanation in terms of experience. With this orientation, it is not surprising that the entire body of Rorschach literature has contributed practically nothing to our knowledge of causal factors in perception, even though the test is a perceptual task.

In a recent study at the University of Pittsburgh, as yet unpublished, Abramson (5) has shown that a set to see wholes, induced by one minute of instructions, increases the average number of whole responses by 50 per cent, decreases the number of detail responses by 50 per cent, and causes significant changes in many other scoring categories. Corresponding but opposite effects were caused by an experimentally induced set to see details. These two sets influenced the Munroe Inspection score in opposite directions. If such perceptual changes can be brought about by brief instructions, it seems likely that sets induced by enduring cultural differences could result in even more striking changes. That such alterations in perception are accompanied by modifications of personality, in accordance with Rorschach theory, remains to be proved. It may well be that the treatment of the Rorschach as related to personality, ignoring the many other variables which affect perception, is a serious weakness of the projective approach. Among the variables affecting the Rorschach, certainly culture must be included.

It is not necessary, of course, to go to primitive groups to study cultural factors in Rorschach responses. Rorschach himself felt that he observed differences in responses between two Swiss cantons. There are variations within our population which almost certainly will make their influences felt in perceptual tasks. Interesting comparisons of occupational and religious groups, and of many other groups, await the investigator.

The Rorschach Test: Cultural Factors in Interpretation.   Thus far in discussing the Rorschach we have been concerned with the effect of culture upon the subject's responses.   Let us turn now to a no less crucial topic, the influence of cultural factors in determining the way in which the psychologist perceives these responses as indicators of personality.

In seeing Rorschach responses as indicators of personality, the proponents of the Rorschach believe that their interpretations are based upon experience.   We know that "experience" of this type is a poor proof of validity.   Mesmer's views concerning animal magnetism were based on experience, the users of the dowsing rod can point to hundreds of successful applications of their method, and Watson was completely sincere in believing that he had seen three, and only three, infant emotions.   In view of the frequency of such errors of experience, it would be wise for all beginning textbooks in psychology to start with illustrations of the fallibility of perceptions, judgments, memories, and generalizations and to stress the need for rigorous checking for human errors.

As psychologists we cannot consider that we have demonstrated effectively the simplest principle concerning perception if it does not become incorporated into our own behavior.   It is useless to point our finger at the employer who sees the man in overalls as lacking in ambition so long as we see the man who gives certain Rorschach responses as lacking in ambition on the basis of evidence which is no better than that of the employer.   It is anomalous that we should criticize the person who sees "red hair" as an indication of personality while we use color responses for the same purpose, if both judgments are based on a similar type of corroborative experience.

Why should our current researchers in perception be so interested in how large a coin looks to a child so long as we know so little about how the Rorschach looks to the clinician?   Proof that the apparent movement of a light in a dark room is illusory, and that the degree of movement is modified by social norms seem to the writer not half so important a problem as to determine whether in the interpretation of the Rorschach we are reading the psychogram into the psyche in our clinical interpretations.

Perhaps this section of our discussion can end on a somewhat more optimistic note by noting the increasing evidence that, since the ingestion of Rorschach doctrine, our digestive juices are beginning to act upon it.   More and more research is appearing which is not partisan. It is aimed not at proving that the Rorschach will do everything, or that it will do nothing, but at finding patiently and carefully what can and what cannot be done with it.

Nor do we need to feel that psychologists have been unusually susceptible to perceptual errors in viewing their subject matter. The chemists earlier had their phlogiston, now nonexistent but once as palpable as fog. The biologists perceived the spontaneous generation of maggots in meat as readily as recent citizens have seen flying saucers in the sky. Many present-day physicists seem to perceive the destruction of mankind in every cyclotron, and they may be just as wrong as the spearman who saw the introduction of the bow and arrow as a similar catastrophe. It is the purpose of all scientists to separate the subjective from the objective in their perception of the universe, yet none succeeds completely.

Developmental Factors in Perception

The second part of the present discussion is concerned with the developmental aspects of perception. This is an appropriate supplement to the consideration of social and cultural factors, since social influences obviously are not present in the chromosomes but must have a developmental course in which to embed themselves in the behavior of the individual.

The majority of the studies of perception in children are modeled after experiments with adults. The general nature of experiments on perception was noted at the beginning of this Chapter. One may characterize many studies of perceptual development as being concerned with illusory perception of geometrical figures, constancy of size, color, and shape, the perception of relative rather than absolute differences, and reliability of observation. The most common finding of these studies is that children's perceptions are somewhat more subject to error than are the perceptions of adults. Thus Binet (8) and later Pintner and Anderson (64) found that the Müller-Lyer illusion is greater with children than with older subjects. Studies such as Cruikshank's (24) give evidence for some size constancy even in young infants. Brunswik (19, 20), however, found that the degree of visual size constancy, or the ability to estimate absolute size regardless of distance, improves with age. The *Aussage* experiments (80) with children also show that fulness of report and accuracy of observation increase throughout childhood. In some cases the improvement with age is less than one might suppose.

In line with the emphasis in the preceding discussion, we shall, in the present connection, be interested primarily in the development of types of perception which have more significance to most of us than do visual illusions. In this realm the investigation which is concerned with the earliest age level is that of Bühler, who studied the child's differentiation between a smiling and a scowling face and between a praising and a scolding voice. Bühler (21) found that most children do not make these differentiations until about the age of five months. It is not surprising to find that, apparently, these differentiations must be learned. Nevertheless, the theories of Ribble with regard to the young infant's need for affection would seem to imply that the child has some sense organ which acquaints it directly with a glow of affection emitted by the mother. Clearly the child must learn the traditional signs of affection prevalent in its culture and has no instinctive recognition of the emotional expression of others.

Distinction Between the Familiar and the Unfamiliar.—The perception of the differences between familiar persons and strange persons is a phenomenon which seems to occur spontaneously in nearly all children. This item is included in many developmental scales and is most often placed at the level of the fifth or sixth month. The usual descriptive title is "fear of strangers." Whether fear is the correct word or not, the child is at least shy and retreating. While evidence on this point may not be conclusive, it does seem likely that the reaction to strangers cannot be accounted for on a conditioned response basis. That is, the child need not have had unpleasant experiences with strangers in order to fear strangers. If a child were reared from birth to an age of several months having seen only one person and having had no experiences except with that one person, it appears likely that he would react negatively to any other person (26). Thus, if the writer is correct, something resembling an in-group—out-group distinction is very fundamental in children's perception. It is not instinctive, since, of course, experience is necessary in order for anything to become familiar, but given familiarity with one group of persons, an initial negative reaction to nonmembers may appear spontaneously. This is an example of the type of development which the present writer has called autogenous, or self-originated within the individual (25, 26).

The perception of a distinction between the familiar and the unfamiliar, with an accompanying negative reaction to the latter, is not a specific reaction of children to other persons. It operates in the most general way and applies to the child's clothes, food, and sleeping arrangements as well as to his associates. This view, if correct, has some significance for social psychology as well as for child care. While the child is not born with prejudices, this mechanism would seem to make the development of prejudices inevitable.

Of course, it is not argued that this is the sole origin or the most potent origin of attitudes. Clearly most attitudes toward members of groups are socially transmitted. Yet here, too, is a field in which research has been slight. In one study of the development by white children of stereotypes concerning the Negro, Blake and the present writer (11) found that the youngest children questioned, pupils in the fourth grade, pictured the Negro in a very generally unfavorable way, not even attributing to him such traits as a sense of humor and love for music. As the child grows older, he approaches the adult stereotype which gives some favorable and some unfavorable traits to the Negro.

The study cited is not one of perception, since it is concerned exclusively with associations to the word *Negro*. It serves, however, as an example of one of the shortcomings of most research on attitudes and stereotypes, namely, that they limit themselves to verbally presented situations. Studies are needed in which subjects are brought into contact with specific persons and are then required to describe the characteristics of the individuals. Such studies would soon show, for instance, whether or not the child perceives in the individual Negro the traits which he attributes to Negroes generally when questioned. There is need to move away from verbal studies to studies of the direct perception of personal qualities, such as friendliness, cheerfulness, cleanliness, laziness, etc.

Work of Piaget.—In the remainder of this discussion of the developmental aspects of perception, particular attention will be paid to the work of Piaget. To avoid the accusation of narrowness in devoting so much space to the work of one man, the following defense is offered. In the first place, the allocation of space is not particularly disproportionate from a quantitative point of view, since Piaget has produced more than a dozen books and monographs (49-63 incl.) all bearing on the development of perception. This is a large fraction of the total literature here. A second reason for choosing this emphasis is that Piaget has been so neglected by most American psychologists that an overemphasis in the present instance may help redress the balance. Despite the extent of his contributions, many of our textbooks in child psychology do not even mention Piaget. References to his work in textbooks in other fields are almost equally scanty.

It may be doubted that Piaget is concerned with perception. Much of his work uses the terms *concepts, reasoning,* and *judgment.* It cannot be denied that much of his work lies outside the scope of the present topic. At the same time, a great deal of his work may be included rightfully. He is concerned basically with how the child perceives his world, rather than with how he reasons about it. In fact, it is one of Piaget's hypotheses that the young child perceives the world in such a way that he is relatively incapable of reasoning with regard to it.

The writer does not wish to picture himself as supporting Piaget in all particulars. Following an unfavorable first reaction to his books, the writer attempted to show how outrageous were some of his views and, by gathering data with the expectation of refuting his theories, became convinced that many of them were sound (27). Yet despite a conviction that his hypotheses and observations are brilliant, the writer cannot deny that his work is subject to many just criticisms. His defects are the very ones which are most likely to damn any investigator in the eyes of an American psychologist. The presence of certain weaknesses in his work has probably provided the major reason for the relative inattention of America to a person who may prove to be a major figure in the history of psychology.

The most patent criticism of Piaget is his disregard of and probable dislike for statistics. He attempts to prove a hypothesis by citing an observation which agrees with the hypothesis. If he thinks further proof is needed, he cites a second observation. His age norms are not norms at all. He is not concerned with regard to whether his subjects are representative of any group. He computes percentages and means; no other statistics are presented. If two means or two percentages differ, no question of the significance of the differences is raised. Since no measures of variability are presented, it is not possible to test the reliability of the observed differences. In some of his publications, an extensive interpretation is developed to explain differences which, for all one can tell, may be of a very low order of significance.

Other criticisms of Piaget's work can also be made. His methods of observation and of experimenting frequently are not standardized. The reliability of his classifications of his data ordinarily is not checked. The absence of such treatment was characteristic of many fields of psychology in America as well as in Europe when Piaget began his work in the 1920's. It seems strange, however, that he should be so unaware of, or at least so uninfluenced by, the advances in research methodology since that time. But we may as well accept the fact that Piaget can neither prove nor disprove his hypotheses. That must be done by others. We turn to Piaget for ideas, not for statistics. Every graduate student of psychology is a better master of statistics than is Piaget, but few will ever be so fertile as he in the development of theories and concepts. This is his forte; it is for this that he should be evaluated.

Piaget's Methods.—The raw data which form the basis for Piaget's hypotheses are observations of the spontaneous speech and conversations of children, interviews with children, and children's explanations of phenomena in experimentally devised situations.

Piaget's aim in questioning the child about some object or event is to learn how he perceives it, how he understands it, how he conceives it. The raw data always refer to a specific object or event—a stone, a floating cork, a moving cloud, etc. However, Piaget, like any scientist, is impelled to classify what he observes. When he does so, he finds trends in the child's experience to which he gives names such as egocentrism, realism, immanent justice, artificialism, etc. It should be kept in mind that these are not names for entities or functional units but are classifications of phenomena. Furthermore, they are not mutually exclusive. For example, a child's description of a dream may be, in Piaget's terminology, realistic, animistic, and artificialistic, at one and the same time. Let us now examine some of the aspects of the child's thought, or of the child's perception of the world.

Children's Perceptions.—According to Piaget, the young child, when he is first able to discuss simple objects and events, sees in them many traits and characteristics which educated adults ordinarily perceive only in the higher animals. In other words, he is animistic. The child sees objects as being aware of their position, their state of rest or motion, and as conscious of their immediate surroundings. He sees them as having feelings and desires, as operating from motives, and as achieving purposes. Furthermore, certain experiences which educated adults ordinarily refer internally are given an external reference by the child. In Piaget's terms, this is child realism. Whatever the child perceives, such as a dream, he assumes to be external and visible to others. Whatever he knows, such as a name, he assumes to be known to other persons and to surrounding objects. Information is not perceived as subjective but as widespread as the air and the sunshine. Similarly the ethical and moral qualities of an action are as observable as the location and vigor of the act itself. That breaking a window is naughty is as obvious as that the window is broken. The wickedness which is involved is absolute, unqualified by circumstances. To break a window is naughty in itself regardless of person, intention, or motivation.

Perhaps several aspects of child experience can best be illustrated by one of the stories used by Piaget as a basis for questioning. It is the story of a boy, a foot-bridge and stolen fruit, and it runs somewhat as follows:

A boy went to an orchard and stole some fruit. On the way back he had to cross a foot-bridge. As he crossed the bridge, the bridge broke.

Questions and answers illustrating various points are given below. No one child would be asked all of these, nor would the questions asked necessarily be in the sequence which is used here.

Why did the bridge break? *Because the boy stole the fruit.*
Did the bridge know that he had stolen? *Yes, of course.*
If he had not stolen the fruit, would the bridge have broken? *No.*
Was the bridge living? *Yes.*
Why? *Because you could walk on it.*
Is it living now? *No, because it's broken.*
Tell me again, why did the bridge break? *To punish the boy.*
Suppose the boy thought it was his father's orchard. Would that make any difference? *No, he was stealing.*
Suppose the boy was lost. He had no lunch and no dinner and was very hungry? *It would make no difference.*

Without further-elaboration, the present writer believes that what he has just presented, if it be taken as representative, shows how greatly the young child's world differs from that of an adult, who would consider the bridge to be senseless and inanimate and to have broken purely from physical causes, who would feel that only persons who have seen the boy steal would know of the act, and who would judge the sinfulness of the act in terms of the boy's condition and motivation. The child may be said to live at the center of a sort of animated goldfish bowl which is all-concerned with his activities and his desires and which imposes and enforces his rules of conduct.

In regard to each aspect of experience, Piaget characteristically finds an early childhood interpretation, an educated adult position, and an intermediate view. Typically, he calls the three conceptions three stages. Occasionally, there is more than one intermediate step, in which case there are four or more stages, but the preference is for three categories. By dividing any course of development into stages, however, Piaget seems only to be indicating distinguishable changes. He seems to recognize that the number of categories is often arbitrary.

While the present writer cannot undertake at this point to survey all the evidence for and against Piaget's views, it should be pointed out that there is a considerable amount of data which in a very general way corroborates his observations. Lerner (41) and also Abel (3) found that American subjects responded to questioning concerning the bridge situation in the same manner as did Piaget's subjects. University of Chicago investigators, as well as the present writer (28, 30), have found the same responses among Hopi and Zuñi Indian children. In regard to animism, Russell and the present writer (30, 66, 67, 68, 69, 70) and others (32) have obtained a large number of data substantially in agreement with the observations of Piaget. Where Piaget has not been supported, as in the case of the studies of Mead (44) and Deutsche (31), the methods of investigation employed have been very divergent from those advocated by Piaget.

Significance of Piaget's Views.—If we accept for the sake of discussion the essential correctness of Piaget's views with regard to the young child, what is the significance of these for psychology and particularly for perception and personality?

For one thing, they indicate that social factors permeate the child's perception of his environment from a very early age. He has interiorized certain aspects of his culture by the time that he can first give a description of his perceptions. In fact, he does not distinguish between world and culture. He does not distinguish clearly the objective and the subjective. They are fused. Almost from the beginning some acts are inherently naughty, some good; some people are evil, some benevolent; some things are dirty, some clean; some people are cowardly, some are brave; some are ugly, others are pretty; some objects are personal property, some are not. While society supplies these characteristics, the child sees them as natural.

Although Piaget has been interested in the more universal aspects of the child's view of the world and scarcely at all in cultural differences, it seems likely that different cultures impose different categories of experience upon the child. Some groups particularly emphasize the cowardly-brave distinction, while others put special emphasis upon the clean-unclean dichotomy, some stress the beautiful-ugly division, and so forth. Although divisions such as living and nonliving have been of chief concern to Piaget, it seems likely that his methods could be used to study social influences upon perception at an early age. Undoubtedly, some of the dichotomies of experience developed in childhood by a given society continue throughout life and persistently affect the individual's experience.

Piaget often writes as if he believes the adult and the child are quite different (1, 2). But Piaget's investigations of adults have been cursory. All his research has been with children. He seems to assume that the adult does not require investigation. It is probable that the adult standards with which he compares the child are the standards of a scientist. It may well be that poets, artists, musicians, and many other persons as well continue as adults to perceive the world as having objective beauty and meaning. It is possible that in many respects most adults retain the child's conception of morality.

Only in a few instances known to the present writer have Piaget's questions been applied to adults. Russell (68), however, found that many high school seniors indicate that clouds, rivers, and such objects are living, not limiting life to plants and animals. Practically no Hopi Indian children thirteen and fourteen years old, were found to be in the so-called adult stages in regard to animism and moral realism when the present writer investigated the matter (28), and in collaboration with Mallinger (29) he found a very considerable degree of animism in white subjects beyond seventy years of age. We proposed that these subjects had regressed to childhood conceptions, but whether these subjects regressed or whether they had never held so-called adult conceptions is not clear. The need for research in the age range of fifteen to seventy years is clearly indicated.

Even among adults who give so-called adult answers to the questions used by Piaget, it may be that such objective thinking may be limited to the simple situations which are employed by Piaget. More complicated situations may reveal modes of interpretation which are not brought out by the more elementary examples. Thus, while the breaking of a foot-bridge may not be perceived by the adult as caused by wrongdoing because the natural science explanation of breakage is understood by the average adult, some less well-comprehended event, such as a hurricane, earthquake, or drought may be perceived as a form of punishment. Even William James (40) reported that he personalized and animated an earthquake which he experienced in visiting California. We have failed to investigate the perception of guilt, of danger, or wrongdoing, of supernatural presences, etc., in the occurrence of unusual events. It is to this type of subject matter that Piaget's methods may give us a new means of access.

In regard to perception as a focus for the study of personality, Piaget's techniques suggest several lines of approach. One of these is the matter of regression to infantile or childhood levels. Whether or not abnormal mental conditions constitute regressions has been difficult to establish because, aside from intelligence tests, we have so few measures of age progression in perception and thought. Animism, moral realism, and allied concepts may prove research leads, since these do change from one age level to another, at least in regard to the simple situations and questions used by Piaget.

Similarly in regard to regression under frustration or in the face of emotion or of stress, we may have a research tool as yet unused. In the differentiation of temperaments, where so little has been done, research on habitual modes of perception may be revealing. Do some persons see rules and violations in simple situations where others see no sort of obligation or compulsion? Is the diplomat or the politician one who early realizes that the "rules of the game" are arbitrary social conventions? Does the member of the antivivisection league and the SPCA see exquisite consciousness in the frog and the goldfish? Does the Fascist believe that the experiences which he values are capable of being attained only by himself and his close associates? Does the paranoid find a personal reference in many ordinary events? Is there individual consistency from age to age in these respects? The answers to such questions would bring the study of perception into close relationship with the study of personality. Piaget himself has not suggested such applications of his methods, but the simple and systematic questioning of persons concerning their perception of familiar and recurrent phenomena may contribute more than Piaget has foreseen to the understanding of people.

In conclusion let us state explicitly what has been implied in most of this Chapter. It is this: the study of perception as a focus for understanding personality will require that the psychologist concern himself intensively with areas into which he has seldom intruded in the past. He must deal not only with autokinetic phenomena but also with the Kinsey report: he must be concerned not only with social norms in the laboratory but also with the perception of social status in real life situations. We are on the way to such goals. The present writer is convinced that, if perception is studied in socially significant situations, it will indeed provide a focus for the understanding of personality.

BIBLIOGRAPHY

1. ABEL, T. M. Unsynthetic modes of thinking among adults: a discussion of Piaget's concepts. *Amer. J. Psychol.,* 1932, **44,** 123-32.
2. ABEL, T. M. Primitive and child mentality. *Poznanskie Towarzystwo Psychol.,* 1934, **5,** 5-22.
3. ABEL, T. M. Moral judgments among subnormals. *J. abnorm. soc. Psychol.,* 1941, **36,** 378-92.
4. ABEL, T. M. The Rorschach test in the study of culture. *Rorschach Res. Exch. and J. proj. Tech.,* 1948, **12,** 79-93.
5. ABRAMSON, L. S. The influence of experimentally induced sets with regard to area on Rorschach test results. Dissertation, University of Pittsburgh, 1950.
6. ANSBACHER, H. *Perception of number as affected by the monetary value of the objects.* Arch. Psychol. No. 215. New York, 1937.
7. BARTLETT, F. C. *Remembering.* Cambridge: Cambridge University Press, 1932.
8. BINET, A. La mesure des illusions visuelles chez l'enfant. *Rev. Phil.,* Paris, 1895, **40,** 11-25.
9. BINET, A. *La suggestibilité.* Paris: Schleicher Freres, 1900.
10. BIRD, C. Suggestion and suggestibility. *Psychol. Bull.,* 1939, **36,** 264-83.
11. BLAKE, R. R., & DENNIS, W. The development of stereotypes concerning the Negro. *J. abnorm. soc. Psychol.,* 1943, **38,** 525-31.
12. BLEULER, M., & BLEULER, R. Rorschach's inkblot test and racial psychology: peculiarities of Moroccans. *Character & Pers.,* 1935, **4,** 97-114.

13. BORING, E. G. *Sensation and perception in the history of experimental psychology.* New York: Appleton-Century-Crofts, Inc., 1942.
14. BROWN, W. Individual and sex differences in suggestibility. *Univ. Calif. Publ. Psychol.,* 1916, **2**, 291-430.
15. BRUNER, J. S., & GOODMAN, C. C. Value and need as organizing factors in perception. *J. abnorm. soc. Psychol.,* 1947, **42**, 33-44.
16. BRUNER, J. S., & POSTMAN, L. Emotional selectivity in perception and reaction. *J. Personal.,* 1947, **16**, 69-77.
17. BRUNER, J. S., & POSTMAN, L. An approach to social perception. In W. Dennis (ed.), *Current trends in social psychology.* Pittsburgh: University of Pittsburgh Press, 1948.
18. BRUNER, J. S., & POSTMAN, L. Symbolic value as an organizing factor in perception. *J. soc. Psychol.,* 1948, **27**, 203-8.
19. BRUNSWIK, E. Über Farben-, Grössen- und Gestaltkonstanz in der Jugend. In H. Volkelt (ed.), *Bericht über den XI. Kongress für experim. Psychol.* Jena: Fischer, 1930. Pp. 52-56.
20. BRUNSWIK, E. *Systematic and representative design of psychological experiments.* Berkeley, Calif.: University of California Press, 1947.
21. BÜHLER, CHARLOTTE. *From birth to maturity.* London: George Routledge & Sons, Ltd., and Kegan Paul, Trench, Trubner & Co., Ltd., 1935.
22. COOK, P. H. The application of the Rorschach test to a Samoan group. *Rorschach Res. Exch.,* 1942, **6**, 51-60.
23. CRONBACH, L. J. Statistical methods applied to Rorschach scores. *Psychol. Bull.,* 1949, **46**, 393-429.
24. CRUIKSHANK, R. M. The development of visual size constancy in early infancy. *J. genet. Psychol.,* 1941, **58**, 327-51.
25. DENNIS, W. Infant reaction to restraint: an evaluation of Watson's theory. *Trans. N. Y. Acad. Sci.,* 1940, II, **2**, 202-18.
26. DENNIS, W. Infant development under conditions of restricted practice and of minimum social stimulation. *Genet. Psychol. Monogr.,* 1941, **23**, 143-91.
27. DENNIS, W. Piaget's questions applied to a child of known environment. *J. genet. Psychol.,* 1942, **60**, 307-20.
28. DENNIS, W. Animism and related tendencies in Hopi children. *J. abnorm. soc. Psychol.,* 1943, **38**, 21-36.
29. DENNIS, W., & MALLINGER, B. Animism and related tendencies in senescence. *J. Gerontol.,* 1949, **4**, 218-22.
30. DENNIS, W., & RUSSELL, R. W. Piaget's questions applied to Zuñi children. *Child Develpm.,* 1940, **11**, 181-87.
31. DEUTSCHE, JEAN MARQUIS. *The development of children's concepts of causal relations.* Minneapolis: University of Minnesota Press, 1937.
32. GRANICH, L. *A qualitative analysis of concepts in mentally deficient schoolboys.* Arch. Psychol. No. 251. New York, 1940.
33. HALLOWELL, A. I. The Rorschach method as an aid in the study of personalities in primitive societies. *Character & Pers.,* 1941, **9**, 235-45.
34. HALLOWELL, A. I. The Rorschach technique in the study of personality and culture. *Amer. Anthrop.,* 1945, **47**, 195-210.
35. HALLOWELL, A. I. "Popular" responses and cultural differences: an analysis based on frequencies in a group of American Indian subjects. *Rorschach Res. Exch.,* 1945, **9**, 153-68.
36. HENRY, J. Rorschach technique in primitive cultures. *Amer. J. Orthopsychiat.,* 1941, **11**, 230-34.
37. HERON, W. T. The group demonstration of illusory warmth as demonstrative of the phenomenon of suggestion. *J. abnorm. soc. Psychol.,* 1927, **22**, 341-44.
38. HULL, C. L. *Hypnosis and suggestibility.* New York: Appleton-Century-Crofts, Inc., 1933.
39. ICHHEISER, G. Misunderstandings in human relations. *Amer. J. Sociol.,* 1949, **55**, Sept., Part 2.

40. JAMES, W. *Memories and studies.* New York: Longmans, Green & Co., Inc., 1912.

40A. KINSEY, A. C., POMEROY, W. B. and MARTIN, C. E. *Sexual Behavior in the Human Male.* Philadelphia: W. B. Saunders & Co., 1948.

41. LERNER, E. *Constraint areas and the moral judgment of children.* Menasha, Wis.: George Banta Publishing Co., 1937.

42. MALINOWSKI, B. The psychology of sex and the foundations of kinship in primitive societies. *Psyche,* Lond., 1923-24, **4,** 98-129.

43. MALINOWSKI, B. Psychoanalysis and anthropology. *Psyche,* Lond., 1923-24, **4,** 293-333.

44. MEAD, MARGARET. An investigation of the thought of primitive children with special reference to animism. *J. R. anthrop. Inst.,* 1932, **62,** 173-90.

45. MESMER, F. A. *Mémoire sur la découverte du magnétisme animal.* Paris, 1779. Trans. G. Frankau, *Mesmerism.* London: Macdonald & Co., Ltd., 1948.

46. OBERHOLZER, E. Rorschach's experiment and the Alorese. In Cora Du Bois, *The people of Alor.* Minneapolis: University of Minnesota Press, 1944, chap. xxii.

47. PASTORE, N. Need as a determinant of perception. *J. Psychol.,* 1949, **28,** 457-75.

48. PERKY, C. W. An experimental study of imagination. *Amer. J. Psychol.,* 1910, **21,** 422-52.

49. PIAGET, J. *The language and thought of the child.* New York: Harcourt, Brace & Co., Inc., 1926.

50. PIAGET, J. *Judgment and reasoning in the child.* New York: Harcourt, Brace & Co., Inc., 1928.

51. PIAGET, J. *The child's conception of the world.* New York: Harcourt, Brace & Co., Inc., 1929.

52. PIAGET, J. *The child's conception of physical causality.* New York: Harcourt, Brace & Co., Inc., 1930.

53. PIAGET, J. *The moral judgment of the child.* London: Kegan Paul, Trench, Trubner & Co., Ltd., 1932.

54. PIAGET, J. Principal factors determining intellectual evolution from childhood to adult life. Papers presented at a symposium of the Harvard Tercentenary Conference of Arts and Sciences, Aug. 31-Sept. 12, 1936. Harvard Tercentenary Publications.

55. PIAGET, J. *La construction du réel chez l'enfant.* Neuchâtel and Paris: Delachaux & Niestle, 1937.

56. PIAGET, J. *Le mécanisme du développement mental et les lois du groupement des opérations: esquisse d'une théorie opératoire de l'intelligence.* Neuchâtel: Delachaux & Niestle, 1941.

57. PIAGET, J. *La genèse du nombre chez l'enfant.* Paris: Delachaux & Niestle, 1941.

58. PIAGET, J. *Le développement de quantités chez l'enfant: conservation et atomisme.* Paris: Delachaux & Niestle, 1941.

59. PIAGET, J. *Introduction a l'étude des perceptions chez l'enfant et analyse d'une illusion relative a la perception visuelle de Cercles concentriques (Delboeuf).* Neuchâtel: Delachaux & Niestle, 1942.

60. PIAGET, J. *La comparaison visuelle des hauteurs a distances variables dans le plan fronti-parallèlle. Le problème de la comparaison visuelle en profondeur (constance de la grandeur) et l'erreur systématique de l'entalon par.* Neuchâtel: Delachaux & Niestle, 1943.

61. PIAGET, J. *Essai d'interprétation probabiliste de la loi de Weber et de celle des centrations relatives.* Neuchâtel: Delachaux & Niestle, 1945.

62. PIAGET, J. *La formation du symbole chez l'enfant; imitation, jeu et nève, image et représentation.* Paris: Delachaux & Niestle, 1945.

63. PIAGET, J. *Les notions de mouvement et de vitesse chez l'enfant.* Paris: Presses Universitaires de France, 1946.

64. PINTNER, R., & ANDERSON, M. M.   The Müller-Lyer illusion with children and adults.   *J. exp. Psychol.*, 1916, **1**, 200-10.
65. PROSHANSKY, H., & MURPHY, G.   The effects of reward and punishment on perception.   *J. Psychol.*, 1942, **13**, 295-305.
66. RUSSELL, R. W.   Studies in animism.   II.   The development of animism.   *J. genet. Psychol.*, 1940, **56**, 353-66.
67. RUSSELL, R. W.   Studies in animism.   IV.   An investigation of concepts allied to animism.   *J. genet. Psychol.*, 1940, **57**, 83-91.
68. RUSSELL, R. W.   Studies in animism.   V.   Animism in older children.   *J. genet. Psychol.*, 1942, **60**, 329-35.
69. RUSSELL, R. W., & DENNIS, W.   Studies in animism.   I.   A standardized procedure for the investigation of animism.   *J. genet. Psychol.*, 1939, **55**, 389-400.
70. RUSSELL, R. W., DENNIS, W., & ASH, F. E.   Studies in animism.   III.   Animism in feeble-minded subjects.   *J. genet. Psychol.*, 1940, **57**, 57-63.
71. SCHACHTEL, A. H., HENRY, J., & HENRY, Z.   Rorschach analysis of Pilaga Indian children.   *Amer. J. Orthopsychiat.*, 1942, **12**, 679-712.
72. SCHAFER, R., & MURPHY, G.   The role of autism in a visual figure-ground relationship.   *J. exp. Psychol.*, 1943, **32**, 335-43.
73. SELIGMAN, C. G.   The vision of the natives of British Guinea.   In *Report of the Cambridge anthropological expedition to Torres Struits,* 1901, ed. A. C. Haddon. Cambridge University Press, Vol. II.
74. SHERIF, M.   *A study in some social factors in perception.*   Arch. Psychol. No. 187.   New York, 1935.
75. SHERMAN, M.   The differentiation of emotional responses in infants.   I.   Judgments of emotional responses from motion picture views and from actual observation.   *J. comp. Psychol.*, 1927, **7**, 265-84.
76. SLOSSON, E. E.   A classroom demonstration of suggestion.   *Psychol. Rev.*, 1899, **6**, 407-8.
77. THOMPSON, LAURA, & JOSEPH, ALICE.   *The Hopi way.*   Chicago: University of Chicago Press, 1944.
78. VERNON, M. D.   *Visual perception.*   Cambridge: Cambridge University Press, 1937.
79. WATSON, J. B., & MORGAN, J. J. B.   Emotional reactions and psychological experimentation.   *Amer. J. Psychol.*, 1917, **28**, 163-74.
80. WINCH, W. H.   *Children's perceptions: an experimental study of observations and report in school children.*   Educ. Psychol. Monogr. No. 12.   Baltimore: Warwick and York, 1914.
81. WOODWORTH, R. S.   *Experimental psychology.*   New York: Henry Holt & Co., Inc., 1938.

CHAPTER 7

THE ROLE OF LANGUAGE IN THE PERCEPTUAL PROCESSES

By Alfred Korzybski [1]

It is my particular privilege, as I am not a specialist in the field of psycho-logics,[2] to participate in this symposium dealing with such a vital subject. The topic and main divisions of this Chapter were suggested to me by the organizers of the symposium, and I am glad to abide by them.

In my work I have found that there are some simple principles underlying the subject matter which I will attempt to convey here. More details may be found in the bibliography given, and the large amounts of other related literature available.

Not dealing with the problem of "perception" directly in my work, I shall use this term here in the vernacular sense. I do not consider myself qualified to define it, and so shall use quotation marks to indicate my nontechnical treatment of this type of human reactions. I cannot avoid dealing with the problems of "perception" indirectly but will do so from a different angle.

The Effect on Perceptual Processes of the Language System

Perhaps a story from the European underground under Hitler would be a good illustration. In a railroad compartment an American grandmother with her young and attractive granddaughter, a Romanian officer, and a Nazi officer were the only occupants. The train was passing through a dark tunnel, and all that was heard was

---

[1] Alfred Korzybski died on March 1, 1950, while doing the final editing of this paper. Miss Charlotte Schuchardt, his editorial secretary, in a letter made the following statement regarding the final form of the manuscript: "It should be stated that he did not complete the final editing of this paper. The editing which I did after his death was minor, and I am grateful for the assistance of some members of the Institute staff. Yet I must assume the responsibility both for the slight editing, and also, particularly, for not making editorial changes which he might have made."

[2] On the special uses of hyphens and other printed symbols as "extensional devices" in this chapter, see pages 192-93.

a loud kiss and a vigorous slap. After the train emerged from the tunnel, nobody spoke, but the grandmother was saying to herself, "What a fine girl I have raised. She will take care of herself. I am proud of her." The granddaughter was saying to herself, "Well, grandmother is old enough not to mind a little kiss. Besides, the fellows are nice. I am surprised what a hard wallop grandmother has." The Nazi officer was meditating, "How clever those Romanians are! They steal a kiss and have the other fellow slapped." The Romanian officer was chuckling to himself, "How smart I am! I kissed my own hand and slapped the Nazi."

Obviously it was a problem of limited "perception," where mainly "hearing" was involved, with different interpretations.

Another example of "perception" could be given which anyone can try for himself. In fact, I suggest that this simple demonstration should be repeated by all readers of this paper. The demonstration takes two persons. One, without the knowledge of the other, cuts out large headlines of the same size from different issues of a newspaper. The subject remains seated in the same position throughout. He is shown one of the headlines at a certain distance. If he is able to read it, it is discarded. Then he is shown another, different, headline at a somewhat farther distance away. Again, if he is able to read it, it is discarded. This process is repeated until the subject is unable to read the headline. Then the demonstrator tells him what is in the headline. The amazing fact is that the subject will then be able to *see and read* the headline the moment he "knows" what is there.

Such illustrations could be multiplied indefinitely. These examples are enough to illustrate the impossibility of separating sharply the "perceptual," "seeing," "hearing," etc., and "knowing," a division which cannot be made, except superficially on verbal levels.

In a non-Aristotelian orientation we take for granted that all "perceptual processes" involve abstracting by our nervous system at different levels of complexity. Neurological evidence shows the selective character of the organism's responses to total situations, and the papers in this symposium also corroborate the view that the mechanisms of "perception" lie in the ability of our nervous system to abstract and to project.

Abstracting by necessity involves evaluating, whether conscious or not, and so the process of abstracting may be considered as a *process of evaluating stimuli,* whether it be a "toothache," "an attack of migraine," or the reading of a "philosophical treatise." A great many factors enter into "perceiving," as suggested by the content of this symposium. As this seems to be a circular process, it is considered here on lower and higher levels of complexity (see page 200).

Processes of Abstracting.—Our knowledge today indicates that all life is electro-colloidal in character, the functioning of the nervous system included. We do not as yet know the intrinsic mechanisms, but from an electro-colloidal point of view every part of the brain is connected with every other part and with our nervous system as a whole. With such a foundation, even though it becomes necessary to investigate different aspects of the processes of abstracting for purposes of analysis, we should be aware that these different aspects are parts of one whole continuous process of normal human life.

Let us consider what our nervous system does when we "perceive" a happening or event. The term "event" is used here in the sense of Whitehead as an instantaneous cross-section of a process. Say we drop a box of matches. Here we have a first-order happening, which occurs on *nonverbal* or what are called the "silent" or "un-speakable" levels. The reflected light impinges on the eye, we get some sort of electro-colloidal configurations in the brain; then, since we are sentient organisms, we can react to those configurations with some sort of "feelings," some evaluations, etc., about them, on "silent" levels. Finally, on the verbal levels, we can speak about those organismal reactions. Newton may have said, about the falling matchbox, "gravitation"; Einstein may say "space-time curvature." Whatever we may *say* about it, the first-order happening remains on the silent levels. How we will *talk* about it may differ from day to day, or from year to year, or century to century. All our "feelings," "thinkings," our "loves," "hates," etc., *happen* on silent un-speakable levels, but may be affected by the verbal levels by a continuing interplay. We may verbalize about them, to ourselves or others, intensify, decrease them, etc., but this is a different problem.

In the following diagram (Figure 35) is given an extensional analysis of the process of abstracting from an electro-colloidal non-Aristotelian point of view. It is oversimplified and could be made more exhaustive. However, it is satisfactory for our purpose of explaining briefly the most general and important points.

Most of us *identify in value* levels I, II, III, and IV and react *as if* our verbalizations *about* the first three levels were "it" (see page 183 ff.). Whatever we may *say* something "is" obviously *is not* the "something" on the silent levels. Indeed, as Wittgenstein wrote, "What *can* be shown, *cannot* be said." In my experience I found that it is practically impossible to convey the differentiation of silent (un-speakable) levels from verbal levels without having the hearer

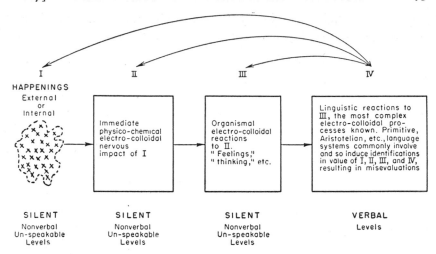

FIG. 35.—The process of abstracting from an electro-colloidal non-Aristotelian point of view.

or reader pinch with one hand the finger of the other hand. He would then realize organismally that the first-order psycho-logical direct experiences are not verbal. The simplicity of this statement is misleading unless we become aware of its implications, as in our living reactions most of us identify in value the entirely *different* levels, with often disastrous consequences.

Unfortunately, people in general, including many scientists, *disregard levels II and III completely,* and react as if unconscious that IV "is not" I. In other words, we do not take into account the mechanisms of the human nervous system or "think electro-colloidally" about our reactions. Such a disregard leads to misunderstandings, heated two-valued ("either-or") debates, hostilities, prejudices, bitterness, etc. In the history of "philosophy," for example, the metaphysical fight about "solipsism" simply ceases to be a problem when we become conscious that the only possible link between the inherently different silent (nonverbal) and verbal levels is found in their similarity of structure, expressed in terms of relations, on which the present non-Aristotelian system is based.

An awareness of the processes of abstracting clarifies the *structure* of a great many of our interpersonal, professional, etc., difficulties, which may become trivial or nonexistent if we become conscious of the identifications involved. Self-made problems often turn out to be no problems.

Statements are verbal; they are never the silent "it." One may have a nightmare that he "is" a Stalin. That may be innocent enough. One may have daydreams of being a Stalin. That is more serious.

One may proclaim consciously, "I am Stalin," and *believe in it,* and begin to shoot people who disagree with him; usually such a person is locked up in a hospital, and he usually is a hopeless case.

We see how the above diagram indicates human semantic (evaluational) mechanisms in the average individual who is hovering between sanity and semantic illness. It is well known that what would be only a dream to a "normal" person, "is reality" to a dementia praecox patient, who lives and acts accordingly.

These mechanisms also function pathologically in infantile adults, who live in a fictitious world built up on identifications.

The verbal levels, in the meantime, are of unique human importance because we can abstract on higher and higher verbal levels from I, II, III, etc. In human life, IV represents means for intercommunicating and transmitting from individual to individual and generation to generation the accumulated experiences of individuals and the race. I call this human capacity the "time-binding" characteristic.

The symbolic levels of behavior differentiate most sharply *human* reactions from signal reactions of lower, less complex forms of life. If those accumulated experiences are not properly verbalized, it may seriously twist or even arrest human development.

This simple diagram represents most complex processes, involving "perception" on different levels, problems of interpretation, verbal formalism, etc. Every type of human reactions from the lowest to the highest levels involves these mechanisms, the nonawareness of which may lead to disturbing, frustrating, or disastrous mis-evaluations and consequences. We will find later how this diagram applies to primitive and Aristotelian language structures.

I have stressed the serious or tragic aspect of our processes of abstracting here because I am attempting to convey the heavy life-value of what may otherwise appear too simple and obvious.

Verbal and Nonverbal "Thinking."—It will be noticed that I have put quotation marks around the word "thinking." This term usually implies a more "cortical" activity, indicating verbally some sort of a split between the functioning of the cortical and thalamic *regions* of our nervous system where there is actually no such split, but an interaction and integration on different levels.

"Is all thinking verbal?" Some say "yes," some say "no." If, however, we limit ourselves to verbal "thinking," we are caught in our old linguistic ruts of bygone generations, socio-culturally trained and neurologically canalized in the inherited forms of representation. Under such conditions we are unable or unfit to see the outside or inside world anew, and so we handicap scientific and other creative work. We speak so glibly about "freedom," never considering Willard Gibbs' *degrees of freedom* on which all our advance depends. A non-Aristotelian system involves that new orientation which ultimately leads to creative "thinking." Thus, an automobile has indefinitely more degrees of freedom than a street-car, which is "canalized" in its rails. Unfortunately and perhaps tragically, the majority of us "think" verbally, so characteristic of the Aristotelian subject-predicate orientation, and thus are handicapped in or prevented from creative "thinking." The physico-mathematical and so scientific way of "thinking" broke through those handicaps, and thus is at the foundation of creative scientific work, which brings to mankind so many benefits.

There is a tremendous difference between "thinking" in verbal terms, and "contemplating," inwardly silent, on nonverbal levels, and then searching for the proper structure of language to fit the supposedly discovered structure of the silent processes that modern science tries to find. If we "think" *verbally,* we act as biased observers and project onto the silent levels the structure of the language we use, so remaining in our rut of old orientations which make keen, unbiased observations ("perceptions"?) and creative work well-nigh impossible. In contrast, when we "think" without words, or in pictures or visualizations (which involve structure and, therefore, relations), we may discover new aspects and relations on silent levels, and so may formulate important theoretical results in the general search for a similarity of structure between the two levels, silent and verbal. Practically all important advances are made in that way.

Jacques Hadamard, the great mathematician, has made a study of how some outstanding mathematicians and scientists "think." I refer to his valuable little book on *The Psychology of Invention in the Mathematical Field* (11). The majority of these creative men reported that they "think" in terms of visual structures. "Most generally images are used, very often of a geometrical nature," he found (11, p. 114). I may mention here one of the questions which Hadamard asked in his questionnaire, to which Einstein gave an answer of particular interest to us here:

Question: It would be very helpful for the purpose of psychological investigation to know what internal or mental images, what kind of "internal word" mathematicians make use of; whether they are motor [kinesthetic], auditory, visual or mixed, depending on the subject which they are studying (11, p. 140).

Answer: The above mentioned elements are, in my case, of visual and some of muscular type. Conventional words or other signs have to be sought for laboriously only in a secondary stage, when the mentioned associative play is sufficiently established and can be reproduced at will. . . . In a stage when words intervene at all, they are, in my case, purely auditive, but they interfere only in a secondary stage as already mentioned (11, p. 143).[3]

Personally, I "think" in terms of pictures, and how I *speak* about those visualizations later is a different problem. I also notice a severe strain on my eyes when doing creative work, due to that visualizing, which seems to be related somehow to "perception."

In this connection I may refer also to a most important essay on "Mathematical Creation" by the great mathematician, Henri Poincaré (34), which was delivered in the first years of this century as a lecture before the Psychological Society in Paris.

Language becomes then a *medium* through which we eventually talk to ourselves or to others, with its own definite limitations. "The relation between language and experience is often misunderstood," Sapir found (40). "Language is not merely a more or less systematic inventory of the various items of experience which seem relevant to the individual, as is so often naïvely assumed, but is also a self-contained, creative symbolic organization, which not only refers to experience largely acquired without its help, but actually *defines experience for us* by reason of its formal completeness and because of our unconscious projection of its implicit expectations into the field of experience" (italics mine).

As Santayana said, "The empiricist . . . thinks he believes only what he sees, but he is much better at believing than at seeing" (21, p. 1).[4]

In *An Essay on Man,* Ernst Cassirer (7) discusses the "hunger for names" which every normal child shows at a certain age.

By learning to name things a child does not simply add a list of artificial signs to his previous knowledge of ready-made empirical objects. He learns rather to form the concepts of those objects, to come to terms with the objective world. Henceforth the child stands on firmer ground. His vague, uncertain, fluctuating perceptions and his dim feelings begin to assume a new shape. They may be said to crystallize around the name as a fixed center, a focus of thought.

But herein lies an important aspect of "naming" or "labeling":

The very act of denomination depends on a process of classification . . . they [the classifications] are based on certain constant and recurring elements

---

[3] By permission of Princeton University Press.
[4] Arabic-numbered page references to Korzybski's *Science and Sanity* are correct for all editions. References in Roman numerals are to the third edition; for corresponding pages in the second edition, subtract five.

in our sense experience. . . . There is no rigid and pre-established scheme according to which our divisions and subdivisions might once for all be made. Even in languages closely akin and agreeing in their general structure we do not find identical names. As Humboldt pointed out, the Greek and Latin terms for the moon, although they refer to the same object, do not express the same intention or concept. The Greek term (*mēn*) denotes the function of the moon to "measure" time; the Latin term (*luna, luc-na*) denotes the moon's lucidity or brightness. . . . The function of a name is always limited to emphasizing a particular aspect of a thing, and it is precisely this restriction and limitation upon which the value of the name depends. . . . in the act of denomination we select, out of the multiplicity and diffusion in our sense data, certain fixed centers of perception (7).[5]

A "name" (label) involves for a given individual a whole constellation or configuration of labeling, defining, evaluating, etc., unique for each individual, according to his socio-cultural, linguistic environment and his heredity, connected with his wishes, interests, needs, etc.

Cassirer makes some interesting comparisons between a child learning its first language and an adult learning a foreign language. I may add here that it happens that I was born into four languages (three different roots), and this has helped me not to be bound by words as I might have been if I had learned only one language as a child.

We see the seriousness of terminology, which is affected by *and also determines* our general *Weltanschauung*. In 1950 we must visualize the world in general as a submicroscopic, dynamic electronic process and life in particular as an electro-colloidal process of still much higher complexity (1, 2). What has made it possible for us to visualize an "object" and life in this way? Theories, verbalizations, built up for thousands of years, up to the latest discoveries of modern science. Thus, we find again that ceaseless circularity (see pages 200 ff.). The fact that we can "perceive" happenings, objects, or persons in this way has very important bearings on that whole process, as we will find later in our discussion.

Primitive Language Structures.—All languages have a structure of some kind, and every language reflects in its own structure that of the world as assumed by those who evolved the language.[6] Reciprocally, we read mostly unconsciously into the world the structure of the language we use. Because we take the structure of our own habitual language so much for granted, particularly if we were born

---

[5] By permission of Yale University Press and Mrs. Toni Cassirer.
[6] For the research supporting this theory, see Korzybski's *Science and Sanity*.

into it, it is sometimes difficult to realize how differently people with other language structures view the world.

The *structure* of anything, whether it be a language, house, machine, etc., must be in terms of *relations*. To have "structure" we must have a complex or network of ordered and interrelated parts. The only possible link between the nonverbal and verbal levels is found in terms of relations; and, therefore, relations as factors of structure give the sole content of all human knowledge. Thus, we may realize the importance of the structure of a language, any language. Bertrand Russell and Ludwig Wittgenstein were the important pioneers in devoting serious attention to the problem of structure (38, 39, 51). I cannot go into this problem in more detail here, except to try to convey its fundamental importance.

Among primitive peoples with one-valued "pre-logical thinking" the "consciousness of abstracting" is practically nil. The effect upon an individual produced by something inside his skin is projected outside his skin, often acquiring a demonic character. The "idea" of an action or object is identified with the action or the object itself.

The "paralogical" state is a little more advanced. Here the identifications are based on *similarities,* and differences are neglected (not consciously, of course). Lévy-Bruhl describes this primitive evaluational level by formulating the "law of participation," by which all things which have *similar* characteristics *"are the same"* (29; 21, p. 514). A primitive "syllogism" runs somewhat as follows: "Certain Indians run fast, stags run fast; therefore, some Indians *are* stags." This evaluational process is entirely natural at this level and lays a foundation for the *building of language* and higher order abstractions. We proceeded by similarities, much too often considered as identities.

Primitive men do not discuss abstract "ideas." As Boas has found, "The Indian will not speak of goodness as such, although he may very well speak of the goodness of a person. He will not speak of a state of bliss apart from the person who is in such a state." However, Boas concludes, "The fact that generalized forms of expression are not used does not prove inability to form them, but it merely proves that the mode of life of the people is such that they are not required" (3, pp. 64-67).

The use of abstract terms, such as a term for "goodness as such," made possible an enormous economy in communication, also a great increase in human time-binding progress, and ultimately it made modern science possible. In the meantime, the fact that we do abstract on higher orders becomes a danger if we are not conscious that we are doing so and retain the primitive confusions or identifications of orders of abstractions.

The following quotation [7] from "Being and Value in a Primitive Culture" by Dorothy D. Lee shows the extensional (by fact, rather than higher order verbal generalizations; see pages 190-93) type of language structure of the Trobrianders (25, p. 402):

If I were to go with a Trobriander to a garden where the taytu, a species of yam, had just been harvested, I would come back and tell you: "There are good taytu there; just the right degree of ripeness, large and perfectly shaped; not a blight to be seen, not one rotten spot; nicely rounded at the tips, with no spiky points; all first-run harvesting, no second gleanings." The Trobriander would come back and say "Taytu"; and he would have said all that I did and more. Even the phrase "There are taytu" would represent a tautology, since existence is implied in being, is, in fact an ingredient of being to the Trobriander. And all the attributes, even if he could find words for them at hand in his own language, would have been tautological, since the concept of taytu contains them all. In fact, if one of these were absent, the object would not have been a taytu. Such a tuber, if it is not at the proper harvesting ripeness, is not a taytu. If it is unripe, it is a bwabawa; if over-ripe, spent, it is not a spent taytu but something else, a yowana. If it is blighted it is a nukunokuna. If it has a rotten patch, it is a taboula; if misshapen, it is an usasu; if perfect in shape but small, it is a yagogu. If the tuber, whatever its shape or condition, is a post-harvest gleaning, it is an ulumadala. When the spent tuber, the yowana, sends its shoots underground, as we put it, it is not a yowana with shoots, but a silisata. When new tubers have formed on these shoots, it is not a silisata but a gadena. . . .

As being is identical with the object, there is no word for *to be;* as being is changeless, there is no word meaning *to become.*

It is significant, also, to find that the *temporal* differentiations and *temporal* generalizations which we have are absent among the Trobrianders:

Trobriand verbs are timeless, making no temporal distinctions. History and mythical reality are not "the past" to the Trobriander. They are forever present, participating in all current being, giving meaning to all his activities and all existence. A Trobriander will speak of the garden which his mother's brother planted, or the one which the mythical Tudava planted, in exactly the same terms with which he will refer to the garden which he himself is planting now; and it will give him satisfaction to do so . . . (25, p. 403).

The Trobriander has no word for history. When he wants to distinguish between different kinds of occasions, he will say, for example, "Molubabeba in-child-his," that is, "in the childhood of Molubabeba," *not a previous phase of* this *time, but a different kind of time* (25, p. 405; italics mine).

Many excellent papers and books have been written by anthropologists, psychiatrists, linguists, etc., on how different primitive

---

[7] By permission of *Journal of Philosophy* and the author.

people or different nationalities dissect nature differently in accordance with the structure of their language.[8]

The main characteristics of primitive or "pre-logical" and "paralogical" language structures may be summarized in their identifications of different orders of abstractions and their lack of abstract terms. The "perceptions" of people on primitive levels are often different from ours, different in the degree to which higher order abstractions are confused, identified with, and projected on lower order abstractions. They identify or ascribe *one value* to essentially many-valued different orders of abstractions and so become impervious to contradictions with "reality" and impervious also to higher order experience.[9]

Aristotelian and Non-Aristotelian Language Systems

Aristotelian Language Structure.—In mankind's cultural evolution, our current abstractions became codified here and there into

---

[8] Among the documentations of this are (25) and other works by Dorothy D. Lee; also (44).

[9] The following note was supplied by Miss Schuchardt: "It may be clarifying to elaborate briefly on some of Korzybski's views on primitive types of orientation and his use of the term 'primitive,' as I interpret them. It seems to me that he refers to certain complex socio-cultural, psycho-logico-linguistic, etc., levels of development and their attendant orientations found in different areas in the world. Considering our human class of life as a whole, we may assume that developments from 'primitive' to more advanced types of 'pre-scientific,' to 'scientific 1950' orientations, proceeded in degrees here and there, not linearly but, rather, 'spirally' in accordance with our understanding of ourselves and our environments (see pages 201-2). The developments of one culture were usually eventually intermingled with and carried along with transformations by other cultures.

"The reader is referred to (18), in which Korzybski first formulated his new definition of human beings as a 'time-binding class of life,' unique in that one generation can (potentially) begin where the former left off. This process can be handicapped or stifled in many ways. Korzybski stated in another context that 'The human understanding of time-binding as explained here establishes the deductive grounds for a full-fledged "science of man," where both inductive and deductive methods are utilized. . . . I had to include neuro-linguistic and neuro-semantic (evaluational) environments as environments, and also had to consider geographic, physico-chemical, economic, political, ecological, socio-cultural, etc., conditions as factors which mould human personalities, and so even group behaviour' (23).

"So far the highest orders of abstractions made by man, and those giving the greatest degree of predictability, may be observed in mathematical forms of representations (such as the tensor calculus). To bring to fuller expression the constructive potentialities of man in his ethical, socio-economic, etc., activities, and so keep pace with the achievements in mathematics, science, etc., and their technological consequences, was one of the main aims of Korzybski beginning with *Manhood of Humanity* in 1921.

"There seems no doubt that some primitive types of evaluation still survive in the orientations of most people in present-day Western cultures (and perhaps other cultures also, of which I feel incompetent to speak), involving dichotomies and conflicting premises, as in 'science *versus* religion,' etc. (23).

"I am aware that there are some who take exception to the findings of Lévy-Bruhl, Boas, and others. Korzybski, as far as I know, felt that they conveyed something of value in the analysis of these problems which still remain problems, and will continue to be analyzed with different interpretations and terminologies.—C.S."

systems, for instance the Aristotelian system. The term "system" is used here in the sense of "a whole of related doctrinal functions" (the doctrinal functions of the late Professor Cassius Keyser [17]). We are concerned with this structure here because of its still enormous influence on those of us whose language structure is of the Indo-European type.

I wish to emphasize here that in discussing the inadequacy of the Aristotelian system in 1950, I in no way disparage the remarkable and unprecedented work of Aristotle about 350 B.C. I acknowledge explicitly my profound admiration for his extraordinary genius, particularly in consideration of the period in which he lived. Nevertheless, the twisting of his system and the imposed immobility of this twisted system, as enforced for nearly two thousand years by the controlling groups, often under threats of torture and death, have led and can only lead to more disasters. From what we know about Aristotle and his writings, there is little doubt that, if alive, he would not tolerate such twistings and artificial immobility of the system usually ascribed to him.

Space limitations prevent my going into details here, and I can but refer the reader to my larger work on this subject, *Science and Sanity: An Introduction to Non-aristotelian Systems and General Semantics* (21). A rough summary in the form of a tabulation of Aristotelian and non-Aristotelian orientations given in that volume (21, pp. xxv ff.) may help to convey to the reader the magnitude of this problem.

Here I will stress some of the main structural considerations of the Aristotelian system and their effects on our world outlook, evaluations, and, therefore, even "perceptions." Practically since the beginning of Aristotle's formulations, and particularly after their later distortions, there have been many criticisms of them, mostly ineffective because unworkable. One of their most serious inadequacies was very lately found to be the belief in the uniqueness of the subject-predicate form of representation, in the sense that every kind of relation in this world can be expressed in that form, which is obviously false to facts and would make science and mathematics impossible.

I will quote the following remarks [10] of Bertrand Russell, who did epoch-making work in his analysis of subject-predicate relations :

The belief or unconscious conviction that all propositions are of the subject-predicate form—in other words, that every fact consists in some thing having some quality—has rendered most philosophers incapable of giving any account of the world of science and daily life . . . (37, p. 45; 21, p. 85).

[10] By permission of Harcourt, Brace & Co., Inc.

Philosophers have, as a rule, failed to notice more than two types of sentence, exemplified by the two statements "this is yellow" and "buttercups are yellow." They mistakenly suppose that these two were one and the same type, and also that all propositions were of this type. The former error was exposed by Frege and Peano; the latter was found to make the explanation of order impossible. Consequently, the traditional view that all propositions ascribe a predicate to a subject collapsed, and with it the metaphysical systems which were based upon it, consciously or unconsciously (39, p. 242; 21, p. 131).

Asymmetrical relations are involved in all series—in space and time, greater and less, whole and part, and many others of the most important characteristics of the actual world. All these aspects, therefore, the logic which reduces everything to subjects and predicates is compelled to condemn as error and mere appearance (37, p. 45; 21, p. 188).

In this connection I may quote some remarks by Alfred Whitehead, who also did most important work on this subject:

. . . the subject-predicate habits of thought . . . had been impressed on the European mind by the overemphasis on Aristotle's logic during the long mediaeval period. In reference to this twist of mind, probably Aristotle was not an Aristotelian (49, pp. 80-81; 21, p. 85).

The evil produced by the Aristotelian "primary substance" is exactly this habit of metaphysical emphasis upon the "subject-predicate" form of proposition (49, p. 45).[11]

The alternate philosophic position must commence with denouncing the whole idea of "subject qualified by predicate" as a trap set for philosophers by the syntax of language (48, p. 14; 21, p. 85).[12]

In his "Languages and Logic" Benjamin Lee Whorf makes an analysis of primitive and other language structures (50, pp. 43-52).

The Indo-European languages and many others give great prominence to a type of sentence having two parts, each part built around a class of words—substantives and verbs—which those languages treat differently in grammar. . . . The Greeks, especially Aristotle, built up this contrast and made it a law of reason. Since then, the contrast has been stated in logic in many different ways: subject and predicate, actor and action, things and relations between things, objects and their attributes, quantities and operations. And, pursuant again to grammar, the notion became ingrained that one of these classes of entities can exist in its own right but that the verb class cannot exist without an entity of the other class, the "thing" class. . . . Our Indian languages show that with a suitable grammar we may have intelligent sentences that cannot be broken into subjects and predicates.[13]

---

[11] From A. N. Whitehead, *Process and Reality.* Copyright 1929 by The Macmillan Co., and used with their permission and that of Mrs. A. N. Whitehead.
[12] By permission of Cambridge University Press and T. North Whitehead.
[13] Reprinted from *The Technology Review,* April, 1941, edited at the Massachusetts Institute of Technology.

The subject-predicate structure of language resulted from the ascribing of "properties" or "qualities" to "nature," whereas the "qualities," etc., are actually manufactured by our nervous systems. The perpetuation of such projections tends to keep mankind on the archaic levels of anthropomorphism and animism in their evaluations of their surroundings and themselves.

The main verb through which these outlooks were structuralized in our language is the verb "to be." Here I will give a very brief analysis of some uses of the little word "is," and what important effects its use has had on our "thinking." A full investigation of the term "is" has been found to be very complex. The great mathematician and logician, Augustus de Morgan, one of the founders of mathematical logic, has justly said, in his *Formal Logic* (1847) (8, p. 56):

> The complete attempt to deal with the term *is* would go to the form and matter of everything in *existence,* at least, if not to the possible form and matter of all that does not exist, but might. As far as it could be done, it would give the grand Cyclopaedia, and its yearly supplement would be the history of the human race for the time.

Here, following Russell, we can only state roughly that in the Indo-European languages the verb "to be" has at least four entirely different uses (36, p. 64):

1. As an auxiliary verb: It is raining.
2. As the "is" of existence: I am.
3. As the "is" of predication: The rose is red.
4. As the "is" of identity: The rose is a flower.

The first two are difficult to avoid in English, and relatively harmless. The other two, however, are extremely pertinent to our discussion. If we say, "The rose is red," we falsify everything we "know" in 1950 about our nervous systems and the structure of the empirical world. There is no "redness" in nature, only different wave lengths of radiation. *Our reaction* to those light waves is only our individual reaction. If one is a Daltonist, for example, he will see "green." If one is color-blind, he will see "gray." We may correctly say, "We see the rose as red," which would not be a falsification.

The fourth, the "is" of identity, if used without consciousness of the identifications implied, perpetuates a primitive type of evaluation. In some languages—the Slavic, for instance—there is no "is" of identity. If we say, "I classify the rose as a flower," this is structurally correct, and implies that our nervous system is doing the classifying.

The importance of that "is" of identity embedded in the structure of our language can hardly be overemphasized, as it affects our neuro-evaluational reactions and leads to mis-evaluations in the daily life of every one of us which are sometimes very tragic.

Here let us recall the "philosophical grammar" of our language which we call the "laws of thought," as given by Jevons (12; 21, p. 749):

1. The law of identity. Whatever is, is.
2. The law of contradiction. Nothing can both be, and not be.
3. The law of excluded third. Everything must either be, or not be.

These "laws" have different "philosophical" interpretations, but for our purpose it is enough to emphasize that (*a*) the second "law" represents a negative statement of the first, and the third represents a corollary of the former two; namely, no third is possible between two contradictories; and (*b*) the verb "to be," or "is," and "identity" play a most fundamental role in these formulations and the consequent semantic reactions.

"Identity" as a "principle" is defined as "absolute sameness in 'all' ('every') respects." It can never empirically be found in this world of ever-changing processes, nor on silent levels of our nervous systems. "Partial identity" or "identity in *some* respects" obviously represents only a self-contradiction in terms. Identification, as the term is used here, can be observed very low in the scale of life. It may be considered the first organic and/or organismal relating of "cause" and "effect," order, etc., when lower organisms responded effectively to signals "as if" they were actualities. On lower levels such organismal identifications have survival value. Laboratory observations show that the amoeba will exhibit reactions to artificial stimulations, without food value, similar to its reactions to stimuli with food value. The amoeba as a living bit of protoplasm has *organismally identified* an artificial, valueless-as-food, laboratory stimulus with "reality." Thus, although the reaction was there, the evaluation was inappropriate, which does not change the biological fact that without such identifications, or automatic response to a stimulus, no amoeba could survive.

Advancing in the scale of life, the identifications become fewer, the identification reactions become more flexible, "proper evaluation" increases, and the animals become more and more "intelligent," etc.

If identifications are found in humans, they represent only a survival of primitive reactions and mis-evaluations, or cases of underdevelopment or regression, which are pathological for humans.

Many of our daily identifications are harmless, but in principle may, and often do, lead to disastrous consequences. Here I give three examples of identification, one by a psychiatric hospital patient, another by a "normal" student of mine, and a third by a group of natives in the Belgian Congo.

When I was studying psychiatry in St. Elizabeths Hospital, a doctor was showing me a catatonic patient who was standing rigid in a corner. For years he had not spoken and did not seem to understand when spoken to. He happened to have been born and spent part of his life in Lithuania, where the people had been trained for several generations by the czar to hate the Poles. The doctor, without that historical knowledge, introduced me to the catatonic by saying, "I want you to meet one of your compatriots, also a Pole." The patient was immediately at my throat, choking me, and it took two guards to tear him away.

Another example is of a young woman who was a student in my seminar some years ago. She held a responsible position, but in her whole orientation she was pathologically fearful to the point of having daydreams of murdering her father because he did not defend her against her mother, who had beaten her and nagged her. During her childhood her brother, who was a number of years older and the favorite of their mother, patronized her, and she hated him for this attitude.

In this particular interview I was especially pleased with her progress and so I was speaking to her smilingly. Suddenly she jumped at me and began to choke me. This lasted only about five seconds. Then it turned out that she identified my smile with the patronizing attitude of her brother, and so she was choking "her brother," but it happened to be my neck.

There is another incident I want to tell you about that will indicate the problems we have to deal with (35, p. 52). We have all seen a box of Aunt Jemima Pancake Flour, with the picture of "Aunt Jemima" on the front. Dr. William Bridges of the New York Zoological Society has told this story about it: A United States planter in the Belgian Congo had some 250 natives working for him. One day the local chieftain called him and said he understood that the planter was eating natives, and that if he did not stop, the chief would order his men to stop work. The planter protested that he did not eat natives and called his cook as a witness. But the cook insisted that he did indeed eat natives, though he refused to say whether they were fried, boiled, stewed, or what not.   Some weeks later the mystery was cleared up when the planter was visited by a friend from the Sudan who had had a similar experience. Between them they figured out the answer. Both had received shipments of canned goods from the United States. The cans usually bore labels with pictures of the contents, such as cherries, tomatoes, peaches, etc. So when the cooks saw labels with the picture of "Aunt Jemima," they believed that an Aunt Jemima must be inside!

A structure of language perpetuating identification reactions keeps us on the level of primitive or prescientific types of evaluations, stressing similarities and neglecting (not consciously) differences. Thus, we do not "see" differences, and react *as if* two objects, persons, or happenings were "the same." Obviously this is not "proper evaluation" in accordance with our knowledge of 1950.

In analyzing the Aristotelian codifications, we have to deal also with two-valued, "either-or" types of orientation. Practically all humans, the most primitive peoples not excluded, who never heard of Greek philosophers, have some sort of "either-or" types of orientations. It becomes obvious that our relations to the world outside and inside our skins often happen to be, *on the gross level,* two-valued. For instance, we deal with day *or* night, land *or* water, etc. On the living level we have life *or* death, our heart beats *or* not, we breathe *or* suffocate, are hot *or* cold, etc. Similar relations occur on higher levels. Thus we have induction *or* deduction, materialism *or* idealism, capitalism *or* communism, Democrat *or* Republican, etc. And so on endlessly on all levels.

In living life many issues are not so sharp; therefore, a system which posits the general sharpness of "either-or" and so objectifies "kind" ("properties," "qualities," etc.), is too distorted and unduly limited. It must be revised and made more flexible in terms of "degrees." The new orientation requires a physico-mathematical "way of thinking." Thus if, through our unconscious assumptions, inferences, etc., we evaluate the event, the submicroscopic process level, *as if it were the same as* the gross macroscopic object which we perceive before us, we remain in our two-valued rut of "thinking." On the macroscopic level, if there are two apples side by side, for example, we perceive that they may "touch" *or* "not touch" (see Figure 36). This language does not apply to the submicroscopic process level, where the problem of "touch" or "not touch" becomes a problem of degree. There are continual interactions between the two on submicroscopic levels which we cannot "perceive." In accordance with the assumptions of science[1950], we must visualize a *proc-*

ess.[14] It follows that this is the way we should "think" about an apple, or a human being, *or a theory.*

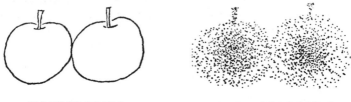

MACROSCOPIC   SUBMICROSCOPIC

FIG. 36.—Macroscopic view and submicroscopic process level of two apples, side by side.

There is no "perception" without interpolation and interpretation (21, pp. xxviii ff.). We cannot stop it. But we can visualize the latest achievements of mathematical physics and other sciences and read these into the silent un-speakable processes going on around us and in us.

The Aristotelian language structure also perpetuated what I call "elementalism," or splitting verbally what cannot be split empirically, such as the term *mind* by itself and the terms *body, space, time,* etc., by themselves. It was only a few years ago (1908) that the outstanding mathematician Minkowski said in his epoch-making address entitled "Space and Time," delivered at the 80th Assembly of German Natural Scientists and Physicians at Cologne, "The views of space and time which I wish to lay before you have sprung from the soil of experimental physics, and therein lies their strength. They are radical. Henceforth space by itself, and time by itself, are doomed to fade away into mere shadows, and only a kind of union of the two will preserve an independent reality" (32, p. 75).

This "union" of what used to be considered distinct separate entities had to be accompanied by a change in the structure of the language, in this particular case by the formulation of Minkowski's new four-dimensional geometry of "space-time," in which "space" and "time" were permanently united by a simple grammatical hyphen, thus making the general theory of relativity possible.

The old elementalistic structure of language built for us a fictitious, anthropomorphic, animistic world not much different from that of the primitives. Modern science makes imperative a language structure which is non-elementalistic and does not split artificially what cannot be split empirically. Otherwise, we remain handicapped by neuro-evaluational blockages, lack of creativeness, lack of understanding, and lack of broad perspectives, etc., and disturbed by inconsistencies, paradoxes, etc.

---

[14] For the significance of the date in small figures, see pages 191-92.

The points I have touched upon here: namely, the subject-predicate type of structure, the "is" of identity, two-valued "either-or" orientations, and elementalism, are perhaps the main features of the Aristotelian language structure that molded our "perceptions" and hindered the scientific investigations which at this date have so greatly, in many instances, freed us from the older limitations and allowed us to "see the world anew." The "discovery of the obvious" is well known to be the most difficult, simply because the old habits of "thinking" have blocked our capacity to "see the old anew" (Leibnitz).

Non-Aristotelian Language Systems.—As usually happens with humans, when we come to an impasse and find that revisions and new approaches are necessary, we do something about it. In this case, with the tremendous advances in science, a structure of language which did not falsify modern discoveries became imperative. As I do not know of any other non-Aristotelian system at this date, I must ask the reader's indulgence that I will have to speak rather exclusively about my own formulations. Many others have made applications, but here I will deal mostly with the theoretical side.

The new system is called "non-Aristotelian" since it includes the prevailing systems of evaluation as special cases within a more general system. Historically the Aristotelian system influenced the Euclidean system, and both underlie the consequent Newtonian system. The first non-Aristotelian revision parallels and is interdependent with non-Euclidean and non-Newtonian developments in modern mathematics and mathematical physics. To satisfy the need to unify exact sciences and general human orientations was one of the main aims of the non-Aristotelian revision, historically the latest, because of its much greater complexities (21, esp. p. 97).

The non-Aristotelian system grew out of the new evaluation in 1921 of human beings as a time-binding class of life (18). This evaluation is based on a *functional* rather than zoölogical or mythological approach and considers "man" as "an organism-as-a-whole-in-an-environment." Here the reactions of humans are not split verbally and elementalistically into separate "body," "mind," "emotions," "intellect," or different "senses," etc., by themselves, which affects the problems of "perception" when considered from a non-elementalistic point of view. With a time-binding consciousness, our criteria of values, and so behavior, are based on the study of human potentialities, not on statistical averages on the level of *homo homini lupus* drawn from primitive and/or un-sane evaluational reactions which are on record (23).

Common sense and ordinary observations make clear that the average so-called "normal" person is so extremely complex as to practically evade a nonsegmented, non-elementalistic analysis. In order to make such an analysis, it became necessary to investigate the main available forms of human reactions, such as mathematics, mathematical foundations, many branches of sciences, history, history of cultures, anthropology, philosophy, psychology, "logic," comparative religions, etc. It was found essential to concentrate on the study of two extremes of human psycho-logical reactions: (*a*) reactions at their best, because of their exceptional predictability, validity, and lasting constructiveness in the time-binding process, as in mathematics, the foundations of mathematics, mathematical physics, exact sciences, etc., which are manifestations of some of the deepest human psycho-logical reactions; and (*b*) reactions at their worst, as exemplified by psychiatric cases. In these investigations it became obvious that physico-mathematical methods have application to our daily life on all levels, linking science, and particularly the exact sciences, with problems of sanity in the sense of adjustment to "facts" and "reality."

In fact it was found that, to change the linguistic structure of our prevailing Aristotelian system, methods had to be taken bodily from mathematics. Thus, the structure of our language was changed through the use of extensional devices without changing the language itself. This will be explained briefly a little later.

When the premises of this new approach had been formulated, I found unexpectedly that they turned out to be a denial of the old "laws of thought" and the foundation for a non-Aristotelian system, the *modus operandi* of which I have named "General Semantics." The premises are very simple and may be stated by means of an analogy:

1. A map *is not* the territory. (Words *are not* the things they represent.)
2. A map covers *not all* the territory. (Words cannot cover all they represent.)
3. A map is self-reflexive. (In language we can speak *about* language.)

We notice that the old prescientific assumptions violate the first two premises and disregard the third (20, pp. 750 ff.; 24).

The third premise turns out to be an application to everyday life of the extremely important work of Bertrand Russell, who attempted to solve self-contradictions in the foundations of mathematics by his theory of mathematical or logical types. In this connection the term *self-reflexive* was introduced by Josiah Royce. The theory of mathematical types made me aware of new kinds of linguistic perplexities to which practically no one, except a very few mathematicians, had paid attention before. The realization and analysis of such difficulties led me to the discovery that the principles of different orders of abstractions, multi-ordinality of terms, $\frac{over}{under}$ defined terms, second-order reactions ("thinking" about "thinking," doubt of doubt, fear of fear, etc.), thalamo-cortical interaction, the circularity of human knowledge, etc., may be considered as generalizing the theory of mathematical types.[15]

The degrees to which we are "conscious of abstracting," which includes, among others, the above, becomes a key problem in the way we evaluate and therefore to a large extent may affect the way in which we "perceive." If we can devise methods to increase our "consciousness of abstracting," this would eventually free us from the archaic, prescientific, and/or Aristotelian limitations inherent in the older language structures. The following structural expedients to achieve this I call the *extensional devices,* and the application of them automatically brings about an orientation in conformity with the latest scientific assumptions.

Extensional Devices. 1. *Indexes,* as in x_1, x_2, x_3 . . . x_n; chair$_1$, chair$_2$, chair$_3$ . . . chair$_n$; Smith$_1$, Smith$_2$, Smith$_3$ . . . Smith$_n$, etc. The role of the indexes is to produce indefinitely many *proper names* for the endless array of unique individuals or situations with which we have to deal in life. Thus, we have changed a *generic* name into a *proper* name. If this indexing becomes habitual, as an integral part of our evaluating processes, the psycho-logical effect is very marked. We become aware that most of our "thinking" in daily life as well as in science is hypothetical in character, and the moment-to-moment consciousness of this makes us cautious in our generalizations, something which cannot be easily conveyed within the Aristotelian struc-

---

[15] In this connection see the following from Korzybski's paper on *Time-binding: The General Theory* (1926): "In my independent inquiry I came across difficulties and had to solve them or quit. My solution is given in the G. T. [General Theory] and the A. [Anthropometer or Structural Differential]. It is found that this theory covers the theory of mathematical types invented by Russell. . . . I knew about the theory of types long before. . . . I could not *accept* the theory of types because it is not general enough and does not fit in my system; as far as my work is concerned I had to dismiss it. Scientific method led automatically to a solution of my difficulties; and perhaps no one was more surprised and happy than myself when I found that the G. T. covers the theory of types" (22, second paper, p. 7).

See also *Science and Sanity,* p. 429: "The author was pleasantly surprised to find that after his *Ā*-system was formulated, this . . . *non-el* [non-elementalistic] theory covers the theory of mathematical types and generalizes it" (21). C. S.

ture of language. A generic term (such as "chair") deals with classes and stresses similarities to the partial exclusion or neglect or disregard of differences. The use of the indexes brings to consciousness the individual differences, and thus leads to more appropriate evaluation, and so eventually "perception," in a given instance. The harmful identifications which result from the older language structures are often prevented or eliminated, and they may become supplanted by more flexible evaluations, based on a maximum probability orientation.

2. *Chain-indexes,* as in $chair_{1_1}$ (in a dry attic), $chair_{1_2}$ (in a damp cellar) . . . $chair_{1_n}$; $Smith_{1_1}$ (under normal conditions) or, say (on the ground), $Smith_{1_2}$ (under extreme starvation conditions) or, say (in a plane at extreme altitudes). $Smith_1$'s reactions are entirely different in many ways under the different conditions.

The role of the chain-indexes is to provide a technique for the introduction of environmental factors, conditions, situations, etc. On the human level, these would include psycho-logical, socio-cultural, etc., factors.

In a world where a given "cause" has or may have a multiplicity of "effects," each "effect" becomes or may become a "cause," and so on indefinitely. As we know from psychiatry, for instance, a single happening to an individual in childhood may start a chain-reaction series, and color and twist his psycho-logical or even psycho-somatic responses for the rest of his life. Chain-indexes also convey the general mechanisms of chain-reactions, which operate not only in atomic fission, but everywhere in this world. We are particularly interested here that this includes organic processes, human inter-relations, and also the processes of time-binding, as expressed in the "spiral theory" of our time-binding energy (18, 1st ed., pp. 232 ff.).

Chain-indexes (indexing an index indefinitely) are not new in mathematics. They have been used automatically, but to the best of my knowledge a general pattern was not formulated for their application in everyday life. For an example of their use in a scientific problem, see "On the Use of Chain-indexing to Describe and Analyze the Complexities of a Research Problem in Bio-chemistry" by Mortimer B. Lipsett (30).

To recapitulate, for better or worse, we are living in a world of processes, and so "cause-effect" chain-reactions, and we need to have linguistic means for ourselves and others to manage our evaluations in such a world. Perhaps the formulation of a linguistic chain-index pattern will help this.

3. *Dates,* as in $Smith_1^{1920}$, $Smith_1^{1940}$, $Smith_1^{1950}$ . . . $Smith_1^t$. The use of dates places us in a physico-mathematical, four-dimen-

sional (at least) space-time world of motion and change, of growth, decay, transformation, etc., yet the representations of the *processes* can be *arrested* at any given point by linguistic means for purposes of analysis, clarity, communication, etc. This gives us techniques to handle dynamic actualities by static means.

Thus, it probably would make a good deal of difference whether a given automobile is a 1930 or a 1950 model, if we are interested in buying one. We are not as a rule similarly conscious of "dating" our theories, creeds, etc., however, although it is "well known" to what extent dates affect science, theories, books, different customs and cultures, people and all life included.

As another example, if we read the *Communist Manifesto* by Karl Marx and Friedrich Engels (31) we find the word "modern" on many pages. It is easy to evaluate the "modern" as "1950," which apparently many readers do. My suggestion is that when we find that word we put on the margin by hand the date "1848." With that dating, many arguments become antiquated, and so obsolete, because we are living in the world of 1950, which is entirely different.

4. *Etc.* The use of "etc." as a part of our evaluating processes leads to awareness of the indefinitely many factors in a process which can *never* be *fully* known or perceived, facilitates flexibility, and gives a greater degree of conditionality in our semantic reactions. This device trains us away from dogmatism, absolutism, etc. We are reminded of the second premise (the map does *not* cover *all* the territory) and indirectly of the first premise (the map *is not* the territory).

Incidentally, in the "etc." we find the key to the solution of mathematical "infinity," with important psycho-logical implications (21, chap. xiv).

5. *Quotes,* as in "body," "mind," "emotion," "intellect," etc., forewarn us that elementalistic or metaphysical terms are not to be trusted, and that speculations based on them are misleading or dangerous.

6. *Hyphens.* The use of hyphens links linguistically the actual empirical complex inter-relatedness in this world. There are most important structural implications involving the hyphen which represent recent advances in sciences and other branches of knowledge.

For example, the hyphen (*a*) in *space-time* revolutionized physics, transformed our whole world-outlook, and became the foundation of non-Newtonian systems; (*b*) in *psycho-biological* marks sharply the difference between animals and much more complex humans (in my interpretation of it). This differentiation is also on the basis of the present non-Aristotelian system, where "man" as a "time-

binder" is not merely biological, but psycho-biological. The hyphen
(c) in *psycho-somatic* is slowly transforming medical understanding,
practice, etc.; (d) in *socio-cultural* indicates the need for a new
applied anthropology, human ecology, etc.; (e) in *neuro-linguistic*
and *neuro-semantic* links our verbal, evaluational reactions with our
neuro-physiological processes; (f) in *organism-as-a-whole-in-an-
environment$_n$* indicates that not even an "organism-as-a-whole" can
exist without an environment, and is a fiction when considered in
"absolute isolation."

In regard to "psycho-biological" and "psycho-somatic," the original workers have missed the importance of the hyphen and its implications and used the terms as one word. This becomes a linguistic
misrepresentation, and these pioneers did not realize that they were
hiding an extreme human complexity behind an apparent simplicity
of a single term. They did this on the unjustified, mistaken assumption that one word implies unity; in the meantime, it is misleading
to the public because it conceals the inter-acting complexities.

Theoretical and Practical Implications. The simplicity of the
extensional devices is misleading, and a mere "intellectual understanding" of them, without incorporating them into our living evaluational processes, has no effect whatsoever. A recanalization and
retraining of our usual methods of evaluation is required, and this is
what is often very difficult for adults, although comparatively easy for
children. The revised structure of language, as explained briefly
here, has *neuro-physiological effects,* as it necessitates "thinking" in
terms of "facts," or *visualizing processes, before* making generalizations. This procedure results in a slight neurological delay of reaction, facilitating thalamo-cortical integration, etc.

The old Aristotelian language structure, with its subject-predicate
form, elementalism, etc., hindered rather than induced such desirable
neuro-physiological functioning. It led instead to verbal speculations
divorced from actualities, inducing eventually "split personalities"
and other pathological reactions.

We may recall the pertinent statement by the outstanding mathematician, Hermann Weyl, who wrote in his "The Mathematical Way
of Thinking": "Indeed, the first difficulty the man in the street
encounters when he is taught to think mathematically is that he must
learn to look things much more squarely in the face; his belief in
words must be shattered; he must learn to think more concretely"
(47).

Healthy normal persons naturally evaluate to some degree in
accordance with the extensional methods and with some "natural

order of evaluation," etc., without being aware of it. The structural formulation of these issues, however, and the corresponding revision of our old language structure, make possible their analysis and teachability, which is of paramount importance in our human process of time-binding.

There are many indications so far that the use of the extensional devices and even a partial "consciousness of abstracting" have potentialities for our general human endeavor to understand ourselves and others. The extent of the revision required if we are to follow through from the premises as previously stated is not yet generally realized. Our old habits of evaluation, ingrained for centuries if not millenniums, must first be re-evaluated and brought up to date in accordance with modern knowledge.

In what way does a non-Aristotelian form of representation bring about a change in evaluating processes and effect deep psycho-logical changes? We have seen how the structure of a language often determines the way we look at the world, other persons, and ourselves. My experiences, and the experiences of many others, confirm that we can and do evaluate stimuli differently as the result of the application of the non-Aristotelian extensional methods.

In practically all fields of human endeavor there are indications that new, more flexible, etc., attitudes can be brought about, with resulting influences on the interrelationships of the given individual with himself and others. A majority of these are in the field of education, but they include fields as diverse as psycho-somatic medicine, psychiatry, psychotherapy, law, economics, business, architecture, art, etc., political economy, politics, social anthropology, reading difficulties, etc.

The non-Aristotelian principles have been utilized in the United States Senate Naval Committee in connection with extremely important national problems such as "Establishing a Research Board for National Security" (45, p. 6), "A Scientific Evaluation of the Proposal that the War and Navy Departments be Merged into a Single Department of National Defense" (46), "Training of Officers for the Naval Service" (42, pp. 55-57). To the best of my knowledge today even on some ships in active duty the personnel are trained in some principles of general semantics (see also 33, esp. chap. i).

One of the main characteristics of the differences in orientation is that the Aristotelian language form fosters evaluating "by definition" (or "intension"), whereas the non-Aristotelian or physico-mathematical orientation involves evaluating "by extension," taking into consideration the actual "facts" in the particular situation confronting us.

For example, some older physicians still attempt to cure "a disease" and not the actual patient in front of them whose psychosomatic malfunctioning and manifestations, observed or inferred from the patient's behavior or record, involve a multiplicity of individual factors not covered by any possible definition of "a disease." Fortunately, today the majority of physicians try to cure the patient, not "a disease."

In his paper on "The Problem of Stuttering" Professor Wendell Johnson (13) speaks of the significance of the diagnosis of a child as "a stutterer":

Having *called* the child a "stutterer" (or the equivalent), they react less and less to the child and more and more to what they have called him. In spite of quite overwhelming evidence to the contrary, they assume that the child either cannot speak or has not learned. So they proceed to "help" him speak. . . . And when, "in spite of all their help" he "stutters worse than ever," they worry more and more. . . . There has been and still is a great deal of controversy among speech pathologists as to the most probable cause of stuttering. . . . But no one outside of general semantics has ever suggested that *the diagnosis* of stuttering was a cause of it, probably because no one outside of general semantics has appeared to realize the degree to which two persons talking about "stuttering" could be at variance in what they were talking about, and could be influencing what they were talking about. The uncertainty principle which expresses the effect of the observer on what he observes can be extended to include the effect of the speaker on what he names (pp. 189-93).[16]

Changes in *attitudes,* in our ways of evaluating, involve intimately "perceptual processes" at different levels. Making us *conscious* of our *unconscious assumptions* is essential; it is involved in all psychotherapy and should be a part of education in general. In this connection the extremely important and relevant work of Dr. Adelbert Ames, Jr., at the Hanover Institute and Princeton University, etc., is very useful in bringing about such consciousness. For example, Dr. J. S. A. Bois (4), consulting psychologist in Montreal and past president of the Canadian Psychological Association, in his report on "Executive Training and General Semantics" writes of his class in a basic training course in the non-Aristotelian methodology to seven key men of an industrial organization:

I proceeded to disequilibrate their self-assurance by demonstrating that our sensory perceptions are not reliable. . . . We ended by accepting the fact that

---

[16] By permission of M. Kendig, editor, *Papers from the Second American Congress on General Semantics* (Lakeville, Conn.: Institute of General Semantics, 1943), and of the author.

the world which each one of us perceives is not an "objective" world of happenings, but a "subjective" world of *happenings-meanings.*

They were quite ready to accept these new views, but I felt that it was necessary to make them conscious of the fact that it is not sufficient to "understand" certain principles and to accept them "intellectually." It is imperative to change our habitual methods of thinking, and this is not so easy as it seems. To bring this last point home, I explained to them the senary number notation system, and gave them some homework on it: making a multiplication table, long additions, subtractions, multiplications and divisions. The following day they were conscious that it is annoying, irritating, and not so easy to pass from one method of thinking to another. They realized that keeping accounts in the senary system would mean a revolution in the office and the factory, would demand new gears in the calculating machines, etc., etc. I felt the stage was set for the main part of the course. . . . It is impossible to evaluate quantitatively the success or failure of such a course. The fact that the top group wanted it to be given to their immediate subordinates is already an indication that they found it helpful.[17]

Bois reported further that the men made their own evaluations in terms of increased efficiency, better "emotional" control and maturity, better techniques of communication among themselves and with their subordinates, etc.

Observations made of a formalized group procedure at Northwestern University by Liston Tatum suggest that when people are forced to follow the "natural order of evaluation" (evaluating by facts first, then making generalizations) they talk to each other differently (43).

The effect of language on our visual evaluations is shown in a study reported by L. Carmichael, H. P. Hogan, and A. A. Walter (5, pp. 74-82) entitled "An Experimental Study of the Effect of Language on the Reproduction of Visually Perceived Form." It was investigated whether the reproduction of visual forms was affected when a set of twelve figures was presented with a name assigned to each figure. The subjects were to reproduce the figures as accurately as possible after the series was over. The same visual figure was presented to all subjects, but one list of names was given to the figures when they were presented to one group of subjects, and the other list of names accompanied the figures given to a second group. For example: kidney bean canoe. The results indicated that "the present experiment tends to confirm the observations of previous experimenters in this field, and to show that, to some extent at least, the reproduction of forms may be determined by the nature of words

---

[17] By permission of J. S. A. Bois.

presented orally to subjects at the time that they are first perceiving specific visual forms."

Professor Irving Lee has been trying out the above procedures on students in his classes in general semantics at Northwestern University and reports (in a personal communication to me) that so far his students do *not* react as the subjects in the above experiment did, but that his students "drew the pictures far less influenced by the labels applied."

Of his teaching of non-Aristotelian methodology to policemen, Lee has written a preliminary report of a three-year pilot study with 140 policemen, from patrolmen to captains, enrolled in the Traffic Police Administration Course in the Northwestern University Traffic Institute (27). From the reports of the instructors and interviews and information from a cross-section of the students after completion of the course, Lee writes, the results indicate that the policemen saw themselves and their work in the school in quite different light after advice on the extensionalizing processes.

Psychologists and others may be interested in the following personal communication giving preliminary data which indicate new fields of investigation in criminology, personality development, etc. Dr. Douglas M. Kelley, professor of criminology at the University of California at Berkeley, has recently written me:

At present I am concerned with the introduction of general semantics into two areas—interrogation and personality development. The first field is covered in a course which I give for 3 units, Detection of Deception, which consists to begin with of a half semester of straight general semantics, beginning with a discussion on the futility of words in communication and carrying right through to the various devices. The latter half of the course is concerned with the emotional relation of words as demonstrated by various types of lie detectors, and with report writing, where again the problems of multi-ordinality, etc., are dealt with at great length. A survey of all the existent literature indicates a complete lack of information in this area, and this approach purely based on your work reports an entirely new notion and opens up interrogative techniques and vistas hitherto unknown. It is my opinion from talking with a number of police officers that this approach will yield one of the most valuable results achieved from application of general semantics. In addition, I am teaching the same material to the Berkeley police force.

In my course on the Psychiatric Aspects of Criminology, a large amount of discussion is included, based upon your work, as a method of indicating how and why people behave like human beings, and what possibly can be done about it. The students are all most favorably inclined toward the general semantics orientation, and I expect within a year or so to have a real program developed.[18]

---

[18] By permission of Douglas M. Kelley, M.D.

During the Second World War Kelley [19] employed the basic principles of non-Aristotelian methodology with over seven thousand cases in the European Theater of Operations, reported on in his article "The Use of General Semantics and Korzybskian Principles as an Extensional Method of Group Psychotherapy in Traumatic Neuroses" (15). The principles were applied (as individual therapies and as group therapies) at every treatment level from the forward area to the rear-most echelon, in front line aid stations, in exhaustion centers, and in general hospitals. "That they were employed with success is demonstrated by the fact that psychiatric evacuations from the European Theater were held to a minimum," Dr. Kelley states (16, pp. vi-vii). "[The] other techniques are, of course, of value but these two simple devices [indexing and dating] proved remarkably potent in this type of neurotic reaction" (15, p. 7).

An example of the effect of indexing and dating, the main devices by which the structure of our language is made similar in structure to the world, may be seen by the reactions of a veteran from the Pacific Theater of War. This veteran was a student of Professor Elwood Murray at the University of Denver. I quote from the veteran's report:

An example of pure identification comes out in the veteran's dislike for rice. His first view of the enemy dead was that of a Jap soldier which was in the process of deterioration. The bag of rice the soldier had been carrying was torn open and grains of rice were scattered over the body mixed in with maggots. When the veteran, to this day, sees rice, the above described scene is vivid and he imagines grains of rice moving in his dish. To overcome this, he has eaten rice several times trying to remember the rice before him is not the same as that on the body. Though the food is not relished, he has succeeded in overcoming the vomiting reflex at the sight of rice (19, p. 262).

These mechanisms of evaluating or "perceiving" *similarities* and neglecting, or not being fully aware of, the differences are potentially present in every one of us, but usually not in such extreme degrees. This involves the lack of differentiation between the silent and verbal levels and nonawareness of our processes of abstracting. The different orders of abstractions are identified, an inference is evaluated *as if* it were a description, a description *as if* it were the nonverbal "object" our nervous system constructed, and an "object" *as if* it were the nonverbal, submicroscopic, dynamic process.

In our non-Aristotelian work we deal very little, if at all, with "perceptions" as such. As our attitudes, however, are bound to be

---

[19] During the war Dr. Kelley was Chief Consultant in Clinical Psychology and Assistant Consultant in Psychiatry to the European Theater of Operations; also Chief Psychiatrist in charge of the prisoners at Nuremberg.

involved with our "perceptions," it would appear that the investigation of the structure of language becomes relevant indeed.

A great deal of work has been and is being done in struggling with the problem of prejudices. Analyses show that the mechanisms of prejudices involve identifications of verbal with nonverbal levels. That is, an individual or group is evaluated by the label and not by the extensional facts (26, pp. 17-28; 28). In a discussion of mechanisms of prejudice and a report on his teaching of general semantics to approximately six hundred people where he stressed the confusion of observation and inferential statements, the response to labels as if they labeled more than aspects, etc., Lee reports one of his findings as follows:

Teachers reported greatly reduced tension when students came to apply what they heard to differences of opinion in the class discussions. The questions "Could they be called anything else?" "Is that an inference?" "Is that what could be observed?" put to a member making a sharp statement created a kind of game atmosphere. An example typical of many occurred in one discussion concerned with what people say about Negroes. Two of the participants most vocal in their assertions that "Negroes won't take advantage of education even if made available" were brought to scrutinize those assertions without the antagonism that results in the usual pro and con debating (28, p. 32).

It is of particular interest to consider the methods of the magicians, who have highly developed their art and even science for purposes of entertainment. Their methods of magic, however, have a deep underlying psychology of deception, self-deception, and misdirection. They have their own literature, so important for psychology, psychiatry, and daily life.

I quote from the paper by Dr. Douglas Kelley[20] entitled "The Psycho-logical Basis of Misdirection: An Extensional Non-aristotelian Method for Prevention of Self-deception" (14, pp. 53-60):

While the artist in conjuring never hypnotizes his audience, not even in India, he accomplishes much the same results by his ability to create illusions by giving a wrong direction to their expectations and assumptions. By this means he can make his public fail to see what is in front of their very eyes, or believe that they see what is not there (p. 53). . . . A general though unconscious belief in the three aristotelian "laws of thought" plays a part of major importance in the success of such misdirection, since there is a general tendency to react in terms of those "laws."

---

[20] By permission of M. Kendig, editor, *Papers from the Second American Congress on General Semantics* (Lakeville, Conn.: Institute of General Semantics, 1943), and of the author.

For instance, Dr. Kelley explains,

If a hat is faked with a false bottom, it may be shown to be apparently empty by the camouflaged lining in the bottom. If it is then tossed about in a reckless fashion, it simulates an empty hat since nothing drops out. Since, according to the two-valued "law of the excluded middle," an existent thing has certain "properties" or does not have them, and since most people following this law expect to see objects if they are present in a hat and expect them to fall out when it is inverted, they are easily fooled by the misdirection employed and consequently are unable to predict the appearance of the rabbit which is eventually drawn forth by the conjurer (p. 57).

Magicians find that children are much more difficult to deceive than adults, as the structural implications of our language have not yet to such an extent put their limitations on the ability of children to "perceive."

The Circularity of Human Knowledge

The electronic or electro-colloidal processes are operating on sub-microscopic levels. From the indefinitely many characteristics of these processes, our nervous system abstracts and integrates a comparatively few, which we may call the gross or macroscopic levels, or the "objective" levels, all of them not verbal. The microscopic levels must be considered as instrumentally aided "sense data" and I will not deal with them here. Then, abstracting further, first on the labeling or descriptive levels, we pass to the inferential levels, and we can try to convey to the other fellow our "feeling about feeling," "thinking about thinking," etc., which actually happen on the silent levels. Finally, we come to the point where we need to speak about speaking.

Scientifically it is known that the submicroscopic levels are not "perceptible" or "perceptual." We do not and cannot "perceive" the "electron," but we observe actually the results of the eventual "electronic processes." That is, we observe the "effects" and assume the "causes." In other words, as explained before, our submicroscopic knowledge is hypothetical in character. The world behaves as if its mechanisms were such as our highest abstractions lead us to believe, and we will continue to invent theories with their appropriate terminologies to account for the intrinsic mechanisms of the world we live in, ourselves included. We read into nature our own latest highest abstractions, thus completing the inherent circularity of human knowledge, without which our understanding of nature is impossible.

Because of what was explained in the first part of this chapter (pages 172-74), and aided by the extensional methods and devices, we must come to the conclusion that inferential knowledge is often much more reliable *at a date, after cross-verification,* than the original "sense data," with which historically we had to start and which have been found to be wanting.

In scientizing, the inferential data must converge. If they do not, we usually have to revise our theories. It is well known that when a new factor is discovered our older generalizations have to be revised for the sake of the integration of our knowledge (21, pp. xxviii ff.).[21]

Our inferences, as abstractions on other levels than the "sense data," may also be on lower or higher orders of abstractions. The structure of our recent knowledge is such that we read into, or project onto, the silent, submicroscopic process levels the highest abstractions yet made by man, our hypotheses, inferences, etc.

Thus, all our fundamental deeper knowledge must be, and can never be anything but, hypothetical, as what we see, hear, feel, speak about, or infer, is never *it,* but only our human abstractions *about* "it." What kind of linguistic form our inferential knowledge is cast in thus becomes of utmost importance. As Edward Sapir has put it, "We see and hear and otherwise experience very largely as we do because the language habits of our community predispose certain choices of interpretation" (41, p. 245).

This circular process of our nervous systems in inter-action with the environments turns out to be a "feedback system," a most happy term which has been introduced lately and which exactly depicts the situation. According to Lawrence Frank (10):

> We are shifting our focus of interest from static entities to dynamic processes and the order of events as seen in a context or field where there are inter-reactions and circular processes in operation. . . . The concept of teleological mechanisms, however it may be expressed in different terms, may be viewed as an attempt to escape from these older mechanistic formulations that now appear inadequate, and to provide new and more fruitful conceptions and more effective methodologies for studying self-regulating processes, self-orienting systems and organisms, and self-directing personalities. . . . Thus, the terms *feedback, servomechanisms, circular systems,* and *circular processes* may be viewed as different but equivalent expressions of much the same basic conception (10, pp. 190, 191).[22]

The mechanisms of "feedback" have been brought to their culmination in humans, and the process of time-binding itself may be considered as an unprecedented, unique organic spiraling of feedbacks.

---

[21] See (21, pp. xxviii ff.).
[22] By permission of *Annals of the New York Academy of Sciences* and the author.

In the exponential "spiral theory" given in my *Manhood of Humanity* (18, pp. 232 ff.), our time-binding capacity is obviously based on feedback mechanisms, chain-reactions, etc., without which humans as humans could not exist. The new understanding of humans as a time-binding class of life, free from the older crippling mythological or zoölogical assumptions, is one of the pivotal points toward a new evaluation of the unique role of humans in this world. It encourages or sponsors better understanding of ourselves, not only in relation to the world at large, but also toward ourselves.

I believe it is essential to begin with an entirely new functional formulation, with the implications which this involves for the study of "man" as "an organism-as-a-whole-in-an-environment," including our neuro-semantic and neuro-linguistic environments as environment.

In closing, I can find no more fitting summary than to quote the passages given below, which so beautifully and profoundly express the foundation of human knowledge.

It was Cassius J. Keyser who said:

. . . for it is obvious, once the fact is pointed out, that the character of human history, the character of human conduct, and the character of all our human institutions depend both upon what man *is* and in equal or greater measure upon what we humans *think* man is (17, p. 424).[23]

This inescapable characteristic of human living has been formulated differently, but just as aptly, by Dr. Alexis Carrel:

To progress again, man must remake himself. And he cannot remake himself without suffering. For he is both the marble and the sculptor (6, p. 274).

Arthur S. Eddington expresses himself in different words:

And yet, in regard to the nature of things, this knowledge is only an empty shell—a form of symbols. It is knowledge of structural form, and not knowledge of content. All through the physical world runs that unknown content, which must surely be the stuff of our consciousness. Here is a hint of aspects deep within the world of physics, and yet unattainable by the methods of physics. And, moreover, we have found that where science has progressed the farthest, the mind has but regained from nature that which the mind has put into nature.

We have found a strange foot-print on the shores of the unknown. We have devised profound theories, one after another, to account for its origin. At last, we have succeeded in reconstructing the creature that made the foot-print. And Lo! it is our own (9, p. 200).[24]

---

[23] By permission of Mrs. C. J. Keyser.
[24] By permission of Cambridge University Press.

BIBLIOGRAPHY

1. ALEXANDER, J.   Successive levels of material structure.   In J. Alexander (ed.), *Colloid chemistry.*   New York: Reinhold Publishing Corp., 1944.   Vol. V.
2. ALEXANDER, J.   *Life: its nature and origin.*   New York: Reinhold Publishing Corp., 1948.
3. BOAS, F.   Introduction.   In Smithsonian Institute, U. S. Bureau of American Ethnology, *Handbook of American Indian Languages.*   Part I. Washington, D.C.: U. S. Government Printing Office, 1911.
4. BOIS, J. S. A.   Executive training and general semantics.   Lakeville, Conn.: Institute of General Semantics, 1949.   (Mimeographed.)
5. CARMICHAEL, L., HOGAN, H. P., & WALTER, A. A.   An experimental study of the effect of language on the reproduction of visually perceived form.   *J. exp. Psychol.,* 1932, **15**, 73-86.
6. CARREL, A.   *Man the unknown.*   New York: Harper & Bros., 1935.
7. CASSIRER, E.   *An essay on man.*   New Haven, Conn.: Yale University Press, 1944.
8. DE MORGAN, A.   *Formal logic or the calculus of inference, necessary and probable.*   London: The Open Court Co., 1926.
9. EDDINGTON, A. S.   *Space time and gravitation: an outline of the general relativity theory.*   Cambridge: Cambridge University Press, 1920.
10. FRANK, L. K.   Foreword.   In L. K. Frank, G. E. Hutchinson, W. K. Livingston, W. S. McCulloch, & N. Wiener, Teleological mechanisms.   *Ann. N. Y. Acad. Sc.,* 1948, **50**, 189-96.
11. HADAMARD, J. S.   *An essay on the psychology of invention in the mathematical field.*   Princeton, N. J.: Princeton University Press, 1945.
12. JEVONS, W. S.   *The elements of logic.*   New York: American Book Co., 1883.
13. JOHNSON, W.   The problem of stuttering from the point of view of general semantics.   In M. Kendig (ed.), *Papers 2d Amer. Cong. General Semantics.*   Lakeville, Conn.: Institute of General Semantics, 1943.
14. KELLEY, D. M.   Mechanisms of magic and self-deception: the psycho-logical basis of misdirection; an extensional non-aristotelian method for prevention of self-deception.   In M. Kendig (ed.), *Papers 2d Amer. Cong. General Semantics.*   Lakeville, Conn.: Institute of General Semantics, 1943.
15. KELLEY, D. M.   The use of general semantics and Korzybskian principles as an extensional method of group psychotherapy in traumatic neuroses.   Lakeville, Conn.: Institute of General Semantics, 1948.   (Mimeographed.)
16. KELLEY, D. M.   Report in Preface.   In A. Korzybski, *Science and sanity: an introduction to non-aristotelian systems and general semantics* (3d ed.).   Lakeville, Conn.: International Non-aristotelian Library Publishing Co., 1948.
17. KEYSER, C. J.   *Mathematical philosophy: a study of fate and freedom.*   New York: E. P. Dutton & Co., Inc., 1922.
18. KORZYBSKI, A.   *Manhood of humanity: The science and art of human engineering* (1st ed.).   New York: E. P. Dutton & Co., Inc., 1921.   Same (2d ed.).   Lakeville, Conn.: International Non-aristotelian Library Publishing Co., 1950.
19. KORZYBSKI, A.   A veteran's re-adjustment and extensional methods.   *Etc.: A Review of General Semantics,* 1946, **3**, 254-64.
20. KORZYBSKI, A.   A non-aristotelian system and its necessity for rigour in mathematics and physics.   In *Science and sanity: an introduction to non-aristotelian systems and general semantics* (3d ed.) by the same author.   (Supplement III, first edition of *Science and Sanity,* 1933.)   Lakeville, Conn.: International Non-aristotelian Library Publishing Co., 1948.   Supplement III, pp. 747-61.
21. KORZYBSKI, A.   *Science and sanity: an introduction to non-aristotelian systems and general semantics* (1st ed., 1933; 2d ed., 1941; 3d ed., 1948).   Lakeville, Conn.: International Non-aristotelian Library Publishing Co.

22. Korzybski, A. *Time-binding: the general theory, Two Papers: 1924-1926.* Lakeville, Conn.: Institute of General Semantics, 1949.

23. Korzybski, A. What I believe. In *Manhood of humanity* (2d ed.) by the same author. Lakeville, Conn.: Institute of General Semantics, 1950.

24. Korzybski, A., & Kendig, M. Foreword. In *A theory of meaning analyzed: Critique of I. A. Richards' Theory of Language* by Thomas C. Pollock, and J. Gordon Spaulding, Elementalism: the effect of an implicit postulate of identity on I. A. Richards' *Theory of poetic value.* Gen. Semantics Monogr. No. III. Lakeville, Conn.: Institute of General Semantics, 1942.

25. Lee, Dorothy. Being and value in a primitive culture. *J. Philos.,* 1949, **13,** 401-15.

26. Lee, I. J. A mechanism of conflict and prejudice. In M. Kendig (ed.), *Papers 2d Amer. Cong. General Semantics.* Lakeville, Conn.: Institute of General Semantics, 1943.

27. Lee, I. J. The assumptions of the arrogant. *Education,* 1950, **70,** 509-11.

28. Lee, I. J. *How do you talk about people?* ("Freedom Pamphlets.") New York: American Education Fellowship, 1950.

29. Lévy-Bruhl, L. *Primitive mentality.* New York: The Macmillan Co., 1923.

30. Lipsett, M. On the use of chain-indexing to describe and analyze the complexities of a research problem in bio-chemistry. *General Semantics Bull.,* 1949-50, **1** & **2,** pp. 8, 9.

31. Marx, K., & Engels, F. *Manifesto of the communist party.* Translated by S. Moore. New York: International Publishers Co., Inc., 1932.

32. Minkowski, H. Space and time. In H. A. Lorentz, A. Einstein, H. Minkowski, and H. Weyl, *The principle of relativity: A collection of original memoirs on the special and general theory of relativity.* New York: Dodd, Mead & Co., Inc., 1923.

33. Naval Leadership. Annapolis, Md.: U. S. Naval Institute, 1949.

34. Poincaré, H. Mathematical creation. *Sci. American,* 1948, **179: 2,** 54-57.

35. *Reader's Digest,* March, 1947.

36. Russell, B. *Principles of mathematics.* Cambridge: Cambridge University Press, 1903.

37. Russell, B. *Our knowledge of the external world as a field for scientific method in philosophy.* La Salle, Ill.: The Open Court Publishing Co., 1915.

38. Russell, B. *Introduction to mathematical philosophy* (2d ed.). New York: The Macmillan Co., 1920.

39. Russell, B. *The analysis of matter.* New York: Harcourt, Brace & Co., Inc., 1927.

40. Sapir, E. Conceptual categories in primitive languages. *Science,* 1931, **74,** 578.

41. Sapir, E. As quoted in I. J. Lee, *The language of wisdom and folly.* New York: Harper & Bros., 1949.

42. Saunders, J. A. Memorandum: the new science of general semantics. In *Training of officers for the naval service: hearings before the Committee on Naval Affairs, U. S. Senate,* on S. 2304. June 13 and 14, 1946.

43. Tatum, G. L. *Preliminary investigation of a procedure for conditioning for discussion.* Unpublished master's thesis, School of Speech, Northwestern University, Evanston, Ill., 1948.

44. Thompson, L. In quest of an heuristic approach to the study of mankind. *Phil. Sci.,* 1946, **13,** 53-66.

45. U. S. Senate Calendar No. 549, Report No. 551, July 28, 1945. *Establishing a research board for national security,* submitted by Senator Byrd.

46. U. S. Senate Committee on Naval Affairs. *A scientific evaluation of the proposal that the War and Navy Departments be merged into a single Department of National Defense, March 13, 1946.* Washington, D. C.: U. S. Government Printing Office, 1946.

47. Weyl, H. The mathematical way of thinking. *Science,* 1940, **92,** 437-46. (See

also H. Weyl in *Studies in the history of science.* Philadelphia: University of Pennsylvania Press, 1941.)
48. WHITEHEAD, A. N. *The principle of relativity with applications to physical science.* Cambridge: Cambridge University Press, 1922.
49. WHITEHEAD, A. N. *Process and reality.* New York: The Macmillan Co., 1929.
50. WHORF, B. L. Languages and logic. *The Technology Review* (Mass. Inst. of Technology), 1941, **43**, No. 6. Also in M. Kendig (ed.), *Papers 2d Amer. Cong. General Semantics.* Lakeville, Conn.: Institute of General Semantics, 1943.
51. WITTGENSTEIN, L. *Tractatus logico-philosophicus.* New York: Harcourt, Brace & Co., Inc., 1922.

ADDITIONAL READINGS

CANTRIL, H., AMES, A., JR., HASTORF, A. H., & ITTELSON, W. H. Psychology and scientific research. *Science,* 1949, **110**, 461-64, 491-97, 517-22.
CASSIRER, E. *Substance and function and Einstein's theory of relativity.* Translated by W. C. SWABEY and MARIE C. SWABEY. La Salle, Ill.: The Open Court Publishing Co., 1923.
FARRINGTON, B. *Greek science: its meaning for us (Thales to Aristotle).* Harmondsworth, England: Penguin Books, 1944.
FRANK, P. *Einstein: his life and times.* New York: Alfred A. Knopf, Inc., 1947.
FRANK, P. *Modern science and its philosophy.* Cambridge, Mass.: Harvard University Press, 1949.
GEORGE, W. H. *The scientist in action: a scientific study of his methods.* New York: Emerson Books, Inc., 1938.
HALL, R. A., JR. *Leave your language alone!* Ithaca, N. Y.: Linguistica, 1950.
KEYSER, C. J. *The human worth of rigorous thinking.* New York: Columbia University Press, 1925.
KEYSER, C. J. *Mathematics as a culture clue; and other essays.* New York: Scripta Mathematica, Yeshiva University, 1947.
LEE, I. J. *The language of wisdom and folly.* New York: Harper & Bros., 1949.
LÉVY-BRUHL, L. *How natives think.* Translated by LILIAN A. CLARE. New York: Alfred A. Knopf, Inc., 1923.
MEYERS, R. The nervous system and general semantics. III. Perceptual response and the neurology of abstraction. *Etc.: A Review of General Semantics,* 1949, **6**, 169-96.
WIENER, N. *Cybernetics.* New York: John Wiley & Sons, Inc., 1948.

CHAPTER 8

TOWARD AN INTEGRATED THEORY OF PERSONALITY [1]

By URIE BRONFENBRENNER, Ph.D.

The Problem

It is now almost twenty years since Kurt Lewin expressed the conviction that psychology was ready to grow "beyond schools" and to strive for what he called "homogenization"—that is, the formulation of a unified body of theory, analogous to that of modern physics, to which all psychological phenomena might be referred (16). It is noteworthy also that the person whom he credited with having contributed more than almost any other to the achievement of this objective was Sigmund Freud.[2] It is the thesis of this paper that a synthesis of the ideas of Lewin and Freud provides a basis for the beginnings of an integrated system of psychological theory and that this system can be further extended and refined in the light of a number of contemporary and more recent contributions. The result will still be, in Lewin's words, "far from complete." Indeed, it may even leave matters in a less satisfactory state than Freud or Lewin had left them, but that is a risk which the present generation of psychologists must take if they wish to extend and solidify their science.

---

[1] This paper was prepared for the symposium on *Perception: An Approach to Personality* conducted at the University of Texas during 1949-1950. The ideas presented in the paper were developed in response to the needs of the planning phase of an interdisciplinary research program on constructive personality development recently initiated by the Department of Child Development and Family Relationships at the New York State College of Home Economics at Cornell University. For the stimulus of their questions, suggestions, and encouragement, the writer is indebted to his colleagues on the Planning Staff of the Research Project on Social Growth: Robert Dalton, Harold Feldman, Mary Ford, Doris Kells, Alexander Leighton, Dorothea Leighton, Robert MacLeod, and Robin Williams.

[2] "Freud's doctrine especially—and this is one of its greatest services—has contributed largely to the abolition of the boundary between the normal and the pathological, the ordinary and the unusual, and hereby furthered the *homogenization* of all the fields of psychology. This process is still far from complete but it is entirely comparable to that introduced in modern physics by which heavenly and earthly processes were united" (16, p. 22; see also pp. v-vi).

Prominent among the areas which remain virtually neglected in the present discussion is the biological sphere. While both Freud and Lewin imply that their theories are rooted in biology, neither indicates how the connection is made nor specifies the neurological and physiological correlates of psychological processes. In like manner, the other theories advanced in this chapter have little to offer on this score. This is not to imply the view that physiology is only of incidental importance to psychology. Rather, it reflects the opinion that neither field has as yet developed far enough at the molar level to permit a substantial theoretical fusion.[3] In any event, the fact remains that until the relationship between the physiological and psychological can be concretely specified, such theoretical integration as is achieved can only be regarded as partial. The present effort at synthesis is, of course, partial in many other respects as well. To take note of them would be to lengthen inordinately an already substantial introduction. Moreover, the most serious errors of "partiality"—in both senses of the terms—are not likely to be those of which the writer is aware.

In bypassing the biological sphere, both Freud and Lewin take as the focus for the development of theory the concept of personality. This seems entirely appropriate, for it is precisely the human personality which represents the first-order totality that psychology seeks to describe. As indicated in the title, the present chapter adopts a similar orientation. In view of this fact, the question naturally arises regarding the relevance of the discussion for a symposium on perception. It is true that any presentation of psychological theory must deal with this phenomenon implicitly if not explicitly. The role of perception[4] in the discussion to follow, however, is not merely a perfunctory one. Rather, it constitutes one of the major foci around which the theoretical material is organized. Specifically, the position is taken that perception—in particular the perception of interpersonal relationships—is the principal vehicle for the process of personality development. One needs only to add the questions of motive force and direction of movement to arrive at a statement of the core problems of psychology as a science.

The Function of Theory.—Before essaying the main body of discussion, it appears desirable to make explicit what is conceived

---

[3] The writer is not sufficiently trained either in physiology or in physics to weigh critically the significance of such developments as are now occurring in the theory of servo-mechanisms or in Koehler's work on psycho-physiological isomorphism. From what he can gather from his colleagues, these developments do not appear to warrant modification of the view expressed above.

[4] The term *perception* is used in its broadest sense as signifying the way in which the person structures his world and himself.

to be the role of theory in scientific method. For the purposes of this chapter, theory may be defined as an integrated system of concepts and hypotheses. This definition highlights the fact that a theory implies more than a series of propositional statements. There is the prior assumption of a particular set of constructs which dictates the selective organization of experience. In other words, a theory implies a particular way of perceiving the world.

This fact has considerable significance for the functional relationship between theory and observation. The beginning student of science frequently thinks of the former as distinct from and necessarily subsequent to the latter; that is, theories, if they are to deserve respect, must be based on facts, and facts are determined independently of theory. Such a notion is surely comforting, for it implies that there is a hard and fast line between fact and fiction and that the scientist begins and ends his explorations on the firm ground of objective reality. It is, of course, discomfiting to discover that this is not so. The scientist deals not with realities but with observations and, as has been repeatedly noted in this symposium, these two are by no means identical. From this point of view the problems of science are basically problems in perception; that is, scientific method, taken as a whole, represents man's attempt to recognize and overcome his limitations as a perceiving organism.

One of the functions of theory, then, is to provide the conceptual framework necessary for observation. Since observations are in part a function of this framework, it is well to make the concepts explicit from the outset, for only in this way is it possible for the observer or his colleagues to become aware of the omissions or distortions which the framework imposes. Moreover, it follows from the preceding discussion that the development of a conceptual system may make possible the perception of phenomena that otherwise would remain unobserved. From this point of view, a theory may be of great value even if it does not contain a single testable hypothesis but merely suggests a new way of looking at things.

This statement deserves special emphasis in view of the somewhat narrow conception of theory prevalent in large segments of our American psychology. For us a theory exists to be tested (and—one might add—to be found wanting). Ours is an attitude of determined skepticism that demands the immediate reduction of all theoretical propositions to hypotheses stated in operational form. That this is an ultimately desirable goal cannot be questioned, for without it we cannot achieve the aim of science, which is to demonstrate the necessary and sufficient conditions under which particular phenomena are observed to occur. But to exact this requirement at the very outset is to make the dubious assumption that scientfic wisdom increases by steps significant at the 5 per cent level. In the face of such exacting standards, it is not surprising that American psychology has created little theory of its own; we may modify or implement, but for original contributions we rely almost entirely on our European-trained colleagues.[5] Moreover, it is difficult for the would-be theorist to avoid being forced in one of two dissociated directions. If he covets his reputation as a scientist, he is under pressure to confine himself to the analysis of relatively simple phenomena where the variables are few, discrete, and susceptible to rigorous experimental control. The most significant aspects of human behavior, however, are not likely to be found in this category, for they are characteristically elusive and multideterminate. To wrestle with these at a realistic level and at the same time to face up to the expectations and criticisms of fellow-scientists take more time, energy, patience, and self-integration than many able men command. It is far easier to remain free of such demands by doing one's theorizing in a non-scientific context. As a result, it is perhaps possible to say—with only moderate exaggeration—that the study of human behavior in America shows a bimodal distribution with undisciplined speculation at one mode and rigorous sterility at the other.

Viewed in the perspective of this discussion, hypotheses should do more than serve as cannon fodder for the statistician. If we wish to grapple with the molar as well as molecular problems of human behavior, we must be ready to begin with vague gropings which only gradually begin to approach the clarity and specificity we have come to expect of hypotheses. If the problems of science are indeed problems in perception, this is simply a restatement of the manner in which the perceptual processes develop; that is, in the beginning perceptions are characteristically diffused, and only gradually do they differentiate to achieve precision and stability.

This view carries with it the implication that a great deal of observation and exposure to phenomena may be necessary (22) before one can—or perhaps even should—attempt to formulate and subject to statistical test precise statements of functional relationship. If, as many seem to prefer, the term "experiment" is to be reserved only for those situations in which such rigorous conditions are met, then much if not most of the work which awaits the psychological scientist cannot be called experimental. The term "explora-

---

[5] This is a personal opinion. The writer knows of no specific research on the subject, but it is his impression that studies of the comparative incidence of European- and American-trained psychologists among those who have made original contributions to theory would reveal a ratio overwhelmingly in favor of the former.

tory," however, would seem to be altogether acceptable. Taken in this sense, both exploration and experiment involve hypotheses. It may, therefore, be useful to distinguish between the *terminal hypothesis* designed to meet the requirements of rigorous experimental test and the *intermediate hypothesis* formulated for the sole purpose of guiding observation. The former must be couched in operational terms; the latter, although it strives for clarity and precision, need not be stated in testable or even communicable form. To serve its function it has only to make possible the extension or further differentiation of perception, thus yielding new observational data: In the last analysis, the intermediate hypothesis, like the conceptual framework from which it derives, is valuable only in so far as it leads ultimately to testable hypotheses of crucial significance for science.

The reader may suspect that the preceding discussion was undertaken partly in the hope of inducing him to be less critical of shortcomings in material to follow. Since professionally the present writer is at least one-third clinical psychologist, such motivations cannot be denied. It is true that the theories offered hereafter do not abound in hypotheses stated in operational terms. Even less conspicuous is the citation of supportive experimental evidence. In other words, such contribution as the theories represent lies chiefly in the areas of conceptual framework and intermediate hypotheses. The principal purpose of this introductory exposition is to suggest that it is precisely in these areas that most of our work must be done if we are to achieve maturity as a science.

In the discussion to follow we are concerned primarily with the work of five men. In addition to Freud and Lewin, these include Otto Rank, William McDougall, and Harry Stack Sullivan. Since it is manifestly impossible to deal with the major contributions of each in their entirety, it will be necessary to restrict discussion to those aspects which appear most significant for an attempt at theoretical integration. In this connection it appears important to note not only points that are critical for or consonant with a general theory but also those that are strikingly incompatible or leave crucial questions unanswered. Even with material thus confined, it will be necessary to resort to condensation and, in many instances, to forgo elaboration or example that might otherwise illuminate the discussion.

Lewin's Topological Theory of Personality

As indicated in the preceding section, the first problem with which any theory must come to grips, knowingly or unknowingly, is that of conceptual structure. Since, of the five men, only Lewin addresses himself directly to this question, it seems appropriate to begin with a consideration of his views (16, 17).

Lewin takes as his point of departure an almost militant position in behalf of the field—vs. class—theoretical approach to the study of human behavior: As evidenced by his use of this very dichotomy, he is not opposed to classification as such. His quarrel is with a conceptual system that requires organization of the phenomenal world in terms of rigid, mutually exclusive categories. For Lewin, nothing exists in isolation—each object is part of a large configuration encompassing other objects. It is literally a matter of wheels within wheels. Accordingly, the scientist is enjoined to order his perceptions not in terms of static categories but of dynamic interacting systems which manifest a greater or lesser degree of separateness or—in Lewin's terms—*abscission.*

The Psychological Field.—Consistent with this general view, Lewin emphasizes that personality can be understood only if it is viewed, not in isolation, but in relation to the field in which it operates. This leads directly into the most familiar aspect of Lewin's theory—his emphasis on the importance of the environment as a determinant of behavior and his analysis of the environmental field in terms of physicomathematical concepts—such as *valence, vector, barrier, detour,* and the like. Lewin stresses that, almost from the very beginning of life, these structural properties of the field are defined in large measure by social forces—by the intervention, control, approval, and example of other persons. Thus for the most part, the psychological field is determined by social rather than physical facts: In this connection it is important to recognize that for Lewin what is most relevant in the environment is not what is objectively there—the physical field—but what is perceived—the psychological field.[6] Thus it is perception that gives psychology its unique content and significance as a science.

This orientation illuminates three of the most provocative aspects of Lewin's theory. The first of these is his insistence on an ahistorical approach.[7] Proceeding from the thesis that cause and effect are necessarily contemporaneous, Lewin argues that the past as such is irrelevant to a consideration of the present, for only those forces can be operative that exist in the immediate situation; or to state this in more familiar language, history is relevant only to the extent that it lives in the here and now. Note, however, that with the immediate

---

[6] The objective reality is nevertheless important. (Cf. discussion of the "foreign hull," 17, p. 75.) Lewin is somewhat unclear and contradictory on this point.

[7] Cf. the excellent discussion of this problem by Chein (2).

situation defined not by what is objectively there but by what is perceived, a great deal of the past can and does become part of the active behavioral field.[8]

Second, for Lewin, the psychological environment includes not only the objective situation in which the individual finds himself but also his idiosyncratic distortions and fantasies—or what Lewin called the *plane of unreality*. Although the inclusion of this "private world" as part of the environment seems incongruous, it is, of course, fully consistent with the view that it is the situation *as perceived* that constitutes the life space.

Finally, the perceptual orientation puts in somewhat different perspective Lewin's emphasis on the power of the environment to evoke and direct activity. There is no question that, in terms of his theory, it is possible to change the person's behavior by changing the external situation, particularly its interpersonal aspects, but this is not be be interpreted simply as a direct influencing of the person from without. Lewin takes pains to specify that the "steering" of behavior is always "by the *perceptual field*" (16, pp. 48, 271, italics mine); that is, only those aspects of external reality can be effective which are selectively attended to, often with distortion, by the individual himself. Even such a concept as valence, which upon first consideration appears to be an attribute of the object, is seen upon analysis to arise from needs or tensions within the perceiving organism—the person:

> The close connection . . . between the perceptual field and the course of the process must not let us forget that the forces which control the course of the process remain without effect or simply do not arise when no psychical energies are present, when there exists no connection with tense psychical systems which keep the process in motion (16, pp. 50-51).

The Structure of the Person.—All of this focuses attention upon the central problem of personality itself. In line with his general orientation, Lewin conceives of the personality as a "differentiated region of the life space" (17, p. 216), a "more or less unitary and more or less closed" organization of interrelated *psychical systems* (16, p. 206). Although he never formally defines this last concept, it is readily apparent from his discussion that the psychical system denotes a disposition to respond in a particular way to selective aspects of the psychical field. Thus, the process of perception is seen to assume focal importance not only in Lewin's general theoretical

---

[8] Cf. Lewin's statement: "History, as the child has experienced it, is also a psychologically essential constituent of the things of the environment" (16, p. 77).

outlook but in his specific conception of personality structure and function.

Psychical systems are characterized by differences in degree of energy ("tension"), differentiation, and rigidity.[9] In the beginning they are few in number, relatively undifferentiated, and separated from each other and from the surrounding life space by boundaries that are comparatively fluid. It is this, says Lewin, which accounts both for the lability and the limited repertoire of infant behavior. The process of personality development is the gradual expansion, differentiation, and stabilization of psychical systems. This process, in turn, is to a large degree a function of the situational field; that is, although the person's view of objective reality is controlled by the psychical systems in existence at a particular point in his development, these systems are to some extent flexible and hence are altered by experience. The nature of this experience determines the modification, reorganization, and further differentiation of psychical systems.

> The effect of experience always consists in the fact that a person, upon the repetition of a situation, reacts not in the same way but in another way than that in which he reacted the preceding time . . . the effect of experience is always a change of the person or of the psychological meaning of the environment (16, p. 269).

In this connection experiences with other people play a major role. Specifically, the way in which adults structure the life space for a growing child dictates the intrapsychic structure. For example, if the psychological field is constricted, this induces rigidity of systems in the person; conversely, if the field is unstructured, the personality remains diffusely organized. From the developmental point of view, limitations of the child's own abilities call for a fairly complete structuring of his world by other persons, but as he grows older and becomes able to supply this structure for himself, increased freedom becomes essential if optimal differentiation is to occur.

This principle has special significance for the differentiation between reality and unreality. Lewin stresses the danger for the child's development of forcing too early and sharp separation between these two planes, for in the beginning, the child, in view of his undifferentiated structure, finds this discrimination very difficult. If achieved at all, it can be accomplished only at the risk of producing rigid boundaries which make it impossible for the person to shift readily from one level to the other, with the result that he can never

---

[9] These concepts are, of course, not new with Lewin; all three are found in classical Gestalt theory. Lewin's contribution is the extended application of the concepts to personality structure, function, and development.

articulate the two. Thus, he cannot recognize possibility for transition from the existing reality to one as yet unreal which might prove more rewarding. In Lewin's words, "Important as a sufficiently clear separation of these planes is, the kind of relation obtaining between them remains decisive of, among other things, all creative behavior. . . ." (16, p. 106).

In summary, Lewin views personality development as the resultant of a progressive reciprocal relationship—a kind of dynamic isomorphism—between personality structure and field structure. A change in the one necessarily evokes a change in the form, and presumably the content, of the other.

Critique and Summary.—This brings us to a critical gap in Lewin's theorizing. Although he disarmingly admits to incompleteness, his attitude toward one major question leaves him open to the criticism of evasion. Specifically, while in describing the psychological field he speaks of content as well as form (e.g., the field is composed of attractive and repelling objects, persons who control, punish, and reward, etc.), in discussing psychical systems, Lewin deals only with their organization and repeatedly shies away from specification of their source or content. Moreover, on at least three occasions when he finds himself face to face with this problem, he simply dodges it. The following comment is typical: "This is not the place for a more comprehensive discussion of the internal structure of personality" (16, p. 107).[10] Yet Lewin himself stresses that even though the structure of two individuals may be the same, "the content corresponding to the systems may be different and constitute *decisive psychological differences of the person*" (16, p. 209, italics mine). It is noteworthy that the first quotation above appears as a footnote to Lewin's most extended discussion of the self. Of the multiplicity of psychical systems which apparently exist, the self-system is the only one which he identifies by name. Even here, he talks all around it, points out that under certain conditions its boundaries become weakened, but never ventures to have a look inside (16, pp. 61-62, 106-10).

This is indeed an unfortunate oversight, for it is tantamount to evasion of the fundamental problem of motivation. We are told that there are systems of forces acting within and between the individual and his environment, but what these forces are, whence they come,

---

[10] Cf. "We cannot here discuss the possible sources of psychical energy as to content" (16, p. 52) ; also "The psychic tensions arise of themselves . . . by means of certain dynamic processes which we shall not here discuss" (16, p. 56).

and whither they impel, remain unanswered questions. True, Lewin does speak of needs, presumably of biological origin, which underlie the psychical systems and determine the forces of the psychological environment, particularly in the early years of life, but he never specifies what these needs are or how they establish connection with psychical systems. He merely resorts to the now familiar formula: "By a process of development (which I cannot here discuss more fully) in the course of the first year of life a psychological environment is formed . . . " (16, p. 175). Moreover, at one point, contrary to his own doctrine of the inadmissibility of exceptions (16, p. 24), Lewin states that "there also occur, occasionally, rather abrupt regulation phenomena (e.g., the sort of thing usually spoken of as the intervention of self-control or a willing) which cannot be deduced from the principles originally taken as a basis," but again, "It cannot here be discussed whether the explanation may always be attained in this way . . . ," for "Here we are faced with questions which embrace the whole field of life" (16, p. 65). A strange rationale, indeed, for avoiding the issue! Finally, one may argue that Lewin does offer directive principles for behavior in postulating that personality tends toward the attainment of dynamic equilibrium (16, p. 58), differentiation, and a happy medium between fluidity and rigidity. But, what is it that is being equilibrated, differentiated, and stabilized? Or, to put it bluntly, what is man? Lewin has given us a skeleton without flesh and blood, a moving skeleton perhaps—but still not a living human being. In a sense, in doing this, Lewin has achieved his ideal of a mathematical theory for psychology. His is a psychological calculus, complete with differentiation and integration, and with empty symbols for the variables. So long as the variables remain unspecified, the theory, as he himself implies, can offer no solutions to the problems of life.

Lewin, of course, did not stop at this point. He applied the theory in a variety of contexts—perceptual, genetic, and social; but, unfortunately, he never returned from these explorations to refine his formulation and give it body. "The place for a more comprehensive discussion of the internal structure of personality" was evidently not in this world. It remained for other theorists to make possible the filling in of the empty spaces in Lewin's brilliant topological map of the personality. Before turning to these contributions, it may be helpful to summarize the major principles explicit or implied in Lewin's position that appear most relevant for the development of an integrated view. It is convenient to organize these principles under two headings, as follows:

Personality Structure

1. Personality is conceived as a hierarchical organization of psychical systems. The latter may be defined as dispositions to respond in particular ways to selected aspects of the psychical field.
2. The self-system occupies a dominant position in this hierarchy and is distinguished by its relatively high level of segregation from the rest of the psychical structure.

Personality Development

1. Personality development is the process of gradual extension, differentiation, and stabilization of psychical systems.
2. Personality development is a function of changes in the environment—notably of the social environment—as they are perceived by the person.
3. At any point in its development, the personality structure both *affects* and *reflects* the structure of the psychological field in general and the interpersonal field in particular.
4. The forces determining personality structure exist only in the present. Hence, personality change can be effected only through modification of the immediate psychological situation.
5. Optimal conditions for personality development involve tolerance for unreality and a gradual shift from firm to fluid structure of the interpersonal field.

Freud's Genetic Theory of the Personality

When one speaks of Freud's theory, it is as with Van Gogh's art; one must specify the period if not the exact year. For just as both sought to lay bare man's inner being and did so in a fashion that was consistently recognizable, so also did each paint man somewhat differently over the course of the years. Freud specifically, though he expected orthodoxy of his disciples, himself never hesitated to alter psychoanalytic theory in the light of his experience. Moreover, conveniently both for the limited pocketbook and perseverance of most of us, he has on two occasions summarized his prolific ideas in a series of introductory lectures, the first completed in 1917 (9), the second [11] in 1932 (6). It is the latter which is taken as the principal text for our discussion, not only because it represents the

---

[11] There is also a third summary (11) which Freud was still working on at the time of his death in 1939. In view of its brevity and incompleteness, it is not comparable to the two sets of introductory lectures.

fruits of Freud's mature thinking, but also because the ideas there expressed seem more promising for the development of integrated theory.

Freudian Theory at Two Levels.—What are these ideas? At first glance, they seem hardly compatible with those of Lewin. Indeed, they border precisely on the kind of thinking to which Lewin objects so strongly, for Freud's is a theory which focuses on the past and abounds in either-or categories, autonomous instincts, and anthropomorphic divisions of the psyche. In true class-theoretical fashion, behavior is explained in terms of the category to which it belongs or by reference to its location in a spatial or temporal system. If one injures others, it is because of the death instinct in the id; if one sucks his thumb, bites his lip, collects paper matchbox covers, chases fire engines, has a crush on his teacher, or a pal, or the girl next door —it is because he is passing through, or has settled at, a stage in a predetermined sequence regulated by the inexorable clockwork of his sexual machinery. This brings us to the foundation of Freud's theoretical structure—a curious combination of biological and cultural determinism. On the one hand is the id with its genetically founded instincts and complexes which account for everything from minor "doodles" to God himself in terms of frustrated impulses of sex and aggression. On the other hand is the equally inevitable and demanding superego which "perpetuates the past," "the traditions of the race," and "the age-long values which have been handed down . . . from generation to generation" (6, pp. 95-96). Caught between these irresistible forces, and in addition exposed to the buffetings of a frustrating reality, is the ego—a rational and mild mediator in an irrational world of passion and power. In such a world, life at best can be no more than a self-deceiving compromise in which one is forced to deny the gratifications of direct instinctual expression and seek what solace one can from disguised, attenuated displacements.

Here, presumptuously condensed into a paragraph, is Freudian personality theory at its literal level—class-theoretical, instinct-ridden, culture-bound, and fatalistic. The presentation has been deliberately oversimplified and overstated in order to set into relief another somewhat contrasting view—one which, the writer believes, is also Freud's, but is not so readily discernible. To borrow Freud's own distinction, it is as if his theory existed at two levels—one the manifest, which we have just described; the other latent and elusive but, in a sense, more valid. To follow this analogy one step further: In undertaking to interpret latent content, one of course runs the risk of secondary elaboration. By this the writer wishes to indicate that what follows is likely to involve in significant measure a distortion of Freud's true views. It is, therefore, not altogether correct to say that it is Freudian theory; rather, these are inferences based on Freud's exposition.

The first postulate, however, involves no risks in interpretation; it speaks for itself. We have said that Freud's conceptual framework is class-theoretical. That this is true in many respects cannot be contested. But, at the same time, it is necessary to take note of passages such as the following:

I have no doubt that you are dissatisfied with the fact that the three qualities of the mind in respect to consciousness and the three regions of the mental apparatus do not fall together into three harmonious pairs, and that you feel that the clarity of our conclusions is consequently impaired. My own view is that we ought not to deplore this fact but that we should say to ourselves that we had no right to expect any such neat arrangement. Let me give you an analogy; analogies prove nothing, that is quite true, but they can make one feel more at home. Let us picture a country with a great variety of geographical configurations, hills, plains and chains of lakes, and with mixed nationalities living in it, Germans, Magyars and Slovaks, who, moreover, are engaged upon a number of different occupations. Now the distribution might be such that the Germans lived in the hills and kept cattle, the Magyars on the plains and grew corn and vines, while the Slovaks lived by the lakes and caught fish and plaited reeds. If this distribution were neat and exact it would no doubt give great satisfaction to a President Wilson; it would also be convenient for giving a geography lesson. It is probable, however, that you would find a less orderly state of affairs if you visited the region. Germans, Magyars and Slovaks would be living everywhere mixed up together, and there would be cornfields too in the hills, and cattle would be kept on the plains as well. One or two things would be as expected, for one cannot catch fish on the mountains, and wine does not grow in water. The picture of the region which you had brought with you might on the whole fit the facts, but in details you would have to put up with departures from it (6, pp. 102-3).

When you think of this dividing up of the personality into ego, super-ego and id, you must not imagine sharp dividing lines such as are artificially drawn in the field of political geography. We cannot do justice to the characteristics of the mind by means of linear contours, such as occur in a drawing or in a primitive painting, but we need rather the areas of colour shading off into one another that are to be found in modern pictures. After we have made our separations, we must allow what we have separated to merge again. Do not judge too harshly of a first attempt at picturing a thing so elusive as the human mind (6, p. 110).

One could hardly ask for more lucid statements of the field-theoretical view than these. Indeed, when so described, Freud's concept of personality structure does not seem so far removed from Lewin's organization of psychical systems. But before exploring this possibility further, it is well to take note of another theme in Freud's thinking that is not so explicit. We have noted that for Freud the attachments and antagonisms one experiences toward objects or persons are founded in the biologically determined psycho-sexual sequence and its critical turning point—the Oedipus complex. Yet, quite often throughout Freud's writings, particularly in the examples he cites, one gains the impression that not only the course but even the character of these feelings can be influenced by the conditions of life and, even more specifically, by the way in which one is treated by other people. Curiously enough, in the *New Introductory Lectures* this point is made most clearly not when Freud is presenting his own theory, but when he criticizes an errant disciple (Adler) for presuming to have "satisfied all the demands of psychoanalysis." He takes issue with Adler's doctrine of the "inferiority complex" by stressing that what is important is not the objective physical inferiority but how it is reacted to by others—whether they reject the child on account of his handicap or try to compensate for it with an extra amount of affection. "If you will bear in mind the importance of mother-love for the mental life of the child," says Freud, "you will be able to make the necessary corrections" in the misguided theory. He then follows this example with emphasis "upon an overwhelmingly important biological fact no less than upon a momentous psychological fact, namely the lengthy dependence of the human child on its parents and the Oedipus complex: These facts, moreover, are closely bound up with each other" (6, pp. 93-95). Here is a somewhat different approach to the biological basis of the oedipal situation. The classic attachment to the mother is seen primarily not in terms of tempestuous sexual desire but as the product of an inevitable dependency relationship.

Nor is this an isolated instance. Freud touches on the same theme in the exposition of a concept basic to his theoretical system—that of anxiety (7). Anxiety, he tells us, is the "perception of an affective state" involving the threat of libidinal discharge in the face of actual or anticipated danger. This reaction has its roots in the experience of the birth trauma but "the danger attending birth has still no psychic content" (7, p. 73). In other words, true anxiety is not merely a physiological but a psychological phenomenon involving perception. But what is it that is being perceived? Freud supplies the answer in very concrete terms.

Only a few instances on the expression of anxiety in infancy are intelligible to us; we shall keep to these. Thus, the three situations of being left alone, being in the dark, and finding a strange person in place of the one in whom the child has confidence (the mother), are all reducible to a single situation, that of feeling the loss of the loved (longed-for person). From this point forwards the way is clear to an understanding of anxiety . . . anxiety thus seems to be a reaction to the perception of . . . separation from a highly valued object. . . . The most basic anxiety of all . . . arises in connection with separation from the mother (7, pp. 75-76).

This central theme reappears in Freud's analysis of the oedipal conflict in women. He designates the dissolution of a dependency relationship as the crux of the problem; (in the place of fear of castration) " . . . for the other sex is found loss of love, obviously a continuation of the fear of the infant at the breast when it misses its mother" (6, p. 121). It is important to note Freud's use of the word "love" in each of these predominantly feminine contexts. While it does not exclude the connotation of eroticism and sexual possession, in both examples cited, it involves much more than this for here love clearly implies nurturant, supportive, and protective aspects. It becomes not merely an erotic experience but an affective relationship. That this broad interpretation is completely in accord with Freud's ultimate position is indicated by the following definitive statement.

I hope it will have been easy to gather the nature of my extension (on which so much stress has been laid and which has excited so much opposition) of the concept of sexuality. That extension is of a twofold kind. In the first place sexuality is divorced from its too close connection with the genitals and is regarded as a more comprehensive bodily function, having pleasure as its goal and only secondarily coming to serve the ends of reproduction. In the second place the sexual impulses are regarded as including all of those merely affectionate and friendly impulses to which usage applies the exceedingly ambiguous word "love." I do not, however, consider that these extensions are innovations but rather restorations; they signify the removal of inexpedient limitations of the concept into which we had allowed ourselves to be led (10, pp. 67-68).

One wonders why this broad concept of sexuality does not appear in Freud's exposition of the classical Oedipus complex. Specifically, why, in terms of Freud's argument, is not the fear of loss of love equally relevant for the male child? Freud does not answer this question.[12] What is even more significant for our purposes, however, is his change in view regarding the primary determinants of the oedipal anxiety.

It is true that the boy is afraid of the demands of his libido, in this case of his love for his mother. . . . But this being in love seems to him to be an internal danger . . . only because it involves an external danger-situation. And in every case we have investigated we have obtained the same result. It

---

[12] A speculative answer is suggested below; see pages 225-26.

must, however, be confessed, that we were not prepared to find that the internal instinctual danger was only a half-way house to an external and real danger-situation (6, p. 120).

Thus, even here, at the very crux of Freudian theory, we find a somewhat grudging reorientation away from narrow biological determinism toward emphasis upon forces in the external world, notably those emanating from interactions between people.

Parallelism in Freud and Lewin.—This brings us back to our comparative analysis of Freud and Lewin. It would seem that their incompatibilities lie principally at what Lewin would call the phenotypic level. If we go behind what might be termed the jargon of psychoanalysis, possibilities for reconciliation appear. Not only does Freudian theory have its field-theoretical aspects, but also, at a secondary level, it focuses attention on interactive processes as they are perceived and mediated through interpersonal relationships. Here indeed is a possible parallelism in theory. The writer would like to suggest that the correspondence is not limited to generalities but can be discerned as well in many of the specific constructs of each system. One needs only to follow Freud's own example. First, just as he has done with the divisions of the personality, we can divest other psychoanalytic concepts of their class elements and view them in terms of their possible meaning in a field theory. Second, having made these alterations we can examine their applications in the field of interpersonal relationships.

Let us begin with that die-hard of Freudian mythology—the instinct. We shall have to fetch up this lecherous creature from the depths of his abode in the reservoir of instincts and emotions and drag him onto the dry land of a situational field. In this setting, our Proteus takes on a more familiar shape. An instinct, Freud tells us, has a source, an object, and an aim; a *vector,* Lewin has said, has strength, direction, and a point of application. The strength of the vector is easily recognized as the energy of the instinct—the libido. Both the instinct and the vector have as their aim the discharge or redistribution of this energy. As with vectors, the energy of the instincts can be combined or displaced to other objects (cf. Lewin's substitute activity). In short, the properties of an instinct have their corresponding terms in the properties of the vector with one exception—the source. And we have already taken Lewin to task for his omissions on this score.

Having transmuted the instincts into vectors, it is far less difficult to find parallels in Freud for other dimensions of field structure. The cathexis—the investment of an object with libido—is readily translated as valence. Reality, as Freud sees it, is the barrier which produces the detours and substitutions that are the classical defense mechanisms of psychoanalysis. One of these, projection, becomes the equivalent for Lewin's unreality. But there is an important difference here. Freud, too, emphasizes the necessity of learning to distinguish between the real and unreal, but, unlike Lewin, he views the latter as an unmitigated evil. The task of the ego is to see the world as it is and to come to terms with it. To see it otherwise is to project—to distort reality. Such distortions are not to be tolerated. In Freud's words, "The ego has to observe the external world and preserve a true picture of it . . . it has to eliminate any element in this picture of the external world which is a contribution from internal sources of excitation" (6, p. 106). If such distortions persist, they are to be dealt with through therapy in which one is encouraged to bring one's projections to the surface, to look at them against the cold light of the analyst's ceiling, and to recognize them for the perversions that they are. Such a view is opposed to that of Lewin who, as we recall, insisted that the level of unreality is essential for optimal personality functioning, for it alone makes it possible for the individual to change the world and bring it into harmony with his own needs. Viewed from this perspective, Freud, with his implicit designation of objective reality as the ultimate value, appears, of all things, as the conformist—the defender of the status quo who despairs of any possibility to change the conditions of life. It is not within man's power to alter the world in his own image; the best he can hope for is to come to terms—to achieve what in recent years (and the writer suspects, under the influence of psychoanalytic thinking) we have aptly called *adjustment*. Here is a difference between Lewin and Freud which, indeed, seems irreconcilable. It is significant that the focus of this difference is a problem in perception—the degree to which man's needs are to play a part in the structuring of his world. To pursue this problem further, it is necessary to extend our comparative analysis of Freud and Lewin from the situational field to the person himself.

The Ego and the Self.—We have already noted the structural parallelism between Freud's divisions of the personality and Lewin's psychical systems. In so far as the latter's limited description permits, this parallelism may be applied to the two specific constructs of the Freudian ego and the Lewinian concept of self. Both occupy a central position in the personality structure; both maintain a relatively high degree of segregation or independence. Freud, however, goes much further than Lewin in indicating the character of this focal concept. For him it is more than a region with boundaries; it is a functioning agent, the uniquely psychological organ that perceives and interprets experience. Moreover, despite the fact that it is weak, the ego is not merely a passive entity, but exerts a measure of active direction over the forces that play upon it. This tendency is manifested particularly in relation to the phenomenon of anxiety, for it is the ego which, through mechanisms of inhibition and displacement, prevents the complete eruption of libidinal energies. Lawrence Kubie has described this situation in memorable terms:

> Anxiety is the ego's reaction to a state of tension (dis-equilibrium) which arises in the nervous system when the Mississippi threatens to overflow its banks—i.e. when excitatory processes are threatening to break through inhibitory barriers to flood the nervous system (14).

In this connection we have an interesting parallelism with the Lewinian concept of regression. The breakdown of inhibitory ego barriers in the face of overwhelming anxiety and the retreat to more rigid systems of defense corresponds closely to the dedifferentiation and return to more primitive psychical systems which Lewinian investigators described in the behavior of persons under conditions of increased tension (4). Under ordinary conditions of life, however, the ego maintains active control over the forces of the id. In Freud's own anthropomorphic language:

> On behalf of the id, the ego controls the path of access to motility, but it interpolates between desire and action the procrastinating factor of thought, during which it makes use of the residues of experience stored up in the memory. In this way it dethrones the pleasure principles, which exerts undisputed sway over the processes in the id, and substitutes for it the reality principle, which promises greater security and greater success (6, p. 106).

Not only does the ego exert control, but it accomplishes this through the aid of a cognitive process which makes possible the abstraction and organization of experience. This brings us to what Freud designates as the most distinctive aspect of ego-functioning—its integrative role.

> What, however, especially marks the ego out in contradistinction to the id is a tendency to synthesize its contents, to bring together and unify its mental processes. . . . It is this alone that produces the high degree of organization which the ego needs for its highest achievements (6, p. 107).

But it would be unlike Freud to close the discussion on so positive a note. In the very next paragraph he hastens to remind us that "the ego after all is only a part of the id. From a dynamic point of view it is weak." It cannot hope to achieve a genuine integration but must resort to "tricks" and be content with compromises. We can more readily understand why this must be so if we inquire into the origins of the constructive trend. Presumably it is rooted in Eros, the instinct of life, which "strives towards the synthesis of living substance into larger wholes." But side by side with Eros there is the death instinct "which acts against that tendency" and "whose aim is destruction." Thus, the former can never achieve its goal and the latter proves victorious in the end. Still, it is important to take note of a new emphasis in the functioning of personality—the tendency to integration.

The ego, of course, has yet another function. It observes, sets goals for, and punishes itself. This task requires the detachment of the ego from itself—a separation within the larger whole of a part that has the specialized function of self-judgment. This is the familiar superego [13] which, in Freud's words, is a "separate entity . . . in the ego . . . that enjoys a certain independence" (6, pp. 86-87). Here we verge again on the problem of personality development, but before we become involved in this it is important to note a major division implied in Freud's conception of personality structure which he himself seems to have overlooked. If there is a separation within the ego there must be at least two parts. One of these is the superego—but what is the other? Freud suggests the answer when he points out that the ego, in order to perform its judgmental function, must take itself as an object. To accomplish this, the ego becomes split into two parts—the observer and the observed. The first is, of course, the superego—the second can only be that which is perceived—the phenomenal self. We have then, in Freud's concept of ego three overlapping but, nevertheless, distinguishable entities. The first encompasses the other two and may be described as a functional system which strives to interpret, control, and integrate all psychic experiences. Occupying a special place among such experiences are those pertaining to an entity perceived as the self. The self, in turn, is interpreted and dealt with against a framework of expectations and standards derived from the culture as mediated by the family; this is the superego. While the self and the superego may be distinguished, it is important to note that one cannot exist without the other. Thus, the superego can have meaning only in terms of a self to which prescriptions and proscriptions are to be applied. Conversely, the self can be recognized only against the

---

[13] Within the superego, Freud distinguishes still another substructure—the ego-ideal—the standard of perfection by which the ego measures itself. The ego-ideal has a counterpart in Lewin's concept of level of aspiration. The latter, however, is far more a function of immediate experience and has little of the punitive character of the superego.

background of other selves—the society—or, to anticipate our theoretical development, what George Herbert Mead has called the *generalized-other* (23). This means, in effect, that self and society constitute complementary sides of a single whole. This totality has been designated by Cottrell as the "self-other" system (3). Freud's concept of ego is thus seen to have two major interdependent aspects; it is both a regulatory-integrative system and a self-other system. The first refers primarily to function; the second to content.

There is one fine point to be noted before we complete our discussion of Freudian personality structure. In his earlier writings Freud subdivided the personality into regions of consciousness and unconsciousness and spoke of conflicts between the ego and the unconscious system. In the second series of introductory lectures he repudiates this view. The term "unconscious" is no longer to denote a "mental province" but rather "a quality which mental things have." The reason for this change, Freud points out, is that unconsciousness cannot be restricted to a single system. There is one region which is totally unconscious—henceforth to be called the id—but parts of the ego and superego are also unconscious. What is this quality and what is its possible relationship to a field theory of personality structure? "We call unconscious," says Freud, "any mental process . . . of which we are not directly aware." In other words, there are aspects of the ego and superego—of the self-other system—which the self does not recognize. Or, to put it directly into Lewinian language, there are subsystems within the region of the self which are not in communication with each other, which are in a state of marked abscission. For Freud this condition is of special importance, for it bespeaks a failure in integration. To re-establish communication between regions and to articulate them with the impulses and energies of the id is the principal aim of therapy. It is Freud's battle cry: "Where id was, there shall ego be" (6, p. 112).

Personality Development.—We are now ready to return to the question of personality development. Is there any evidence that here too beneath the class-theoretical surface we may find a field-theoretical base? This question provokes an immediate answer from the material we have just examined. The ego, we have noted, is a "part of the id that has been modified by its proximity to the dangers of reality," and the superego in turn emerges out of the ego. This certainly suggests a process of differentiation, but let us look into the matter further. What is the specific course through which the ego develops? Freud supplies the answer in two concepts: object cathexis and identification. Impelled by the erotic impulses of the id, the ego invests libido in external objects and then incorporates them. The prototype for this reaction is the oral sucking orientation of the infant. The first object to be incorporated is the mother's breast, but this is rapidly generalized to the mother as a totality. Thus early in life, the principal object cathexes become other human beings. Identification, which follows upon object choice, is to be distinguished from it by the fact that the actual object is separated from the ego, but in its place there is retained a libidinally invested representation. In Freud's words, "If one has lost a love-object, or has had to give it up, one often compensates oneself by identifying oneself with it; one sets it up again inside one's ego, so that in this case object choice regresses, as it were, to identification" (6, p. 91). The process reaches its climax in the resolution of the Oedipus complex. The child is forced to give up the intense object cathexes which it has formed toward its parents and, to compensate for the loss, identifies with the parents; this "precipitate of the abandoned parent-cathexis" is the superego. Here we see the basis for Freud's classic statement: "The superego is the heir of the Oedipus complex."

But if we have maintained our field-theoretical set, we recognize in this two-phase process a familiar sequence—the extension (object cathexis) and differentiation (identification) of psychical systems. Moreover, we have a further indication of the process through which the structure of the interpersonal field is transmuted into the structure of the psyche. Personality develops through the integration into the psychical organization of the significant persons in the environment.

But what about the psychosexual zones which form the core of the Freudian developmental process? Let us examine these more carefully. At the manifest level they represent a series of stages—oral, anal, phallic, and genital—dictated by successive physiological maturation of erogenous areas. Upon further analysis, however, we discover that at the beginning the infant is polymorphous-perverse—that is, all modes of sexual expression are potentially open to him. It does not seem to be stretching the point to construe this as meaning that he is sexually undifferentiated. Also, in his second set of introductory lectures, Freud repudiates the view that each psychosexual stage gives place to the next; rather "each earlier phase persists side by side with, and behind, later organizations" (6, p. 137). In other words, we have a gradual expansion and differentiation of the sexual organization. Finally, we learn that this process is not restricted to the physiological sphere but extends into the realm of psychic structure. Thus from autoeroticism, where libidinal experience is limited to gratifications of his own body, the infant proceeds to narcissism in which "the ego behaves as if it were in love with itself" (6, p. 141). Moreover, "This narcissism is the universal original condition out of which object love develops later" (9, p. 360). This new development begins in the latter part of the anal stage in which "out of love for the person who looked after him" (6, p. 138) the infant begins to control his anal expulsiveness. "In the middle of this (anal) phase," says Freud, "there appears for the first time a consideration for the object, which is the forerunner of a later relation of love toward the object" (6, p. 136). This process, of course, reaches its climax in the genital phase, which is distinguished from the phallic in that it involves a genuine affective relationship. Thus we find that psychosexual genesis itself carries us, via a process of expansion and differentiation, from the soma to the self to the self-other. But if this is so, why is it that so much of Freud's discussion seems to focus on the erogenous zones? We have a possible answer for this question if we recall that he dealt primarily with neurotics, for these are precisely the persons who, because they cannot establish affective relationships with others, regress to or remain fixated at earlier levels. In Freud's language, the object libido is withdrawn or retained as ego-libido so that affective satisfactions are derived primarily from the self and its immediate somatic sensations. We have here a parallel to Lewin's concept of the "encystment of the self" in which the child confronted by an inescapably disagreeable situation" contracts physically and psychically" (16, p. 94).

Finally we should not leave Freud's theory of psychosexual genesis without taking note of an important developmental principle. Though ultimately it may pass beyond the soma and the self, psychological growth is initially provoked and paced by physiological changes in the growing organism. All bodily processes possess an affective charge, so that as new organs and systems mature (e.g. "the cutting of the teeth, the strengthening of the musculature, the control of the sphincters"; pubertal development), they impose demands for utilization and affective discharge. Such discharge of necessity implies invasion of the external world, particularly the world of other people. Thus, personality development becomes a function of the degree and manner in which the somatically rooted affective impulses find expression in the interpersonal context into which they inevitably intrude. If the process is facilitated by the persons who make up the psychological field, it culminates in the affective investment and differentiation of others as individuals in their own right.

Having reached the genital level, we can travel no further in Freud's conceptual domain, and since we are past midway in our journey, it is well to take stock of our theoretical possessions. Most of the principles which Lewin gave us still stand, but many gaps have been filled and much has been added. Above all, we no longer deal with mere shells of humanity bereft of flesh or feeling. Freud has provided the living clay for the Lewinian scaffolding. Indeed, as in the Greek myth, the statue seems all too real—nay, a veritable image of its maker. Perhaps it is this which explains the curious idiosyncrasies—the hopeless battle with a distant and threatening father, the guilt over sexual expression, and the preoccupation with the classical theological dilemma of good and evil. All these were the problems of the upper middle-class Austrian culture in which Freud grew up. They were what he saw in his patients and perhaps suspected in himself: Freud is reputed to have described himself as a cured neurotic and designated the *Interpretation of Dreams* (8) as the protocol of his analysis. If so, may all of us have as productive consequence for our self-therapeutic efforts.

Summary and Prospect.—But we have wandered from our task. We have yet to specify the additions to our theoretical structure made possible by Freud's contribution. Again, these are conveniently organized under two headings.

Personality Structure

1. The psychical systems comprising the personality are seen to have affective as well as cognitive aspects. In other words, the dispositions to respond differentially to selective aspects of the psychical field are always emotionally charged.
2. The self-system, or ego, is conceived not only in terms of structure but also in terms of function (regulative-integrative) and content (self-other).
3. The regulative-integrative function is made possible by a maturing capacity for abstraction and cognitive organization.
4. The self-system includes substructures which maintain a high level of abscission. In other words, the ego contains dispositions toward the self and toward others which are not accessible to awareness.

Personality Development

1. Personality development involves not merely the differentiation but also the progressive integration of psychical systems.
2. Psychological growth is provoked and paced by physiological changes in the growing organism. This physiological development involves cumulative differentiation of affectively toned processes which require for their expression invasion and consequent emotional investment of ever-widening dimensions of the environment—notably its interpersonal aspects.

3. The importance of the interpersonal field derives from the child's lengthy period of dependence on others for his comfort and survival. The interpersonal field thus becomes the principal context for the ever-widening investment of affective impulses.

4. As a result, the objective condition of dependence on others becomes a psychological dependence. The child comes to experience the need to be cared for by the persons in his environment.

5. It follows that at any point in its development, the personality reflects not only the structural properties of the psychological field but also its affective interpersonal content. In other words, the child's perception of whether he is loved is as important for his personality development as his awareness of the limits and expectations that others may impose. We shall designate these two dimensions of the psychological field as *structure* and *support*.

6. Personality development occurs chiefly through the integration into the ego of the other selves that are perceived in the psychological field.

7. Finally, it follows that the maximal extension, differentiation, and integration of psychical systems is achieved only when the individual has been able to relate affectively to the persons comprising his developmental life space.

But along with the progress he has enabled us to make, Freud has also added to our problems. First of all, there are a number of fundamental aspects of his theory which cannot be incorporated into the Lewinian framework that we have taken as our point of departure. Chief among them is the dualistic doctrine of motivation represented by the opposing forces of Eros and Thanatos (life and death). Second, there is Freud's dissident view regarding the place of levels of unreality in the psychical structure. Third, there is the conflict between Lewin's focus on the present situation and Freud's emphasis upon the past. Finally, much of what we have derived from the so-called latent level of Freud's thinking remains vague and incomplete. This is particularly true with respect to the specific organization of the self-other system and the precise nature of the seemingly osmotic process through which other selves are incorporated into the developing personality. It is for an answer to such unsolved problems that we turn to Rank, McDougall, and Harry Stack Sullivan. We shall find that we can deal with them more expeditiously than with Freud and Lewin, for much of what they have to say will be already familiar to us : This is not to detract from their contribution, for what we were able to achieve with both Lewin and Freud before us, they came to with the help of only one or, in McDougall's case, neither. And what is more, they were able to go beyond both.

Rank's Theory of Will and Relationship [14]

Otto Rank was a pupil of Freud who, like Jung and Adler before him, departed from orthodoxy, was criticized by his master, and ultimately divorced himself from the official psychoanalytic family. Although his thinking is rooted in his extensive experience as a psychotherapist, it has carried him, as indicated by the title of his last volume, *Beyond Psychology* (28), into education (27), esthetics (26), and general philosophy (28). The final statement of his psychological theories is contained substantially in two works, which fortunately have been translated and published together in a single volume (29).[15]

Although he writes in the now familiar context of psychoanalysis, Rank's ideas are by no means easily understood. Two factors contribute to this difficulty. First, he introduces a number of new concepts—such as will, life fear, and death fear, which lack the concreteness made possible by Freud's anthropomorphism, but at the same time, because of their abstract semitheological character, are no more congenial to the scientifically minded reader. But even if, by virtue of our experience in analyzing Freud, we are ready to look for psychological principles in nonscientific garb, our problems of comprehension are by no means solved. You may remember that in the introduction to this chapter it was argued that hypotheses may serve a highly important function even if they cannot be stated in communicable terms. We are about to reap the bitter fruits of this doctrine, for if difficulty in communication is any criterion of ultimate theoretical worth (which the writer trusts it is not), then Rank is a candidate for a very honored place in the gallery of science. In this connection let the writer make clear from the outset that there is no pretension here to understand all of what Rank is saying. Even where one thinks he sees the light, it would be presumptuous to say that one has grasped exactly what Rank had in mind. If one must read Freud at two levels, Rank is simpler at least by the criterion of parsimony; virtually everything is beneath the surface. Thus, once again the

---

[14] The writer is indebted to Dr. Max L. Hutt for introducing him to Rankian ideas and brilliantly elucidating their application in clinical practice.

[15] An excellent though understandably oversimplified statement of Rankian theory as applied in child therapy appears in Allen (1).

formulations to follow are to be regarded not as restatements of the theory but as interpretations of it.

One further fact is to be noted before we proceed with the discussion proper. Rank's statement of his theory preceded that of Lewin by several years and, insofar as can be determined, neither was familiar with the work of the other.[16] The relevance of this fact will become apparent upon consideration of Rank's principal differences with orthodox Freudian theory. Since they constitute an excellent introduction to his own views, we begin with an examination of them.

Past vs. Present.—First of all, Rank takes issue with Freud's emphasis on history and his assumption that therapy requires a restructuring of the past. In a somewhat different vocabulary, Rank states independently the now familiar Lewinian thesis that the past is relevant only to the extent that it lives in the present.[17] Specifically, he criticizes Freud for failing to recognize that unconscious impulses cannot be stored away but must be operative in the immediate situation.

At first Freud maintained that all experiences are thus retained [in the unconscious], then only certain traumatic ones and finally that the individual only regresses temporarily to certain experiences. The next step he did not trust himself to make, although he comes close to it in certain of his conceptions, possibly because the results would have overthrown the whole theory of repression into the unconscious, this literal picture of a heap of unreleased or traumatic experiences. In this sense there certainly are no unconscious complexes, nor even an unconscious in the topical sense of the word. The undischarged, unreleased, or traumatic experiences are not repressed into the unconscious and there preserved, but rather are continued permanently in actual living, resisted, carried through to an ending or worked over into entirely new experiences. Here in actual experience, as in the therapeutic process, is contained not only the whole present but also the whole past, and only here in the present are psychological understanding and therapeutic effect to be attained (29, p. 28).[18]

Here we have a position that is fully in accord with Lewin's, not only in terms of its ahistorical orientation, but also with reference to per-

---

[16] This information is based on conversations with Dr. Frederick H. Allen, one of the principal interpreters of Rank's work in this country (1).

[17] At some points, Rank approaches Lewin even in terminology (with due allowance for the translation in both instances); e.g., ". . . psychology itself, a pure psychology, cannot be historically oriented, cannot be static but only dynamic. In this sense pre-analytic psychology which occupied itself with the processes of feeling, willing, perception, thinking, was more psychological than psychoanalysis . . ." (29, p. 42).

[18] Cf. the following statement in the translator's introduction: "The content of the unconscious so far as set forth by analysis, might be conceived as a portrayal of what takes place in the analytic situation between analyst and patient projected into the individual's historical past" (29, p. xvii).

sonality structure. Rank completes the redefinition begun by Freud.
The unconscious is no longer even a quality, let alone a province of
the mind; rather it is an active dispositional system existing in abscission within the total personality organization.

Rank's emphasis on the primacy of the present has an important
corollary for therapy, for it implies that the person's childhood feelings toward his parents need not be worked through in their original
context. To the extent that they are important, and Rank agrees
that they are, they will be projected into the therapeutic relationship,
where they may be dealt with directly. This leads to Rank's second
major criticism of orthodox analytic theory and practice. He cen-
sures Freud for failing to grasp the constructive significance of resistance, projection, and other distortive mechanisms and for setting up
a false value in objective reality. It is only via such distortions, Rank
argues, that the person can learn to utilize reality creatively. This is
again Lewinian theory, but in more concrete and emphatic terms.
Psychoanalysis, Rank charges, makes a "secret ideal of the much
prized adaptation to reality which breeds patient docile Philistines"
(29, p. 200). This is not to imply that reality has no value. On the
contrary,

> The so-called "reality" upon which most neurotics and theories of neuroses
> place all the blame for neurotic suffering, proves to be the greatest help in the
> struggle of the individual against his internal ethical will conflict, because it
> affords him unburdening and objectification, displacement and rationalization,
> personification and denial, even more than the night time dream, which actually
> throws the ego entirely on itself, and accordingly is either painful or in waking
> reveals all these illusory mechanisms as deceiving or disillusioning. . . .
> The creative expression of the personality in real experience with all the
> deception of its emotional displacement and denial, is constructive (29, pp.
> 90, 92).

Rank's Major Constructs.—We can already discern the general
tenor of Rank's objection to the views of his teacher. He feels that
Freud has seen only the negative side of psychic phenomena and failed
to recognize in them the expressions of a positive force. This positive
force Rank identified as the *will*. Such a term understandably evokes
discomfort among those of us schooled in the American behavioristic
tradition. Lest we be confused by the personal connotations it has
for us, let us take careful note of what Rank means by this (for him)
central concept. In characteristic fashion, Rank prefaces his definition with a disavowal of any similarity to Freudian conceptions.

> The objection has been made that I am essentially saying nothing new
> because I simply use the word "will" in place of the Freudian "wish." There

is hardly an objection that would do Freud as well as myself greater injustice. Freud's psychology is anything but a doctrine of will, which he not only does not recognize but actually denies since he conceives of the individual as ruled by instinctual life (the id) and repressed by the super-ego, a will-less plaything of two impersonal forces. On the contrary, I understand by will a positive guiding organization and integration of self which utilizes creatively, as well as inhibits and controls the instinctual drives (29, pp. 111-12).[19]

But for us this is not an unfamiliar idea, for we met its prototype, paradoxically enough, in our analysis of Freud's concept of the ego. We shall have occasion to inquire into this paradox later. At the moment we have the task before us of examining the properties of the will and their implications for personality development.

The will, first of all, works to maintain and extend the integrity of the self and hence resists all attempts at limitation or external control. It is primarily this, and not the forces of repression from the past, which in Rank's view, explains the phenomenon of resistance encountered in orthodox psychoanalytic treatment. Thus what the Freudian analyst regards as weakness—the triumph of the forces of the death instinct over the forces of life—is for Rank a sign of a constructive process. Instead of attempting to oppose this process, the therapist should ally himself with it, for only then can the patient turn his energies from the maintenance of his self-system to its further development. This principle has an important corollary, for in Rank's view, the recognition of the existence and nature of the will makes Freud's postulation of the death instinct both unnecessary and invalid. What Freud regarded as forces of destruction are to be understood as manifestations of the active constructive struggle of the ego to preserve its integration in the face of therapeutic attack. Thus in Rank's view, Freud's introduction of the death instinct is to be understood as a rationalization, both for his patients and for himself, of his therapeutic inadequacy; the death instinct has no basis in fact (29, pp. 116-17).

There does exist, however, a death fear which is of major importance to the functioning of the will. In order to understand where the death fear comes from and what it is, we must take note of a second fundamental principle in Rank's theoretical system and one which also is not entirely new to us. Rank conceives of personality development as a series of progressive weanings from the primordial dependency relationship with the mother. This is the meaning of his concept of the trauma of birth, which, as he himself notes, has been interpreted too literally and thus robbed of its more important symbolic significance.

---

[19] For a strikingly similar but independent formulation, see Lecky's *Self-Consistency: A Theory of Personality* (15).

In order to prevent misunderstandings, I wish to call attention to the fact that my theory of the birth trauma is applied not so much from the point of view of content, as has been concluded from my first presentation (1923) but dynamically, as a universal symbol of the ego's discovery of itself and of its separation from the momentary assistant ego, originally the mother, now the therapist (29, p. 108).

Although this conception is similar to what we have already encountered in Freud (who gives Rank credit for contributing to its development), it differs fundamentally in one respect. For Freud, separation is inevitably a frustrating experience forced upon the infant from without. For Rank, it is an autonomous expression of the will. This does not mean, however, that the process does not involve conflict; for the act of separation requires the dissolution of an existing integration in favor of a new one, and this cannot be accomplished without anxiety. In Rank's words, there is "the fear both of going forward and of going backward" (29, p. 124). The latter Rank has designated as the death fear—"the fear of the loss of individuality" through remaining dependent. The former is the "life fear"—"the fear of birth," of moving out toward independence and thus disrupting the existing level of integration. Unlike Eros and Thanatos, however, the life fear and the death fear are not to be viewed as dichotomous entities derived from disparate sources. In Rank's words:

The two forms of fear which we have differentiated as life fear and death fear seem on closer examination to reduce themselves to a primal fear of the individual which only manifests itself differently in different situations. This ambivalent primal fear which expresses itself in the conflict between individuation and generation, is derived on the one side from the experience of the individual as a part of the whole, which is then separated from it and obliged to live alone (birth), on the other side, from the final necessity of giving up the hard-won wholeness of individuality through total loss in death (29, p. 134).

It is not difficult to recognize behind the symbolic terminology the familiar processes of differentiation and integration. It is important to note, however, that in Rank's conception the processes are operative not merely within the self but between the self and other persons. The nature of this interplay and its relationship to ego structure and ego development is indicated in the following description of the dynamics of the therapeutic process.

[The preceding discussion] . . . points to the multiplicity of roles falling to the therapist in the course of a treatment which are inherent in the case itself. Regardless of whether the patient gives to the therapist the role of a parent or spouse, of a brother, sister or friend, of a superior or inferior, temporarily or persistently, the therapist must penetrate beyond the concrete content to the ego of the patient and its division, if he is to understand and utilize the dynamics therapeutically. For the patient assigns to the therapist alternately the roles of a partial ego, whether it be now the impulsive ego, now the willing ego, or again the restraining fear ego, and of these selves the life relationships of the moment (parents, spouses, etc.) are only symbolic representatives (29, p. 168).

The projection of a part of the self upon the therapist, which we have designated as a first unburdening of the inner conflict, appears on the other side as the vanishing of the differences between the self and the other, the not-self (reality) (29, p. 176).

These passages illustrate how Rankian theory complements and extends the conception which emerged from our synthesis of Lewin and Freud. Here we see personality development as the successive expansion, differentiation, and integration of external self-other relationships which is paralleled by like processes within the intrapsychic self-other system.

Having established the general character of the Rankian growth process, we can now examine it in further detail. The first question that confronts us is that of the circumstances which are most likely to impede or facilitate successful self-other differentiation. In answer to this question, Rank points to "two great principles which oppose each other in every kind of emotion relation . . . love and force" (29, p. 64). The first is to be identified primarily with the role of the mother; the second with the father. We recognize in these principles the field dimensions of structure and support (see above, page 229), but Rank sees them as dynamically interrelated. The two principles are in opposition because love approves the will, enabling the individual to accept himself, while force challenges the will, provoking self-assertion. Both are necessary if the developmental process is to reach its goal, but a delicate balance must be kept between the two. For love without force tends to perpetuate the existing symbiotic relationship, while force without love creates an impossible situation in which the existing level of integration is threatened but nothing is offered in return. In either event, the will is confronted by a dialectic dilemma which can be resolved either through compliance or through active resistance.[20]

---

[20] An almost identical dialectic principle is advanced by Goldstein (12, 13). The following quotation is representative: "Normal, ordered life asks for a balanced relation between compliant and encroaching behavior. Only then can the individual realize himself, and assist others in their self-realization. Furthermore, the highest forms of human relationships, such as love and friendship, are dependent on the individual's ability and opportunity to realize both these aspects of human behavior. This is evident so far as self-restriction is concerned, but encroachment also belongs to every relationship between individuals. Love is not merely a mutual gratification and compliance, it is a higher form of self-actualization, a challenge to develop both one's self and another in this respect. This challenge involves aggression inasmuch

The Neurotic *vs.* the "Average Man."—This brings us to the principal focus of Rank's difference with Freud. In the words of Jessie Taft, Rank's translator and American editor:

> If one were to pick out the particular attitude which finally led Rank to a new comprehension of the therapeutic task on which he had worked in association with Freud for so many years, one might well select his complete respect for the personality of the neurotic patient (29, p. xi).

Rank's respect for the neurotic derives from the view already noted that resistance and symptom formation are expressions of strength— of the unwillingness of the ego to sacrifice its integrity to external demands or to accept conditions which are inimical to its own growth. From this it follows that the neurotic stands at a higher level of psychological development than the so-called healthy person who conforms to reality at the expense of his individuality and creative powers. In Rank's words "the neurotic . . . stands nearer to the creative type than to the average man" (29, p. 127). It is in defense of this thesis that Rank sounds the battle cry against the theories and methods of his teacher: In a preface, he states, "If psychoanalysis has emphasized in the creative individual, the human, yes, even the less than human instincts, I attempt to show in the neurotic the superhuman, divine spark" (29, p. 99). He then proceeds to take Freud to task for his superior attitude toward the patient. Psychoanalysis, he charges, is based on the "tacit assumption that the therapist, on the basis of his knowledge, is in the right and that the patient must be wrong, of which his suffering is the only proof" (29, p. 99). This orientation leads into the error of placing at the center of the therapeutic stage not the patient and his feelings but the therapist and his interpretations. On this last score, ironically enough, Rank accuses Freud of overintellectualization and underestimation of the role of emotional experience.

> The sick person actually does not need to be initiated into all the theoretical presuppositions and consequences which do not help him therapeutically and may easily lead him to the idea that he himself might become a therapist. Not only less theory but less "art of interpretation" is necessary since what is essential is the production and solution of reactions in the therapeutic situation (29, p. 5).

---

as it involves influencing—perhaps even coercing—another to do things which sometimes seem foreign to him. Self-restriction is experienced as inherent in human nature; it corresponds to what we call the ethical, to the norms. Our intrusion upon others is often experienced as a suffering that has to be endured, as one of the difficulties of life that must be borne. It is experienced as suffering because interference with one's own freedom or that of others has the appearance of injustice. But if one understands the necessity of such interference for one's own or another's sake, one can tolerate or enact it without self-accusation, and with less harm to others" (13, p. 207).

Knowledge alone does not liberate, but freeing through experience can bring the insight afterwards, although even this is not essential to the result (29, p. 106).

Rank goes further to assert that in our present age we suffer from too much consciousness. With a remarkable sense for the role of culture in the determination of mental disease, he traces the history of the modal types of neurosis from the Middle Ages to the present time and points to the gradual decrease in the frankness and frequency of hysterical symptoms in the face of the growing self-consciousness of the population from which psychiatrists draw their patients. In Rank's view the situation has come to the point where

. . . already there is a class of neurotics, or better said, of people, who essentially suffer from consciousness in that they are too conscious of themselves. To burden them with still more consciousness as the purely analytic therapy does, means to make their condition worse. What they need is an emotional experience which is intense enough to lighten the tormenting self-consciousness (27, p. 52).

But we must turn to our last major question. If the neurotic is but one step removed from the top of the developmental ladder, what is it that prevents him from attaining the summit? Rank's answer is twofold. In the first place, the neurotic suffers from guilt which immobilizes the will. This guilt stems from his unresolved dependency relationships and his efforts to free himself from their bonds. Moreover, he can see this struggle only in terms of its genesis in the past.[21] Accordingly he does not utilize the therapeutic possibilities available in present reality. Thus, in Rank's words, "the neurotic is a person who expresses his creative will exclusively within his own ego" (29, p. 154).[22] But in this restricted context growth is impossible, for ego development can occur only through the differentiation of relationships with other people.

The second difficulty follows from the first. Because he has been incapable of differentiation, the neurotic remains disintegrated. This lack of integration is evidenced both in his external relationships with

---

[21] This does not mean that the neurotic does not strive actively to alter his retrospective focus. "If the neurotic is a man who has need to forget more, or to repress more intensely, then it follows not only that he is more fixated in the past, but also that he struggles more actively to get free from it. If one emphasizes the former tendency more, then one accepts the infantile character; if, on the contrary, one emphasizes the latter aspect, then one recognizes therein the constructive striving of the individual to loosen himself from the past in order to be able to live independently of it in the present. That the neurotic comes to grief in this is no proof that he lacks this tendency, rather the opposite, for only he can wreck himself who attempts something" (29, pp. 34-35).

[22] Cf. Lewin's concept of encystment and Freud's withdrawal of object libido.

others and in his ego-structure. In terms of the former, he is incapable of differential response and can only resort to all-or-none reactions—to give or withhold himself completely. In terms of the latter, the neurotic is segmentalized; the various aspects of ego-functioning are carried on in isolation from each other.[23] It is this, Rank points out, which explains the sexual preoccupation, overt or covert, of the neurotic, which Freud seized upon as the basis for his theory.

It is not the biological form of sexuality which creates conflicts but the attitude of the individual, the relation of his personality to sexuality as such, which opposes itself to the ego as an alien force . . . (29, p. 137).

In contrast to the neurotic, the successfully differentiated person finds integration through creative action—the extension of the ego into the world of reality. Moreover, for ego-development to occur, such creativity must inevitably involve other people. Having begun as an integrated whole with the mother, the person can never find integrity within himself. He moves from dependence not to independence but to interdependence. By giving himself to others he receives in return the gift of the other's ego necessary for his own integration. Thus, the person may be said to create himself through contributing to the creation of other selves in the environment.

Now the creative can never be purely individual; the individually constructive must at the same time be collective, or at least work collectively in order even to attain constructive meaning (29, p. 99).

. . . [The creative type is the] artist who works in living human material, who seeks to create men not like parents, physically, but spiritually like God. . . . this likeness to God corresponds to a creating of one's self in another (29, p. 128).

Lewin, Freud, and Rank—A Summary.—The language is theological, perhaps mystical, but the parallelism with our earlier theoretical development is unmistakable. Rank represents a fusion of Lewinian and Freudian modes of thought. In a sense, he outdoes both at their own game. Not only does he advance Lewinian principles of growth, but he applies them in the new context of human relationships. As for Freud, he elevates to a primary role the experiential, interpersonal, and integrative themes we found buried beneath the surface. There remains the paradox of Rank's failure to comment on the presence of these trends in the work of his teacher and his sharp criticism of the man from whom the seeds of his own theory unquestionably spring. An answer to this paradox suggests itself when we

---

[23] The parallel with a rigid dedifferentiated organization of psychical systems is here self-evident.

recall the nature of the relationship between the two men. As a pupil of Freud, Rank in all probability was analyzed by him in accordance with the orthodox pattern—the impact of which he has eloquently described. At the time when he began differing from the views of his teacher, he wrote a book called *The Trauma of Birth* (25), which was originally dedicated to Freud. Following the latter's sharp criticism of this work, Rank, by his own decision, broke with his mentor. At the time of the separation, he wrote *Will Therapy* and *Truth and Reality*. Of the three volumes, the first emphasized the conflictful nature of separation; the remaining two stressed the rewards of differentiation in the form of creativity. It is perhaps significant also that Rank describes the concluding state of therapy as one in which the patient sees the therapist no longer as a positive force but as "the essential hindrance to his freedom of will and expression" (29, p. 189). The ending phase, he states, "can be represented as a battle for life heightened to the utmost between two individuals, one of whom must die that the other may live" (29, p. 179). In terms of Rank's own interpretive principles, it is not difficult on the basis of such symbolism to speculate why he found it necessary to emphasize his difference from Freud and to focus upon the limitations in the latter's work. Moreover, if these speculations be valid, we have concrete evidence in support of Rank's theory, for as the result of his separation he has arrived at a new level of integration—both personal and theoretical. The latter is summarized in the form of *additions* under the two familiar headings.

Personality Structure

1. The "regulatory-integrative system" of the ego is not merely reactive; it actively encroaches upon and creatively restructures objective reality in line with the dispositional sets of the psychical organization.[24]

Personality Development

1. The basic force motivating personality growth is a generalized impulse to integrated affective expression. Whether this im-

---

[24] This conception of the ego finds striking parallelism in the work of Hermann Rorschach (30). It is unfortunate that preoccupation with the technical aspects of his test has distracted attention from the theory which underlies it. The Rorschach determinants are in effect the perceptual expression of the dimensions of ego-functioning that have been delineated in the present paper. Thus, we have the factors of integration (W, D, Dd, and their interrelationships), regulation ($F+$), affective charge (color and shading), creativity (M), and articulation of relationships (FC and H). Here again is evidenced the intimate connection between personality theory and perception.

pulse appears externally as destructive or constructive depends on the dialectic balance between the forces of structure and support encountered in the interpersonal field.

2. Personality development is a function of progressive expansion, differentiation, and integration of external self-other relationships which is paralleled by like processes within the intrapsychic self-other system.

3. The developmental process progresses through the creative restructuring of objective reality. To be effective, this creativity must encompass the sphere of reciprocal interpersonal relationships. Thus, the person moves from the receptive dependence of infancy to the creative interdependence and self-determination of mature adulthood.

It is noteworthy that we have been able to add little under the heading of personality structure. It is as if Rank had taken heed of his own warning regarding the dangers of looking into the self. Thus, while Rank has resolved for us the conflicts presented by Freudian theory (the primacy of the past, Eros and Thanatos, and the role of the unreal), he still leaves unanswered questions regarding the content of the self-system and the manner in which this content is incorporated from other selves. For further wisdom in these matters we turn next to William McDougall.

McDougall's Theory of the Sentiments

One wonders whether the course of American psychology would have been any different had William McDougall begun his books not with a discussion of the instincts but of the sentiments. It is by token of the former that McDougall is known, and thereby he is condescendingly dismissed by many of us. The first four chapters of his *Social Psychology* (18) are about as much as most students can manage of his seemingly endless parade of innate tendencies reminiscent of the discredited faculty psychology of a bygone era. Yet, if one but steps over the threshold of chapter v, one finds himself among ideas that, far from echoing the past, are in the forefront of developments in current social psychology. True, the tone and phraseology partake of nineteenth-century morality and decorum, but this only sets in bolder relief the modernity of McDougall's formulations.

The Concept of Sentiment.—Central to all of these is the concept of the sentiment. Although McDougall acknowledges a debt to the English psychologists Stout (21, p. 307) and Shand (18, p. 126) for originating this construct, it has been justly said that "he passed beyond both in developing a full-bodied and consistent theory of the sentiments" (5, p. 253). His first statement of the theory appeared in 1908 with the publication of the first edition of *Introduction to Social Psychology* (18), and underwent a number of revisions over the course of the next twenty years (19, 20, 21). These developments have been excellently summarized by French (5). The best concise definition of sentiment is contained in McDougall's initial presentation; it is defined as "an organized system of emotional dispositions about the idea of some object" (18, p. 164). McDougall emphasizes that the sentiment is an integrate involving affective, conative, and cognitive dimensions. The first two are intimately linked and represent the functional aspect of the system; the last contributes the structural framework (21, pp. 308-10). The total number of possible sentiments is very large. McDougall suggests two ways in which they may be classified: (*a*) according to broad categories of content such as love, hate, and respect, or (*b*) in terms of level of generality ranging from the concrete (e.g., love for a particular child) to the abstract (e.g., love of justice). Through the association of emotions and objects in experience sentiments grow cumulatively. Thus, "each sentiment has a life history, like every other vital organization. It is gradually built up, increasing in complexity and strength and may continue to grow indefinitely . . . " (18, p. 168). The nature of the total sentiment organization comprising the personality is conveniently summarized by McDougall himself.

Development of integrated character consists in the growth of a harmonious system of the sentiments, a hierarchial system in which the working of the sentiments for the more concrete objects is regulated and controlled by the sentiments for general and more abstract and ideal objects, such as devotion to the family, the clan, the occupational or civic group, the nation, or mankind, the love of justice, humanity, liberty, equality, fraternity; and by hatred for cruelty, for injustice, for oppression, for slavery. And volition in the full and higher sense implies that this hierarchy of sentiments culminates in and is presided over by a sentiment of self-regard which, by incorporating in its system these higher abstract sentiments, has become an ideal of self, an ideal of character and of conduct to which our daily actions must conform and with which our long-range motivations, our ambition and personal loyalties, must harmonize (21, p. 337).

It is unfortunate for present-day psychological theory that D. K. Adams of Duke University has not as yet put to paper his brilliant comparative analysis of McDougall and Lewin. Adams asserts that not only can McDougall's theory be directly translated into Lewinian language but that, in addition, it carries through the logical implications of Lewin's conception further than he was able to do himself. For example, the structure and development of sentiments can be directly compared to the organization and differentiation of psychical systems [25] and the usually dominant sentiment of self-regard corresponds to Lewin's central concept of the self. McDougall goes beyond Lewin, however, in his emphasis on the affective dimension (21, pp. 233-35), his focus upon the integrated character of the system, his stress upon the concept of volition, and above all in his specification of the content and development of the self and the self-regarding sentiment. For our purposes, the first two require no further comment, the second calls for only brief elaboration, but the last deserves a careful examination, for it contributes new elements to the theoretical picture.

McDougall defines volition as "the supporting or re-enforcing of a desire or conation by the cooperation of an impulse excited within the system of the self-regarding sentiment" (18, p. 255). For him, the role of volition is essentially a moral one; it permits "mastery over some stronger, coarser desire of our primitive animal nature" by adding itself "to the weaker ideal motive" (18, p. 254). But this aspect of the problem is not our concern. We need only take note that the concept includes the active quality which is the crux of the Rankian idea of will and that volition, like will, is a property of the self-system. In short, McDougall anticipates the conceptualization of the ego as a self-determining active agency.

The Development of Self.—We can now turn our attention to the problem of the nature and development of the self and its counterpart, the self-regarding sentiment. You may already have recognized in this pair of concepts an old friend. If not, McDougall's own description will leave no doubts, for he uses the very terms we have already adopted.

For we find that the idea of the self and the self-regarding sentiment are essentially social products; that their development is affected by constant interplay between personalities, between the self and society; that, for this reason, the complex conception of self thus attained implies constant reference to others and to society in general, and is, in fact, not merely a conception of self, but always of one's self in relation to other selves (18, p. 185).

Here in still another theoretical context we see the independent formulation of the concept of the self-other system.[26] In describing

---

[25] Following Lewin, French (5) has explicitly incorporated the concepts of differentiation and integration in a restatement of the theory of sentiments.

[26] With the subsequent development of psychoanalysis, McDougall took note of possible correspondence in terms: "I take it that 'the censor' on the one hand, and

the development of this system, McDougall likewise speaks in familiar language.

As the differentiation of persons and inert objects proceeds, persons continue to be the more interesting to the young child, for they continue to be the main sources of his pains and pleasures and satisfactions. . . . But much more important than the actions of the people about him are the feelings and emotions that prompt them. . . . [The child] widens his experience and his understanding of the emotional attitudes and motives of others by copying them in his imitative play; he puts himself into some personal relation he has observed, assumes the part of parent or teacher or elder sister, makes some smaller child, a dog, a cat, or a doll, stand for himself, and acts out his part, so realizing more fully the meaning of the behaviour of other persons. In this way the content of his idea of his self and its capacities for action and feeling grows hand in hand with his ideas of other selves . . . he gets his idea of his self in large part by accepting the ideas of himself that he finds expressed by those about him (18, pp. 190-91).

McDougall distinguishes four stages in the development of the person.

These are (1) the stage of instinctive behaviour modified only by the influence of the pains and pleasures that are incidentally experienced in the course of instinctive activities; (2) the stage in which the operation of the instinctive impulses is modified by the influence of rewards and punishments administered more or less systematically by the social environment; (3) the stage in which conduct is controlled in the main by the anticipation of social praise and blame; (4) the highest stage, in which conduct is regulated by an ideal of conduct that enables a man to act in the way that seems to him right regardless of the praise or blame of his immediate social environment (18, p. 186).

We note here a parallelism with the Freudian levels of psychosexual genesis, particularly when they are viewed in terms of their interpersonal implications. Thus, McDougall's first stage corresponds to the oral period during which the pleasure principle reigns supreme; the second stage may be likened to the anal phase when external controls are imposed to regulate the impulsive life; the third stage is that prior to the resolution of the Oedipus complex when the child's ego is still fused with that of the parents; and the last stage represents the differentiation of self following upon the resolution of the oedipal conflict.

Active Sympathy.—McDougall approaches previously examined theory even more closely in his designation of "two principles" which

'the Ego' (together with the 'Ego-Ideal') on the other are two alternative designations for that part of the developed personality which I have called the sentiment of self-regard" (19). (This statement was made prior to Freud's formulation of the superego.)

determine the process of the development of self: " . . . on the one hand the influence of authority or power . . . on the other hand the impulse of active sympathy towards harmony of feeling and emotion with our fellows" (18, p. 207). This second principle, however, appears somehow different from the simpler notion of love or support, and we shall do well to examine it further. Upon investigation, we discover that "active sympathy" is a somewhat complex affair which has no necessary connection with love although it is frequently, and happily, associated with it. McDougall describes active sympathy in the following terms.

> It involves a reciprocal relation between at least two persons; either party to the relation not only is apt to experience the emotions displayed by the other, but he desires also that the other shall share his own emotions; he actively seeks the sympathy of the other, and, when he has communicated his emotion to the other, he attains a peculiar satisfaction which greatly enhances his pleasure and his joy, or, in the case of painful emotion, diminishes his pain (18, p. 173).

Active sympathy impels the person "not only to seek to bring the emotions of his fellows into harmony with his own, but also . . . to bring his own into harmony with theirs" (18, p. 206). In this way there develop new aspects of the self in relation to the other. It follows that a person in whom the sentiment of self-regard is highly developed "will be constantly observant of other's feelings in regard to him and so will develop his powers of perceiving and interpreting the signs of the more delicate shades of feeling that do not commonly find deliberate expression" (18, p. 207). In contrast, one whose self-regarding sentiment is poorly developed "will be moved only by the coarser expressions of general approval and disapproval, by open praise and blame" (18, pp. 208).

Active sympathy reaches its highest expression when combined with the "reciprocal sentiment of love" to which it is likely to give rise. But love can exist without active sympathy; this occurs quite frequently in the expression of pity or mutual encouragement: "But such a sentiment of love without active sympathy brings little joy and is likely to be troubled by frequent jars and regrets" (18, p. 174). Moreover, active sympathy may occur in relation to painful emotions such as anger, fear, and revenge. This poses a problem in motivation. Why should one be impelled to seek out and share the unpleasant feelings of another? Confronted by this riddle of his own making, McDougall retreats to the line of last defense, " . . . we must, I think, fall back on the gregarious instinct" (18, p. 175). He who lacks this instinct is devoid of active sympathy and "is content to bury his joys and his sorrows in his own bosom" (18, p. 176). He who is generously endowed by nature can find no peace in solitude and must share every experience—be it pleasant or unpleasant—with someone else. Such persons, McDougall acidly remarks "wear out their wives, or others about them, by their constant demands for sympathetic emotion, regardless of the strain they put upon their companions, who cannot always be in the mood to sympathize" (18, pp. 177-78).

The concept of active sympathy has been discussed at some length, because, setting aside its instinctivistic origins, it anticipates by almost forty years what has by some been regarded as a revolutionary development in our own time. I refer to the work of the American psychiatrist Harry Stack Sullivan, who places at the center of his theory of interpersonal relationships a phenomenon he identifies as *empathy* which, *mutatis mutandis,* has virtually the same structural and developmental significance as McDougall's concept of sympathy. We shall proceed directly to a consideration of Sullivan's views, since these views will permit a more satisfactory statement of the theoretical propositions to be derived from McDougall's theory of the sentiments.

Sullivan's Theory of Interpersonal Relations

With Harry Stack Sullivan we once again experience difficulties in communication, for he writes in a compressed, obscure style that partakes of the very autistic quality which he so observantly noted in his patients—a style which provoked a friendly critic to remark: "Nothing can justify condensing two paragraphs into one sentence" (34, p. v). Sullivan did not write a great deal. Most of his work appears in scattered, unsystematic papers in psychiatric and sociological journals (e.g., 31, 32, 33). Only once did he attempt to present a statement of his theory as a whole (34). The shortcomings of this presentation will be quickly identified by taking note of the fact that it was prepared for delivery in lecture form; it is discursive, disorganized, and incomplete in many vital respects. Fortunately, Sullivan had his editorial Boswell in the person of Patrick Mullahy, who on the basis of many personal conversations, has supplemented and clarified his mentor's cryptic prose. These addenda appear in the form of two essays, the first included as an appendix in the last edition of Sullivan's monograph (34) and the second as a chapter in a volume reviewing current psychoanalytic theories (24). In order to avoid the error of double interpretation, we shall try to base our discussion on Sullivan's original text wherever possible, but there are a number of focal concepts (e.g., prototaxis, syntaxis) for which we have to rely entirely on Mullahy's careful secondhand reports.

The Meaning of "Interpersonal Relations."—The focus of Sullivan's thinking is reflected in his definition of psychiatry as "the study of interpersonal relations" (34, p. v). Even the behavior of the acutely schizophrenic patient, he asserts, "is made up of interpersonal processes" (34, p. 7). In line with this orientation, Sullivan defines personality as "the relatively enduring patterns of recurrent interpersonal situations which characterize a human life" (34, p. vi). Having been warned regarding the idiosyncratic nature of his concepts, we shall do well to examine carefully the implications of the term "interpersonal relations" as Sullivan uses it. At the very outset we discover that the relationship centers about a perceptual process and a perceptual problem.

. . . our ordinary relation between an object and a percept has as a generally overlooked but nonetheless necessary link the act of perceiving. . . . Now, when it comes to the matter of perceiving another person, not only is there the object, this other person, and the perception of emanations from that person . . . but also the distorting and confusing and complicating factor of our past experience with other people who looked like this, who sounded like this, who made those statements, who had certain implications that happen to be irrelevant here, and so on. In other words, the central synthesis of acquaintance, the percept in our mind, concerning another person is fabulously more complicated than is the case with non-personal reality (34, p. 5).[27]

But what is there about this phenomenon to make it the focus of all psychiatric and psychological inquiry? In reply, Sullivan states his case as follows:

When we speak of impulse to such and such action, of tendency to such and such behavior, of striving toward such and such goal, or use any of these words which sound as if you, a unit, have these things in you and as if they can be studied by and for themselves, we are talking . . . about something which is observably manifested as action in a situation. The situation is not any old thing, it is you and someone else integrated in a particular fashion which can be converted in the alembic of speech into a statement that "A is striving toward so and so from B." As soon as I say this, you realize that B is a very highly significant element in the situation. Many situations are inte-

---

[27] Sullivan proceeds to develop this theme in terms of its implications for methodology. "So complex is this synthesis that it is practically impossible to elaborate techniques by which we can make our objective contact with another individual reasonably good. . . . We can improve our techniques for participant observation in a situation in which we are integrated with our subject-person. . . . I urge it as implying the root premise of psychiatric methodology" (34, p. 5). In other words, instead of attempting to maintain objectivity by staying out of the situation, the social scientist is enjoined to become involved as an active participant. Only in this way can he establish the kind of subject-object relationship in which valid perception of another human being becomes possible (34, p. 122).

grated in which A wants deference from B, and B, mirabile dictu, wants deference from A. It looks as if there were something in A and something in B
that happened to collide. But when one studies the situation in which A and
B pursue, respectively, the aim of getting from the other person what he himself needs and what the other person needs, we find that it is not as simple as
it looks. The situation is still the valid object of study, or rather that which
we can observe (34, p. 24).

We learn further that there may be dynamic components on either
side of the relationship which are "dissociated from the awareness
of the person" (34, p. 24). Also, we discover that a situation involves
two or more people "all but one of which may be illusory"; that is,
the other person may be real or fantasied (24, p. 282). Finally, and
here Sullivan, like McDougall before him, points directly to the
familiar features behind the verbal façade, the interpersonal relationship is alternately referred to as the "conceptual me and you" (34,
p. 45). In short, once again we have come upon the "self-other."
As in previous contexts, it is situationally determined, is an integrate
containing subsystems in abscission, and has manifestations both in
the psychological field and within the intrapsychic structure. In
Mullahy's paraphrase of Sullivan: " . . . the self-system is the
limit, the containing manifold, the enveloping matrix of the 'me-
you patterns' " (34, p. 134). Thus in his conception of personality
structure, Sullivan offers us little that is new beyond the terminology.
In considering personality development, however, we shall find a
somewhat different story.

   Power and Security.—For Sullivan the forces motivating psychological growth are of two kinds. Forces of the first kind, which he
calls *satisfactions,* are biologically founded. They include the usual
appetites for food, drink, sleep, but all of these impulses are secondary
in importance to "the motive toward the manifestation of power or
ability." As an illustration of what he means by this motive, Sullivan cites the example of an infant's reaching for the moon, and, inter-
estingly enough, failing in the attempt:

   An oft-told story beautifully illustrates the early appearance of what I am
discussing. . . . The infant seeing for the first time the full moon, reaches for
it. Nothing transpires. He utters a few goos and nothing transpires; then he
starts to cry in rage, and the whole household is upset. But he does not get
the moon, and moon becomes "marked" unattainable. This is an instance of
the frustration of the manifestation of power . . . (34, p. 6).

Mullahy (with his mentor's tacit approval—34, p. 5) has more to
say on the subject. The power motive underlies "the organism's
efforts not merely to maintain himself in stable balance with and in

its environment, but to expand, to 'reach out' to, and interact with widening circles of the environment" (34, p. 121). In short we have a counterpart to the Rankian concept of will. The similarity in views is underscored by statements such as the following: ". . . personality tends toward the state that we call mental health or interpersonal adjustive success . . . the basic direction of the organism is forward" (34, p. 48).

> . . . healthy development of personality is inversely proportionate to the amount, to the number, of tendencies which have come to exist in dissociation. Put in another way, if there is nothing dissociated, then whether one be a genius or an imbecile, it is quite certain that he will be mentally healthy (34, p. 22).

In other words, the self-system tends toward integration both internally in terms of its subsystems and externally in terms of interpersonal relationships.

To understand how the power motive functions in personality development, we must first examine the other class of "sought end states" which determine the course of growth. These are described under the general heading of *security*. In Sullivan's usage, this term refers to all those artifacts which man has learned to need in the course of growing up in a particular culture. Thus it includes language, customs, and even "movements," and "reveries" that have been "imbedded in a particular individual" (34, p. 6). The role of security in personality development is to be understood in terms of its relationship to the power motive.

> The full development of personality along the lines of security is chiefly founded on the infant's discovery of his powerlessness to achieve certain desired end states with the tools, the instrumentalities, which are at his disposal. From the disappointment in the very early stages of life outside the womb— in which all things were given—comes the beginning of this vast development of actions, thoughts, foresights, and so on, which are calculated to protect one from a feeling of insecurity and helplessness in the situation which confronts one. This accultural evolution begins thus, and when it succeeds, when one evolves successfully along this line, then one respects oneself so one can respect others. That is one of the peculiarities of human personality that can always be depended on. If there is a valid and real attitude toward the self, that attitude will manifest as valid and real toward others. It is not that as ye judge so shall ye be judged, but as you judge yourself so shall you judge others; strange but true so far as I know, and with no exception (34, p. 6).

Having probed the obscurity of Rankian prose, we may be able to discern in this passage a restatement of the dialectic relationship between will and dependence with its resultant precipitate in the progressive formation of self. If so, we are still on familiar ground. If not, be not dismayed, for Sullivan proceeds to describe the process stage by stage beginning with infancy.

Stages in the Growth of Awareness.—Infant behavior is characterized by several terms which, since they are basic to the total theoretical structure, require special explanation. The first of these is *empathy*. Empathy refers to the tendency of the infant to respond to the emotional state of the mother. For example, if the mother is disturbed during feeding time, the infant will experience feeding difficulty. If the mother is relaxed, the infant—other things being equal—is likewise in a benign state. Sullivan defines empathy as "the peculiar emotional linkage that subtends the relationship of the infant with other significant people" (34, p. 8). It is a kind of "emotional contagion or communion" which precedes "signs of any understanding of emotional expression." Before awareness can occur, there must be development in another sphere—that of symbolic activity. This is an expression of the power motive which is manifested first in a highly rudimentary state which Sullivan designates as "prototaxic." [28] Prototaxic symbolization occurs without reference to space, time, or self—none of which is as yet developed. It is confined to momentary impressions of vaguely demarcated "proto-concepts." Thus, the infant may "prehend," in contradistinction to "perceive," the "mothering one" who subsequently may be grossly distinguished as the Bad Mother and the Good Mother. In such primitive conceptualization there is no movement of thought. Prototaxic symbolization is succeeded by the *parataxic,* which is manifested verbally by *autism.* "With the development of the parataxic mode of symbol activity," says Mullahy, "the original undifferentiated wholeness, oneness of experience is broken. But the 'parts,' the diverse aspects, the various kinds of experience are not related or connected in any logical fashion. Various experiences just happen together . . . " (34, p. 126). In other words, in parataxis there is differentiation without integration. Thus, the term also applies to those interpersonal situations in later life which include dissociated elements. Specifically the projections or transferences that develop in the therapeutic setting are examples of parataxic activity (34, p. 45). In order for such fragmentations and discrepancies to be eliminated there must occur a process of *consensual validation* through the medium of an interpersonal relationship. In Sullivan's words,

---

[28] This term does not appear in Sullivan's published papers. It is discussed at length by Mullahy (34, pp. 125, 136-37) as representing an important aspect of Sullivan's later thinking.

. . . one has information about one's experience only to the extent that one has tended to communicate it to another—or thought about it in the manner of communicative speech (34, p. 91).

When such integration of experience has been achieved, the person is said to have attained the *syntaxic* level (24, p. 291). The parallelism between the developmental sequence we have just examined and previously noted theoretical formulations is so clear as to require no further elaboration.

Anxiety and the Self.—But we have gone far ahead of our story and must return to our infant; fortunately we left him in a benign state basking empathetically in his mother's contentment. But, in Sullivan's view, this happy condition is not likely to continue for long. With the acquisition of the "rudiments of language habits," the infant enters the state of childhood, where he is exposed to increasing restraint and disapproval. Moreover, by virtue of his developing powers of symbolization, the child not only feels such disapproval empathetically but becomes capable of "perception" (34, p. 9). Implicit in this distinction is an important theoretical point. For Sullivan, perception involves the symbolic or cognitive organization of an affective interpersonal experience (empathy). Furthermore, the development of the capacity for perception gives rise to two other phenomena of critical psychological significance. The first of these is *anxiety,* which, concisely defined, is the perception of empathized disapproval. Anxiety is of focal importance for the second phenomenon made possible by perception—the development of the self-system. In Sullivan's words, "the self dynamism is built up out of (the) experience of approbation and disapproval" (34, p. 9), or to put it more succinctly, the self is the organization of perceived empathic experience.

Thus the experience of empathy, and its prototype in McDougall's concept of sympathy, are seen to have a crucial role in personality development. Specifically, they represent the osmotic process through which the emotional content of other selves is incorporated into the self-system. We have yet to account, however, for empathy as a phenomenon. Here Sullivan is not too helpful. Though he does not go as far as McDougall, he apparently posits something like an instinct of gregariousness (34, p. 120) and seems to imply that empathy is closely connected with biological states,[29] but the point remains un-

---

[29] "It is biological for the infant when nourished to show certain expressive movements which we call the satisfaction-response, and it is probably biological for the parent concerned to be delighted to see these things. Due to the empathic linkage, this, the reaction of the parent to the satisfaction-response of the infant, communicates good feeling to the infant and thus he learns that this response has power" (34, p. 8).

clear. It would seem, however, that one can establish a basis for the phenomenon in terms of principles already available in our general theoretical structure as well as in Sullivan's specific formulation. Thus, the reliance of the infant upon the mother for his affective integration (34, p. 15), taken together with his capacity for learning, would appear to set all the conditions necessary for empathic responses to occur. (This assumes, of course, that the feelings of the mother are in some way reflected in her behavior; e.g., through muscle tensions, abortive movements, etc.; nothing in Sullivan would seem to contraindicate such an assumption.)

We return once again to a consideration of the formation of the self. Although we have already noted some of the properties of this system in our discussion of Sullivan's concept of personality structure, the developmental perspective illuminates several other important characteristics. The first additional point to be noted is the effect of anxiety in restricting the perceptual range of the self. Sullivan likens the self-system to a microscope: "You don't see much except what comes through the channel."

So with the self dynamism. It has a tendency to focus attention on performances with the significant other person which get approbation or disfavor. . . . In other words, it is self-perpetuating, if you please, tends very strongly to maintain the direction and characteristics which it was given in infancy and childhood. For the expression of all things in the personality other than those which were approved and disapproved by the parent and other significant persons, the self refuses awareness, so to speak. It does not accord awareness, it does not notice; and these impulses, desires, and needs come to exist disassociated from the self, or *dissociated* (34, p. 10).

We may note in passing that Sullivan's usage of the term "self" is more restrictive than previous conceptions have been; it is limited to those integrated subsystems which are not in abscission. But, as Mullahy points out, "the dissociated tendencies are analogous to the self because they definitely involve the existence of others" (34, p. 138). There is the further question of the degree to which the self is capable of flexibility. Sullivan's answer is found in his discussion of the third stage of development, the juvenile era. This is characterized "by the appearance of an urgent need for compeers" (34, p. 17). Sullivan does not specify whence this need arises, but an answer is clearly forthcoming in terms of his general theory of expansive differentiation. What is most significant about this period is the opportunity it offers for the limited redirection of the developing self-system.

Still gradually, gradually, because other children who are now important put up with this, take it for granted, seem to think that it is perfectly natural; because of this powerful support or validation of the novelty, the self may expand somewhat. This is always a difficult achievement; but the self may come as it were to doubt certain of the harsh puritanical restrictions which have been incorporated in it, and while perhaps they do not disappear and in times of stress throughout life may manifest themselves clearly, still the experience of the school may head the self dynamism in another direction which will make for much greater opportunity for contented living, for mental health (34, pp. 18-19).

Following in the wake of the juvenile period comes what Sullivan has called "the quiet miracle of pre-adolescence" (34, p. 39). There is nothing "dramatic or exciting about its appearance," but it is miraculous in Sullivan's view because "now for the first time since birth" there appears the capacity for genuine love. And here, also for the first time, we are offered a definition of this powerful force in personality development.

When the satisfaction or the security of another person becomes as significant to one as is one's own satisfaction or security, then the state of love exists (34, p. 20).

Love, by virtue of the intimate interpersonal relationships it creates, results "in a great increase in the consensual validation of symbols" (34, p. 20). This, in turn, broadens one's range of affiliation within the total human community. "In other words," says Sullivan, "the feeling of humanity is one of the aspects of the expansion of personality which comes in pre-adolescence" (34, p. 21). Finally, it is in this period that "for the first time one can begin to express one's self freely" (34, p. 20). All of these tendencies are enhanced in the ensuing phases of adolescence and adulthood, culminating in "the establishment of durable situations of intimacy such that all the major integrating tendencies are freely manifested within awareness in the series of one's interpersonal relations" (34, p. 28).

Retrospect and Prospect.—Thus, once again we have attained the genital level, and, after such repetition, there is surfeit even in this acme of human experience. Also, there is little to add, for Sullivan's views seem to fall comfortably into places that already await them in our developing theoretical framework.[30] But one final task remains:

---

[30] Surprisingly enough, Sullivan himself would probably have been the last to anticipate or welcome identification with his fellow-theorists in this paper. Although he expressed indebtedness to Freud (34, p. 3), he explicitly rejected his theoretical constructs, including not only the more vulnerable notions of the death instinct and infantile sexuality (34, pp. 30, 48), but also the structural concepts of ego and super-ego. In reference to both of the latter, Sullivan states unequivocally: "I have not

To summarize the major theoretical propositions developed in our attempt at theoretical integration, incorporating in this statement the additions and modifications derived from the contributions of McDougall and Sullivan.

Personality Structure

1. Personality is conceived as a hierarchial organization of psychical systems.
2. Psychical systems are dispositions to respond in a particular way to selected aspects of the psychical field.
3. The psychical system is an integrate involving conative, affective, and cognitive dimensions. The first two are intimately linked and represent the functional aspect of the system: the last contributes the structural framework.
4. The self-system or ego occupies a dominant position in the total hierarchy.
5. The ego is conceived both in terms of function (regulative-integrative-creative and content (self-other).
6. The regulative-integrative-creative functions are made possible by a maturing capacity for abstraction and perceptual reorganization.
7. The self-other system is a perception of the self in relation to other selves.
8. The self-other system includes substructures which maintain a high level of abscission. In other words, the ego contains dispositional systems toward the self and toward the other which are not accessible to awareness.

Personality Development

1. From the outset, the human organism is conceived as a system. As such, it has the following properties (after MacLeod, 22):
   a) It possesses boundaries which segregate it from the rest of the field and which are selectively permeable in both directions.
   b) It functions as a unit—acts and is acted upon as such.
   c) It maintains a dynamic equilibrium (i.e., it maintains a level of excitation) both within itself and with the external milieu.

---

found these conceptions useful in formulating problems" (34, p. 48). McDougall and Rank fare even more poorly. The former is branded with the instinct label and dismissed from the scene; the latter is cast aside as an advocate of "the medieval view" of man as "a creature of . . . transcendental powers between or among which he may choose allegiance" (34, p. 14).

2. From birth, the human organism manifests an active impulse to growth; that is, to extension, differentiation, and integration both within itself and in relation to the external milieu. This impulse is holistic and undifferentiated as to content. It has three aspects which are intimately intertwined.

    a) *Conative:* an impulse to action, to utilization of maturing physiological organs and tissues (this is analogous to the activity drive of classical psychology).

    b) *Affective:* an impulse to affective expression and investment of ever-widening dimensions of the organism and its milieu.

    c) *Cognitive:* an impulse to utilize the capacity to abstraction (12, 13), to organize experience in terms of concepts.

3. The conative-affective aspects precede the cognitive in both the order and the rapidity of their development. Conative-affective impulse activity is referred to as *experience.* The cognitive organization of experience is designated as *perception.*

4. The advent of perception marks the beginning of psychological (as distinguished from physiological) development. The conatively-affectively-cognitively organized impulse to activity (i.e., a dispositional organization) is designated as a psychical system.

5. Personality development involves the progressive expansion, differentiation, and integration of psychical systems.

6. Psychological growth is provoked and paced by physiological changes in the growing organism. This physiological development involves cumulative differentiation of affectively toned processes which require for their expression invasion and consequent emotional investment of ever-widening dimensions of the environment—notably its interpersonal aspects.

7. The importance of the interpersonal field derives from the child's lengthy period of dependence on others for his comfort and survival. The interpersonal field thus becomes the principal context for the ever-widening investment of affective impulses.

8. The reliance of the infant upon the mother for his affective integration, taken together with his capacity for learning, leads him to become reactive to changes in the affective organization of the mother—and later other persons—as such changes are manifested through muscle tensions, abortive movements, and other behavioral signs. Such experience of another's emotional state is designated as *empathy.*

9. With the development of perception, the objective condition of dependence on others becomes a psychological one, that is, the

child begins to perceive others as they are related to his impulses and needs.

10. Personality development is a function of the degree and manner in which the biologically rooted affective impulses find expression in the interpersonal context into which they inevitably intrude.

11. The interpersonal field has two broad interrelated dimensions which may be distinguished as *structure* and *support*. The former refers to the boundaries, prescriptions, and proscriptions that are perceived in the life space of the developing person. The latter refers to the manner and degree to which dependence needs are met. Whether the impulse to conative-affective-cognitive expression appears externally as destructive or constructive depends on the dialectic balance between the forces of structure and support.

12. Personality development is a function of progressive expansion, differentiation, and integration of self-other relationships which is paralleled by like processes within the intrapsychic self-other system. This osmotic-like isomorphic process takes place through the medium of *empathy*.

13. The forces determining personality structure exist only in the present. Hence personality change can be effected only through modification of the immediate psychological situation.

14. Optimal conditions for personality development involve tolerance for unreality and a gradual shift from firm to fluid structure of the interpersonal field.

15. The developmental process progresses through the creative restructuring of objective reality. To be effective, this creativity must encompass the sphere of reciprocal interpersonal relationships. Thus, the person moves from the receptive dependence of infancy to the creative interdependence and self-determination of mature adulthood.

Where does this summary leave us? We see that our initial prophecy has come true in that we have achieved little more than a conceptual framework filled in, here and there, by intermediate hypotheses—some of them barely in communicable form. Along with the prophecy, however, there was expressed the conviction that it was precisely these areas that required development if we were to make progress as a science. Specifically, it was argued that the formulation of a conceptual framework would permit the observation of phenomena hitherto unnoted or at least unutilized. One of the embarrassing aspects of science is that one is committed to put his convictions to this test. Accordingly, there has been initiated at Cornell University (under the sponsorship of the Department of Child Development and Family Relationships in the New York State College of Home Economics) a long-range program of research designed to explore the processes of constructive personality development. The program is organized on an interdisciplinary basis with representation from the fields of child development, experimental psychology, clinical psychology, social psychology, sociology, anthropology, psychiatry, and social work. In order to weld together a working interdisciplinary team and to develop a common conceptual framework, the division was made to set aside a period of a year for theoretical exploration. The ideas expressed in this Chapter are the product of one man's efforts to meet the challenge of this exploratory p_.:.' The project is now in the second and last year of its planning phase. We are currently in the process of trying out techniques and completing the design for the long-range program of research. This is not the place to outline this design in detail—suffice it to say that it involves systematic observation and study of children and adults over extended periods of time, paralleled at the earliest opportunity by controlled experiments designed to refine and test the specific hypotheses derived from the initial and continuing theoretical and empirical explorations. Such an undertaking is fraught with risks, technical difficulties, and unexpected results, but, for some of us at least, it offers the best hope for enhancing our understanding of what human beings are and what they may become.

BIBLIOGRAPHY

1. ALLEN, F. H. *Psychotherapy with children.* New York: W. W. Norton & Co., Inc., 1942.
2. CHEIN, I. The genetic factor in ahistorical psychology. *J. gen. Psychol.*, 1947, **36**, 151-72.
3. COTTRELL, L. S. The analysis of situational fields in social psychology. *Amer. sociol. Rev.*, 1942, **7**, June, 370-82.
4. DEMBO, TAMARA. Der Aerger als dynamisches Problem. *Psychol. Forsch.*, 1931, **15**, 1-144.
5. FRENCH, VERA V. The structure of sentiments. I. A restatement of the theory of sentiments. *J. Personal.*, 1947, **15**, 250-82.
6. FREUD, S. *New introductory lectures in psychoanalysis.* New York: W. W. Norton & Co., Inc., 1933.
7. FREUD, S. *The problem of anxiety.* New York: W. W. Norton & Co., Inc., 1936.
8. FREUD, S. Interpretation of dreams. In A. A. Brill (ed.), *The basic writings of Sigmund Freud.* New York: Random House, Inc., 1938.
9. FREUD, S. *A general introduction to psycho-analysis.* New York: Garden City Publishing Co., 1943.
10. FREUD, S. *An autobiographical study* (2d ed.). London: Hogarth Press, Ltd., & Institute of Psychoanalysis, 1946.

11. FREUD, S.   *An outline of psycho-analysis.*   New York: W. W. Norton & Co., Inc., 1949.
12. GOLDSTEIN, K.   *The organism.*   New York: American Book Co., 1939.
13. GOLDSTEIN, K.   *Human nature in the light of psycho-pathology.*   Cambridge, Mass.: Harvard University Press, 1947.
14. KUBIE, L. S.   A physiological approach to the concept of anxiety.   *Psychosom. Med.,* 1941, **3,** 263-76.
15. LECKY, P.   *Self-consistency: a theory of personality.*   New York: Island Press, 1945.
16. LEWIN, K.   *A dynamic theory of personality.*   New York: McGraw-Hill Book Co., Inc., 1935.
17. LEWIN, K.   *Principles of topological psychology.*   New York: McGraw-Hill Book Co., Inc., 1936.
18. McDOUGALL, W.   *An introduction to social psychology* (13th ed.).   Boston: John W. Luce & Co., 1918.
19. McDOUGALL, W.   *Outline of abnormal psychology.*   New York: Chas. Scribner's Sons, 1926.
20. McDOUGALL, W.   *The energies of men.*   New York: Chas. Scribner's Sons, 1933.
21. McDOUGALL, W.   The organization of the affective life.   *Acta Psychol.,* 1937, **2,** 233-346.
22. MacLEOD, R. B.   The phenomenological approach to social psychology.   *Psychol. Rev.,* 1947, **54,** 193-210.
23. MEAD, G. H.   *Mind, self and society.*   Chicago: University of Chicago Press, 1934.
24. MULLAHY, P.   *Oedipus: myth and complex.*   New York: Hermitage Press, 1948.
25. RANK, O.   *The trauma of birth.*   New York: Harcourt, Brace and Co., Inc., 1929.
26. RANK, O.   *Art and artist.*   New York: Alfred A. Knopf, Inc., 1932.
27. RANK, O.   *Modern education.*   New York: Alfred A. Knopf, Inc., 1932.
28. RANK, O.   *Beyond psychology.*   Published privately by friends and students of the author, 1941.
29. RANK, O.   *Will therapy and truth and reality.*   New York: Alfred A. Knopf, Inc., 1947.
30. RORSCHACH, H.   *Psychodiagnostics.*   Berne: Hans Huber, 1942.
31. SULLIVAN, H. S.   Socio-psychiatric research: its implications for the schizophrenia problem and for mental hygiene.   *Amer. J. Psychiat.,* 1931, **10** (o.s. 87), 977-91.
32. SULLIVAN, H. S.   A note on the implications of psychiatry . . . for investigations in the social sciences.   *Amer. J. Sociol.,* 1937, **42,** 848-61.
33. SULLIVAN, H. S.   Psychiatry: introduction to the study of interpersonal relations.   *Psychiatry,* 1938, **1,** 121-34.
34. SULLIVAN, H. S.   *Conceptions of modern psychiatry.*   Washington, D. C.: The William Alanson White Psychiatric Foundation, 1947.

CHAPTER 9

UNCONSCIOUS PROCESSES AND PERCEPTION

By James G. Miller, M.D., Ph.D.

Let us turn our attention to the psychology of ignorance—how each of us handles the fact that he is not omniscient. A good way to enter this little-discussed realm of the sciences of man is with the children's story [1] about the man who was sitting in the center of a great plain, completely surrounded by all the people of the world; and he was eating junket. And he asked the curious world: "Why don't you guess what I am thinking about?" "But first," he said, "let me tell you what I am *not* thinking about." He was not thinking, he said, about a walrus with an apple on his back nor about a year-old lion blowing out the candle on his birthday cake nor about a cow with her head in a bag. On the basis of this useful information the others then tried to guess what was on his mind, offering as suggestions a kangaroo jumping over a glass of orange juice and various other animals doing other interesting things. In the end it turned out he was thinking about junket.

This story was called to my attention by a philosopher who said that he believed this was the way the medieval scholastics defined the attributes of God. Omnipotence meant that there was no way in which He was limited. He was omnipresent, which signified that there was no place where He wasn't. And He was omniscient, which meant that there was nothing He did not know. This is the way many think about unconscious processes: There is nothing that can be said about them directly; the only statements that can be made concern what is not true about them. Let us take a different approach, trying to see what can be said positively about them, and investigating what is their relationship to the problems of perception.

The paucity of specific statements about unconscious processes is not the result of neglect of the subject. Many pages about it have flowed over the presses. At least sixteen meanings of *unconscious* are to be found in psychological literature (44, pp. 16-44). Like many other words frequently used in this science—*instinct,* for exam-

---

[1] Due acknowledgment is made to the charming fantasy by Mrs. Dorothy Kunhardt, *Junket Is Nice,* New York: Harcourt Brace & Co., 1933.

ple, or *intuition*—there exists a multitude of meanings of the same term, and much of our confusion about the problems involved derives from the fact that the words are being worked overtime by various of their employers and they have no union to protect them.   A clear statement of what unconscious processes are is not easily available.

The writer's own interest in this field began several years ago while sitting with a number of other students in the observation gallery of a surgical amphitheater watching a well-known surgeon operate on a woman who had abdominal complaints.   At the end of the operation he ordered that the general anesthesia be discontinued and then turned to us who were observing and, standing next to the patient, said, "This woman has been having these symptoms ever since her husband was sent to the penitentiary two years ago. We had to do this exploratory operation in order to be sure there was no malignancy, but I didn't expect to find any and we have discovered no organic grounds for the complaint.   It seems to me most likely that this condition is psychogenic, and I intend to tell her when she returns to consciousness that she has had an operation which will probably be helpful to her, and that we hope the symptoms will be relieved.   I will, therefore, use the power of suggestion in appealing to her unconscious mind."   A number of us discussed this statement later on.   It seemed to us that, regardless of what opinion one holds about the adequacy of his psychotherapy—and it did seem a little blunt— or the ethics of his treatment, the surgeon was making an assumption concerning the patient lying near him which was not justified. He said that he was going to deal with her "unconscious mind" and yet he had no way of knowing that, although she was still asleep from the operation, she was not in some important sense perceiving everything he said.   Perhaps, indeed, he had at that moment as direct access as he ever could to her "unconscious mind," and the information he was giving to us might very well directly frustrate any effect that could be wrought by the suggestive therapy he was planning to use.   Later we shall discuss some research motivated by this incident, which was done in an effort to approach the whole matter experimentally.   But the point which can be made at the moment is that the surgeon was assuming, as so many others do, that "the mind" is unitary and that, consequently, if a patient is unconscious as a result of being anesthetized, the whole mental mechanism is inoperative.   There are multiplex grounds for doubting the legitimacy of this assumption, and these facts have important implications for the theory of perception.

We said that we shall consider the psychology of ignorance—how the individual deals with the gaps in his knowledge.   In doing so we may be able to get our scalpel into the tissues of the problem of unconscious processes and find how closely it is located to the heart of perception. When Sergeant York captured 132 Germans single-handed at one time during the first World War and brought them back to the American lines, it is rumored that on being asked how he did it he replied, "Oh, it was simple: I just surrounded them." The humor of this remark lies in its caustic comment concerning the relative weakness of the individual. For an instant we are buoyed up by empathizing with a human being who is so superbly in control of his environment. There are numerous such jokes and legends that reflect one of the central predicaments of humans, namely that we are small and relatively impotent individuals in the midst of many sorts of threatening influences, some of which can be dangerous, surroundings about which we have relatively little knowledge. What do we do about this ignorance?

Development of Protections Against Ignorance

In the developing embryo the ectodermal layer seems to attain the function of protecting the rest of the organism, either by a skin which envelops it or by that part which turns into the neural ectoderm that forms the brain, spinal cord, nerves, and retina. This latter part protects by relaying to the organism accurate news about the world. The mechanism by which the various derivatives of neural ectoderm do what is possible to overcome the ignorance of the organism and to assuage the natural anxieties that arise from the threatening surroundings makes a fascinating story of which we have only the first glimmerings of understanding, but which is very basic to problems of perception.

Throughout our discussion we shall repeatedly refer to material presented in earlier chapters of this symposium. This is because unconscious factors in perception have already been abundantly illustrated to the reader, since a number of the processes which have been described are clearly unconscious. The present writer hopes to be able to organize some of these data into a pattern which will throw light on our particular problem. Dennis (14) has reviewed the research which indicates how the infant and child improve in the accuracy of their understanding of what is the veridical universe. These studies have demonstrated in general that, as they get older, children perceive the external world more accurately. The research of Binet (5) and of Pintner and Anderson (46) showed that the Müller-Lyer illusion was more profound to children than to older subjects; Brunswik (8, pp. 52-56) discovered that perception of color, size, and shape constancy improves with age up until adolescence, declining somewhat in adulthood; and Cruikshank's evidence (13) indicates that there is some size constancy even in infants. Fulness of report and accuracy of observation also increase throughout childhood, as was shown by Winch (66) in *Aussage* experiments with children. Dennis's own research (14) has led him to conclude that the fear of strangers, reported as appearing first at the fifth or sixth month, is best considered as the perception of a distinction between familiar and unfamiliar, because it is elicited not only by persons who are strange but also by objects not seen before. He believes this indicates that there is an initial withdrawal of the organism from parts of the environment not contacted previously. This protective mechanism appears early and is one of the ways that the organism deals with ignorance—by withdrawal, which is frequently interpreted as fear. Hebb (26) reports that chimpanzees raised in captivity show similar fear. Blake and Dennis (6) discovered a similar mechanism in the development of prejudices toward Negroes. They found that white children, even as young as fourth-graders, had a stereotyped notion of the Negro which put him in a generally unfavorable light that was clearly inaccurate, not even attributing to him such positive traits as being religious and being cheerful. Perceptions of older children were somewhat more accurate by adult standards even though still stereotyped, as is the case with many adults. But the recognition of both favorable and unfavorable traits in the Negro made their perceptions of the external world more nearly correct.

All this research suggests that with increasing age, as the organism matures and continues experiencing, it views the external environment more accurately and the factor of ignorance is thus diminished. A more and more veridical concept of reality appears, even though, as was shown in Morgan's excellent summary (Chapter 2 above), the task of getting a correct picture of this sort with the various sensory and perceptual mechanisms incorporated in the human nervous system is by no means an easy one. And the task of understanding how we do get such accurate photographs is even more difficult.

From Ambiguity to Stability

Now let us consider briefly the goals of the perceptual process dealing with the external environment which were listed by Hilgard (Chapter 4). He stated that he believed one of the goals of perception is the achievement of environmental stability. Discussing the demonstrations of perceptual phenomena developed by Ames and Lawrence (38)—the remarkable illusions whereby a man standing in a specially designed room seems to be smaller than his young son, water seems to flow uphill, and so on—Hilgard concluded that in such illusions the background is less likely to appear altered than the objects on it because the general purpose of environmental stability is more effectively served by this solution of the ambiguity. This suggests that the fear or anxiety which might arise from the constant threat of an uncertain environment can be diminished in this manner. Bruner and Postman (7) have stated that an individual, stimulated in a way which is threatening or capable of arousing anxiety, is likely to misperceive a stimulus presented to him very rapidly on tachistoscopic exposure either by blocking—that is, by not perceiving anything at all—or by seeing jumbled, nonsensical, or incomplete stimuli, or even by seeing something which is derogatory or contradictory to the character of the actual stimulus. As they say, (7, p. 25), "These phenomena suggest to the guileless investigator the image of the superego peering through a Judas eye, scanning incoming percepts in order to decide which shall be permitted into consciousness." This sort of defense against anxiety, which appears to be nearly conscious, is in many ways similar to the defense against the anxiety aroused by instability which is suggested by Hilgard's comments.

Hilgard (Chapter 4) stated that another of the goals of perception is the achievement of definiteness. There are many sorts of research evidence on perception, some of which he listed, which suggest that the organism would, as it were, prefer to see something—anything—rather than remain indefinitely uncertain about what is going on out in the environment. As Hilgard says, "The tendency to structure into figure and ground is one indication of the strain toward definiteness and thing-quality. The tendency is to construct concrete things out of the patterns we perceive, for concrete things have definiteness" (page 104). This is illustrated by the point made by Ichheiser (30), that we often assume that a small segment of behavior of a person of whom we have slight acquaintance must be an important, repeating characteristic, an assumption which frequently results in prejudice toward him. Frenkel-Brunswik (20), in her research comparing "prejudiced" and "unprejudiced" children, came close to the heart of the matter. She demonstrated by a number of different perceptual situations that the children who had more "rigid" personalities, more "prejudice," were also more likely to insist on clarity in their perceptions, even though the perception might be wrong, rather than be tolerant of an ambiguous perception. She relates this to the aspect of personality dynamics which the psychoanalysts have referred to as ambivalence and believes that there are marked individual differences in the ability to maintain such ambivalent attitudes. She finds that those who tend to hold and express rigid and moralistic attitudes appear to do so in order to feel certain about those toward whom the attitudes are directed. They have in effect to relieve their anxieties by having rapid closure in cognitive and perceptual reactions as well as in emotional and social spheres. Frequently, this effort at immediate knowledge about the environment is maladaptive, because it results in a sort of superficial clarity which cannot be supported by the realities of the veridical environment. There is more than a suggestion in Frenkel-Brunswik's work that this is a basic personality difference between two types of individuals, which is exemplified throughout a gamut of responses from simple perceptual activities to complicated social matters. This is a way in which some organisms handle the problem of ignorance by coming to a conclusion—any conclusion—in order to avoid the anxiety that would otherwise arise. When we do not know certainly about something, we make a guess as to its character and then, as we shall see frequently occurs, are more insistent upon the guess than we would be upon something more factual, because we wish to fend off the anxiety which will arise if we admit to ourselves that we do not have sound grounding for our perception.

All this process which we have been discussing seems to be closely related to what scientists, particularly in psychology, frequently try to avoid, the tendency to reify—to believe in the existence of some thing when there is really no entity. Whitehead (64, p. 11) has called this deceptive mode of thought "the fallacy of misplaced concreteness" and points to the numerous occasions when scholars in many fields have believed that just because something is given a name it exists as a concrete reality. To realize how common such conceptualization is in psychology, we need only think of how often id, ego, and superego have served as the names for egregious homunculi that live in the brain. It would seem that a sort of determining tendency drives thinking toward reification.

Perhaps the most frightening manifestation of this at present is found in the phenomena of group behavior elicited by the Iron Curtain. This process of demanding quick closure in order to get certainty is insidiously linked with the defense mechanism of projection. When there is ambiguity, as there is in any block to communication between one group and another, be they races, social classes, or in the case of the Iron Curtain, two cliques of nations, there are unresolved ambiguities. Because of ignorance concerning the external environment, members of the group sense threat just as a small child feels threatened by strange faces. Finally, to resolve the ambiguous situation, we Americans often project into this unstructured situation the concept that the Russians harbor the same sorts of hostilities that fear has engendered in us. Then the desire for concreteness reifies this malign influence. This false interpretation of the environment in order to do away with ignorance is repeated in many fields of life—for example, in those skeptical attitudes we have about persons we know slightly which so frequently change as acquaintanceship ripens.

Anxiety and Perceived Threat

In the process of perceiving the world, anxiety plays an important role. We have already referred to the evidence presented by Bruner and Postman (cf. page 262) that anxiety affects perception of materials presented tachistoscopically and also to the work of Frenkel-Brunswik (cf. pages 262-63) that the individual who manifests anxiety in the presence of ambiguity works for too rapid closure and superficial clarity of perception of external reality because of intolerance of ambiguity. Hilgard (Chapter 4) has reported the research he has under way with Kaplan and Jones on discriminatory eyelid conditioning using two illuminated windows, a left and a right, the light in the right window always being followed by a puff of air to the cornea, making it threatening. On the basis of the Minnesota Multiphasic Personality Inventory he has separated anxious subjects from those who are more normal and obtained some moderately convincing evidence that anxious subjects may find the air puff more threatening than those not classed as anxious by the Minnesota criterion.

Such data, together with various sorts of clinical evidence, suggest that anxiety is a signal flag which appears in the subjective experience of an individual when he is uncertain about the nature of his environment and therefore fears that it may be threatening. This is only one origin of anxiety; as we shall see later, anxiety can be aroused by events within the organism as well. There seem, however, to be individual differences in the amount of anxiety that can be tolerated, or perhaps there are differences in the amount of anxiety which one has to begin with and therefore in the total amount which occurs with uncertainty about the external world. However that may be, when this anxiety becomes intolerable, the evidence seems to be that the organism makes an effort to get security by insisting on rapid closure of perception, regardless of how representative it is of the veridical environment.

In his paper (Chapter 8) Bronfenbrenner referred to the following relevant quotation from Freud (21, pp. 75-76) :

Only a few instances of the expression of anxiety in infancy are intelligible to us; we shall have to keep to these. Thus, the three situations of being left alone, being in the dark, and finding a strange person in place of the one in whom the child has confidence (the mother), are all reducible to a single situation, that of feeling the loss of the loved (longed for) person. From this point forwards the way is clear to an understanding of anxiety. . . . Anxiety thus seems to be a reaction to the perception of the absence of the object, and there at once spring to mind the analogies that castration anxiety has also separation from a highly valued object as its content and that the most basic anxiety of all, the "primal anxiety" of birth, arises in connection with separation from the mother.

Freud, with his particular emphasis on the importance of early infantile interpersonal relations, here states that separation from the mother is the most fundamental anxiety. Whether or not he is right, this would seem to be one of the most significant forms of lack of support or threat from the external environment, and much clinical evidence suggests that it is likely that the insecurity arising from such loss is reflected in the whole pattern whereby anxiety is aroused in the child and later the adult. But this is only a special case of the general principle that anxiety develops when the environment becomes threatening.

Internal Processes

Let us now turn our attention from the perception of the external environment to processes occurring inside the organism. Claude Bernard (4) has suggested the concept of the internal environment of the organism, referring particularly to the biochemical and physiological processes which condition behavior. (In our discussion it is useful to expand this notion to include also neural activities going on at various levels of the nervous system.) There is another problem of ignorance which, for the individual, is as difficult as, or perhaps more difficult than, his ignorance of the external environment, and this is lack of knowledge of what goes on within his body. It is on this whole area of unconscious processes that Freud turned the searchlight of investigation as he began to formulate psychoanalytic theory, and it is the recognition of this field which William James (31, p. 233) called "the most important step forward that has occurred in psychology since I have been a student of that science." Let us see how this problem of ignorance affects perception.

Beach (Chapter 3) has already brought to the attention of this symposium illustrations of the effects of variations in the chemistry of the body, the constituents of the blood stream and tissue fluids, upon human behavior. For example, he mentioned the research of

Franklin, Schiele, Brozek, and Keys (19) on the effects of six months of semistarvation on thirty-six men. After having an ample diet for three months, they were limited to 1,570 calories a day for the next half-year. This diet produced the large average body weight loss of 24 per cent. There were many changes in behavior at the same time, including increased irritability and depression as well as withdrawal from social contacts. In the field of perception, marked changes in ways of viewing and behaving toward food were observed. The subjects were increasingly aggressive in their manner of getting food and increasingly possessive of what they got. In addition, bizarre behavior which was related to the altered perceptions but which might almost be considered worthy of psychotherapy occurred, with cookbooks becoming preferred reading and the men on shopping trips sometimes buying kettles, frying pans, and similar utensils, though they had no use for them. Frequently, they were unable to explain (were in a sense unconscious of) why they had made these purchases. In other words, perceptions had been altered but the individuals were unaware of why. The men also lost interest in the company of women, and their sexual activity in general was diminished—another field of changed perceptions. All this reminds one of reports of Shackleton, the Antarctic explorer, and others who have been on expeditions when food ran low, that they could not keep their thoughts, fantasies, and dreams away from the particular kinds of food of which they had been deprived (52, pp. 333, 356). As time went on and they lost fat from the deposit areas of the body, their interests turned more and more toward fatty foods, so that even seal's and whale's blubber became increasingly desirable (53, p. 112). There is also the work of Sanford (48) with school children, in which he found that before meals they gave twice as many food responses in a word-association test as afterward. There is the evidence of Nowlis (45) that chimpanzees change their social roles so that a normally submissive partner may become dominant if he has not been satiated while the other animal was.

Seventeen centuries ago Galen (22) reported that he performed a caesarean section on a goat and allowed the kid immediately, without seeing its mother, to choose food from vessels of oil, wine, honey, and milk. It smelled them all and then drank the milk. Many generations later Richter, Holt, and Barelare (47) as well as others have studied similar matters by permitting animals to choose their diets freely from various pure essential foods—casein for protein, dextrose and sucrose for carbohydrates, olive oil for fats, inorganic salts, vitamins, and water. The animals made selections that permitted excellent growth. In some ways the animals were able to make the proper perception of the food in order to maintain adequate adjustment, but it is unthinkable that they could have explained what determined their behavior even if they had been such verbalists as the menageries of Aesop or Disney.

The intervening mechanisms for such activities are extremely difficult to understand, but it is clear that many of the necessary perceptions are made unconsciously and that the organism is ignorant of the determinants of its behavior. The classical work of Cannon and Washburn (11) proving that hunger pangs are temporally related to stomach contractions is in point. Certainly most individuals are not aware that their stomachs are contracting in many circumstances when they feel hunger, and yet we have the perceptions of hunger and if things get bad enough we see images of what will satisfy us. Beach (Chapter 3) has given other illustrations of how chemical changes in the body related to diet affect perceptions and behavior, and the evidence is overwhelmingly in favor of the existence of processes of this sort, which are part of what has been called the "visceral unconscious."

There are indications that the ability to judge time intervals is grounded in a physiological pace-setter which is either part of the inherited structure of the body or is acquired early in life. The mechanism by which time estimates are made is, like the mechanism of diet choice, not available to introspection. Hoagland (27) and others have carried out investigations indicating that the temporal pace-setter by which periods of time are estimated, located somewhere in the nervous system, operates more rapidly in a feverish state than at normal body temperatures. The changes with temperature closely follow Arrhenius' law concerning the increased rate of chemical reaction as heat increases, and this would suggest that the pace-setter is a biochemical mechanism. As the temperature of the body goes up with a fever, time seems to pass more rapidly, giving us the impression of so many more hours in a day as to make the day seem inordinately long. Conversely, this might lead one to speculate that one reason bears can tolerate spending all winter in hibernation is because, once their body temperatures are lowered, less time seems to have passed by than really has elapsed. Though we need not insist on implicit acceptance of this last speculation, it would seem clear that perceptions of time are affected by functions of the internal environment of which most persons are ignorant.

There is also the remarkable aspect of language behavior which has been described by Zipf (70). He has shown that in nearly any type of written or spoken speech there is an almost invariable relationship between the rank order of the words used, in terms of their commonness in the passage, and the frequency of occurrence of the words. It would seem, indeed, as if this were some sort of quasi-biological rhythm affecting both perception and linguistic behavior.

Beach (Chapter 3) has also made reference to the effects of various drugs on perception—the well-known colored hallucinations produced by mescal, for example. No one who has been under the influence of alcohol can doubt that drugs do affect perception. The remarkable thing is the great specificity of these effects: laughing gas, for example, producing the characteristic behavior which has given nitrous oxide its nickname, and ether usually resulting in expansive, philosophical dreams with a satisfactory feeling of closure and community with the universe.

Neural Thresholds

In explaining these phenomena various hypotheses have been advanced. The most common suggestion is that the effect of the internal environment is ultimately accomplished by alteration of neural thresholds. These are lowered or raised in some way so that stimulation which had not been possible formerly is now possible, or, alternatively, stimulation to which the organism was ordinarily receptive is now prevented. It is, of course, known that certain chemicals definitely can affect neural thresholds, and this, consequently, makes a convenient hypothesis even though much of the required evidence is still lacking. There has been a great deal of research on the threshold or the limen which relates to the psychology of perception. Many of these studies have attempted to connect the notion of threshold to the unconscious processes, and often it has been suggested that there is a hierarchy of thresholds within the nervous system, different levels of neural integration. For example, Bruner and Postman (7) have interpreted their research on perception which we have mentioned (cf. p. 262) as possibly indicating that veridical report of an accurate perception has one threshold and that the affective avoidance response has another threshold which is frequently lower than that for veridical report. They concluded that in such situations there is a hierarchy of response thresholds—a hierarchy which can alter as determining conditions change.

Klein and Schlesinger (35) have also given the concept of threshold an important role in their analysis of perception. They refer to the work of the Slaters, who studied large numbers of British neurotics and normals (56) and found (57) a deficiency of visual and auditory acuity in neurotics, and to Eysenck's findings (18) that dark adaptation is abnormal in hysterics, anxiety neurotics, and depressives. They mention also differences in cutaneous sensitivity in neurotics found by Malamud and Nygard (41), and a continuation of their research, by Klein and Leavitt (34), that showed that sensory changes occur in hypnotic states. All of which, they conclude, makes it appear that these alterations of the threshold involve central participation and result in altered perceptions. They go ahead to point out that various sorts of neuro-physiological evidence adduced by Dusser de Barenne, Garol, and McCulloch (16), and Barker and Gellhorn (2) suggest that there are cortical areas with suppressor functions, stimulation of which influences the reactivity of the cortex to afferent impulses and consequently alter perceptions. Research by Heymans (58), Spencer and Cohen (59), Dodge (15), Collier (12), Kravkov (36), Hartmann (23, 24), Beitel (3), and Karn (33) on "Heymans' law," which states that concomitant stimulation can inhibit sensory processes, leaves one in some doubt about the validity of the law because of the conflict of evidence but seems to make it clear that such concomitant stimulations can definitely affect the level of the threshold.

There are also data which support the position that there are levels of functional integration in the nervous system which have different thresholds. The most convincing study is that of Burge, Wickwire, Orth, Neild, and Elhardt (10), who investigated in anesthetized dogs the electrical potentials of the cerebral cortex. Under these circumstances, they found the cortex was electropositive in relation to the sciatic nerve, but as the depth of anesthesia diminished the polarity was reversed. When further anesthetic was administered, the polarity changed again. Similar results were obtained when the animals were unconscious from bleeding or suffocation, and the investigators concluded that below a certain threshold potential animals lose consciousness. Since inactive tissue is electropositive and active tissue electronegative, the assumption is that consciousness bears some relationship to activity of the cortex. Although there are some conflicting researches, they by no means cancel out these positive findings. These, furthermore, are bolstered by the fact that deepening anesthesia results in an orderly, progressive disappearance of various reflexes, another confirmation that there are differential levels of neural integration.

Subliminal Stimulation

There is a long history of investigation of another related problem, the effect of subliminal stimulation on behavior. This research, which the writer has reviewed in detail elsewhere (43), began in the middle of the last century with the work of Suslowa who, with the aesthesiometer, a compass for determining the two-point limen, found that under subliminal electrical stimulation sensitivity was lowered, a result which seems to illustrate the operation of "Heymans' law." Throughout the years the research in this area became increasingly precise and well controlled, and it makes an interesting history. The most recent studies are probably the most convincing.

Both Baker (1) and Williams (65) have recently illustrated, for auditory and visual modalities, that discrimination among subliminal stimuli is possible. Some years ago the writer (42) also conducted a similar research, which was published soon after the work of Baker and Williams. In this study the five different geometrical figures on the ESP cards of Rhine were projected upon the back of a transparent mirror at an intensity well below the threshold. Certain subjects, facing the other side of what appeared to them to be an ordinary mirror, did not realize that the images were being projected through it. They were told that they were to assist in the telepathic experiment of guessing the geometrical figures, using the mirror like a crystal to help them. There were also sophisticated subjects who did know that the figures were being projected. It was found that, for both sorts of subjects, projecting the figures demonstrably improved the guesses, even though the subjects did not communicate that they saw images on the mirror. As the illumination was increased, the accuracy of calling the cards also improved. When the naïve subjects discovered finally, after the experiment was finished, that they were seeing real images, they showed reactions of surprise.

One may ask whether it is possible to learn to improve subliminal perception, and to answer this question this research (43) was carried on in the form of a learning experiment. The first motivations to learning employed were simple desire to please the experimenter, apparent increasing success, and monetary reward and punishment (the subject betting with the experimenter that he would guess the figure correctly). One of the difficulties with this last method seemed to be that under real financial inducement failure was more depressing than success was encouraging. At any rate none of these motivations produced learning. When, however, an arrangement was made whereby the subject was punished with an electric shock immediately if he gave the wrong response and received praise if he gave the right one, it was found that learning occurred.

This research was a direct consequence of the event mentioned previously when the surgeon addressed the gallery in the presence of the anesthetized patient. Continuing to work on this general issue, Sterling and the writer (61) tried to discover whether it is possible to form conditioned responses under deep anesthesia. Settlage (51) had already demonstrated it was possible for conditioning to occur at

a light level, and we were interested in seeing whether we could produce it at that deep, surgical plane where the patient was when the
surgeon was talking.   Under sodium evipal anesthesia, we found that
in eight cats out of thirty it was possible to condition the eyelid-
closing response, produced by a puff of air, to a sound so that the conditioning would be apparent the next day, when the animal had re-
covered full consciousness.   With all this evidence that learning and
perception can occur unconsciously, it would be highly desirable for
similar researches to be carried on with human beings, to learn, among
other things, what types of perception can go on in anesthetized
unconsciousness.

There are other investigations, with human subjects, which demonstrate convincingly that unconscious perception of subliminal stimuli is possible.   Wolff (67, 68, 69), for example, presented to each of
his subjects the subject's own voice, profile, shape, picture of hands,
mirrored writing, and other forms of expression, for comparison with
similar forms of expression by other subjects.   Often the subject did
not recognize his own forms of expression as being such.   Only 16
per cent of the judges recognized their own voices as their own, for
example.   In spite of this, most subjects usually judged their own
forms of expression more favorably than they judged the mean of the
others.   Seldom were subjects neutral about their own forms of expression, though sometimes they rated them most unfavorably.   Huntley (29) has done an experiment like Wolff's work under much more
carefully controlled conditions.   He obtained definite statistical evidence that in most cases a subject preferred his own form of expression, though often he was unaware that his was in the series.   Several
times a subject, on being told that one of the forms was his own,
showed evidence of surprise.   When asked to point out their own
forms of expression, subjects often could not comply.   This proves
that the differentiating characteristics in such cases were subliminal.
Why a subject rated his own forms of expression higher, and why
(as Huntley found) this rating was more extreme when he was unable to report that he was rating his own, are fascinating issues concerning unconscious motivation worthy of study to see why and how
the existence of consciousness thus alters behavior.

Work of McGinnies (40) is closely related to this.   He used as
stimuli words which were emotionally toned and socially taboo but
otherwise of comparable character to others which were emotionally
and socially neutral.   Both kinds of words were presented tachistoscopically at exposure levels which were below the threshold of report.   At each exposure before recognition of the word the subject's
galvanic skin response was recorded and he was asked to tell what he

had seen. It was shown that a significantly greater galvanic skin response was elicited by unrecognized emotional words than by unrecognized neutral ones. McCleary and Lazarus (39) tackled the same problem by comparing tachistoscopically presented nonsense syllables which were associated with electric shock to nonsense syllables not so associated. They found that, even though the words were presented so briefly that they were not recognized, nevertheless there was a reliably greater galvanic skin reaction in response to the nonsense syllables associated with shock, which would suggest that unconscious perception had occurred. This work, together with that of Bruner and Postman mentioned earlier, and other research, clearly points to the fact that under many conditions the affective response precedes the rational response; and this will fit in well with our concluding remarks indicating the relatively secondary importance of rational processes. In comments on a recent symposium on perception, Tolman (63) complained that we do not at present have enough brain models of what goes on in perception and suggested that someone should stick his brain model out even though he expects to have it excised. The hypotheses implied could then be attacked experimentally. The suggestion of Bruner and Postman that there are types of hierarchies of perceptual organization is closely congruent with a notion that has been popular for some time as a sort of vague neurological model of what goes on in conscious and unconscious perception. Schilder (49), for example, has explained by such means certain psychopathological cases that show signs of disturbance of motor and tonic functions involving the extrapyramidal and autonomic nervous systems. We have already had occasion to refer to other research which confirms this notion of levels.

Neural Vigilance

Head (25) developed a concept of "neural vigilance," that is, a state of high-grade physiological efficiency at some part of the nervous system. These neural centers, he said, react to similar stimuli with more or less physiological efficiency, according to their vitality at that moment. Vigilance of the higher centers results in consciousness, just as its existence at lower centers produces adaptive and purposive reflexes. A high level of vigilance results in easier elicitation of responses, and the responses give the appearance of being more adaptive or purposive than when vigilance is low. Structural changes in the central nervous system, toxins, or any other factor which cuts down physiological capacity can lower vigilance. It was Head's position that vigilance disappears from a part of the nervous system through which neural impulses do not pass.

Now, if we accept the brain model of a nervous system which operates at different levels, each having its own threshold, and add to that the notion of vigilance and the possibility of appearance and disappearance of this vigilance at different levels, then we have the first outlines of a model which will explain a number of phenomena related to perception above and below the threshold. Texts in introductory psychology frequently refer to the situation of the physician and his wife asleep in bed together. The baby cries and she awakens, but he goes on sleeping. Then the telephone rings and he awakens, but she goes on sleeping. Each is sensing, each is perceiving, but for one the sort of vigilance is different from that for the other, because of their differing motivations.

In terms of nervous system function we can say that all these cases represent a sudden redevelopment of vigilance in the highest integrating centers. The organism, like a fire department, always has a guarding point on watch, and when the alarm sounds it summons all necessary forces at once. Conscious perception takes the place of unconscious perception when the lazing organism is faced point-blank with a change in environment which may be beneficial or harmful. The determination of that comes second. First, attention to the new stimulus must develop.[2]

In human beings it is usual for communications or expressions indicating surprise to occur with these sudden flashes of consciousness. The writer would like to suggest that the characteristic responses of surprise known to us all are the external criteria that perception which was subliminal has suddenly come above the threshold. Few besides poker players, diplomats, and facial paralytics can avoid these outward signs. They are among the surest and most objective evidences available of the change from unconsciousness to consciousness. They indicate that some part of the environment concerning which the individual was ignorant in the past has changed its character and that he is no longer ignorant of it. Let us investigate a few examples of this sort of behavior recorded in psychological literature.

Jastrow and West (32) did research with the automatograph, a scientific Ouija board. They found among other things that subjects involuntarily moved their fingers on the board toward objects to which they were told to attend. Also, the fingers moved the board

---

[2] Much of the material in this and the following five paragraphs is condensed from *Unconsciousness* by James A. Miller, by permission of John Wiley & Sons, Inc., publishers.

in time with ticking sounds. They stated that "the movements are sometimes unconscious but always involuntary, there is often great surprise at the result" (32, p. 407).

Sidis (54) had each of his subjects guess what letters were shown to him at such a great distance that they appeared to be merely blurred dots. The subjects complained that they would have just as much basis for guessing if they shut their eyes. Sidis reported that they were much surprised when they learned after the experiment that they frequently had named the letter correctly.

We have referred to the research of Huntley (cf. page 271), in which subjects judged their own forms of expression in comparison with those of others. When the subjects discovered they had been judging their own hands, their own handwriting, and so on, they gave various exclamations of surprise. They had been astonished to find that the purpose of the experiment had been so different from what they thought it was. A similar result occurred in the writer's own research, in which subjects discriminated geometrical figures projected on the back of a transparent mirror when they did not know that actual images were there and thought they were doing a clairvoyance experiment. The same element of surprise was obvious when these subjects, who had known nothing of the purpose of the research, found they had been receiving actual physical visual stimuli and looking at the mirror again saw the outlines that had been invisible before. Subject A said: "I was positively amazed when the setup was explained to me." Subject B: "I was very surprised when I saw it." And so on for each of the other subjects.

Observers watching the experiment were continually astonished that these naïve subjects did not see the images at the higher voltages of illumination when it was perfectly obvious to them that the images were present, because they knew of the actual physical stimulation. Even an experienced subject who understood the setup before beginning his observing, after discussing the experiment with other psychologists, declared: "I could not get that group to feel as surprised as I did about the effect of cues that refuse to be available to introspection. Apparently my attitude is due to the fact that I was a subject." He had been ignorant of a characteristic of his environment, and when he found it was different from what he had expected he felt surprise.

The Nonunitary Organism

All this leads us to a statement of the most important principle concerning the ignorance of the individual about his own operations. This is a principle definitely opposed to that enunciated by Skinner

(55), who believes that the individual should be observed as a unit bounded by his skin, and no effort should be made to "lift up the hood" and see how the motor works inside. We have had much comment about the unitary character of the organism, the whole man, and in one sense it is extremely important to realize that every part of the individual is related to every other and interdependent. But in another sense which is equally significant, the organism is not unitary. Frequently, it operates as several relatively independent machines. Sometimes they are hooked up in one sort of hierarchy, sometimes in another, but from time to time they operate at different levels nearly independently. It is this great fact about human beings which we still frequently find so hard to realize that makes it clear why it is possible for unconscious perception to occur. It is to this that Freud's genius called our attention when he talked about the mechanism of repression. Various researches, like those reviewed by Sears (50), confirm the presence of such a mechanism in the individual which separates various aspects of his operation one from another.

We have spoken earlier of the anxiety that arises when the individual is ignorant of his external environment. It is reasonable that the anxiety might be much greater when he recognizes that there are mechanisms, processes, going on in himself of which he is ignorant. This very likely has been the reason why man has been so slow in coming to recognize that actually he is unconscious of many of the internal determinants of his own behavior. As Kubie (37, p. 271) said: "Anxiety is the Ego's reaction to a state of tension which arises in the nervous system when the Mississippi threatens to overflow its banks—i.e., when excitatory processes are threatening to break through inhibitory barriers to flood the nervous system." This is an anxiety often even more overwhelming than that which arises from ignorance of the outside, and yet it comes basically from the same feeling of insecurity, which in this case derives from inability to understand and control one's own organism.

Throughout all this discussion we have been talking as if the individual proceeded in a rational fashion to get stability and security in relation both to the external and to the internal environment. This has been a shortcoming of the writer's words, for it has not been intended to imply that these mechanisms of conscious and unconscious perception are by any means carefully worked out by a complete hypothetico-deductive process. When Tolman talks about his "organizing state of affairs" and his "hypotheses" and his "cognitive maps," he also is talking as if these processes of organization were carried out rationally by the organism. But certainly this is not so, and he doesn't think it is.

The writer would like to draw attention now to a final principle which it is believed can explain most of the phenomena of perception with which we have been dealing in this symposium. It is not a new principle, and it has been called by many names. When Hume (28) wrote about it, he called it "belief." Many think of Hume as a skeptic who at the end of the first book of his treatise had destroyed all rational basis for believing in causality, the existence of an external world, or the identity of individuals, who found himself in a hopeless predicament. And this is true of Hume at the end of his first book, but many do not go on and read the second book where he talks about the principle of "human nature" or about "belief." It is for him a characteristic of the human mind very similar to the classical determining tendency, which is as unavoidable for him as a skeptic as it is for anyone else. He said if someone should hit his head against a wall enough times, regardless of what his rational processes might tell him, he will come to believe in the solid reality of that wall. When he comes back to his quarters after being out, he says that he is forced by this tendency of belief to recognize that the fact the backgammon pieces have been moved means there has been an agent to do this—that there is causal relationship. Similarly, when he looks at the embers dying away in his fire, he cannot but believe they are the remnants of the blazing logs he left when he went out. They have not changed their identity. These are conclusions to which he came by a process of induction—an irrational, nonlogical process—rather than by deduction. And over and over again in discussions on perception we find references to the inductive process. For example, Hilgard has already quoted in Chapter 4 the conclusions of Lawrence concerning his and Ames's work on perception (38):

1. . . . your perceptions are based, not on one phenomenon, but on the statistical averages you use as presumptions.
2. . . . these statistical averages you used as presumptions are based on a great many past experiences.
3. . . . your perceptions result from an apparent weighing your mind makes of a very large number of indications and . . . this weighing of numerous factors goes on swiftly and unconsciously.
4. . . . your mind takes conflicting indications into account.

Hypotheses: Perceptions of Probability

Here we deal with the question of statistical averages and presumptions arising from probability. Statistics is the mathematics of ignorance. It gives us reasonable ways to come to conclusions when we do not know the character of the whole population. And it is this scientific process which is of the nature of every scientific law, because laws are generalizations beyond the population observed. Brunswik (9) has demonstrated with a T-maze that animals can learn to perceive in terms of experienced probabilities of reward in a learning situation. They can perceive probability. It has been observed by Bruner (Chapter 5) that it is even possible to propose a general hypothesis about the utilization of ambiguous information. Briefly, the hypothesis is this: The stronger the hypothesis, the more will ambiguous information be suitable for confirming hypotheses. This implies, in short, that personality and motivational and experiential factors, having a maximum effect upon the kinds of hypotheses adopted, will therefore have a maximum effect upon the emergence of perception in situations where information is ambiguous. In other words, the personality of the individual enters more and more into the perception as ambiguity or his ignorance increases.

It is probable that a better way to state this is in the reverse, which is that the greater the ambiguity existing and the greater the ignorance, then the more it is necessary for the organism to create a strong hypothesis in order to maintain its equilibrium, its homeostasis, and to relieve it from anxiety concerning the potential threat which develops from its ignorance. (Ignorance causes anxiety because the potential, unknown threat may overwhelm the organism. Dispelling ignorance will reduce anxiety—and even create constructive curiosity —if it is clear that the organism can master the situation. If mastery is not certain, anxiety will remain even after ignorance has gone.)

Induction

The writer believes that all this can lead us to hypothesize a general principle which might be called homeostasis, or perhaps by Rogers may be called the growth principle, which perhaps may be called the principle of *Prägnanz* or by Tolman the hypothesis-creating principle or organizing state of affairs—a basic and primitive tendency of the organism to find security by making inductive guesses on the basis of what probabilities can be estimated from experience, jumping from them to some form of certainty. This is carried out in a way similar to that outlined by Harry Stack Sullivan in his discussion of empathy. It is illustrated early in life by the response of the infant to the emotional state of the mother, the response of the individual to his environment. Perhaps best of all it is illustrated by the way Helen Keller, at the age of six, suddenly one day felt her teacher write the word "w-a-t-e-r" on one hand while the other was held under the stream from a faucet. Thus "the mystery of language was revealed" to her and she was enabled for the first time to make the induction to the existence of the external world and to the meaningfulness of symbols—symbols which up to that time because of her blindness and deafness she had been utterly unable to comprehend. From then on she was able, on the basis of this single induction and the many that followed from it, to develop for herself a perception of the external world.

This process of inductive belief—jumping to conclusions from inadequate premises—is the most essential cognitive process in the organism. It is necessary to maintain homeostasis with the external and internal environment and to remove anxiety. It is necessary to protect the organism from threat and onslaught. It is a highly effective process, as evidenced by the skill with which the human race carries on and the amount of agreement concerning external reality which exists among us. Sometimes, particularly in situations of great ignorance or ambiguity, this process goes awry and results in rigidity of perception and the prejudice, the illusions, and the misinformation which have been the subject of so much research on perception. An important thing to realize about this mechanism is that a very large part of it goes on entirely unconsciously—like the iceberg, it is mostly under water.

Perhaps it would be profitable to compare this basic principle of the organism to the principle of immunity. The body has developed biochemical methods whereby the entrance of foreign protein into the body is resisted by increase in temperature, by flocculation of particles in the blood stream, and by similar measures. This mechanism of maintaining homeostasis in the body is extremely valuable when the foreign proteins are dangerous, as they are in the case of many bacteria. It is this that enables us to fight off infection. But sometimes this process (and one much like it) works a disservice to the body when such other foreign proteins as house dust or ragweed pollen produce a similar effect and result in the disease known as allergy. Similarly perception, which usually is extremely effective in adjusting the organism to the environment, in certain cases goes awry, as with hallucinations, delusions, illusions, and the perception of the stereotypes of prejudice. It works to disadvantage when, in an unstructured situation like the Iron Curtain, the organism fearfully perceives threat on the other side because in his ignorance he can see nothing else.

In our culture there is a greater demand for rationality than in some other civilizations. Perhaps because of the ascendancy of science and the evidences of the accomplishments of the touted human frontal lobes, we increasingly find that we are required by our culture

to give rational explanations for all our acts.   We can be held account-
able for them in court, and we can be punished if we are not ready
with an explanation for what we have done.   Particularly apt is
Ellis's description of the rationality of consciousness (17, pp. 10-11).
"Sleeping consciousness, we may even imagine as saying to itself in
effect: 'Here comes our master, Waking Consciousness, who attaches
such mighty importance to reason and logic and so forth.   Quick!
gather things up, put them in order—any order will do—before he
enters to take possession.' "

If an individual is to live in peace with his fellows, his explanations
of his acts must be framed so as to make them appear to arise logically
from standards or purposes which are considered proper in his society.
In order to protect himself from the wrath of this group, one often
does not tell all he knows about his desires, purposes, and acts, simply
because he cannot make them appear to follow rationally from accepted
principles of his culture.   But even more than that, he is in trouble
when his behavior is determined by perceptions whose character he
does not understand, by inductions whose bases he does not know,
or by stimulation which he received at a subliminal level.

Stein (60) projected Rorschach cards at various tachistoscopic
speeds and found that, in general, more primitive responses of autistic
character occur at rapid exposure rates, while the defense mechanisms
of the personality become more evident at slower speeds.   This would
tend to suggest, as much other evidence also does, that the basic processes of belief and induction which lead to the assumptions we make
in perception are more primitive phylogenetically and ontogenetically
and less likely to be destroyed than the icing of rationality which we
put over it all.   Mankind, weak and limited in his power and knowledge, surrounded by ignorance, nevertheless is doing an effective job
of adjusting to his environment.   But our reason is beginning to show
us that the chief explanation for this effectiveness, the primary principle behind our perceptual processes, conscious and unconscious, is
not deductive rationality but the inductive process of irrational belief.

BIBLIOGRAPHY

1. Baker, L. E.   The influence of subliminal stimuli upon verbal behavior.   *J. exp. Psychol.*, 1937, **20**, 84-100.
2. Barker, S. H., & Gellhorn, E.   Influence of suppressor areas on afferent im-
   pulses.   *J. Neurophysiol.*, 1947, **10**, 133-38.
3. Beitel, R. J., Jr.   Spatial summation of subliminal stimuli in the retina of the
   human eye.   *J. gen. Psychol.*, 1934, **10**, 311-27.
4. Bernard, C.   *Leçons sur les phénomènes de la vie communs aux animaux et aux
   végétaux.*   Paris: J. B. Balliète et fils, 1878-79.
5. Binet, A.   *La Suggestibilité.*   Paris: Schleicher Frères, 1900.

6. BLAKE, R., & DENNIS, W.   The development of stereotypes concerning the Negro.   *J. abnorm. soc. Psychol.,* 1943, **38**, 525-31.
7. BRUNER, J. S., & POSTMAN, L.   Perception, cognition, and behavior.   *J. Personal.,* 1949, **18**, 14-31.
8. BRUNSWIK, E.   Über Farben-, Grössen- und Gestaltkonstanz in der Jugend. In H. Volkelt (ed.), *Bericht über den XI. Kongress für experim. Psychol.* Jena: Fischer, 1930.   Pp. 52-56.
9. BRUNSWIK, E.   Probability as a determiner of rat behavior.   *J. exp. Psychol.,* 1939, **25**, 175-97.
10. BURGE, W. E., WICKWIRE, G. C., ORTH, O. S., NEILD, H. W., & ELHARDT, W. P. A study of the electrical potential of the cerebral cortex in relation to anesthesia, consciousness and unconsciousness.   *Amer. J. Physiol.,* 1936, **116**, 19-20.
11. CANNON, W. B., & WASHBURN, A. L.   An explanation of hunger.   *Amer. J. Physiol.,* 1912, **29**, 441-54.
12. COLLIER, R. M.   An experimental study of the effects of subliminal stimuli. *Psychol. Monogr.,* 1940, **52**, No. 236.
13. CRUIKSHANK, R. M.   The development of visual size constancy in early infancy. *J. genet. Psychol.,* 1941, **58**, 327-51.
14. DENNIS, W.   Infant development under conditions of restricted practice and of minimum social stimulation.   *Genet. Psychol. Monogr.,* 1941, **23**, 143-91.
15. DODGE, R.   Theories of inhibition.   Part II.   The refractory phase hypothesis of inhibition.   *Psychol. Rev.,* 1926, **33**, 167-87.
16. DUSSER DE BARENNE, J. G. GAROL, H. W., & McCULLOCH, W. S.   The "motor" cortex of the chimpanzee.   *J. Neurophysiol.,* 1941, **4**, 287-303.
17. ELLIS, H.   *The world of dreams.*   Boston: Houghton Mifflin Co., 1911.
18. EYSENCK, H. J.   *Dimensions of personality.*   London: Kegan Paul, Trench, Trubner & Co., 1947.
19. FRANKLIN, J. C., SCHIELE, B. C., BROZEK, J., & KEYS, A.   Observations of human behavior in experimental semistarvation and rehabilitation.   *J. clin. Psychol.,* 1948, **4**, 28-45.
20. FRENKEL-BRUNSWIK, ELSE.   Intolerance of ambiguity as an emotional and perceptual personality variable.   *J. Personal.,* 1949, **18**, 108-43.
21. FREUD, S.   *The problem of anxiety.*   New York: W. W. Norton & Co., Inc., 1936.
22. GALEN, C.   De locis affectis.   In *Medicorum Graecorum Opera.*   Lipsiae: C. Cnoblochii, VIII, 1824.   Lib. 6, Cap. 6.
23. HARTMANN, G. W.   I.   The increase of visual acuity in one eye through the illumination of the other.   *J. exp. Psychol.,* 1933, **16**, 383-92.
24. HARTMANN, G. W.   II.   Changes in visual acuity through simultaneous stimulation of other sense organs.   *J. exp. Psychol.,* 1933, **16**, 393-407.
25. HEAD, H.   The conception of nervous and mental energy (II).   *Brit. J. Psychol.,* 1923, **14**, 127-47.
26. HEBB, D. O.   On the nature of fear.   *Psychol. Rev.,* 1946, **53**, 259-76.
27. HOAGLAND, H.   The physiological control of judgments of duration.   *J. gen. Psychol.,* 1933, **9**, 267-87.
28. HUME, D.   *A treatise of human nature.*   Selby-Bigge ed.   Oxford: Clarendon Press, 1896.
29. HUNTLEY, C. W.   Judgments of self based upon records of expressive behavior. *J. abnorm. soc. Psychol.,* 1940, **35**, 398-427.
30. ICHHEISER, G.   Misunderstandings in human relations.   *Amer. J. Sociol.,* 1949, **55**, Sept., Part 2.
31. JAMES, W.   *The varieties of religious experience.*   New York: Longmans, Green & Co., Inc., 1902.
32. JASTROW, J., & WEST, H.   A study of involuntary movements.   *Amer. J. Psychol.,* 1892, **4**, 398-407.

33. KARN, H. W.   The function of intensity in the spatial summation of subliminal stimuli in the retina. *J. gen. Psychol.*, 1935, **12**, 95-107.
34. KLEIN, G. S., & LEAVITT, M.   Sensory thresholds in the hypnotic state. (In preparation.)
35. KLEIN, G. S., & SCHLESINGER, H.   Where is the perceiver in perceptual theory? *J. Personal.*, 1949, **18**, 32-47.
36. KRAVKOV, S. W.   Über eine zentrale Beeinflussung der Sehschärfe. *Graefes Arch. f. Ophthal.*, 1930, **124**, 76-86.
37. KUBIE, L. S.   A physiological approach to the concept of anxiety. *Psychosom. Med.*, 1941, **3**, 263-76.
38. LAWRENCE, M.   *Studies in human behavior.*   Princeton: Princeton University Press, 1949.
39. MCCLEARY, R. A., & LAZARUS, R. S.   Autonomic discrimination without awareness. *J. Personal.*, 1949, **18**, 171-79.
40. MCGINNIES, E.   Emotionality and perceptual defense. *Psychol. Rev.*, 1949, **56**, 244-51.
41. MALAMUD, W., & NYGARD, W. J.   The role played by the cutaneous senses in spatial perceptions. II. Investigations in mental diseases. *J. nerv. ment. Dis.*, 1931, **73**, 465-77.
42. MILLER, J. G.   Discrimination without awareness. *Amer. J. Psychol.*, 1939, **52**, 562-78.
43. MILLER, J. G.   The role of motivation in learning without awareness. *Amer. J. Psychol.*, 1940, **53**, 229-39.
44. MILLER, J. G.   *Unconsciousness.*   New York: John Wiley & Sons, Inc., 1942.
45. NOWLIS, V.   The relation of degree of hunger to competive interaction in chimpanzee. *J. comp. Psychol.*, 1941, **32**, 91-115.
46. PINTNER, R., & ANDERSON, M. M.   The Müller-Lyer illusion with children and adults. *J. exp. Psychol.*, 1916, **1**, 200-10.
47. RICHTER, C. P., HOLT, L. E., JR., & BARELARE, B.   The effect of self selection of diet—food (protein, carbohydrates and fats), minerals, and vitamins—on growth, activity and reproduction of rats. *Amer. J. Physiol.*, 1937, **119**, 388-89.
48. SANFORD, R. N.   The effects of abstinence from food upon imaginal processes: a preliminary experiment. *J. Psychol.*, 1936, **2**, 129-36.
49. SCHILDER, P.   *Brain and personality.*   Nerv. ment. Dis. Monogr. Ser. No. 53. New York, 1931.
50. SEARS, R. R.   *Survey of objective studies of psychoanalytic concepts.*   Soc. Sci. Res. Coun. Bull. No. 51. New York, 1943.
51. SETTLAGE, P.   The effect of sodium amytal on the formation and elicitation of conditioned reflexes. *J. comp. Psychol.*, 1936, **22**, 339-43.
52. SHACKLETON, E. H.   *The heart of the Antarctic.*   Philadelphia: J. B. Lippincott Co., 1909. Vol. I.
53. SHACKLETON, E. H.   *South.*   New York: The Macmillan Co., 1920.
54. SIDIS, B.   *The psychology of suggestion.*   New York: D. Appleton & Co., 1899.
55. SKINNER, B. F.   *The behavior of organisms.*   New York: Appleton-Century-Crofts, Inc., 1938.
56. SLATER, E.   The neurotic constitution: a statistical study of two thousand neurotic soldiers. *J. Neurol. Psychiat.*, 1943, **6**, 1-16.
57. SLATER, E., & SLATER, P.   A heuristic theory of neurosis. *J. Neurol. Psychiat.*, 1944, **7**, 49-55.
58. SPENCER, L. T.   The concept of the threshold and Heymans' law of inhibition. I. *J. exp. Psychol.*, 1928, **11**, 88-89.
59. SPENCER, L. T., & COHEN, L. H.   The concept of the threshold and Heymans' law of inhibition. II. *J. exp. Psychol.*, 1928, **11**, 194-201.
60. STEIN, M. I.   Personality factors involved in the temporal development of Rorschach responses. *Rorschach Res. Exch. and J. proj. Tech.*, 1949, **13**, 355-414.

61. STERLING, K., & MILLER, J. G. Conditioning under anesthesia. *Amer. J. Psychol.,* 1941, **54**, 92-101.
62. TOLMAN, E. C. Cognitive maps in rats and men. *Psychol. Rev.,* 1948, **55**, 189-208.
63. TOLMAN, E. C. Discussion. *J. Personal.,* 1949, **18**, 48-50.
64. WHITEHEAD, A. N. *Process and reality.* New York: The Macmillan Co., 1929.
65. WILLIAMS, A. C., JR. Perception of subliminal visual stimuli. *J. Psychol.,* 1938, **6**, 187-99.
66. WINCH, W. H. *Children's perceptions—an experimental study of observations and report in school children.* Educ. Psychol. Monogr. No. 12. Baltimore: Warwick & York, 1914.
67. WOLFF, W. Selbstbeurteilung und Fremdbeurteilung im wissentlichen und unwissentlichen Versuch. *Psychol. Forsch.,* 1932, **16**, 251-328.
68. WOLFF, W. The experimental study of forms of expression. *Character and Pers.,* 1933, **2**, 168-76.
69. WOLFF, W. Involuntary self-expression in gait and other movements. *Character and Pers.,* 1935, **3**, 327-44.
70. ZIPF, G. K. *The psycho-biology of language.* Boston: Houghton Mifflin Co., 1935.

CHAPTER 10

PERCEPTUAL ORGANIZATION AND BEHAVIOR PATHOLOGY

By NORMAN CAMERON, M.D., Ph.D.

The field of psychopathology—or *behavior pathology,* as the present writer prefers to call it—is often treated as though it somehow lay outside the boundaries that enclose the legitimate behavioral sciences. To many students of human activity, what goes on in pathological behavior seems absurd, unpredictable, irregular, and unnatural. It is difficult for them to believe wholeheartedly that techniques of investigation and interpretation useful in this outlying and perhaps foreign region can be organically related to techniques appropriate to the more central and familiar normal areas. Such implicit ostracism, of course, merely repeats the skepticism and rejection with which the physical sciences long ago greeted the rise of the biological sciences. It repeats the skepticism and rejection with which both physical and biological sciences not so long ago greeted psychology. It provides a nice illustration of the increase in rigidity which is so common a defense against the disorganizing threat of innovation.

In view of this still widespread attitude, it is noteworthy that this symposium on perceptual organization gives a rather prominent place to behavior pathology, not only in the present chapter, but throughout. Students of behavioral sciences have recently grown apprehensive lest the stepchild, perception, turn upon its parent and engulf it —so that psychology may eventually survive only as it can be incorporated into the once neglected stepchild. If this apprehension should some day become reality, the writer hopes that the new perceptualists will continue to recognize that they cannot develop and maintain a healthy psychological organism unless they remain alert to the vital significance of pathology.

If the writer were to attempt to relate perceptual organization to the whole field of behavior pathology in a single chapter, the reader would quickly become confused and the writer would get lost. We propose, instead, to confine the discussion to what is directly relevant in delusional development and the formation of pseudocommunities. Since the *principle of continuity* is basic to this presentation, we may

283

begin by restating it here: *All the attitudes and responses found in behavior pathology are in some way related to and derived from normal biosocial behavior* (8, pp. 54, 141, 576). If this is a valid principle, of course, it implies that the yield we may expect from the present resurgence of interest in perception will contribute directly or indirectly to our understanding of pathological phenomena.

As illustrations of this implied relationship, let us take two representative formulations by other members of this symposium which agree in substance. There is Hilgard's statement that the goals of perception are those of maintaining stability and achieving immediate clarity and definiteness (Chapter 4). And there is Bronfenbrenner's statement that perceptions are, in the beginning, characteristically diffuse but gradually differentiate to achieve stability and precision (Chapter 8). At first glance, the role of perception in delusion formation may seem directly to contradict these formulations. But, as we shall see, it is commonly the case that overwhelming need for stability, clarity, and definiteness is responsible for delusion and that the organization of the pseudocommunity may be obviously a movement from diffuseness toward greater stability and precision.

All of us tend continually to complete the incompleteness of our behavioral universe by making inferences that go far beyond the facts, by supplying perceptually what the environment does not immediately provide. This is an important source of what Miller (Chapter 9, page 258) has aptly called "the psychology of ignorance." In his presentation he has chosen to stress unconscious factors—that is, stimulation which remains inaccessible to a person's own self-reactions. But the psychology of ignorance also applies to the conscious or self-accessible. A failure to check on the validity of one's conclusions and the correctness of one's observations, for example, is a common occurrence in relation to self-accessible events as well as to those which are self-inaccessible ("unconscious"). Such failure may permit misinterpretation to lead over into delusional conviction; and delusional conviction, of course, is often a crucial step toward frank pathology.

Organization

In order that we may profitably consider perceptual distortion in delusion and the pseudocommunity, it will be necessary first to review briefly some of the facts concerning organization which the behavior pathologist finds most pertinent. One of these is certainly the maintenance of an *exclusion-inclusion* equilibrium. Closely related to this are the phenomena of *reaction sensitivity* and *progressive reaction sensitization*. The roles played by *communication* and *self-reaction* are also of prime importance for an understanding of delusional developments; and so likewise is the task of *maintaining socialization* in the presence of almost unlimited individualistic trends. To these, accordingly, we shall now turn, before proceeding to a consideration of the techniques of perceptual completion that leads us into delusion and the pseudocommunity.

Exclusion-Inclusion.—The achievement of stability, clarity, and definiteness in perceptual organization, the movement from diffuseness toward precision, depends as much upon what is left out as upon what is admitted. This becomes obvious the moment one observes gross defects in the exclusion-inclusion equilibrium. For example, *overinclusion*—a failure to exclude the irrelevant and inconsequential (5)—leads initially to behavioral disruption. A common defense in such situations is that of meeting the initial disorganization with prompt *overexclusion* (8, p. 373); and this usually results in a simpler and more restricted perceptual reorganization. Such an outcome introduces the danger of serious behavioral impoverishment or distortion, such as we see in conversion hysteria; but the restriction does in effect eliminate the conflict and thus avoids a continuance of the disorganization.

Overexclusion sometimes fails as a defense against disorganization because it deprives a person of behavioral components that happen to be essential to an ongoing act. There may then be a pendular swing back to overinclusion with disorganization. This is apparent when a person in acute conflict reacts with fragmentation because his conflictual responses—which have now been eliminated from the dynamic pattern—were themselves central to his perceptual organization. Occasionally, in overinclusion, the initial disruption is not successfully countered by a reactive exclusion, or a perceptual reduction that has been instituted cannot be maintained. The organism thus cannot escape the bombardment of stimulation except by leaving the field or by ceasing altogether to respond. Thus we find flight, concealment, and stupor as common reactions early in schizophrenic developments. And when these solutions prove inadequate, there follows the familiar disruption, with its galaxy of perceptual distortions, its diffuseness, its characteristic instability, indefiniteness, and unclarity.

Reaction, Attitude, and Response.—In dealing with perceptual organization and disorganization, it is often necessary to distinguish between the behavioral background and whatever specific behavioral elements appear against or emerge from the background. The writer has more or less arbitrarily chosen the term *reaction* to designate any given segment of behavior under consideration—whether the segment is of brief or extended duration, and regardless of how simple or complex the perceptual structuring may happen to be. *Attitude* and *response* are then defined as aspects of a reaction. The *attitude* is the relatively diffuse, widespread aspect of the reaction. It functions as a behavioral background which prepares for, supports, and prolongs certain responses but not others. The *response* is the specific, localized aspect of the reaction which appears against or emerges from the more sustained attitude and is supported by the attitude (8, pp. 54-58).

This interpretation deviates in certain fundamental respects from traditional ones. It has the advantage of preserving the unity of the behavior segment—the reaction—while at the same time permitting separate emphasis upon the diffuse and the specific aspects. Attitudes are not conceived of as static structures which stand permanently behind behavior, ready to influence it along predetermined lines. Instead, attitudes are always a part of dynamic, ongoing, contemporaneous behavior just as are the responses which they facilitate, support, and prolong. Thus, in disorganization we need not assume that a hidden, static attitudinal structure has been fractured or destroyed. The disruption occurs in the current behavior. The attitudinal disintegration is a disintegration of the behavioral background of an ongoing reaction; and the fragmentation of the responses is only another aspect, with different emphases, of the same phenomenon.

Reaction Sensitivity.—By reaction sensitivity we mean a readiness-to-react selectively to certain components of a stimulating situation and not to others. This selectivity, of course, is the result of one's having acquired systems of related reactions with their attitude and response aspects. It may be considered one of the conditions of expectancy learning, one of the factors responsible for reducing the significance of mere frequency in determining the character of perceptual organization and reorganization. It is certainly of great importance in the development of the differential sensitivities observed in behavior pathology.

Nothing that we know about acquired reaction sensitivity eliminates from consideration the potential effects of variations in receptors, effectors, and the central integrating mechanisms. Indeed, there are definite indications that defective hearing, for example, may result in heightened susceptibility to cumulative misinterpretation. Neither is it possible to dismiss the potential influence of what Hilgard calls "innate preferences" (Chapter 4, page 96). But the *character* of a misinterpretation, its resistance to refutation or modification, and the tendencies toward secondary elaboration exhibit the same relationship to individual need that one finds in normal everyday behavior and in laboratory experiment (15, 16). A similar case can be made for persons suffering from systemic disease, deformity, and cerebral incompetence (1, 13). For such individuals there is greater than average likelihood that damaging reaction sensitivities will develop; but the *directions* of this development in each will be determined largely by individual need.

The development of reaction sensitivity at a relatively simple level may be illustrated by the task of learning to detect râles with the aid of a stethoscope, which every medical student faces. The stethoscope magnifies all chest sounds; and the sound of râles is among the least intense and least regular of these. But by persistent practice, the student learns selectively to exclude responses to the thundering heart and the coarser breathing noises, and to respond in this setting only to the minute crackling sounds which he has come to identify. Eventually his perceptual organization becomes such that, when he is listening for râles, they come through clearly, definitely, and reliably.

Through his acquisition of selective anticipant attitudes, the medical student's original multiple expectancy has been replaced by a single expectancy; and this has the effect of maximizing one kind of stimulus component while minimizing all others. Indeed, so great may an individual's reaction sensitivity to râle-like sounds become that he cannot always trust his hearing. If, for example, his diagnostic bias raises a strong urge to find râles present—if, in other words, his hypothesis is so strong that he tends to supply appropriate information, through his own behavior, when the appropriate stimulus via the stethoscope is lacking—he will turn to a trained colleague for help in guarding against his own too great need.

Reaction sensitivity introduces distortions into otherwise veridical perception because it represents a personal selective factor. The visual perception of one's home town as seen from the air will not correspond to an aerial photograph; and the greater one's eagerness to land, or one's fear, the less close will be the correspondence. The far greater complexity of social interbehavior affords infinite opportunity for misinterpretation to develop out of a person's specific sensitivities. The perpetually anxious individual, for example, tends to structure the environment he shares with others in much more threatening terms than they do (9).

Individuals whose personal inadequacies dominate their thinking —whether this characteristic is accessible to their self-reaction ("conscious") or not—are likely to perceive slights, insinuations, and hostility in the behavior of those around them to a degree that is foreign to adequate individuals. And because persons who are hypersensitive to the opinions of others are often grossly deficient in social skills,[1] they have considerable difficulty in avoiding the evolution of pseudo-communities in their thinking. We may say of such a paranoid person that, in the areas of sensitivity, his hypotheses become so strong that they not only maximize relevant confirming information, but also tend to be confirmed by ambiguous, and eventually by inappropriate, information.

Progressive Reaction Sensitization.—A newly acquired reaction sensitivity tends, of course, to generalize. The perceptual reorganization that enables a medical student to detect râles while the whole thorax is in action helps him also to isolate and identify obscure patterns of sound in the heart and the great vessels. Likewise, the brooding patient, whose perceptual reorganization leads him to suspect that a fellow-worker is defaming his character, will soon conclude that other persons are exhibiting similar attitudes toward him. His multiple expectancy is narrowed, in terms of his hypothesis, to something approaching single expectancy; while his single suspicion expands into a general conspiracy.

Progressive reaction sensitization is related to such generalization. Once a person has become sensitized in some specific direction, he is likely to develop further sensitivity in the same direction on the basis of successive acquired reactions. Thus his initial reaction sensitivity, which may have been more or less fortuitously acquired, gives him a perceptual organization that favors further sensitization along related lines. This further sensitization cannot be considered fortuitous. The significance of progressive reaction sensitization for behavior pathology is threefold.

1. It may determine the degree of an individual's *immunity* or *susceptibility* to behavior disorder. A selective readiness-to-react not only increases the ease with which a person responds to certain excitants; it also has the reciprocal effect of restricting his range of behavior. Perceptual reorganization, in other words, involves exclusion as well as inclusion. If a process of progressive reaction sensitization results in the successive elimination of culturally desirable and socially valid reactions, the outcome is bound to be one of severe impoverishment. The final step may be the development of a dominant hypothesis with something approximating full monopoly; and in this sense a

---

[1] "Skill" and "technique," as used in this chapter, always mean far more than a mechanical knack or a trick of some kind. It should be especially noted that among the most important of all social skills are those involving direct affectional relationships. Indeed, as the writer has pointed out (8, pp. 72-80), the visceral contribution, so characteristic of emotional reactions, is in the background of *all* behavior.

fixed delusion, based upon a single expectancy, is likely to approach unit strength.

2. Progressive reaction sensitization is also operative in the development of *cumulative* behavior pathology. In ordinary everyday life, information is always somewhat ambiguous, and not infrequently it becomes maximally ambiguous. A strong hypothesis is likely to crystallize by accretion under these circumstances. Thus a person whose anxiety level has been sharply raised will develop a perceptual organization that increases selectively his tendencies to respond to threatening aspects of his environment. His expectancy range becomes progressively narrowed, and his response threshold within that range is lowered. Such responsiveness, in turn, raises further the anxiety level and renders the person still more susceptible to apparent danger. In this way, uneasiness sometimes spirals through acute anxiety into paranoid panic and may terminate in disruption that leads into chronic schizophrenic disorganization.

3. Finally, progressive reaction sensitization is often responsible for the *differentiation* of pathological reactions into specific behavior disorders. Relatively slight deviations from the normal in basic personality patterns—as, for example, the utilization of an overt defensive ritual by one person and of unshared hostile daydreams by another—can lead persons further and further along increasingly divergent paths to widely dissimilar end points. The first will develop compulsive disorder, while the second will go into an agitated depression following the *crucial shift* (8, pp. 527-28). Both of these syndromes, when they are fully developed, can be described operationally as hypotheses with a high degree of monopoly.

Communication and Self-Reaction.—The beginning of life marks the commencement of socialization for the individual; and socialization continues thereafter throughout most of a person's existence. The child is inducted into the surrounding culture through his membership in the family group; and the price he must pay for this membership is conformity with the group customs and mores. The social learning by means of which conformity is acquired and maintained, of course, goes on in a social context. The family, the neighborhood, and the community provide the social setting in which children carry on their endless task of role-taking in real life and in play. Through this never-ceasing activity they enter into relationships of affection and reciprocal dependence, of cooperation and competition, of dominance and submission.

The outcome of this process is that the potential confusion and fluctuation of the perceived environment become organized into perceptual clarity, definiteness, and stability. The routinization of behavior eliminates much of the necessity for choosing among alternatives. The acquisition of skill in arriving at socially valid decisions enables a child to deal with the relatively clear-cut conflict in whatever alternatives remain. And in acquiring such skill, he learns also to meet the inevitable frustrations of delay and thwarting. Two outstanding achievements make human socialization possible. One is *communication,* and the other is *self-reaction.* The first frees us from strict bondage in space and time. The second makes it possible to develop individual self-regulation which in large part reflects social demand. Both communication—with its product in socially oriented thinking—and the systems of self-reaction are essential for adequate role-taking; and both may be gravely impaired in perceptual distortion.

As a child grows skilled in the techniques of communication, socially oriented thinking, and self-reaction, he becomes capable of taking an enormous number of social roles in talk and in fantasy. In these symbolic forms, he can practice and vary roles indefinitely, and he can learn to shift deftly from one role to another, with corresponding shifts in social perspective. He can, in other words, go on learning even in the absence of appropriate objects and situations through the use of his acquired symbolic systems. And he learns, at the same time, skill in social evaluation through the critiques his self-reactions help provide. Of course, this unavoidable emphasis upon word and thought must not lead us to forget the prime importance of direct, nonsymbolic activity—the perception of object arrangements and of the apparent sequence and concomitance of events. For no human being is socially competent whose perceptual organization is inadequate in *either* the symbolic or the nonsymbolic.

Maintaining Socialization.—The mature person enters adulthood an intricately organized, dynamic perceptual system. He has acquired manipulative and locomotory skills. He is practiced in the techniques of communication, self-reaction, fantasy, and role-taking. He is schooled in interpersonal behavior and communal participation. The mature adult is not confined to the present, nor is he dependent upon the momentary opinions of others for his own self-regulation. He has achieved perceptual stability without becoming changeless and rigid. For the human being must actively maintain throughout life a dynamic equilibrium between fluidity and fixity if he is to continue to engage successfully the ceaseless fluctuation of the environment in which he is immersed (4).

To attain to adulthood means only to reach a level of maximal growth and physiological adequacy. It means that one is biosocially capable of taking a variety of culturally structured roles from which he has previously been barred. For the *maintenance* of adult socialization the most essential condition, of course, is that the individual participate wholeheartedly in the activities of everyday living. This must involve perceptual organization that includes genuine communication, the social modification of one's individualistic interpretations, and a free interchange of perspectives with others. The perceptual organization of the socialized human being must encompass the reciprocal behavior of other persons as well as his own reactions. The maintenance of such interbehavior is the price everyone must pay for the preservation of social validity in the face of environmental organization that is rarely, if ever, completely structured.

Incompleteness and Perceptual Organization.—In all ongoing behavior, perceptual organization necessarily keeps ahead of environmental developments. For when action is completely structured, it always includes *anticipant attitudes* which are oriented toward the temporally or spatially absent. In everyday life we are all constantly engaged in supplementing facts with inferences—what can be seen, heard, and felt with what cannot, the present with the past and the expected future, and distortion with correction. Everyone must be continually acting on the basis of incomplete and uncertain data. We see a crowd and infer an accident; the telephone rings and we anticipate a specific call; we catch a glimpse of a hat, an overcoat, trouser legs, and shoes going by, and we reconstruct an acquaintance; we hear a few word fragments and react as though we had heard a complete statement which we then stand ready to reproduce in its entirety. Indeed, in everyday life, as in deliberate experimentation, the illumination is commonly inadequate, things are seen and heard obscurely, fleetingly, under suboptimal conditions.

We are able to perform effectively on the basis of perceptually supplementing such fragmentary and unfinished patterns because we have already operated successfully hundreds or thousands of times under closely similar conditions. In other words, we have already achieved skill in constructing operative hypotheses with the support of minimal data. But the fact that we have gained skill in reacting adequately in relation to incomplete stimulus organization by no means insures us against serious error. The crowd we saw at a distance may turn out to be a street-corner audience, not witnesses of an accident; the telephone call may come from a radio program survey; the man wearing clothes that seemed familiar may be a total stranger; and the words we partly heard may not even approximate what they aroused in our perceptual organization.

These situations constitute what Bruner and Postman designate the *problem of incongruity* (3). The perceptual expectancies are not confirmed by subsequent environmental developments, and a prompt reorganization must ensue if confusion is to be avoided. Behavioral adequacy under such circumstances will be measured in terms of the ease and celerity with which errors of supplementation are replaced by a more realistic closure.

As indicated above, we are perpetually responding to ongoing activity, to behavior that we must predict, *as we respond,* in terms of what we anticipate. A person's hand begins to move forward. This movement may terminate in rejection or a welcome, in a greeting or a blow, in our being given something or deprived. It may turn out to have no direct reference to us, but to be aimed beyond us or beside us. Whenever the context of such an act is ambiguous or unstructured, our response will be largely in terms of personal need, fear, and anticipation. And here we have the foundation upon which anyone may build delusion and evolve a pseudocommunity.

The situation in even the most complex role-taking behavior is basically no different from this. For while we are living our own social roles, we must at the same time include in our perceptual organization the roles of cooperating, competing, or reciprocating other persons. In so doing we must anticipate their next moves, reciprocate with their unfinished ongoing activity, and be able to understand its implications after it is completed. These are the inescapable conditions of everyday interbehavior. And they make it perfectly clear that *completeness and certainty are, at most, mere fleeting incidents which quickly give place to further instability, unclearness, and lack of definition.* Many of the gaps remaining in the configurations of social interbehavior are completed by imaginal supplementation, while a given behavior is developing or, retrospectively, after it has run its course. Many gaps are never filled. There is no need in some instances; in others there is no time, no opportunity, or no adequate behavioral technique at hand.

Perceptual Reorganization

If need, time, and the opportunity are present, however, human beings show irresistible tendencies to supplement the fragmentary pattern, to terminate a series once begun, to group scattered objects and complete an unfinished statement, to make a pointless incident into a meaningful story. They embrace isolated perceptual elements within a coherent whole that is integrated by their need and by the thinking which satisfies the need. In achieving this, human beings develop a number of well-recognized techniques which usually go by the name of psychological mechanisms. It is my purpose to present certain of these adjustive devices or mechanisms as *techniques of completion and elaboration* and therefore of *perceptual reorganization*. The three selected for discussion—compensation, rationalization, and projection—are all distortive from the standpoint of veridical perception, and all are of the utmost significance for an understanding of delusion and the pseudocommunity.

Compensation as Perceptual Completion.—Regardless of the character of compensatory behavior, it is obvious that techniques of compensation lead to the completion and elaboration of a vast number of trends which, for any one of many reasons, cannot be directly consummated. This is true of overt as well as of covert activities. As we all know, overt activities which in their original form are prohibited by social taboo become acceptable when they have been restructured along lines that coincide with prevailing mores. This process, in effect, permits the completion and elaboration, in substitutive form, of an infinite variety of unconsummated reaction patterns. It results in the enrichment of one's overt behavioral repertory, which must otherwise remain limited and poor. The personal costliness of modern industrial civilization is to a large extent indemnified by many compensatory satisfactions which are lacking in preliterate societies. Among these may be mentioned rapid changes of scene, almost effortless transportation, entertainment without responsibility, tolerance of many nonconformities, and the social institutions which provide vicarious excitement, hostility, revenge, and erotic pleasure through an endless procession of newspapers, magazines, cinemas, and radio dramas.

For the student of delusion and the pseudocommunity, the most important source of compensatory fulfilment lies in the almost inexhaustible potentialities of covert fantasy. We all understand the disadvantages and the hazards that may attend compensatory completion and elaboration in unshared, unvalidated thinking. But a further word needs saying about the benefits. All participants in group living are subject to the pressures of never-ceasing frustration and demands for compromise. The restriction of freedom which such pressures induce would inevitably result in much greater behavioral impoverishment than is actually the case were it not that our fantasy gives us a vast perceptual region which is relatively free from social restraint.

The widespread depreciation of dreaming and daydreaming which is characteristic of Western industrial civilization undoubtedly has interesting implications for behavior pathology. It is customary in our culture to regard the dream as something magical, capricious, or altogether meaningless and to look askance at daydreaming as an idle preoccupation with trivialities. Most persons appear to take little responsibility for their dreams and daydreams even if they recall them clearly. Thus, dreaming which is frankly erotic, grandiose, or murderous merely surprises and entertains the awakened dreamer, who characteristically does not accept such chimerical phenomena as his own behavior. Likewise, few persons hesitate to disown the daydream or the passing thought if it seems not to belong to their conception of themselves which they have organized in their self-reactions.

Nonetheless, it is true that compensatory completion and elaboration in fantasy of an incomplete, unconsummated perceptual organization can lead an individual into chronic ineffectuality and ultimately into personal disaster. Thinking, as we all know, can be carried on successfully in the absence of social validation—successfully, that is, from the standpoint of achieving increasing perceptual stability, clarity, and precision. Few organizations are more stable, clear, and precise than some of the products of delusional sudden clarification. But such an achievement involves unrealistic magnifications, reductions, and distortions.

Indeed, daydreams and night dreams—both those accessible and those inaccessible to one's self-reactions, the conscious and unconscious—often provide maximally effective tension-reduction when they are *not* made to conform to the demands of social validation, to verbal logic, or even to the logic of nonverbal operations (8, pp. 345-46). Nevertheless, it is in these very distortions, condensations, and ambiguities of socially nonvalid thinking, of verbal and nonverbal logic, that the potential dangers exist which become manifest in behavior pathology. For if an individual under stress constructs strong nonvalid hypotheses in fantasy, which makes him reaction-sensitive to confirmatory information from his ambiguous surroundings, he has already begun the organization of a pseudocommunity and started on a delusional career.

Rationalization as Perceptual Completion.—Unlike compensation, rationalization necessarily involves symbolic skills. For the process of selecting and assigning motives [2] cannot be carried on without language or thinking. Like compensation, however, rationalization expresses a trend toward completion of the incomplete— an elaboration of fragmentary certainties and vast unknowns into a structure which seems sure, consistent, and reasonable. The hallmark of rationalization is the inventing and accepting of interpretations that satisfy personal need but are not substantiated by impartial analysis.

Traditional definitions which emphasize social acceptability as characteristic of rationalization are only half right. Rationalization operates not so much in the service of social conformity as in that of *internal consistency and coherence.* This frequently means that a person must ascribe publicly to himself socially inexcusable and unforgivable motives if they result in perceptual coherence and consistency or if they help support a fiction that is vitally important for him to maintain. Thus the depressed person often rationalizes his own conduct and that of others toward him by heaping accusations upon himself. These then seem to justify the hostility which, in the *crucial shift* (8, pp. 527-28), he ceases to visit upon others but turns upon himself instead. Similarly, paranoid and schizophrenic persons employ rationalizations that, it is true, achieve perceptual completeness but at the expense of virtually excluding them and their dominant attitudes from all claims upon human society.

The unwritten law in rationalization seems to be that any explanation is better than none at all. There is a great deal of empirical evidence to indicate, for example, that anxious persons prefer frightening and even catastrophic explanations to suspense, just as patients in a panic reaction, who fear capture and death, sometimes kill themselves rather than endure the intolerable uncertainty. Likewise, in progressive delusional developments, the phenomenon of sudden clarification—to which we shall allude later—frequently involves an absolute conviction which, if sound, would mean confirmation of the patient's worst fears, the end of his hope, and often his sure and imminent death.

The practice of rationalization is itself justified by the satisfaction it provides of this widespread need for explanations, for symbolic extensions beyond the clear trail of fact. When, however, a rationalization is effectually challenged, the need for explanation is at once rearoused; and this can be met only by insistent reassertions and

---

[2] Elsewhere the writer has stressed the fact that all organized reactions are motivated and that what we call *motive* is actually a product of behavior analysis. "In practice we designate, as motive, whatever factor seems to be of special significance in the instigation of a given need-satisfaction sequence, in sustaining such a sequence and in determining its course and its outcome" (8, pp. 127-30).

denials, or by the production of secondary rationalization. Sometimes, for strong personal reasons, one cannot give up a nonvalid explanation. Under these conditions, the elaboration of further defensive assertion, without validation, is likely to favor the perceptual organization of paranoid pseudocommunities. And if, instead, a person retires from the field in order to preserve what he can neither give up nor defend, he will almost inevitably undergo some degree of behavioral disorganization, because he fails to maintain his level of socialization.

Projection as Perceptual Completion.—The writer has elsewhere introduced a distinction between *assimilative* and *disowning* projection (8, pp. 166-70). *Assimilative projection* refers to the assumption by anyone, in the absence of adequate supporting evidence, that others are as he is—that they are behaviorally the same or closely similar. *Disowning projection* arises from the same implicit assumption. However, it is complicated by a denial that the disowning person shares these attributes of his which he ascribes to others. The first says, in effect, "You have the same characteristics that I find in myself." The second says, "I do not have these characteristics at all—*you* have them."

Assimilative Projection. As a technique of completion and elaboration, assimilative projection has unquestionable advantages. It simplifies everyday life tremendously, since it allows a person to dispense with the chore of checking and socially validating every attitude and response he perceives. He assumes that others are like him; and, if the surrounding culture is stable and homogeneous, he will seldom run into serious difficulty with this hypothesis. He can extend assimilative techniques to include animal pets and inanimate things and by so doing actually increase his sense of belonging in his environment. For it is obvious that people, animals, and objects which seem akin to a person—as long as the person is himself secure—will in such case contribute to his security. His assimilative projection makes them all appear to share his own attitudes and to stand ready to meet his expectations.

On the other hand, an insecure and hostile person will, by assimilative projection, attribute hostility to his surroundings and thereby greatly increase his own insecurity. As long as he shows adequate skill in social validation and is able to accept the confirmatory judgment of the consensus, he is in a position to put his assumptions to the test. He can then determine, with some objectivity, the degree to which his own hostility may be provoking hostile reactions in others. But, of course, if he is lacking in the skills necessary for social validation, there will be nothing in his own behavioral organization to minimize the effects of situational components which are relevant to his delusional assumption. In other words, the dominant hypothesis will be free to maximize the confirmatory information contained in the situation. The person must respond to what he perceives as threat with counteraggression, defense, flight, or concealment. This is the situation in a great many persecutory delusions.

Grandiose delusions may arise similarly. The perceptual organization of the expansive, self-assertive, or amatory person is such that he is reaction-sensitive to confirmatory evidence in harmony with his dominant mood. The people in his environment seem prepared to participate reciprocally in his greatness, his aggressiveness, or his love. Actually, the complexity of the ordinary social environment of other persons and cultural objects is so great that any individual with sufficient need can find confirmatory information for any strong hypothesis. It should be pointed out, however, that confirmation depends upon strength of hypothesis as much as strength of hypothesis depends upon confirmation-in-operation by appropriate incoming information. The important thing to remember is that although "appropriate" may mean acceptable—in a nonjudgmental sense—to the person, it can also mean consonant with ongoing or developing behavioral organization.

The determinative trends in delusion have their beginnings in fantasy. A perceptual configuration, thus begun, will operate selectively to respond to whatever material in the surroundings will elaborate and complete it. The grandiose person finds the reflection of his own self-attitude in the apparent attitudes of others toward him which, of course, are actually products of his own selective readiness-to-react to a normally ambiguous environmental field. Like the patient with persecutory delusions, the grandiose individual thus succeeds in building the appearance of unanimity between his own self-attitudes and those he imputes to others, and so he completes his fantasy with confirmatory material borrowed from his surroundings.

Disowning Projection. In disowning projection, a person ascribes to others certain attributes which he does not acknowledge as his own. For example, if he ascribes hostility to others, he himself acknowledges only a reciprocal fearful or submissive role. If he attributes to others amorous attitudes directed toward himself, he makes it plain that he neither encourages nor reciprocates. If he maintains that he is under some irresistible influence (*delusion of influence*), for good or for evil, he takes refuge in an assumption that he himself is reciprocally helpless; and to this he may add repeated assertions that he cannot identify the forces impinging upon him or discover why he has been chosen as the victim. In grandiose delusion, also, the person may deny that his greatness or his destiny is in harmony with his acknowledged trends. Nevertheless, it is abundantly clear that whatever a person ascribes to others, without justification, *is at the time a part of his own perceptual organization*—regardless of the fact that he is unable to recognize his behavioral ownership.

As has already been indicated, each of us learns through acquiring and utilizing adequate anticipant attitudes—overtly and in fantasy —to prepare to meet the ongoing behavior of other persons in advance. In any situation involving reciprocal activity, a person preparing to meet another person's ongoing behavior, or expected behavior, must necessarily *have* some representation of the other person's reciprocal reaction in his own anticipant attitudes. For example, *if anyone takes in fantasy the role of hostile aggressor, he will necessarily include in his own perceptual organization, at the same time, the role of his fearful and injured victim.* The reverse, of course, is equally true. Anyone imagining himself victimized must necessarily take the role simultaneously in fantasy of an attacker and therefore have also his imagined attacker's perspective. These are simply examples of what is meant by the statement that psychological mechanisms or basic adjustive techniques are techniques of completion and elaboration.

The person who believes himself to be under the domination of some good or evil influence likewise *has the role of the power dominating him as an integral part of his own perceptual organization.* The grandiose individual must structure his throng of admirers—the generous, the grudging, and the envious—whose imagined attitudes are present in his perceptual organization as he steps forth into the street. His anticipant attitudes spring inevitably from his need, and they render him reaction-sensitive to whatever responses he detects in his social environment that will confirm his strong hypothesis. As Witkin (17) has shown, even relatively simple and well-structured situations are reacted to by many normal persons as ambiguous. In behavior pathology we are dealing neither with normal individuals nor with relatively well-structured situations. Our subjects are operating with pathologically strong hypotheses, with single rather than multiple expectancy, and in fluid, heterogeneous, and highly unstable social configurations.

This is the pattern of all reciprocal role-taking in fantasy. *The role and its reciprocal are both in the same person's behavioral repertory at the same time.* They can have no other locus. In disowning projection—and hence in the commonest delusional organizations—one behavior is acknowledged as one's own and its reciprocal is ascribed to others. The *origin* of this reciprocal behavior in one's own fantasy is repressed; but the *behavior* obviously is not, since it is openly attributed to other persons and publicly acknowledged in this altered form as fact. The choice as to which behavior the patient will acknowledge as his and which he will disown and project will be determined in part by the balance of anxiety—i.e., which behavior precipitates intolerable anxiety and which does not. It will be determined also, of course, in terms of need, in terms of one's past and of one's immediate perceptual organization.

Thus, for example, if a sadistic component is acceptable as one's own behavior, hostility will be favored as one's acknowledged role. The imagined other will then be a victim. But if hostility is present, and it can be neither acknowledged nor completely repressed, then the sadistic component must be ascribed to others and its origin in one's own fantasy must be repressed. In this case, the person disowning his sadism can *acknowledge* only the reciprocal masochistic role of a fantasied victim. Again, the same general pattern is basic also to delusions of influence and of grandeur—acknowledgment of one behavior, with ascription of its simultaneously present reciprocal to others, and *repression of the source of this reciprocal* in one's own fantasy.

It is clear that, in *disowning projection, perceptual completion and elaboration are achieved through setting up an opposition in one's own behavior.* This pathological technique has distinct economies. For example, a patient may punish himself by means of organizing a pseudocommunity of fantasied persecutors. At the same time, however, he is able to gain the satisfactions that may come from undeserved martyrdom. Moreover, he can now engage in counter-aggressions against persons whom he has cast in the role of his persecutors, thus satisfying his need to injure without putting himself in the wrong. And finally, by such activity he succeeds in provoking real persons to take the punitive roles toward him that he has previously fantasied and feared.

In this way, the patient guarantees that confirmatory information shall emerge from the environmental configuration that will strengthen his persecutory hypothesis. In consequence of the repressive activity, through which the source of one behavior becomes and remains inaccessible, the unacknowledged opposition in the patient's perceptual organization seems to him to arise from a source *outside* himself. It seems to belong to persons over whom he has no control, to groups or imagined communities whose activities appear then to converge upon him.

The Paranoid Pseudocommunity

Definition and Examples.—We have been saying that everyone must be continually responding in terms of ongoing, developing stimulus organizations—supplementing the incomplete, fragmentary, unstable and unclear, anticipating what is not yet present, and inferring an uncertain past. All of us manage to elaborate, round out, complete that which seems reasonably sure by means of techniques or "mechanisms" such as we have just discussed. But we seldom have the leisure or the opportunity of checking and socially validating our inferences; and much of the time we recognize no pressing need to go through the laborious procedures of confirming and infirming the various hypotheses which support our operations.

Under these circumstances, it is inevitable that we should frequently make inaccurate observations, neglect significant aspects of a developing field, misinterpret what we do observe, and draw unsound conclusions. Occasionally this results in a perceptual organization which favors single expectancy and makes the individual seem to himself the focus of some concerted action when actually he is not. It is this kind of dynamic relationship which we call the *pseudocommunity*. Before discussing the implications of this relationship for behavior pathology, we shall first define and then exemplify it. By a *pseudocommunity* we shall mean a *perceptual organization, structured in terms of the observed or inferred activities of actual and imagined persons, which makes an individual mistakenly seem to himself a focus or a significant part of some concerted action.* It is obvious from this definition that pseudocommunities are organizations within a person's own behavior.

The concept of the pseudocommunity was originally developed in relation to behavior disorders (6, 7); but it can just as well be exemplified by normal or near-normal behavior. Suppose, for instance, that a salesman returns from a dramatically successful trip to find the president of his firm and the sales manager at the airport in the company of half a dozen distinguished-looking strangers. The salesman may immediately organize this situation into a triumphant welcome for himself and assign to the strangers the role of a board of directors. When it turns out that the president and the sales manager are seeing off a touring delegation of foreign businessmen, the successful salesman has to effect a rather painful form of that sudden behavioral reorganization which helps to define insight (9).

We shall use, as our other hypothetical example, one involving fear and hostility. The hostile person, we said in discussing projection, is almost sure to make himself the center of reciprocal hostility. By his very actions he tends to arouse defensive measures of rejection and counteraggression in others, and this actual hostility confirms and reinforces his original hypothesis—a relationship that we may call *reciprocal maximation.*

Let us suppose that a hostile man enters a tavern truculently and observes that people seem to stare at him in an unfriendly manner. If at the bar they move to give him place, he sees it as a sign that they are avoiding contact with him. If they do not move over, they are deliberately obstructing him, and therefore they actively dislike him. The level eye of the bartender becomes an enemy's challenge, and his matter-of-fact casual service an intentional slight. As the truculent customer leaves the tavern, he may project and disown even his own relief, and imagine that the other customers seem relieved that he is going; whereas in fact he had been noticed by few and hated by no one. In his own perceptual organization, the entire company is united in a threatening enmity of which he seems unquestionably the object. His hypothesis, the pseudocommunity, approximates unit strength. His expectancy range, in terms of anticipant attitudes, is exceedingly restricted; and this determines the one-track character of his responses.

The illustration just given is certainly that of a paranoid reaction; but it need not necessarily be part of a paranoid disorder. It might, for example, have been a transient, ill-humored displacement from some antecedent frustration or an unsuspected anxiety reaction in relation to anticipated trouble. To justify being called definitely pathological, such an incident would have to be merely the segment of a lasting and pervasive perceptual organization; or it would have to be a phase in a progressive delusional development. It is with the progressive evolution of the delusional pseudocommunity that we are here concerned, and to this we shall now turn.

Some Characteristics of Pseudocommunity Development.—The pseudocommunity, as a behavioral organization, has constructive and creative functions even though what it leads to may not correspond with social fact. Indeed, in Bronfenbrenner's able formulation of steps in the evolution of scientific theory, one can find distinct parallels with delusional operations. For example, he says, "One of the functions of theory, then, is to provide the conceptual framework necessary for observation," and " . . . the development of a conceptual system may make possible the perception of phenomena that otherwise would remain unobserved" (Chapter 8, page 208). This statement might just as well have been made concerning the pseudocommunity, whose salient characteristic is that of rendering a person selectively reaction-sensitive by providing such a framework. Paranoid individuals typically grow more vigilant as the pseudocommunity evolves, and they notice a great many actual phenomena which had previously escaped their observation and that of other persons around them. They develop a particular way of perceiving their world and this determines the direction of their further observation.

The comparison can be carried still further. During the perceptual structuring of a pseudocommunity there may be several intermediate hypotheses—just as there may be during theory construction —and these are often simultaneously present or at least overlap with one another. These intermediate hypotheses, which also can be effective without being in testable or communicable form, are formulated in consequence of observation; and they serve as guides to more observation. Like the scientist, the paranoid patient usually goes through an incubation period, an exploratory phase, during which he does considerable observation before his formations begin to crystallize. In many respects he closely resembles the overenthusiastic scientist who allows himself to be driven for a time by his personal needs against the stream of factual data. Here the comparison begins to break down. For the scientist who showed himself unable to subject his formulation to a competent and unbiased scrutiny would in this performance be no scientist; while the patient who succeeded thoroughly in doing so might cease to be a patient.

The pseudocommunity, like any other perceptual organization, develops in general from a comparatively diffuse, unstructured beginning toward increasing clarity and stability. Early in this evolution, however, it may go through an expansive phase. Particularly under conditions of strong need or anxiety, constructs appear to grow by almost indiscriminate accretion from the surrounding information. In this phase, the relevance-to-irrelevance ratio is low; nearly everything seems in some way related to the dominant, ongoing perceptual crystallization. Ambiguities are frequently distorted so as to support the developing hypothesis, or they remain unobserved. The *generalization gradient,* to use Bruner's term, initially becomes increasingly broadened. If confusion between reality and unreality is complained of in early delusion-formation, it is this relatively undifferentiated structuring that is at least in part responsible; for the discrimination between reality and unreality is itself the product of a learned differentiation.

In acute paranoid stress, with its overwhelming anxieties, the tendency is for ambiguous and distantly relevant material to become organized, along with the directly relevant information, into strong hypotheses. This organization of strong hypotheses, in the evolution of pseudocommunities, then leads directly over into a phase of restrictive and distortive perceptual development. Indeed, the pseudocommunity is one expression of increasing intolerance of ambiguity; it is an attempt to destroy contradictions, to end suspense, complete the incomplete, and replace doubt with certainty.

The phenomena characteristic of this restrictive-distortive phase in an organizing pseudocommunity are strikingly paralleled by those described for the ethnically prejudiced by Frenkel-Brunswik (10, 11, 12). In general, she found the ethnically prejudiced to be suffering from a rigid, cautious segmentary approach—sometimes alternating with disorganization. They resorted to black-white solutions, and arrived at premature closure [cf. Postman and Bruner's "perceptual recklessness" (14)]. Once they made an assumption they tended to repeat it over and over; they could not correct assumptions in the face of new informing evidence; they neglected aspects of reality that threatened the solutions at which they had already arrived. The ethnically prejudiced considered the same trait objectionable in the outgroup but desirable in the ingroup. They ascribed all "good" characteristics to the ingroup and all "bad" ones to the outgroup.

The paranoid patient, likewise, can be said to have a rigid, cautious, segmentary approach to the areas of his unshared prejudices. He characteristically insists upon black-white solutions and arrives at premature closure—sometimes in the dramatic form of *sudden clarification*. Like the ethnically prejudiced, he is unable to take the role of his antagonists and truly share their perspectives, even momentarily. The paranoid individual also falls back upon tireless reassertion, cannot yield to infirming information, and is blind to the contradictions of reality. He ascribes complete villainy and unscrupulousness to his persecutors and complete innocence to himself; and yet he condones in himself the guile and violence which he condemns in the others—just as prejudiced members of an ingroup do with respect to an outgroup. Indeed, so close are the parallels that two possibilities for investigation at once suggest themselves. In the ethnically prejudiced, one could study full-blown nonpsychotic delusion, with a great deal of knowledge of its antecedents; and in the growth of paranoid pseudocommunities, one could study individualistically determined prejudice that is universally opposed—not supported—by the surrounding subculture.

One general behavioral similarity between paranoid patients and the ethnically prejudiced deserves special mention here. Their predominant attitudes with respect to pseudocommunity and outgroup are *spectator* in character rather than *participator*. There is no genuine manipulation of the available perceptual environment in either patient or prejudiced. Each tends to confine himself to watching, with his acquired reaction sensitivities making selections that confirm his favored hypotheses. What experimental data we have tend to support the thesis that manipulation—even intended manipulation—may reduce or obliterate perceptual misjudgment (2). Spectator behavior does not permit genuine manipulation; the spectator cannot put his uncertain material into a variety of contexts which would make checking and a participation in new perspectives possible. The outcome is likely, therefore, to be nonveridical perception which may terminate in socially nonvalid activity.

In relation to perceptual experimentation, Bruner points out that "the less 'ambiguous' the information, the less the effect of past experience in confirming hypotheses, the more the use of input information" (Chapter 5, page 134). A statement that is related to this may be made concerning delusion. It would read as follows: In pseudocommunity developments, the stronger the hypothesis and the greater the effect of past experience in structuring a present dominant need, the less appropriate and the more ambiguous can information be and still be effective as useful input information—useful, that is, in terms of delusion-formation. The reason for this, of course, is that along with the progressive reaction sensitivity characteristic of increasing hypothesis strength there are exceedingly strong tendencies toward distortion of the incongruous, to make it congruent, and toward neglect or denial of contradictory evidence. Things are either made to confirm the hypothesis or they cannot be taken into consideration. Nothing can infirm it.

This restrictive-distortive phase is probably a reaction against the effects of overinclusion in the expansive phase. The pseudocommunity development now acts as a defense against disruption. Overinclusion often introduces greater complexity than a patient can master and hence threatens him with chaos (9). In effect, the patient excludes whatever he cannot handle, regardless of its potential importance. In extreme instances, the multidimensional becomes unidimensional; everything that can be made congruent gets absorbed into the vectors of the developing system, even though this system may not correspond with social fact. The further progress from this point may be to premature closure, as in sudden clarification, or to further overinclusion and disorganization.

Sudden Clarification. Sudden clarification is a dramatic denial of ambiguity. It represents the highest level of personal certainty that can be obtained, together with the lowest level of social validity. "Everything has become clear" to the person; he has abruptly achieved a spurious insight that seems to illumine all his darkness.

The perceptual organization has now become a closed system and the basis for finalistic action. The major defect in this structure has already been alluded to in the discussion of projection. It is that, whereas the individuals who people the pseudocommunity may exist socially and their partial acts may be public, the relationships ascribed to them have validity only in the patient's fantasy. The patient has engaged persistently in *spectator* behavior until he gets himself so actively involved in his structured pseudocommunity that he takes finalistic action which *he* regards as *participative*. Actually, of course, it is purely solitary behavior in the field of social operations, even though it is no longer purely spectator.

Rigidity and Chaos. When a patient essays the operational translation of sudden clarification into an aggressive act—or into any other public consummation—the consequences to him will either destroy his dominant perceptual organization or else make it into something rigid and indestructible. In the latter case, the patient may reach stable equilibrium, a compromise recovery of some kind. If he is completely mastered by his own unassailable perceptual structure, his capacity for social cooperation may be so low that he must live permanently in an artificially restricted environment. If the mastery is incomplete, he may achieve some degree of encapsulation of his pseudocommunity which permits him to operate in some areas—in a majority for some paranoid persons—without special relevance to what he has encapsulated. Eventual return to the social community, of course, is much less likely in the former than in the latter instance.

If, under the impact of social frustration, the pseudocommunity organization disintegrates, there may follow a rather rapid restructuring which meets the now altered circumstances with new compensations, rationalizations, and projections. Such perceptual reorganization, of course, runs the same risks as the old one. In some instances, the patient does not succeed in restructuring a recognizable pseudocommunity but continues to live with the chaotic remnants of the disintegrated one. In either case, the unhappy consequences of putting the first one to the test are likely to encourage the patient to avoid further social testing. This means a retreat into further unreality, that is, a retreat to hypotheses less and less susceptible of social validation.

A final step which some disorganizing patients take is that of transforming the remnants of their disintegrated pseudocommunity into an *autistic community* (8, pp. 486-89). This is an organization of the patient's behavior which confines it to reactions in terms of the imagined activities of imagined persons in a fantasied context. Autistically organized behavior has so little contact with the activities of others and with the objective properties of the environment that there need be little or no correspondence between its dimensions and theirs. Thus we complete a circle in which a strong hypothesis, arising in response to anxiety-provoking uncertainty, begins by broadening the generalization gradient and developing overinclusion, then leads to overexclusion and to intolerance of ambiguity, next is shattered by the impact of social operations, and finally eventuates in a total or subtotal exclusion of the social environment. This is the final destruction of self-salience and the absorption of the whole community into one individual's behavior.

BIBLIOGRAPHY

1. BARKER, R. G., WRIGHT, B. A., & GONICK, M. R. *Adjustment to physical handicap and illness: a survey of the social psychology of physique and disability.* New York: Social Science Research Council, 1946.
2. BRUNER, J. S., & POSTMAN, L. Emotional selectivity in perception and reaction. *J. Personal.*, 1947, **16**, 69-77.
3. BRUNER, J. S., & POSTMAN, L. Perception, cognition, and behavior. *J. Personal.*, 1949, **18**, 14-31.
4. BRUNSWIK, E. Organismic achievement and environmental probability. *Psychol. Rev.*, 1943, **50**, 255-72.
5. CAMERON, N. Schizophrenic thinking in a problem-solving situation. *J. ment. Sci.*, 1939, **85**, 1012-35.
6. CAMERON, N. The development of paranoic thinking. *Psychol. Rev.*, 1943, **50**, 219-33.
7. CAMERON, N. The paranoid pseudocommunity. *Amer. J. Sociol.*, 1943, **49**, 32-38.
8. CAMERON, N. *The psychology of behavior disorders: A biosocial interpretation.* Boston: Houghton Mifflin Co., 1947.
9. CAMERON, N., & MAGARET, A. *Behavior pathology.* Boston: Houghton Mifflin Co., 1951.
10. FRENKEL-BRUNSWIK, ELSE. Dynamic and cognitive categorization of qualitative material. I. General problems and thematic apperception test. *J. Psychol.*, 1948, **25**, 253-60.
11. FRENKEL-BRUNSWIK, ELSE. Dynamic and cognitive categorization of qualitative material. II. Interviews of the ethnically prejudiced. *J. Psychol.*, 1948, **25**, 261-77.
12. FRENKEL-BRUNSWIK, ELSE. Intolerance of ambiguity as an emotional and perceptual personality variable. *J. Personal.*, 1949, **18**, 108-43.
13. LANDIS, C., & BOLLES, M. MARJORIE. *Personality and sexuality of the physically handicapped woman.* New York: Paul B. Hoeber, Inc., 1942, Medical Book Department of Harper & Bros., 1942.
14. POSTMAN, L., & BRUNER, J. S. Perception under stress. *Psychol. Rev.*, 1948, **55**, 314-23.
15. POSTMAN, L., BRUNER, J. S., & McGINNIES, E. Personal values as selective factors in perception. *J. abnorm. soc. Psychol.*, 1948, **43**, 142-54.
16. VANDERPLAS, J. M., & BLAKE, R. R. Selective sensitization in auditory perception. *J. Personal.*, 1949, **18**, 252-66.
17. WITKIN, H. A. The nature and importance of individual differences in perception. *J. Personal.*, 1949, **18**, 145-70.

CHAPTER 11

PERCEPTUAL REORGANIZATION IN CLIENT-CENTERED THERAPY

By CARL R. ROGERS, Ph.D.

In talking about the process and outcomes of psychotherapy, a descriptive phrase which is frequently used by the client as well as the therapist is that the client has come "to see things differently." Is this sort of phrase simply a loose descriptive analogy, or is there some type of perceptual reorganization which takes place in therapy? In this chapter, we shall endeavor to consider the available evidence which exists in relation to this problem, touching on the changes which come about in the perception of the environment and of the self, and proposing a theory of psychotherapy which places heavy emphasis upon the perceptual elements in the process. Though the writer will make certain attempts to link these observations with the chapters which have preceded it in this series, much of this integrative thinking will be left to the reader.

An Examination of Evidence

The Reorganization of Visual Perception—Clinical Evidence. —Counselors are rather frequently struck by statements from their clients which would seem to indicate that perceptions based upon visual stimuli had undergone marked change during therapy. Perhaps some examples may make this clear.

One client, nearing the conclusion of therapy, wrote a note at holiday time to her counselor stating, "It is impossible to put into words what it means to see the same campus that looked so common for several years become a place of beauty." She continued describing other changes—"to have a spot that I preferred not to think of become a home where I desire to go . . . " This change in the appearance of the campus which she mentioned is characteristic of comments which indicate that objects, things, the external world, are seen differently as a concomitant of psychotherapy.

Sometimes the change in the perception of the environment is more dramatic. Take, for example, the experience of Henry, an eleven-year-old boy who came in for play therapy. He had been a social isolate, came from a most unhappy home, and was referred because of his "nervousness." Toward the latter part of therapy, after a great many contacts with a play therapist, the following incident occurred. During one interview he said:

> You know, when I first started coming to you I had so many worries. Now I have just one big worry: how to keep myself from worrying. I have a fear that the Devil will sort of seep into my mind. I don't really believe in the Devil, but in a way I do. I'm just afraid he might seep into my mind. It's sort of a vague feeling. I can't express it.

There was some further talk along this line, but the matter was not resolved. One week later, Henry again brought up his concern.

> *Henry:* Last week I was telling you about my worry over the Devil seeping into my mind. I was afraid he might punish me for telling you. So I decided to think about it. I tried to recapture my feeling about the Devil. I asked myself, "Who is he?" And guess who he is. *Me! I* am the Devil! *I* make myself worry. All this time, the Devil has been me.
> *Therapist:* So that you are your *own* Devil?
> *Henry:* Exactly. I am my own Devil. All this time, I've been fighting a part of myself, using up so much of my energy to fight a part of myself, and keeping myself so tired. Using energy I could have had for other things. Say, what happened to the room?
> *Therapist:* Is there something?
> *Henry:* It suddenly got lighter, like if there was a fog or a mist and an opening, and it got bigger, and the fog lifted and the mist disappeared. (*Incredulously.*) You mean, you don't see it?
> *Therapist:* No. But things look much brighter to you now?
> *Henry:* Yes. It happened when I was telling it to you. It's amazing—hm. Well, that's something. I realize now that I can think through my problems. That's something I just discovered.

Here it seems clear that at a significant moment in therapy the whole immediate environment was perceived so differently that even this bright and sensitive youngster regarded the change as so obvious that he was convinced that it was the stimulus, the room, which had been altered.

Perhaps one more illustration will suffice. This is from a diary kept by an intelligent and articulate woman during her therapeutic contacts. After therapy was over, she showed it to her counselor. During a period of great discouragement with her therapy, she wrote the following:

> And just to make everything worse, you look disapproving. Now I know perfectly well that you don't actually look that way, and in a sense, I don't really care any more whether you approve or disapprove. But you see, last

time your face suddenly looked different—as if it had been black with coal dust, and then was washed clean, to reveal an altogether unsuspected freshness and individuality. I was delighted with that discovery and I'm as blackly disappointed as a child to have lost that clear vision.

Later in the same day, she writes more in her diary, expressing the full depth of her hopelessness and misery. She continues:

As I was crouching there in a miserable huddle, not improved by the fact that my cold is rapidly getting worse, your face with its disapproving expression rose vividly in my mind's eye. Perhaps I was addressing my thoughts to you—really. I can't remember, but anyway, I was carrying on a despairing struggle to solve the riddle of my relationship with my mother, when suddenly, two things happened—and for the life of me I can't remember which happened first, but whichever way it was, they trod right upon each other's heels. For one thing, it suddenly occurred to me that of course Mother, too, has a right to make her own choices and to be any kind of person she chooses to be. As simple as all that, the answer is. The other thing was that as I looked at your face, it was as if a hand reached out and quite literally peeled a heavy shadow from it, revealing the fresh, individual face which I was so disappointed to lose this afternoon. It was the most extraordinarily vivid experience; it wouldn't be at all adequate to say it was *like* a hallucination—it *was* a hallucination. Not the face, that is, that was just a vivid memory, but the shadow of my own feelings which I had projected on it. Isn't it astonishing how that insight corrects, not only present feelings, but reaches back to correct the distortions of stored memories?

Perhaps these examples are sufficient to indicate that even if we define perception in its narrowest terms, as the meaning given to visual stimuli, there is clinical evidence to suggest that perceptual reorganization takes place in some clients, and that this reorganization has a general quality to it, in that it is not merely a change in the objects or persons perceived in the therapeutic hour, but appears to affect the perception of the world at large.

Objective Evidence of Reorganization of Visual Perception.— While such clinical illustrations are of interest, they fall short of being evidence in any scientific sense. There are, however, two studies which bear on this point.

Of the several studies utilizing the Rorschach before and after client-centered therapy, the one by Haimowitz (1) is the most sophisticated. She administered the Rorschach before and after therapy to fifty-six clients receiving either individual therapy or group therapy, or both. She also administered the Rorschach twice to a control group which was similar to the experimental group in age, sex, and education. The period between the first and second administration was equivalent to that in the experimental group, but the control group received no therapy.

In analyzing the Rorschachs, Haimowitz used the index of neurotic signs developed by Harrower-Erickson. She also developed a series of ten rating scales for evaluating the Rorschach in terms of the therapeutic concepts of client-centered therapy. These scales measured such variables as the degree of anxiety, the degree of dependency, the degree of acceptance of emotionality, the degree of integration, and the like.

The results obtained indicated significant change in the therapy group as measured by both methods of analysis. The mean number of neurotic signs dropped from 3.0 to 2.0, the significance of the drop being indicated by a critical ratio of 4.03. The analysis of the ten rating scales showed a mean rating of 3.13 prior to therapy and 3.59 after therapy, a difference in the direction of improved adjustment, with a critical ratio of 6.3.

The control group showed marked contrast to the experimental group. Although there had been important environmental and life changes in several of the control cases between the first and second tests, the number of neurotic signs remained constant (4.0 and 3.9) and the mean rating on the ten scales showed no significant changes (3.0 and 2.9).

As is clear from the description, this study was an investigation of adjustment, not of perception. Yet it is also clear that these findings could not have been obtained if there had not been a significant change in the manner of perceiving, a significant alteration or reorganization of the perception of an unstructured stimulus. This type of change or reorganization does not appear to occur in a group which has not undergone therapy. No study was made, however, of the degree or kind of perceptual change, and the fact of its occurrence is simply inferred from the changes which are evident in the various analyses, changes which could not have been found had there been no change in perception.

We do not have to content ourselves with such an inferential conclusion. Jonietz (3) has studied directly the phenomenological changes in perception of Rorschach blots during psychotherapy. In her investigation there was no attempt to make the usual diagnostic analysis by means of the Rorschach. The blots were, instead, regarded as a simple perceptual task, and it was the purpose to investigate the content of these perceptions and any changes in them. In her study there were twelve experimental subjects to whom the Rorschach was administered before and after a series of therapeutic interviews and a control group of twelve to whom the test was administered at roughly equivalent intervals. Six of the therapy group had a follow-up Rorschach administered six months to a year after the therapeutic interviews had ceased.

The results for the therapy group were significantly different from those for the control group. When the percepts were examined for evidence of change from one administration of the Rorschach to the next, it was found that the therapy group kept fewer percepts the same, dropped a larger number of percepts, altered more percepts, and added more new percepts than the control group. In other words, in every way in which alteration or change of perception could be measured, the therapy group exceeded the control group, and this difference was statistically significant at an .001 level of confidence.

Another line of investigation was to compare, within the therapy group, those cases which were judged more "successful" by counselor evaluation and qualitative Rorschach evaluation with those judged less successful by these criteria. It was found that those which were judged to have shown more improvement showed a greater amount of perceptual change (in terms of percepts kept the same, dropped, altered, or added) than those who were judged as showing less improvement.

Another finding related to the follow-up period of those six cases in which this could be studied. The changes during this period, which followed therapy but in which no therapeutic interviews were held, were compared with the changes which occurred in the control group. It was found that these individuals showed a greater change in perceptions than occurred in the control group; that their percepts showed somewhat less alteration than occurred during therapy; but that they continued to acquire as many new percepts as they did during the therapy period.

What were these changes in perception, in which the therapy group differed from the control? How may they be described? Jonietz analyzes the trends which are most evident. Those who had participated in psychotherapy showed certain trends which were not found, or were found to a lesser degree, in the control group. There was, for example, an increased number of human figures perceived in the ink blots. There was an increase in the number of sexual percepts. There was a decrease in the number of static percepts. There was a decrease in the number of perceptions in which something was being done to the passive subject of the percept, over which he had no control. There was a decrease in the percepts in which abstractions or inanimate objects were perceived in action. Jonietz believes that the implications of these changes is that the individuals in therapy became less repressed and less fearful and felt more adequate to handle their problems.

Whether or not we accept this interpretation, it appears reasonable to draw certain conclusions from this study. These conclusions might be summarized as follows:

1. Change and reorganization of visual perception occurs during psychotherapy, but tends not to occur in a control group.

2. The change which occurs is a generalized one, in that it affects the perception of an unstructured stimulus which was in no way a topic of consideration in therapy.

3. This reorganization of perception is initiated by psychotherapy but does not stop with the completion of the interviews. It appears, therefore, to be generalized in a time sense, affecting perception long after the interviews have ceased.

4. The degree to which change and reorganization occur in visual perception appears to be correlated with the depth or satisfactoriness of the process of therapy as judged by other criteria. It appears, therefore, to be a real indicator of therapeutic change.

5. It appears that the types of perceptual change which occur are among those ordinarily associated with improved adjustment according to subjective clinical judgment.

Reorganized Perception of Others.—A common clinical observation in psychotherapy is that the client comes to perceive others in his personal environment in a very different fashion. A wife perceives her husband as entirely bad, a person who is intentionally hurting her in every way possible. During therapy this picture changes and she sees him as a person who, like herself, is struggling to find happiness, whose intentions are essentially positive, who hurts her unintentionally in his blundering attempts at adjustment. In the same fashion change occurs in the perception of a child by his parent; in the perception of friends, employers, and teachers. These persons are differently perceived as therapy continues.

A brief illustration may be taken from the case of a man who from a diagnostic point of view would be regarded as deeply paranoid. In an early interview he gives the perception he has of his wife as an unfaithful, scheming individual.

Mr. W: We've been quarreling a lot. She's been carrying on with another man, and I've got plenty of evidence to prove it. He's a man who lives next door, see, and I know that he comes in to see my wife after I leave in the morning. She doesn't think I can prove it, but I've got an airtight case against her.

Counselor: You're sure she is carrying on with this man, and you know you can prove it.

Mr. W: My wife claims I imagine all this, and she went to my boss and made lots of trouble for me by saying I was raving mad. But I know what she's doing. (*He goes on with many other details which, for him, prove and confirm the accuracy of his perception.*)

During therapy, in the accepting and nonthreatening atmosphere of the relationship, Mr. W. can examine some of his own experiences more deeply. He tells of boyhood experiences which made him doubt his sexual adequacy and of the fears that were engendered by being told that because of masturbation he could not have children or even get married. He explores the realization that because of this he has felt that he must be rather brutally dominating in marriage in order to prove his adequacy.

Mr. W: I started right in to treat her meaner than dirt. I got to calling her all sorts of names. I got fears that I couldn't measure up (sexually). I sold her on the idea that I was no good. . . . I realize now that she loved me devotedly. All those things that I've thought of her, the names I've called her and all, were really in me. I've driven her to what she's done.

Here it is clear that he has come to perceive his wife not as a wicked, scheming, immoral person but as a devoted wife who has been driven into sexual misbehavior by his own accusations growing out of his own fears regarding his sexual adequacy. Still later in therapy he had a dramatic experience—whether a dream or a type of conversion could scarcely be determined from his description—in which the whole Gestalt of his perceptions came to be viewed in a new fashion, much as the Gestalt figure in a textbook is first viewed as an ascending staircase, and now is seen as descending.

Mr. W: I had a funny experience last night that sorta turned my mind inside out. (*He goes on to describe the strange quality of this dreamlike experience.*) This business about my wife and Jim—that sort of blots out somehow. I can't quite straighten it out. I would like to be sure. I thought it all over. I *could* be mistaken. . . . (*Later.*) I thought, too, about my wife. I put a lot of different little things together, and I realize that I might be mistaken.

Counselor: It made you feel that your suspicions might not be correct.

Mr. W: That's it. I'm reasonably sure that she was right. (*Later.*) The sudden point in this dream, or whatever it was, was this thing about my wife. I see that I'm the one at fault there.

Here the perception has completed a full about-face. The perception of his wife as a shameless, deceitful, adulterous person has shifted completely to a perception of her as an individual devoted to him and not involved in any deceitfulness or sexual misconduct. Concurrently the perception of himself as a righteous and aggrieved husband has changed to a picture of himself as having felt sexually inadequate, and as having imagined his wife's unfaithfulness.

This illustration has been used not because it is typical but to indicate that the change in perception of others, which occurs in lesser degree in the majority of cases, may be so extreme as to produce a perception which is the reverse, in almost every respect, of the perception with which the client started. The change in the way another is seen may be very radical indeed.

There is a certain amount of objective evidence to support this clinical description. Sheerer (10) studied the changes in acceptance of self and acceptance of others as they occurred during client-centered therapy. She found "a marked and fairly regular increase in the measured acceptance of and respect for self from the beginning to the end of the cases. There is also a marked but more uneven rise in the acceptance of others from the beginning to the end" (10, p. 175). While the concept of acceptance of others is not, strictly speaking, a perceptual concept, it is nevertheless clear, when we examine her definition, that it contains many perceptual elements. It involves the degree to which the other is perceived as being worth while, as having a basic equality as a person. It involves perception of the other as having a right to his own opinions, beliefs, values, and standards. It involves perception of the other as a separate and self-directing individual. In all these respects perception becomes reorganized in a positive direction during the course of therapy.

This study by Sheerer, and another somewhat similar study by Stock (12), further uncover the fact that the acceptance of others, the feelings about others, the perception of others, are all positively and significantly correlated with the degree of acceptance of, feelings about, and perception of oneself. This leads to a consideration of a question which the writer regards as most basic: in what way and to what degree do the perceptions of self change or become reorganized during the process of client-centered therapy?

The Reorganization of Self-Perceptions.—To some it may seem unrealistic to speak of the "perception" of anything as intangible or as vaguely defined as the self. Yet it seems no more unreasonable to speak of the perception of self than to speak of the perception of another person, such as a close friend. In the latter case we have had a multitude of sensory stimuli which we perceive as related to this social object, our friend. It is the organized meaning which we attach to these stimuli that is our perception of our friend, and this meaning may be reinstated by very slight or very remote cues, such as a glimpse of his handwriting in a letter. In the same way a multitude of sensory and visceral stimuli appear to be related to us, to ourselves, and the meaning which we attach to those stimuli is the perception we have of self. This perception, as we shall see, seems to be governed by the principles which govern all perception.

It has been a part of the developing theory of client-centered therapy, as will be pointed out later, that the perception of self occupies a central place in the process. We may at this point then ask whether or not alteration or reorganization of this perception of self is characteristic of the course of therapy.

Until very recently our evidence along this line has been meager, fragmentary, and too largely subjective, even though it has tended to confirm our theory. Several studies have had some relationship to this question. In addition to the studies by Sheerer and Stock, mentioned above, Kessler and Natalie Rogers have made small objective studies (4, 9), and Lipkin has made a clinical survey which includes consideration of client self-perceptions (5).

The findings from these studies may be stated in terms of answers to a question. In what way does the individual come to perceive himself differently during therapy, particularly in those cases in which, by common-sense criteria, some "success" seems to have been achieved? The answers given by these studies would be the following.

1. There is a tendency for the "acceptance of self," operationally defined, to increase during therapy. Acceptance of self, according to the definition used, means that the client tends:

 a) To perceive himself as a person of worth, worthy of respect rather than condemnation.
 b) To perceive his standards as being based upon his own experience, rather than upon the attitudes or desires of others.
 c) To perceive his own feelings, motives, social and personal experiences, without distortion of the basic sensory data (10).

2. The individual in "successful" therapy tends:

 a) To perceive his abilities and characteristics with more objectivity and with greater comfort (9).
 b) To perceive all aspects of self and self-in-relationship with less emotion and more objectivity (12).
 c) To perceive himself as more independent and more able to cope with life problems (5, 9).

d) To perceive himself as more able to be spontaneous and genuine (5).

e) To perceive himself as the evaluator of experience, rather than regarding himself as existing in a world where the values are inherent in and attached to the objects of his perception (4).

f) To perceive himself as more integrated, less divided (5, 9).

How may we summarize these changes in self-perception? The essential elements would appear to be that the individual changes in three general ways. He perceives himself as a more adequate person, with more worth and more possibility of meeting life. He permits more experiential data to enter awareness and thus achieves a more realistic appraisal of himself, his relationships, and his environment. He tends to place the basis of standards within himself, recognizing that the "goodness" or "badness" of any experience or perceptual object is not something inherent in that object, but is a value placed on it by himself.

A New Procedure for Measuring Changes in Self-Perception.— These findings are of interest, but they do not tell us enough, and some of the studies upon which they are based contain too large an element of subjective judgment. Recently the *Q* technique, developed by William Stephenson (11) has appeared to provide a much richer and more meaningful approach to this problem and others of a similarly complex sort. No attempt will be made here to give an account of the theoretical statistical thinking out of which the method has grown, but the use made of it in studying the self will be described in a very practical and limited way.

Since the problem we wish to investigate is the way in which the individual perceives himself, the first step is to obtain a trait universe of self-perceptions. Ideally we would like this trait universe to contain samples of all the possible ways in which an individual could see himself. We approximate this by culling from a large number of recorded interviews all the statements which the clients make about themselves. To give a little of the flavor of this trait universe, here are a few statements collected in this manner:

I like to be independent. I don't like to be run over, or obligated to anyone.

I have all the assurance and self-confidence I need.

I don't see how anybody could love me.

I sort of only half believe in myself.

I know from experience that I can't pretend to be something I'm not and get away with it.

I feel sexually inadequate.

I feel I ought to be in a sanitarium. There must be something awfully wrong with me.

I often have the feeling of wanting to be immersed in the group . . . to belong and be just like other people.

I always felt that there was more security at home than out in the world.

I really feel insecure.

I seem to have a real inner strength in handling things. I'm on a pretty solid foundation and it makes me pretty sure of myself.

I know it's impossible to change myself all at once, but that's the thing I'd like to do.

It means a great deal to me to be different. . . . I don't want to be like the mob.

I've gotten so that I'm afraid to try things, because I just know before I start that I'm not going to be able to do them.

Most of my problems revolve around dealing with people.

The possibility of my ever amounting to anything is pretty darn slim.

I'm really a very different person from what people think I am.

To me life is interesting, rich, and colorful.

For our next step let us draw at random from this total population of several hundred items a group of 150. Since it is drawn at random, it may be taken as a limited but representative sample of all the ways in which a person may see himself.

As a further step, let us ask a client before therapy to sort these 150 cards into eleven piles, placing the items most characteristic of himself in the eleventh pile, and those least characteristic in the first, with the others sorted into the intermediate piles depending on how much they are like or unlike his perception of himself. In order to simplify later statistical handling, let us request him to put a given number in each pile so as to give us a normal distribution curve. Thus we will request him to put only four cards in each end pile, but thirty in the middle pile, etc. We now have a complex but statistically manipulable report of the person's self-perception, as it exists before therapy.

We can obtain a similar picture of the self as it exists during therapy. We can again obtain the picture as it is at the conclusion of therapy, and six months or a year or more following the conclusion of therapy. Since each item of the self-picture has been assigned a numerical value by being placed in pile 1 or 3 or 11, etc., the relationships between these various "selves" may be investigated readily by correlating each self-picture with every other. A high degree of correlation would mean, obviously, that there had been little change or reorganization, while a low correlation would mean that change had taken place.

Even this does not exhaust the aspects we may investigate. We may ask the client to re-sort the cards to express the self that he would like to be, wants to be. We might call this his self-ideal. We may further ask him to sort the cards to represent the most unhappy or miserable self he can imagine. Another sorting might give us his picture of the traits of the ordinary person. Since these sortings could be made before, during, and after therapy, we may obtain a very complex correlation matrix expressing all the interrelationships which exist between these various sortings. This may be analyzed further by means of factor analysis, through what would be termed an inverted type of factor analysis.

But without carrying our thinking further into a statistical stratosphere, let us investigate the type of finding that we are getting as we begin to use this technique. The writer is indebted to Hartley (2) for the following data, which come from a study which is still in progress.

Let us consider the findings in the case of Zar, as indicated in Figure 37. Zar was a young woman, a student, who came in for counseling. She sorted the cards for the self she perceived herself as being, and for the self she would like to be. This was done before therapy, after the ninth interview, and again at the end of therapy, which in her case concluded with the thirty-first interview. Some of the intercorrelations are shown in the figure. Studying these, it would seem accurate to draw these conclusions for this case.

1. The perception of self undergoes such change and reorganization during therapy that there is very little relationship between the self as perceived before and as seen after therapy ($r = .15$).
2. Before therapy the self as perceived has little relationship to the self she would like to be ($r = .18$).
3. At the conclusion of therapy she perceives herself as being much more nearly the self she would like to be ($r = .81$).
4. There is only modest change in self-perception in the first part of therapy ($r = .75$) but a great deal in the last portion ($r = .13$).
5. The perception of the self she would like to be remains rather constant throughout therapy ($r = .71$), while the perception of self as it is changes markedly ($r = .15$).
6. During therapy the discrepancy between these two selves grows greater ($r = .04$) before the discrepancy is largely removed ($r = .81$).

7. The self after therapy approximates the self as it was desired before therapy $(r = .70)$.

8. The self before therapy bears no relationship to the sort of self desired after therapy $(r = .00)$.

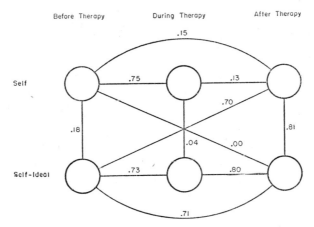

FIG. 37.—Case of Zar. Correlations between self and self-ideal Q sorts before, during, and after therapy.

Let us also examine in a qualitative fashion some of the perceptual changes which have occurred. Before therapy she perceives herself as lacking in energy and dissatisfied with the way things are going for her. She doesn't know what she wants, nor does she have a definite purpose. She is troubled about her relationships with people and needs to have others like her. She feels greatly lacking in confidence, has lived by the standards of others, and feels so unsure that she feels she has to be led around. She thinks it is a slim chance that she will ever amount to much. She sees herself as having lots of ability, but unable to express it effectively. She wants to create. She loves children.

After therapy the picture is decidedly changed. Certain elements, such as her love for children and her desire to be creative, still have a high ranking. But the outstanding elements after therapy are the self-assurance and confidence that she feels and the new sense of goal direction. She perceives herself as having a real inner strength, as being capable of going forward, as confident about the future. She looks at her present situation with optimism and contentment. She desires to learn, knows more clearly what she wants, takes action rather than letting things pile up, is not afraid to try things, feels a sense of purpose. She perceives herself as having a feminine, warm emotionality and a considerable zest for living. Life looks interesting, rich, and colorful, and she can take its problems with calm and serenity. It seems obvious that the perception of self has been rather drastically changed during therapy.

Thus far this elaborate and rewarding method of analysis has been used on but a few cases. Yet since the tentative generalizations which are emerging appear to be congruent with clinical experience, the writer will endeavor to state them, with the warning that they may prove to be incorrect as further evidence is obtained.

1. The perception of the self is the aspect of personality which is most radically changed by the process of therapy.
2. The change appears to be more in the meaning which is given to the stimuli than in the stimuli themselves.
3. The self the person wants to be is reorganized to a much lesser degree in therapy.
4. The hypothesis is very tentatively advanced that the self the person wants to be may be a more accurate description of his organism and its experience than is the description of the perceived self.
5. At the conclusion of the type of reorganization described in 1, 2, and 3 above, the self is perceived as being much more nearly congruent with the desired self or self-ideal.
6. There appears to be much more confidence in this reorganized self.

Now while this section may stand as a reasonably adequate description of the perceptual changes which take place in therapy—to be modified, of course, as the evidence accumulates—it only whets our curiosity as to why and how such changes take place. Any light on these questions can only be given at the present time by a speculative formulation. Consequently, in the section which follows the writer will endeavor to state a current theory of the process of therapy, in terms which contain the clinical and objective evidence of perceptual change, but which go beyond this evidence in giving certain explanations which may help to interpret the facts and may provide hypotheses for further testing.

A Theory of the Process of Therapy and Its Perceptual Changes [1]

The theoretical statement begins with the personality as it exists before a need for therapy develops and carries through the processes which occur in client-centered therapy. Let us begin with the indi-

---

[1] This section of the paper is taken largely from Chapter 4 of *Client-Centered Therapy*, by Carl R. Rogers, by permission of Houghton Mifflin Co., publishers.

vidual who is content with himself, who has no present thought of seeking counseling help. We may find it useful to think of this individual as having an organized pattern of perceptions of self and self-in-relationship to others and to the environment. This configuration, this Gestalt, is, in its details, a fluid and changing thing, but it is decidedly stable in its basic elements. It is, as Raimy says, "constantly used as a frame of reference when choices are to be made. Thus it serves to regulate behavior and may serve to account for observed uniformities in personality" (8). This configuration is, in general, available to awareness.

We may look upon this self-structure as being an organization of perceptual hypotheses for meeting life—an organization which has been relatively effective in satisfying the needs of the organism. Some of its hypotheses may be grossly incorrect from the standpoint of objective reality. As long as the individual has no suspicion of this falsity, the organization serves him well. As a simple example, the star student in a small-town high school may perceive himself as an outstandingly brilliant person, with a mind excelled by none. This formulation may serve him adequately as long as he remains in that environment. He may have some experiences which are inconsistent with this perception, but he either denies these experiences to awareness or symbolizes them in such a way that they are consistent with his general picture.

As long as the self-Gestalt is firmly organized and no contradictory material is even dimly perceived, then positive self-feelings may exist, the self may be seen as worthy and acceptable, and conscious tension is minimal. Behavior is consistent with the organized hypotheses and concepts of the self-structure. An individual in whom such conditions exist would perceive himself as functioning adequately.

In such a situation the extent to which the individual's perceptions of his abilities and relationships were incongruent with socially perceived reality would be a measure of his basic vulnerability. The extent to which he dimly perceives these incongruences and discrepancies is a measure of his internal tension and determines the amount of defensive behavior. As a parenthetical comment, it may be observed that in highly homogeneous cultures, where the self-concept of the individual tends to be supported by his society, rather grossly unrealistic perceptions may exist without causing internal tension and may serve throughout a lifetime as a reasonably effective hypothesis for meeting life. Thus the slave may perceive himself as less worthy than his master and live by this perception, even though, judged on a reality basis, the perception may be false. But in our modern culture, with its conflicting subcultures and its contradictory sets of values, goals, and perceptions, the individual tends to be exposed to a realization of discrepancies in his perceptions. Thus internal conflict is multiplied.

Let us return to our individual, who is not yet ready for therapy. It is when his organized self-structure is no longer effective in meeting his needs in the reality situation or when he dimly perceives discrepancies in himself or when his behavior seems out of control and no longer consistent with himself that he becomes "ripe," as it were, for therapy. As examples of these three conditions, we might mention the "brilliant" small-town high school student who no longer finds himself effective in the university, the individual who is perplexed because he wants to marry the girl yet does not want to, and the client who finds that her behavior is unpredictable, "not like myself," no longer understandable. Without a therapeutic experience, planned or accidental, such conditions are likely to persist because each of them involves the perception of experiences which are contradictory to the current organization of the self. But such perception is threatening to the structure of the self and consequently tends to be denied or distorted, to be inadequately symbolized.

But let us suppose that our individual, now vaguely or keenly disturbed and experiencing some internal tension, enters a relationship with a therapist who is client-centered in his orientation. Gradually he experiences a freedom from threat which is decidedly new to him. It is not merely that he is free from attack. This has been true of a number of his relationships. It is that every aspect of self which he exposes is equally accepted, equally valued. His almost belligerent statement of his virtues is accepted as much as, but no more than, his discouraged picture of his negative qualities. His certainty about some aspects of himself is accepted and valued but so are his uncertainties, his doubts, his vague perception of contradictions within himself. In this atmosphere of safety, protection, and acceptance, the firm boundaries of self-organization relax. There is no longer the firm, tight Gestalt which is characteristic of every organization under threat, but a looser, more uncertain configuration. He begins to explore his phenomenal field more and more fully. He discovers faulty generalizations, but his self-structure is now sufficiently relaxed to consider the complex and contradictory experiences upon which they are based. He perceives experiences of which he has never been aware, which are deeply contradictory to the concept he has had of himself, and this is threatening indeed. He retreats temporarily to the former comfortable Gestalt but then slowly and cautiously moves out to assimilate this contradictory experience into a new and revised pattern.

In understanding the process by which these denied experiences are assimilated, the experimental work of Postman, Bruner, and McGinnies (7) and that of McCleary and Lazarus (6) are highly pertinent. Since this work has been described by Miller earlier in this book (Chapter 9), the description will not be repeated here. Suffice it to say that the client in therapy first "subceives" an experience (to use the term coined by McCleary and Lazarus) as being threatening to self. This creates anxiety, even though there is no awareness of the experience itself. But in the safety of the therapeutic relationship the client can permit the self-Gestalt to be disrupted by actually *per*ceiving, openly, in awareness, the threatening and hitherto denied experience. Then the self-structure is reconstructed, is reperceived, with this new experiential element now owned and included as a part of self.

Essentially this is a process of disorganization and reorganization of percepts and concepts, and while it is going on it may be decidedly painful. It is deeply confusing not to have a firm concept of self by which to determine behavior appropriate to the situation. It is frightening or disgusting to find self and behavior fluctuating from day to day, at times largely in accord with the earlier self-pattern, at times being in confused accord with some new, vaguely structured Gestalt. As the process continues, a new or revised configuration of self is being constructed. It contains perceptions of many experiences which were previously denied. It involves more accurate symbolization of a much wider range of sensory and visceral experience. It involves a reorganization of values, with the organism's own experience clearly recognized as providing the evidence for the valuations. There slowly begins to emerge a new self, which to the client seems to be much more his "real" self, because it is based to a much greater extent upon all of his experiences, perceived without distortion.

Something of the direction which this perceptual reorganization will take has already been predicted by the self-ideal, the self which the person wants to be. In many ways this self-ideal is perhaps nearer to the accurate description of the organism and to the undistorted symbolization of the sensory and visceral stimuli. Whether this is true in all cases or not, the perceived self changes and is reorganized in the direction of fitting more closely the raw experiential aspects of this unique human organism. The feelings in particular are perceived for what they are, and the self is discovered in and abstracted from basic experience, rather than being a formulation or structure which is imposed upon experience.

This painful dis- and re-organization of self-perception is made possible by two elements in the therapeutic relationship. The first is one already mentioned, that the new, the tentative, the contradictory, or the previously denied perceptions of self are as much valued by the therapist as are the rigidly structured aspects. Thus the shift from the latter to the former becomes possible without too disastrous a loss of self-worth or a too frightening leap from the old to the new. The other element in the relationship is the attitude of the therapist toward the newly discovered aspects of experience. To the client they seem threatening, bad, impossible, disorganizing. Yet he experiences the therapist's attitude of calm acceptance toward them. He finds that to a degree he can introject this attitude and can look upon his experience as something he can own, identify, symbolize, and accept as a part of himself.

If the relationship is not adequate to provide this sense of safety or if the denied experiences are too threatening, then the client may revise his concept of self in a defensive fashion. He may further distort the symbolization of experience, may make more rigid the structure of self, and thus may achieve again positive self-feelings and a somewhat reduced internal tension—but at a price of increased vulnerability. Undoubtedly this is a temporary phenomenon in many clients who are undergoing considerable reorganization; but the evidence available suggests that some clients may conclude their contacts at such a juncture, having achieved only an increasingly defensive self.

Where the client does face more of the totality of his experience and where he adequately differentiates and symbolizes this experience, then as the new self-structure is organized it becomes firmer, more clearly defined, a steadier, more stable guide to behavior. As in the state in which the person felt no need of therapy or in the defensive reorganization of self, positive self-feelings return and positive attitudes predominate over negative. Many of the outward manifestations are the same. From an external point of view an important difference is that the new self is much more nearly congruent with the totality of experience—that it is a pattern drawn from or perceived in experience, rather than a pattern imposed upon experience. A change in the manner of perceiving also comes about. Because there is less defensiveness, there is less perceptual rigidity. Sensory evidence can be more readily admitted to awareness. It can be interpreted and perceived in a greater variety of ways and with a greater degree of differentiation. From the client's internal point of view the new self is a more comfortable one. There are fewer experiences perceived as vaguely threatening. There is, consequently, much less anxiety. There is a less insistent need for closure and more tolerance of ambiguity. Thus there is both a greater tentativeness and a greater assurance in the perceptions of the individual at the end of therapy. The tentativeness is due to the lessened defensiveness. The greater assurance arises because perception is more closely rooted in, more influenced by, the direct evidence of experience as conveyed by all the sensory modalities. Values, too, are seen differently. Because values are perceived as originating in self, the value system becomes more realistic and comfortable and more nearly in harmony with the perceived self. Valued goals appear more achievable.

The changes in behavior keep pace with the changes in organization of self, and this behavior change is, surprisingly enough, neither as painful nor as difficult as the changes in self-structure. Behavior continues to be consistent with the concept of self and alters as it alters. Any behavior which formerly seemed out of control is now experienced as a part of self and within the boundaries of conscious control. In general the behavior is more adjustive and socially more sound, because the hypotheses upon which it is based are more realistic.

Thus therapy produces a change in personality organization and structure and a change in behavior which are relatively permanent. It is not necessarily a reorganization which will serve for a lifetime. It may still deny to awareness certain aspects of experience, may still exhibit certain patterns of defensive behavior. There is little likelihood that any therapy is in this sense complete. Under new stresses of a certain sort, the client may find it necessary to seek further therapy, to achieve further reorganization of self. But whether there be one or more series of therapeutic interviews, the essential outcome involves a more broadly based perceptual structure of self, an inclusion of a greater proportion of experience perceived as a part of self, and a more comfortable and realistic adjustment to life.

Relationship to Perception in General.—Hilgard, in Chapter 4 of this book, describes the distorted room devised by Ames and some of the uses which Ames, Cantril, and others have made of the room to further study of the problems of perception. You will recall that the room is grossly distorted and oblique in shape yet so designed as to give all the perceptual cues which we have learned to associate with an ordinary rectilinear room. But Cantril tells an interesting story about his use of the room which provides an analogy to therapy. If a person, looking at this room at the proper point of vision, takes a stick and tries to hit the rubber rat or to strike a spot on the left-hand wall and a (seemingly) corresponding mark on the right-hand wall, he misses badly. This is true even though he may know intellectually that the room is oblique and not rectilinear. This is analogous to much maladjustment. We act in strict accord with our perceptions, but the results of our behavior are ineffective or unsatisfying, and even though we understand the trouble intellectually, it does not help. Cantril reports that if the person continues to practice hitting the rat or striking the marked spots on the walls, he gradually comes to *experience* the proper distance and level at which to strike, and in the process his *perception* of the room changes so that it now *appears* oblique and not rectilinear. This, the writer believes, is therapy.

Let us make the analogy more explicit. Because of his past learnings in his family and culture, a person has come (for example) to perceive himself as of little worth, a self in whom it would not be possible to have confidence. This perception is extremely constant, just as is our perception of the room as rectilinear. Every experience appears to confirm it, just as every look at the distorted room only assures us that it is rectilinear. We may tell the person that he is worth while, that he may have confidence in himself, and he may know this intellectually, but such knowledge is as ineffective as is a view of the floor plan of the oblique room.

In therapy he begins to act on his perceptions, symbolically at least. He is free, in the safe relationship that is therapy, to *be* his worthless self, to express to the fullest his lack of confidence in himself and all that is implied by it. He *is* his worthless self, but finds himself accepted as worth while. He is himself as a person in whom he cannot have confidence, yet he finds that he unerringly chooses the areas of conflict to talk about, that he makes progress in understanding himself, that he is in some odd way confident of the direction in which he is going. He discovers, by acting on them, that his perceptions do not match his immediate therapeutic experience. The sensory and visceral evidence simply does not correspond with the learned aspects of his perception. Gradually, on the basis of the raw data of his immediate experience of the relationship with the therapist, he finds his perception of himself changing. He does not change it—he simply discovers that it *is* changing, just as the person who practices with the stick discovers that his perception of the room is changing.

If we think of perception as a complex phenomenon involving the raw data of immediate experience and the learnings we bring to it from the past, then therapy is a process whereby a safe exploration permits the person to separate and differentiate the elements of this phenomenon. He can feel the immediate experience of himself in this relationship. He can also experience the meaning which his past learnings would tend to cause him to see in himself in this relationship. Where there is discrepancy, the perception becomes reorganized in terms of the immediate experience. He can be what he *is* and can recognize that past learnings would frequently cause him to see himself as something he is not. He acquires a new confidence as he rests his perceptions more securely upon the data of his senses. Perception of self thus becomes what it should be, an adequate hypothesis for living, soundly based on the available evidence, and alterable in the light of new evidence.

But as has been suggested by the data presented earlier, when the individual has reorganized his perception of self, he has reconstructed the most significant learned element that he brings to any experience. Thus we find that, when the self is perceived in reorganized terms, it affects not only the future perception of self but the way the individual perceives his wife, his friends, other persons, the campus buildings, the counselor's face, and even that holy of psychological holies, the unstructured and ambiguous ink blot. It is thus, the writer believes, that psychotherapy reorganizes perception by providing a relationship in which the individual's most basic perception, his perception of himself, can change.

BIBLIOGRAPHY

1. HAIMOWITZ, NATALIE R. An investigation into some personality changes occurring in individuals undergoing client-centered therapy. Ph. D. thesis, University of Chicago, 1948.
2. HARTLEY, MARGARET. *Q* technique—its methodology and application. Ph. D. thesis, in progress, University of Chicago, 1950.
3. JONIETZ, ALICE K. A study of the phenomenological changes in perception after psychotherapy as exhibited in the content of Rorschach percepts. Ph. D. thesis, University of Chicago, 1950.
4. KESSLER, CAROL. Semantics and non-directive counseling. M. A. paper, University of Chicago, 1947.
5. LIPKIN, S. The client evaluates nondirective psychotherapy. *J. consult. Psychol.,* 1948, **12,** 137-46.
6. McCLEARY, R. A., & LAZARUS, R. S. Autonomic discriminations without awareness: an interim report. *J. Personal.,* 1949, **18,** 171-79.
7. POSTMAN, L., BRUNER, J. S., & McGINNIES, E. Personal values as selective factors in perception. *J. abnorm. soc. Psychol.,* 1948, **43,** 142-54.
8. RAIMY, V. C. The self-concept as a factor in counseling and personality organization. Ph. D. thesis, Ohio State University, 1943.
9. ROGERS, NATALIE. Changes in self concept in the case of Mrs. Ett. *Personal Counselor,* 1947, **2,** 278-91.
10. SHEERER, ELIZABETH T. An analysis of the relationship between acceptance of and respect for self and acceptance of and respect for others in ten counseling cases. *J. consult. Psychol.,* 1949, **13,** 169-75.
11. STEPHENSON, W. A statistical approach to typology: the study of trait-universe. *J. clin. Psychol.,* 1950, **6,** 26-38.
12. STOCK, DOROTHY. An investigation into the interrelations between the self-concept and feelings directed toward other persons and groups. *J. consult. Psychol.,* 1949, **13,** 176-80.

CHAPTER 12

THE PERSONAL WORLD THROUGH PERCEPTION [1]

By George S. Klein, Ph.D.

I think I am interpreting correctly the spirit of this symposium when I say that our focus upon perception is secondary to an interest in persons, that perception is for us only a convenient wedge into this larger problem. Our target is a theory which would lead to laws of *perceivers,* not laws of *perception,* a theory which would be not so much concerned with linking generalized field conditions or states of motivation to perception in general as with linking them to the organization of people. Rather than ask, "What effects do values or needs have upon perception?" we would want to know "How are people *constructed* to cope with values among other stimuli?"

Perception is a key site for the study of individual organization. The work of Ames (1) and Cantril (7) which comes from the boldly conceived functionalism of von Helmholtz (39), the facts amassed by Hilgard, the pioneer efforts of Murphy (31), Bruner (4, 5), and their associates and of Egon Brunswik (6) provide evidence enough that purposes, aims, intentions suffuse the very act of perceiving. All of this work challenges the idea of "internal requiredness" or autochthony in the stimulus field, of "field structures" which are so compelling as to have a predestined and universal effect independent of personal intent. It has also helped to bury the older conception of an autonomous perceptual system which is capable of study apart from the larger context of the total system of the person, an idea born out of a myopia to personality theory. Clinical observation has certainly helped at this burial. The hysteric who scotomizes the objectionable, the paranoid's sensitivity to slightest nuances, the hypnotic's distortions of body image—surely the clinician will give you any number of instances of perception giving faithful service to the handling of censored wishes. Perception is *the* point of reality contact, the door to

---

[1] The formulations given here issue from a research program now in progress under a grant from the National Institutes of Health, United States Public Health Service. I am indebted to my coworkers, Herbert J. Schlesinger and Philip S. Holzman, for applying a critical eye to many of the points in this paper.

reality appraisal, and there is no doubt that here especially are the selective, adaptive controls of personality brought into play.

But to pile demonstration upon demonstration of purposiveness in perception is not enough, nor even to show the different qualities and distortions of percepts, or of "hypotheses" and of "subceptions" and to trace these to needs or values. This gets us no nearer a theory of *personalities,* for it speaks still of the nature of *perception*—how *it* is capable of being influenced, that it *can* serve purposes. Our sight must go beyond perception itself to the different requirements, demands, and claims of personality structures (egos).

Requirements for a Personality Theory of Perception

The touchstone of any personality theory is how well it accounts for *differences* among people. In meeting this test, it is not enough to note differences, to classify contents and responses. Another step is necessary. The theory should give us principles—dimensions— which make variations meaningful and point to ego controls of which the one variation is only an instance. If factors outside a person affect his responses, it is the *dealing with* them by his singular filtering processes, not the effects themselves, to which we should point. We may call this concern with the structure of a person a *vertical* approach.

A generalization about personality is always vertical; it contrasts with *horizontal,* cross-person, and system-absent generalizations so common to social psychological thinking. The horizontal approach levels people and considers only the uniform or "general" effects of a situation. Its typical focus is upon *what* is seen—the content of a percept—rather than upon *how* it is seen—the personal organization which frames it. It ignores the "vectors" of personality organization which direct response and reduce the authority of the stimulus field. The horizontal approach does not typify only the classical theories of autochthonous perception but has carried over to most current functional theories. Even an outlook so purposivistic as Ames's speaks of the "purpose" in an act of perceiving as if it were inevitable to the particular situation and invariant from person to person. For him, "purposes" vary with the situation, not with the person; he makes little provision for differences in purpose in the *same* situation. That is why Ames's approach and most other functional theories of perception are as yet only starting points for, but are not themselves, theories of personality.

Two major questions face us here: Just what do we need to assume about the *structure* of personality to justify our studying it in perception? How can we best take systematic account of individual differences in perception so that they become data for a personality theory?

Most personality theories treat the appraisal and mastery of reality. This function of *reality testing* mediates between inner demands and outer imperatives. The placating formulae which a person develops —his equilibrating mechanisms—are his *ego-control system*. It is this that perception can tell us most about. All theories of adaptation assume in one way or another that functioning is directed to resolve tension and to reach an equilibrium between the inner and the outer, and perception helps to accomplish this. But it is not solely a perceptual affair, for all the part-systems of response—perception, motor processes, thinking—are put to *use* in the effort to achieve equilibrium. If we take seriously the idea of the "organism as a whole", then there should be consistency in how all of these functions work. This is something to be demonstrated, of course, but it would be difficult to think of coherence in a person if it were not true. This crucial tenet is required of any theory of personality which would encompass perceptual theory; it is the only basis for making the study of perception relevant to the theory. Conversely, if analyses of perception are to have any relevance to personality theory, they must disclose how the control principles, the equilibrating mechanisms, appear *in* and *through* its functioning.

In speaking of equilibrium, I want to avoid a common but unfortunate implication which follows from thinking too much in physicalistic models, i.e., to think of equilibrium as a fixed and inevitable state to which the person always returns and which takes similar forms in all people; that given the *same* "field conditions" and the *same* "needs" in the *same* intensity, the final state reached in that field and the processes for reaching it will be the same for everyone (14). This is an earmark of the horizontal approach; and the prototype of the person which it describes is like a chemical balance, all varieties of which come to equilibrium in exactly the same way, though of course, the weights in the pans may differ.

The concept of "equilibrium" is useful only if we wholeheartedly recognize that the kind of balance and the means for reaching it are different for different people. Perhaps it would be better to substitute the word "solution" for "equilibrium," meaning the more or less "steady state" which an individual reaches in the face of a task, a problem, or a stimulus as he resolves it in his own way. What determines the form of the steady state as much as anything are the favored and stabilized means of tension-reduction which people settle upon. One man's "equilibrium" is another man's discomfiture. This is a basic datum, and we must begin here.

Our goal then is to seek out in perceptual structure the matter-of-course avenues by which a person resolves disequilibria and to infer from these his central controls.

The entire functionalist emphasis—as in the work of Ames, Bruner, and Brunswik—testifies to how the directedness and purposiveness of perception are in the very *act* of perceiving. If we look at the perceptual system, we find a number of properties which offer the possibility of control by the ego system; they serve ends and answer adaptive requirements. Such properties as thresholds, perceptual latency or recognition time, brightness and size constancy, among others, are favorite textbook chapters. All these may be variants of a more basic property of "hypothesis-forming," as Bruner suggests, or the developing of schema or adaptation levels, in Helson's terms. Considered from the viewpoint of the perceiver, however, they are "tools" or "potentials" which are used in any situation to which he adapts. These qualities of the perceptual system we have elsewhere described as *adaptive properties* (16).

But these "adaptive properties," as we call them, are provided by the physiology and anatomy of the perceiving system. They are the "givens," and all perceivers have them; no one with an intact perceptual system is without thresholds, the quality of latency, the capacity to "schematize" or form adaptation levels. The disclosure of such properties was an important event in the history of psychology, and equally important are the more recent demonstrations that they can serve purposes, needs, and values. But to stop here merely reaffirms a clinical commonplace—that it is indeed possible for "personality to influence perception,"—and this is where most functional emphases have stopped. We *know* that only certain people scotomize, only certain people develop psychogenic anesthesias, and only certain people accentuate a valued stimulus (19). The perceptual apparatus lends itself to adaptive control; its properties are used variously. To sum up all this: People develop definitive modes of meeting the world (ego controls). These controls and the connections among them, both within persons and among persons of the same type, are the "dimensions" of the ego-control system. Now, the next advance should show, *in perceptual terms,* how the modes and patterns of perceiving express the claims of ego controls.

The Concept of *Anschauung*.—For want of a better word, we have tentatively adopted the term *Anschauung* or "attitude" to identify these key principles. A perceptual attitude is a personal outlook on the world, embodying in perception one of the ego's adaptive requirements. A style of reality-testing is expressed through it. It expresses a broader control principle which makes comparable demands upon other systems besides perception.[2] Since it aims to specify in perception more general principles of ego control, the concept supplies the needed conceptual tool—or intervening variable if you like (29)—for making perception the focus of personality theory. It gives us a means of accounting for how and in what respects people differ, and in so doing, it makes generalizations about persons in perceptual terms, also personality principles. It carries us a step beyond mere demonstrations of selectivity and purposiveness and speaks of various kinds of selectivity or different kinds of equilibrating mechanisms in people and leads us to look for these in individual variations.

You will better understand the implications of the concept through descriptions of several attitudes we are working on, but to help fix it in mind I will mention one we have isolated. It is titled "sharpening" —a tendency to be hypersensitive to minutiae, to respond excessively to fine nuances and small differences, to exaggerate change, and to keep adjacent or successive stimuli from fusing and losing identity. I am going to give you further examples of perceptual attitudes, but their meaning will be clearer if first I summarize certain of their general qualities which reach to the ego-control system itself.

An Anschauung Is a "Solution" to an Adaptive Task. For instance, attitudes which we call "leveling" and "sharpening" are ways of resolving disequilibrium when the task is to cope with "differences." There are probably other attitudes or "solutions" which could apply to this same task. I am not clear how best to represent formally all those which we conceivably could get in certain types of situations. Our own definitions are influenced by *quantitative* differences among people, and this has led us to think of attitudes as ranging from "more to less" along a continuum, as from "leveling" to "sharpening." This may be untenable when we learn more about those people who now are the "in-betweens." All the varieties may be *qualitatively* different, and it may be uneconomical to think of any two as "opposites." There is some evidence even

---

[2] The term *Anschauung* is preferable to "attitude" because of the rather more narrow, well-worn connotations of the latter term in American psychologies, particularly in social psychology. Attitude usually implies a quite specific *content* and a direction toward or away from an object. In this common meaning it carries no implications of formal personality structure. But our use of it is precisely in the latter sense, as a genotypic principle of control, having no ties to specific content, not necessarily related to particular conflicts or stresses, and with counterparts in all forms of cognitive behavior. Since the common meanings are so difficult to ignore, the reader would do well to couple *attitude* with *Anschauung,* which better implies the broader meaning.

now that the so-called attitude of "sharpening" is not simply "opposite" to leveling. Perhaps it is better to think of a *cluster* of unique solutions than of a single linear dimension. But this simpler scheme of a continuum anchored by seeming opposites is workable enough for now, and our illustrations will refer to "dimensions" of attitudes. You must keep in mind, however, that the question of continuity is far from settled.

An Anschauung Is a Style of Organization. It is the flavor of an act of perceiving, the organizing theme, or *leitmotiv* of perceptual sensitivity. The "sharpening" attitude, which I will discuss more fully later on, says in effect: "Be alert to all shades and nuances. Let nothing slip by unnoticed." This cast of response should show itself in many tasks and all modalities. A type of order is conveyed by it, what Angyal calls "a system principle" (2). For instance, when we speak of the circularity of something (regardless of content), we mean a formal principle or motif of organization—the equidistance of points from some center. In the same way when we speak of "sharpening," we do not imply a particular perceptual content but a formal principle which shapes the percept; the theme is accentuation, the highlighting of differences.

An Anschauung Is a Syndrome or Patterning of Adaptive Properties. The extent to which adaptive properties participate in a percept is not always known. If it were, we could state our definitions through them, for every variation of an adaptive property acquires its color from a perceptual attitude. Properties we call "schematizing" and "inherence," which I describe later on, take special forms in "sharpening" and "leveling." The particular patterning of adaptive properties that are impressed by an attitude, we call a *syndrome*. Most of the time we do not know the adaptive properties in a situation, but if we understand the kind of solution reached, then the perceptual attitude is definable notwithstanding.

An Anschauung Expresses a Central or "Executive Directive" of the Ego-Control System Which Shapes an Adaptive Solution. Perception is only one facet of the controlling ego system, but through it we see the manner of working of the entire system. In this sense a perceptual attitude has "purpose," but by this I mean only that it expresses a control requirement, a regulative principle. It acts very much as a "selective valve" which regulates intake—i.e., what is or is not to be ignored. Its immediate "purpose" is only what it succeeds in accomplishing. In "leveling," the purpose is the obliteration of differences; in "sharpening," a heightened sensitivity to them. It is a way favored by a person for bringing about an equilibrium.

Parallel attitudes presumably appear in "learning" behavior, in motor activity, or in other functions of the ego. The ego system is independent of any one *part-system,* yet its principles pervade all of them. It is possible that certain kinds of people, say hysterics, need for effective learning overvalue or "technicolored" stimuli. This kind of learning behavior may parallel in perception what we call "leveling." In other words, both tendencies in two very different areas of behavior may be offshoots of a single ego-control principle. But we must leave such cross-functional definitions to the future. Since our focus at present is on perception alone, our definitions had best remain anchored there. Eventually, a more inclusive model of the person's total functioning may allow us to convert the "attitudes" of perception and their counterparts in other systems into a single set of general principles of control.

One implication of the concept is worth a special note: We are encouraged to think of attitudes as having concurrent forms in patterns of physiological behavior, e.g., in electrochemical activity of the brain and in muscle-tonus phenomena. The concept of *Anschauung* frees us from the notion of "levels" of behavior, each organized rather independently of the others. It suggests that what we have meant by "levels" of behavior is really only the multiple expressions of an ego control in operation, and it suggests also that the physiological description can enrich our idea of it. The "reducing" of psychological laws to the physiological in this way becomes a meaningless issue. There is not physiological behavior and psychological behavior. There is only *behavior,* and the levels we speak of are only *conceptual* levels arising from the methods chosen for studying it; they do not refer to the nature of the organism itself. The structure I have outlined gives physiological considerations, especially individual differences in such phenomena, a place in a theory of personality. It makes it possible to unify, with parsimony, behaviors not previously reconciled.

Derivation of a Perceptual Attitude.—Obviously, our propositions regarding the control system of the ego are too crude to allow a purely deductive approach to perceptual attitudes. For this reason, our hypotheses about them have often developed in an informal way —from curiosity about a certain phenomenon, quirks of data, hunches from clinical experiences, intuitions of subjects, and suggestions from typological literature. Most of the time we have followed our noses and let the data lead us to organizing principles that might account for them. The most common starting points are, however, worth special mention.

One of our favorite departure points has been individual differences in a task emphasizing one or several adaptive properties. Through a close study of the experiences of extreme groups, tentative attitudes are formulated to account for these differences. We then seek other perceptual tasks which will highlight these attitudes, and by a process of internal validation see if the separation of our groups is maintained in these as well. This process leads to redefinition of the attitudes in somewhat broader terms. Following this process of confirmation and formulation in *perceptual* terms, we are ready to fan out to concomitant aspects of the attitude, e.g., to get correlates in clinical descriptions, in motor or physiological behaviors, or in other functioning.

We can also start from a hypothesis regarding an ego-control principle derived from clinical experience, translate it into perceptual terms, and then proceed in the manner outlined above. The starting point is a matter of convenience. My examples will furnish illustrations of both kinds of approach.

Before going on to illustrations, let me summarize briefly: We began with the supposition that the organism continually wrestles with and seeks equilibrium between two sources of tension, its inner strivings and the demands of reality. In this task the ego puts perception to use, as it does other systems. Perception lends itself to this by virtue of its "adaptive properties." But these properties, common to all perceivers, are employed idiosyncratically; the personal styles in using them for reality appraisal I have called *perceptual attitudes* or *Anschauungen*. This is as far as we have come. With this structure in mind, I will describe three sets that have been derived and studied at the Perception Laboratory of the Menninger Foundation: (*a*) leveling and sharpening; (*b*) attitudes of resistance to or acceptance of instability; and (*c*) physiognomic and literal attitudes.

Some Perceptual Attitudes

The Dimension of "Leveling" vs. "Sharpening" of Differences. —One set of controls which we call "leveling" and "sharpening" we first isolated in a situation which was as neutral, as anonymous, and as "contentless" as any the psychophysical tradition can conjure up. The starting point was an experiment in visual "schematizing" which had to do with the way people organized and integrated their impressions about the sizes of squares.[3] Actually, when we began, there

---

[3] A collaborative study with Philip S. Holzman (18).

was no idea of "leveling" and "sharpening" in our minds. We were content to ask ourselves only: What sorts of solutions do people reach when they have to cope with stimuli which continually but gradually change in size? We felt that such a situation was "open" enough to draw a wide range of response and left room for a variety of solutions to appear.

Our method was to project one at a time fourteen squares ranging in size from two to fourteen inches. After looking at a square, the subject judged it for size. At first, only the smallest five were shown, until each had been judged three times. Then, without the subject's knowing it, square 1, the very smallest square, was taken out of the series, and square 6, which was larger than any in the series, was added. In this way, by subtracting the smallest square and adding a next larger one, the series gradually and progressively shifted from the smaller end of the range to the larger until all the fourteen squares were exposed, making a total of 150 judgments.

You will notice that the situation had none of the characteristics of so-called projective techniques. It involved no erotic content, excited no mysterious conflicts, triggered off no special traumata or stresses. Most of our subjects, almost all of them patients, felt the test rather easy to cope with; it was even absorbing to some. At the very worst it was monotonous. Our assumptions don't require much more than this, for they presume that a person continually brings to bear in any kind of a situation what for him are "preferred" ways of meeting reality. This is strategic for method: *Anschauungen* can be derived and studied in the laboratory, and we need not require hard-to-reproduce conditions of conflict or significant content; only the *formal* aspects of situations concern us at this stage.

Now just to take one slice of the most relevant findings. I cite only the extremes of our group, for these were the people who became key subjects. Some kept pace with the changing squares and judged size accurately. At the other extreme were those who responded very slowly to change; they kept underestimating more and more—they "lagged." The extent of this "adaptive lag" in some was such that at the close of the experiment they were judging a square of 13 inches to be only 4 inches!

How to account for this? It was as if the "lag" group preferred to ignore, deny, or suppress differences, to "level" them all to some simpler uniformity. Though the squares when placed side by side were obviously different, these persons seeing them successively managed to obscure the differences and to reach a stability of sameness. It was as if an early preconception of the whole series developed that "all the squares were small," and this idea served as a "background" to pull all stimuli toward it, for all squares were judged small without too much regard for actual distinctions.

In the group which shifted appropriately, an opposing formula seemed to be at work. The people here seemed less enslaved by such a preconception of the series; they were better able to consider each stimulus in its own right, and appropriately. They therefore appreciated and noted change. Stability for them meant not suppressing change and difference, but being alert to it.

As we looked further, we found that in those who lagged, inaccuracy was particularly great when a square was no longer vivid, that is, when it was neither largest nor smallest in a series but somewhere in between. Only when a square was conspicuously different and larger than the others did the lagging subjects keep track of it. When it lost its novelty and became integrated into the series, embedded in it, and "lost in the crowd," they were unable to tell it apart from the others. Accuracy increased once more when the stimulus was the smallest and again a prominent member of the series. One subject dropped in accuracy over 90 per cent when the stimulus moved from being the largest in the series to the next largest! Our non-laggers were much more accurate to start with and lost less accuracy as a stimulus moved through the series.

At this point the ideas of "leveling" and "sharpening" came to life; we now looked to other situations for validation. Perhaps the decrease in accuracy, as the square lost its novelty, reflected a difficulty with "embedded," as opposed to vivid, stimuli; perhaps people who lagged would find it harder to extract a particular figure from a masking context. We used Thurstone's version of the Gottschaldt figures to test this (36). The task was to locate a simple figure which was hidden in a more complex one. The lag group did indeed find this extraction task more difficult than did our non-lagging group.

We next used the familiar childhood puzzle of finding hidden faces in a larger picture for another extraction test. Again our lag group found it hard to penetrate the camouflage and to "extract" the hidden faces. Those who sharpened differences could easily spot the hidden faces. In fact, in one case this seemed to reach such unusual projective proportions that picayune details were elaborated into faces.

We reasoned further about this in still another test. In the lag group the preferred tendency should be to reduce the saliency of figures against grounds, to level the differences between them. To test this we are making use of an observation by Koffka and Harrower (22) who observed that a contour has the effect of increasing the saturation of a figure; in segregating a figure, it tends to "heighten" the qualities within it. A black figure looks "blacker" when its contour is firm. We represent this effect by an adaptive property which we call "inherence," a term suggested to us by Fritz Heider.

Since we expect that the lag group will obscure rather than highlight differences, we would suppose too that "inherence" would be given less play in their perceptual life. Contours should be less effective in setting off figure from background for this group. Their reaction should be toward diluting a figure to make it more congruent with the background, and the reverse tendency should hold in the non-lag group. For them the enhancing power of a contour should be greater, and the saturation of the figure should be increased by the fact of segregation alone.

To test this, four small, different gray squares were superimposed on nine different grounds, and subjects compared them with standards ranging from white to black. The effect of the firm contour should be toward making the stimuli seem darker than they actually are. In nearly every case this was so—the figures were judged darker. But the more important thing for the purpose of the experiment was that this tendency is less evident in the lag group. In them, segregation does not increase saturation to the extent of the sharpening group. To sum up, they seem to diminish differences in the perceptual field.

Let us pause for a moment. We began with a single task, our schematizing test, and we tried to account for the individual differences by formulating an opposed pair of attitudes. Then reaching out to other situations to which these attitudes seemed to apply, we came to a more comprehensive principle to which we can refer the results in all these situations. In this procedure we have looked for the consistencies of a person from one task to another; our focus has been the perceiver—how he organizes experience in his own ways. The findings have from the beginning pointed to *individual* prediction.

Notice, we did not immediately correlate individual differences with personality "traits" or diagnostic labels but defined the control principles in perceptual terms. Such premature correlations are more often frustrating than revealing. They only suggest important ties but tell us little of what these are. Our procedure anchors perceptual attitudes to sets of coordinate phenomena and in this way avoids the confusions latent in correlating incoordinate events.

Validation of these attitudes is far enough along that we can look to their ties to clinical behaviors. Remember, in describing the properties assigned to an attitude, we suggested that it should express a control principle of the ego system which gives personal color to the function of reality appraisal. We should expect to see this principle in clinical descriptions too, though it might be couched in terms more congenial to clinical practice.

Our first step was exploratory. We gathered a large number of descriptive statements expressing some thirteen traits defined by Murray, e.g., needs for dependence, independence, dominance, aggressiveness, tendencies toward self-depreciation, and so forth (32). We asked our subjects' therapists to describe their most and least distinctive qualities using the sorting method known in the Q technique. In this way we obtained a patterning of these trait qualities for each subject. We then summarized the relative prominence of the different descriptive "traits" in each extreme group.

The description of the lag or leveling group followed a pattern which we called "self-inwardness" and emphasized a retreat from objects, avoidance of competition or of any situation requiring active manipulation, exaggerated needs for nurture and succor, self-abasement, and rather ingenuous and passive drifting. The avoidance and minimizing of distinctions and nuances in the perceptual sphere thus seems to have its parallel in an avoidant pattern of everyday behavior. Such qualities are much *less* frequent in the sharpening group. The reverse tendency of "self-outwardness" includes traits that are manipulative and active; it describes people who generally find competition and exhibitionism congenial, who have high needs for attainment, who energetically and oftentimes aggressively push themselves forward, and who have a great need for autonomy. The leveling group was, however, more unequivocally linked with "self-inward" qualities than was the sharpening group with the self-outward items. In the non-laggers or sharpeners, self-inward and self-outward items were about equally represented among their most salient qualities, but as a group they were well separated from the other.

This is as far as we have carried our empirical studies of this set of attitudes, enough to give them preliminary definition. There is evidence of their generality and a hint of their ties to some central parameter of ego functioning. But questions about them are far from exhausted.

Figure 38 shows some of the relationships implied by the concept of perceptual attitude, using the leveling-sharpening dimension as an example. It is a sort of conceptual map which diagrams some speculations about the links which these attitudes have beyond the perceptual sphere itself. First of all, it places leveling and sharpening within the broader perspective of the ego-control network operating in perception; it pictures them as only one dimension of a number of control principles. In one sense these attitudes are intervening variables which link individual differences of one situation to those of others and to the larger design of a control system. Since we think of this system as unified and ordered, we would suppose attitudes to be interrelated in any single person and we could regard this as his "type." But I must bypass this problem of typology. The diagram, then, projects a microscopic view of only one set of attitudes—the leveling-sharpening dimension. It takes us through its *internal validation* and expresses the idea that perceptual attitudes are defined through consistencies of behavior in a number of situations and that they are unique patternings of adaptive properties.

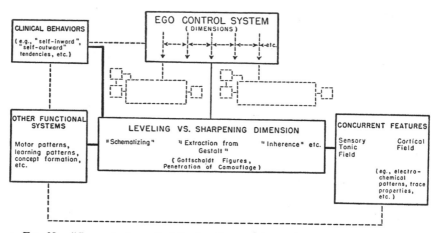

Fig. 38.—"Conceptual map" of the leveling vs. sharpening dimension. The boxes, except for the one labeled "ego control system," indicate areas of behavior where it is possible to look for patterns akin to leveling and sharpening in perception. These links are shown by solid lines. Dotted lines indicate congruencies that may eventually be found among the so-called non-perceptual behaviors. They are as yet completely unexplored, but their existence is also deducible from the conceptual scheme. Other perceptual attitudes are also indicated by dotted lines; these give a perspective of the whole ego control system. A similar mapping out of relationships is possible for each of these other attitudes.

The adaptive properties contained in our tests are called here for convenience "schematizing," "extraction of a Gestalt" (Gottschaldt test and penetration of camouflage), and "inherence."

After the validation process, the diagram leads us to look for wider affiliations. Of course, we have only a hint of these now. On the one side a bond is shown to clinical descriptions. Earlier it was said that *Anschauungen* as we conceive them are only representatives in perception of pivotal ego controls; they may have parallels in other functions. Were we able to get beyond the phenomenological restraints of our definitions, we might be able to give these definitions highly generalized forms from which we could deduce the special cast they take in each of the response systems, perception as well as others. But even now our descriptions of perceptual attitudes offer starting points for considering the meaning of individual differences elsewhere and for approaching the central directives which control all of a person's adaptive behavior. This possibility is shown in the diagram by a connection which leads to congruences of leveling and sharpening in other functions—in motor or expressive behavior, in learning, in concept formation, etc. Consistencies of a person in each of these spheres is a major research problem for the future.

It is possible to go further than this, though these extensions are purely speculative at the moment. We may suppose that the leveling attitude is also a set of distinctive electrocortical events or that it is accompanied by particular variations of postural tonus. Were it possible to record reliable individual differences in these phenomena, we might arrive at descriptions of the attitudes in these terms. To cite one possibility: At various times it has seemed to us that the analysis of schematizing behavior touches common ground with research in the time-error, and through it with neurophysiological conceptions and the study of "satiation" effects (23). Our concept of attitude provides a conceptual leverage for studying individual differences in these events. It is not inconceivable that what we observe as a leveling attitude might also include a distinctive set of events in the cortical field, what Lauenstein reports as "trace assimilation" (27). We may ask: Would assimilative tendencies of the time-error be particularly manifest in our lag group?

Attitudes may have other concomitant aspects. Perhaps the diverse perceptual attitudes of the schematizing and other situations are accompanied by typical patternings of muscle tonus. Our concept leads us then to an interest in the sensory-tonic events to which Werner and Wapner (43) and Purdy (33) have assigned fundamental importance in perceptual experience and to wonder about the significance of individual differences in these behaviors.

Our model thus brings so-called "autochthonous" and "peripheral" factors within the orbit of personality theory. The organismic axiom which the diagram presupposes tells us that it is too limiting to speak of "physiological behaviors" and "psychological behaviors." It is better to think of modes of regulation or control which provide the mold for a person's functioning and that our methods, our preferred concepts, describe them in a variety of ways. Were we to achieve all the alliances pictured in the diagram, we would have a set of laws regarding an ego directive as it operates within the total structure of the person.

The Dimension of Tolerance *vs.* Resistance to the Unstable.—

Curiosity about apparent movement led us to another set of attitudes. We call them tentatively tolerance and intolerance for the unstable or the equivocal. Apparent motion, or the *phi* phenomenon as it is often called, has a long history, but questions about the ease or difficulty of the experience and the reasons for this in the personalities of people are new.

The *phi* phenomenon is a common experience in daily life, in the motion picture, in the moving arrow in neon lights outside a bar, in the flitting of light around a movie marquee. All are impressions of movement gained from stationary stimuli exposed at a critical interval. We know too that the experience depends on several factors— the brightness of the lights, the rate of flashes, and distance between the lights, among others. To us what seemed most striking was that people differed in the *ease* of the movement experience. It was definitely more comfortable for some than for others. In some people, certain combinations of stimuli, two "formless" ones, gave a broader range of apparent movement, i.e., between "alternation" and "simultaneity," than did distinctly "formed" stimuli; figures of no clear-cut form seemed to them to move easily. Also, when the two figures were identical, movement again was easier, i.e., they were seen as moving over a wider range of speeds than when the two were different. When the two figures were not only similar but implied a reasonable movement, as when the two figures were galloping horses, then the range was greatest of all.

Such "facts" of individual differences are in themselves nothing startling; they have been many times reported. But what do they tell us about the control and selective functions of perception? What kinds of "solutions" result in such differences? Put it this way: What problem faces a person in the apparent-movement test? What ways of "solving" it are open to him and what are *his* favored answers? He must look at two alternating figures which become harder and harder to see as such, as the alternation rate steps up. He must either compromise with what he knows and organize the two as one form which he sees as moving, or strain himself to keep seeing the field as he *knows* it to be, as two distinct and alternating stimuli. Now, what we thought was this: An important aspect of reality testing for some people, a requirement which they force on reality, is that it remain stable and unchanging, even rigid, especially in its outward aspects. In order for such a person to remain comfortable, things must appear as they are *known* to be; he desires stability above all. It is as if the externals, the outward form, the shells or containers of experience, perhaps in distinction to their "depth" or emotional meaning, are to be preserved at all costs; these are his anchors in experience.

This enslavement to form came out clearly on the Rorschachs of those who had trouble seeing movement.[4] We grouped our subjects according to their handling of forms on the Rorschach. We found that those who were overconcerned with sharp forms, who were reluctant to project more than the most obvious meaning into the ink blots, who played safe in not elaborating percepts, gave us the narrowest ranges of movement. Those who took to the Rorschach like ducks to water, who fantasied and projected freely, even too freely in some cases, or who could permit themselves to tamper with the form of the blot as given, gave us our broadest ranges of movement.

Thus, an attitude which reflected on the Rorschach in reluctance to project or fantasy, in refusing to attribute qualities to the blots which were known not to be, in finding it difficult to take an "as if" attitude, was also working in the apparent-movement test. Here two forms appear which the subject *knows* are not really moving. As the speed increases and the field becomes harder to organize, rather than accept the easy compromise of one stimulus moving, he acts to resist it. For him the experience of apparent movement violates the integrity of what he knows. Some of these subjects have indeed reported the experience as uncomfortable; they "did not want it to move." We could say that movement meant equivocation, "unsurety," to use an expression of Ames, which only a tenacious holding-on to the forms as known could prevent. They were "form-bound." Among our other group the experience of movement was easily accepted, and we called them "form-labile." Experiencing movement is, in fact, an easier way to organize the field once a certain rate of alternation has been exceeded.

The apparent-movement phenomenon, then, is a situation in which one can observe the degree of dependency upon form in reality appraisal. The two stable states are the experiences of alternation at very slow speeds and of simultaneity at very high speeds. During alternation the two forms are seen separately and the integrity of each is maintained. Between these two states we have an equivocal state of disequilibrium. Ease in experiencing movement indicates the readiness to tamper with forms in order to bring about stability. It is harder to accept this compromise when the two forms are unlike and movement is harder to experience.

The attitudes which lead to form-lability and form-boundedness are not limited to the apparent-movement experiment. Extreme re-

---

[4] A collaborative study with Herbert J. Schlesinger (21).

liance on form perhaps reflects a still more general intolerance of
instability of any kind. We are working with three other situations
in which to test this. In one we induce a sharp distortion of the
entire visual field through the wearing of aniseikonic lenses which
distort the retinal image.[5] This develops subtly, and people vary in
the time it takes to recognize the distortion. Some never do report
any change. They must resist the unfamiliar and hold fast to what
is habitually stable. A second test involves the well-known experience of autokinesis—the "illusory" movement of a pin-point of light
in a dark room. Here, too, stable frameworks are removed and disequilibrium is induced. Will a person *force* the light to remain still
when other supports are absent or will he accept the movement experience? Still a third situation measures the flicker-fusion threshold. Pilot studies suggest that those who show constricted apparent-
movement ranges also show lowered flicker-fusion thresholds. Here
the experience is not so much one of direct dependence upon form
itself for reality testing but the need to stabilize an unsteady field.
Our form-bound people appear to be uncomfortable when they face
such instability and hasten to resolve it. The over-all attitude which
we have abstracted from three related experiences—*phi,* flicker-
fusion, and Rorschach [6]—we have tentatively called "intolerance for
the unstable or equivocal."

It would not surprise us if many of our form-bound group who
show general intolerance for any kind of equivocation are clinically
describable as rigid, pedantic, compulsive persons. We have concentrated on the form-bound group because here the experience and the
attitude involved seem more unitary. Among those who are *not*
characterized by form-boundedness we find some who are truly form-

---

[5] I am grateful to Adelbert Ames of the Hanover Institute for his gift of these
lenses.

[6] A methodological aside is worth your attention. In using the Rorschach, we tried
to avoid a dubious but popular practice in clinical research. There are practically
no convincing demonstrations of clearcut links between cognitive patterns and
Rorschach score categories; yet like the Stanford-Binet years ago, the Rorschach
often turns up as the validating rather than the validated instrument in research
designs. Worse than this: By a questionable twist of circular reasoning, such
validations of *other* measures by Rorschach categories are used on occasion to sell
the validity of the Rorschach itself! Our use of the test was dictated solely by our
attitudinal hypothesis. We did not rely upon the Rorschach as a "criterion" measure
to "explain" for us the behaviors seen in other situations; nor was it the final say
about the personalities of our subjects. The present approach applied *to* the
Rorschach a hypothesis regarding a control principle, the test being only one of a
number of perceptual situations where the control principle might operate. Our
hypothesis was independently derived, free of biased commitments to Rorschach
interpretation, and capable of test by other means as well. In this application
there is perhaps a paradigm for a fresh approach to the validation of the Rorschach
itself and for developing a clearer picture of the ego control principles expressed
through it.

labile, that is, really disregard formal requirements, "project" freely, and flout reality in an extreme manner. But we also find those who would be better described as "flexible" and who merely can tolerate a greater degree of "Ungestalt," to use Stern's term, without discomfort. Our form-labile group is, therefore, not as homogeneous as the form-bound group seems to be. The complexity of the form-labile group is apparent only to qualitative observation, not in the scores. Hence, our dichotomy is probably an overly simple affair—the result of ranging quantitative scores along a single continuum and thereby obliterating some qualitative distinctions. Incidentally, attitudes toward instability, as with all the attitudes we have worked with, are not in themselves pathological, though they may be exacerbated in pathology. Both our extreme groups ran the gamut from normal to psychotic.

As in the case of our leveling-sharpening dimension, we need not stop with the perceptual definition of an attitude and its clinical correlates. It can perhaps lead us to congruent forms in other functional systems and to multiple forms of expression, as seen through the eyes of different methods. Far from being the end of our search, the isolation of an attitude provides only the groundwork for further investigation. I earlier offered one possibility: We can ask, how does an individual adjust to life who is excessively form-bound? Is he unusually "compulsive?" Another question we can ask is whether a particular patterning of sensory-tonic events accompanies the attitudes, a suggestion supported by Werner's theory that movement is a sensory-tonic experience (40). Still another question is whether a particular kind of brain injury, say to the frontal lobe, invariably results in form-boundedness, bringing in its wake particular satiation effects and patternings of sensory-tonic events as well as certain personality qualities. Werner and Thuma (42) have indeed found that for the brain-injured the experience of apparent movement is especially difficult. Interest in the effects of brain injury can in this way have a logical place in the study of an ego-control principle.

The Physiognomic vs. Literal Dimension.—A third set of *Anschauungen* has its roots in well-known observations that percepts are often subtly suffused with an emotional or expressive quality (24, 42, 45). Inanimate objects or events seem to move, become motivated, and assume an expressive and human-like aura. "An object is just as sinister as it is black; in fact, it is sinister first of all" (15). A flickering light is described as "dancing." A schizophrenic feels as he enters a room that "the door is devouring me" (35). No doubt you have your own favorite examples. Colors often have these qualities. It is said that "green is smooth and especially agreeable . . . red is very disagreeable, exciting, obtruding, aggressive, produces nausea." Goethe is quoted to the effect that "yellow-red has an intolerable power; it is active. It seems to penetrate, to pierce the eyes" (10). All these experiences involve a preference for the dynamic and emotive rather than the static and literal.

The physiognomic experience itself has been fairly intensively studied (3), but its relation to the control system of personality has not been stressed. How much reliance do people place on the physiognomic or on the matter-of-fact; on what do their preferences for one or the other depend; how otherwise do people differ for whom one or the other is typical? Questions of this kind regarding the organizing *attitudes* which such experiences reflect shifts interest away from merely cataloging physiognomic experiences. The older work went no further than this, trying to show how it is possible for objects to acquire physiognomic connotations—the mechanics of such an investment.

There are broad hints that physiognomic experiences have the wider importance suggested. Werner (41) reports greater or lesser preference for physiognomic experiencing in different ethnic, developmental, and pathological groups. He believes it to be more typical of "primitive" forms of thought organization. He thinks that in development we shift from a high reliance upon it in childhood toward an emphasis upon the "geometrical and technical" in adulthood. He believes too that in "regressive" states the ego falls back again upon highly physiognomic organization. Bizarre physiognomic experiences are common among schizophrenics (35). Hanfmann (11) reports a schizophrenic's grouping of small, thin, and yellow blocks on the basis of "Don't you think they look sick?" To be able to perceive physiognomically is probably essential to rich and responsive communication between people. But extreme reliance upon it could be pathological. Its complete *loss* may be accompanied by narrowing or dulling of emotional responsiveness of the sort which is so frequently seen in the brain-injured.

We are developing one test [7] for the study of individual differences. We hope eventually to follow the internal validation process followed with other attitudes and also to fan out to relationships with other forms of behavior ("personality qualities").

Our method tests an "active" and a more "passive" physiognomic experience. For the first the test is to draw a line making it be angry, happy, loving, and so forth, following a procedure used by Lundholm

---

[7] Work by the writer in collaboration with Dina Rubinstein.

(28), Kraus (25), and others.   In the larger number of such "free" or "active" productions which we have taken from people of different sexes, age groups, status levels, etc., there are great commonalities. Anger most usually expresses itself in a heavy angular or broken line, resembling a conventionalized lightning flash.   There is an intense pressure to the pencil stroke.   Many variations of response cluster around this common symbol.   A peaceful line is undisturbed, unbroken, and uniform, never excited or very varied.   Lines expressing the quality of loving are nearly always round, a circle often, or two rounded lines which touch.   Previous work has centered on such decisive uniformities, but our interest turns mainly to the equally real and important variations.   We are trying to scale the differences found, to develop criteria of facility, e.g., which moods are hardest to convey for which people, and to take into account deviations from the usual, stereotypy of response, and so forth.   Of what importance is it when a person's responses to all these words are quite similar, when there is no difference among the lines for anger, sadness, or loving?   Perhaps from a clinical standpoint this is a danger signal.   But in using this test with clinical application in mind we look beyond it to the predictive significance of test behavior for other situations.   In a second test subjects try to identify out of a mixed group of lines those which are most appropriate to each feeling.   The designs used in this test were "typical" ones for each mood found in the large group tested in the first situation.   This more "passive" task of physiognomic recognition is to be evaluated with similar stress upon kinds of "errors," disagreements with convention, and difficulty with particular feelings.

Although this work is still in progress, I would like to take you a little way further than we have actually explored to point out a few possible links to other behaviors.

Perhaps a gift for physiognomic organization is implied in behavior usually described as "empathic."   Perceptual components are ignored in usual considerations of "empathy," most of which have been in motor terms.   But the coloring of percepts by subtle affects may very likely be a precondition of "empathic" experience.[8]

The physiognomic-literal dimension is also pertinent to the measurement of subtle changes in ego functioning which follow upon lobotomy.   Jan Frank (8) has reported that lobotomized individuals show unconcern, insensitivity, or ennui in interpersonal relationships, that the experiencing of subtle sentiments and empathy is reduced and a general flattening of emotional life occurs.   If so, the physiog-

---

[8] We plan to test people at the extremes on an independent measure of empathy devised by Dr. Robert Holt of the Menninger Foundation.

nomic capacity should be weakened, impaired, or otherwise affected. Lobotomized people might find the *requirement* to perceive physiognomically quite difficult and might depart from conventions or show other deviations. There is some early evidence that this is so, but our study has only begun. Although this particular study has an immediate practical goal, the findings may give us clues to physiological concomitants of the physiognomic attitude. Possibly one anatomical requirement is an intact frontal lobe. Thus, if our interest takes us into lobotomy because of the relevance of this set of attitudes to a practical question, we will not feel that we have been diverted from the main stream.

Actually, we have already been studying people with *gross* frontal lesions with this in mind, and the few cases we have show striking impairments in their drawings. In one case the literalness and concreteness of physiognomic interpretations were particularly dramatic, since nowhere else in the usual clinical psychological test battery (Rorschach, Wechsler-Bellevue, etc.) was such a striking impairment seen. (There was even some question whether there were *any* psychological effects of the brain injury!) This patient's productions were completely lacking in variety and took such literal forms as the drawing of animals. When he was told that he did not have to draw an actual picture but could use any kind of expressive line, he proceeded to write synonyms such as "shy" for "timid" and "romance" for "loving." We see here an almost complete incapacity to take on a physiognomic attitude; clearly, it plays no role in this person's life, and if the physiognomic attitude in some form is one requirement of emotional communication and empathy, then we should not be surprised by the emotional poverty which this person shows under clinical scrutiny. Further work may reveal that such kinds of impairment typically occur in frontal-lobe injury, though the literalness of this lobectomized patient is the most extreme we have encountered.

Implications and Perspectives for the Future

These three examples of perceptual attitudes have, I hope, given you an idea of the importance of this intervening variable. I have far from exhausted its implications; neither have I summarized all the attitudes we have worked on. You can now perhaps better appreciate how these bridge the gap between perceptual data and personality theory. They do so not by a jumping of levels in which perceptual variation is linked to clinical traits but by directing us to organizing principles in the perceptual sphere itself which give it consistency. They focus upon what horizontal approaches usually overlook, the self-consistent "perceptual character" of the person.

To recap my thesis: Ego control takes form in perception through what I have called perceptual *Anschauungen* or attitudes. These are special ways, distinctive for the person, for coming to grips with reality. They are pervasive and are not only apparent in situations of stress or conflict. As formal mechanisms they can be studied in the laboratory; they are demonstrable in quite neutral circumstances and in the various cognitive functions.

I would like to call attention to some implications of the concept of attitudes for the psychoanalytic concept of defense. Psychoanalysis is perhaps the only theory of personality to give systematic recognition to formal, structural controls of functioning, e.g., the defense mechanisms, and it is important to see how the formal controls we have described for perception fit with the psychoanalytic scheme of things.

Probably our examples have suggested to you that perceptual attitudes share certain of the properties usually assigned to "defenses." With defenses, they are coping mechanisms at the disposal of the ego; they are means of "resolving" tensions and of bringing about stability. Like defenses, they are of several kinds because the requirements for tension-reduction differ among people and among situations. In fact, we might suggest that the defenses observed on the clinical level are counterparts of the controls we are looking for in perception. In making this analogy, we have in mind a rather general conception of defense which refers not to "defense against something" but to a singular means of tension-reduction. For all we know, of course, perceptual attitudes may, like defense mechanisms, begin in psychosexual fixations or traumata. But we must bypass such genetic considerations.

There is one catch in relating these two concepts. Even though it is possible to think of perceptual attitudes as collateral with the defenses of psychoanalytic theory, we have preferred to avoid the term *defense,* especially in the sense of the well-known defense mechanisms. The reason for this is the differences of method which both concepts reflect; perceptual methods are radically unlike those which gave birth to the classical defense mechanisms. Obviously, "methods define concepts" and psychoanalytic concepts are no exception. We therefore distinguish here between the *concept of defense* as required by the psychoanalytic model of ego structure (8, 11, 13) and the *defense mechanisms* derived and defined from clinical observation. The point of contact is that our concept of attitude answers requirements for us similar to those of the concept of defense for clinical observation.

The differences in origin caution us not to expect that particular attitudes will translate into particular defense mechanisms. It is pointless to expect *direct* analogues of "repression" in perception. Repression, though seemingly unitary enough to clinical observation, may, to a different method of observation, disclose itself as several mechanisms all related to the broader clinical designate. At this stage concepts are best linked to operations, and we decided to call the cognitive controls inferred from our observations by the more noncommittal term of perceptual *attitudes*. The possible correspondence between them and classical mechanisms of defense has yet to be demonstrated. Probably they will overlap, but their relationship is an interesting departure point for future research.

The watchword of our approach is that it bases itself firmly in perceptual data; attitudes are developed not by *analogy* to clinical concepts but through a process of internal validation. This avoids the tail-chasing procedure, which Krech (26) has justly criticized, of accepting clinical conceptions uncritically as standards by which to judge the perceptual datum, but which themselves remain untouched by it. Since our attitudes are tension-reduction devices in the service of reality mastery, they must draw the clinician's attention as "means of defense." This may not result in the "changes" in psychoanalytic theory which Krech [9] would like to see, but it must certainly be an enlargement of it, an extension and refinement of one aspect of it—the conception of ego controls—and it also has importance for a more general theory of personality as well.

I want to call your critical attention to the currently favored method of linking individual differences in perceiving to "personality traits" and diagnostic categories. At the risk of sermonizing, I want to underline the essential emptiness of this approach for a theory of personality beyond a certain *demonstrational* value. A correlation is important for systematic theory if it does one of several things: (*a*) if it points to a link *between* perceptual behaviors and thereby contributes to the induction of an organizing principle, i.e., perceptual attitude; (*b*) if it illuminates a concomitant aspect of a perceptual attitude, i.e., establishes a link between the formal organization of perceiving and that of other *functional* systems; or (*c*) if it indicates a relationship of integrative mechanisms within the person. It is hard to see how correlating observed variations in perceptual behaviors with schizophrenia or with "introversion," even if of the order of .95, contributes to any of these. At the most, the correlation *implies* a stable dimension having consequences beyond the perceptual

---

[9] Personal communication.

sphere itself, but neither the organizing principle nor its consequences are in any way clarified by it.

The snare in correlating perceptual behavior with "traits" is the belief that it can disclose a tie with events *outside* perception. But "traits" or diagnostic categories are usually literary or type concepts, the tatters of outworn typologies or global behavioral descriptions, having practical use but no *functional* specificity, and they are, therefore, of little value to systematic theory; there is no way of telling what correlations involving them represent. A "trait" may, in some instances, be merely another and more literary way of couching perceptual behavior, so that what seems like a correlation of two sets of independent events may only be a correlation of two ways of reporting a *single* cognitive process. Are "introversion" and "passivity" kinds of cognitive organizations, motor organizations, types of perceptual behaviors? Very often a correlation with traits is attempted before the crucial intermediate step is taken of accounting for the individual differences through perceptual principles alone. In such cases neither the perceptual datum nor the clinical datum is clarified by the correlations. An example is a study which correlated "preferences for colors" with anxiety. In itself the correlation offered nothing about the *perceptual* principles which accounted for variations in color preferences nor anything about the functional meaning of "anxiety." One might as well correlate moonbeams with cobwebs.

The impasse, then, in clinical research seems to be that it has been concerned too much with correlating any correlatables in the search for differential diagnosis without concern for *process* and functional specificity, and with no model of total functioning which would make such correlations the bases of laws of the individual. That is why one often feels about clinical research as if one is surveying a motley arrangement of curios, no matter how glittering the individual items. The correlations described in connection with the leveling and sharpening attitudes deserve some of this criticism. They *do* have a demonstrational value in pointing to consistency within the person of an organizing principle isolated in perception—indicating that leveling or sharpening have significance beyond perception—but they do not advance us a bit toward our goal of defining the ties to other functional systems.

A brief survey of the gaps in our picture will give you an idea of the future course our work must take.

1. We can say as yet practically nothing about the relationships *among* attitudes within any one person which would make it possible for us to describe his ego-control system as a whole. A perceptual attitude is only one of several available to him for adjustment. All

of them must be seen in some kind of dynamic apposition which we can designate as his "type" of *ego structure*. Other papers (17, 20) have sketched the outlines of a future typology and laid down certain empirical requirements to avoid the pitfalls which trapped type theories of the past. Practically nothing can be said now about types, and here again lies a major question for the future.

2. Even more serious is the difficulty we have at present in distinguishing among attitudes. As yet, even our most generalized definitions seem tied to certain test situations. Because the tests are different, our various attitudes are defined in terms best suited to them. Such definitions in incommensurate terms may give the perhaps spurious impression that the attitudes are themselves actually different, but we have as yet no way of checking on this.

The most ideal solution would be to redefine perceptual attitudes, using commensurate existence concepts and an "as if" *structural* model (30, 37) of total ego functioning. This would permit us to go "beyond phenomenology" toward a tighter, more parsimonious definition of control principles not only of perception but of all functions. There is no time here to choose among the possible models. I will only say now, putting together leads from von Bertalanffy (38) and Rapaport (34), that the most suitable one seems to be a "vertical" scheme of the perceiver, endowed with the properties of an "open system" in self-regulation.

3. I have spoken of each of these sets of attitudes as "preferred modes of control." But what "triggers off" one or another attitude in any situation? Indeed, some of our more disturbed patients have responded to the apparent movement situation in a highly physiognomic manner, though this was not the more usual reaction. To ask the question differently: What determines the "choice" of an attitude? This is probably a question as open as "What determines the choice of a defense mechanism or neurosis?"

4. There is another loophole, one which we share with the entire functionalist position of considering perception as the vehicle of adaptation and reality appraisal. The difficulty is in accounting for synthetic, creative, or other-than-adaptive activities of man. We sometimes speak as if reality appraisal and control were the essence of ego functioning. But this is probably too narrow. It certainly does not give the flavor of a person's life or even his perceptual world to say that all his behavior serves the ends of reality control and mastery. As a friend once remarked, the exquisite delicacy of a piece of lace is not captured when we say of it that "it rips easily" (it has "weak defenses"!). The delicacy of the lace is also a positive quality, and, I might add, perhaps possible *because* of its nega-

tive ones. The same holds for our conception of the ego. It bypasses the leisurely, the contemplative, all those activities which take reality and needs for granted. Qualities of "awe," of the feelings of "mystery" and of "wonderment" are untouched by a model based solely on questions of adaptation.

Despite this gap, we are describing a vital facet of man, his controlling agencies, certainly one of the preconditions which makes possible all other ego activity. For this reason it merits the exclusive attention we are giving to it for the time being.

5. I have spoken of perceptual attitudes as "stabilized" modes of control, thus encasing in a static term what is really a dynamically shifting process. Our picture is that of "a system which comes to rest in a familiar form," and it is the only one which the present scheme provides; it tells us nothing of how easily attitudes are changed within the person, how flexible they are, how easily they are manipulated. Within the "perceptual character," we know nothing yet of special mechanisms directed to particular contents or trauma, of perceptual "resources" which become available in the fright of battle or in the heightened emotion of any sharp break with everyday living. Would these bring out *other* "solutions"?   But even recognizing the importance of such "reserves," could it also be that the consistencies of the person would still call the turn to some degree? In looking to coherence in perception to find the central consistencies of a person, we have at least one basis for thinking that perception *is* personality.

BIBLIOGRAPHY

1. AMES, A., JR. *Nature and origin of perceptions.* Preliminary laboratory manual for use with demonstrations disclosing phenomena which increase our understanding of the nature of perception. Hanover, N. H.: The Hanover Institute. (Unpublished.)
2. ANGYAL, A. The holistic approach in psychiatry. *Amer. J. Psychiat.,* 1948, **105**, 178-82.
3. ARNHEIM, R. The Gestalt theory of expression. *Psychol. Rev.,* 1949, **56**, 156-71.
4. BRUNER, J. S., & GOODMAN, C. C. Value and need as organizing factors in perception. *J. abnorm. soc. Psychol.,* 1947, **42**, 33-44.
5. BRUNER, J. S., & POSTMAN, L. Symbolic value as an organizing factor in perception. *J. soc. Psychol.,* 1948, **27**, 203-8.
6. BRUNSWIK, E. *Wahrnehmung und Gegenstandswelt.* Vienna: Deuticke, 1934.
7. CANTRIL, H. *Understanding man's social behavior: preliminary notes.* Princeton, N. J.: Office of Public Opinion Research, 1948.
8. FRANK, J. Some aspects of lobotomy (prefrontal leucotomy) under psychoanalytic scrutiny. *Psychiatry,* 1950, **13**, 35-42.
9. FREUD, S. Interpretation of dreams. In A. A. Brill (ed.), *The basic writings of Sigmund Freud.* New York: Modern Library, 1938. Chap. vii.
10. GOLDSTEIN, K. Some experimental observations concerning the influence of colors on the function of the organism. *Occup. Ther. Rehabil.,* 1942, **21**, 147-51.

11. HANFMANN, E. Analysis of the thinking disorder in a case of schizophrenia. *Arch. Neurol. Psychol.,* 1939, **41**, 568-79.

12. HARTMANN, H. Ego psychology and the problem of adaptation. In D. Rapaport (ed.), *The organization and pathology of thought.* New York: Columbia University Press, 1951. Chap. xix.

13. HARTMANN, H., KRIS, E., & LOEWENSTEIN, R. M. Comments on the formation of psychic structure. In O. Fenichel and A. Freud (eds.), *The psychoanalytic study of the child.* New York: International Universities Press, Inc., 1946. Vol. II.

14. HOCHBERG, J. E., & GLEITMAN, H. Towards a reformulation of the perception-motivation dichotomy. *J. Personal.,* 1949, **18**, 180-91.

15. KATZ, D. *Gestalt psychology.* New York: The Ronald Press Co., 1950.

16. KLEIN, G. S. Adaptive properties of sensory functioning. *Bull. Menninger Clin.,* 1949, **13**, 16-23.

17. KLEIN, G. S. A clinical perspective for personality research. *J. abnorm. soc. Psychol.,* 1949, **44**, 42-50.

18. KLEIN, G. S., & HOLZMAN, P. S. The "schematizing process": perceptual attitudes and personality qualities in sensitivity to change. In preparation. Abstract in *Amer. Psychologist,* 1950, **5**, p. 312.

19. KLEIN, G. S., MEISTER, D. M., & SCHLESINGER, H. J. The effect of personal values on perception: an experimental critique. *Psychol. Rev.,* March, 1951. Abstract in *Amer. Psychologist,* 1949, **4**, 252-53.

20. KLEIN, G. S., & SCHLESINGER, H. J. Where is the perceiver in perceptual theory? *J. Personal.,* 1949, **18**, 32-47.

21. KLEIN, G. S., & SCHLESINGER, H. J. Perceptual attitudes of "form-boundedness" and "form-lability" in the Rorschach. *J. Personal.,* June, 1951. Abstract in *Amer. Psychologist,* 1950, **5**, p. 321.

22. KOFFKA, K., & HARROWER, M. *Color and organization.* Smith College studies in psychology No. 3. Northampton, Mass., 1932.

23. KÖHLER, W., & WALLACH, H. Figural after-effects. *Proc. Amer. phil. Soc.,* 1944, **88**, 269-357.

24. KOUVER, B. J. *Colors and their character.* The Hague: Martinus Nijhoff, 1949.

25. KRAUS, R. Über graphischen Ausdruck. Beih. 48. *Z. angew. Psychol.,* 1930, **14**, No. 48.

26. KRECH, D. Notes toward a psychological theory. *J. Personal.,* 1949, **18**, 66-87.

27. LAUENSTEIN, O. Ansatz zu einer physiologischen Theorie des Vergleichs und der Zeitfehler. *Psychol. Forsch.,* 1932, **17**, 130-77.

28. LUNDHOLM, H. The affective tone of lines. *Psychol. Rev.,* 1921, **28**, 43-60.

29. MacCORQUODALE, K., & MEEHL, P. E. On a distinction between hypothetical constructs and intervening variables. *Psychol. Rev.,* 1948, **55**, 95-107.

30. McCULLOCH, W. S. A recapitulation of the theory, with a forecast of several extensions. *Ann. N. Y. Acad. Sc.,* 1948, **50**, 259-77.

31. MURPHY, G. *Personality: a biosocial approach to origins and structure.* New York: Harper & Bros., 1947.

32. MURRAY, H. A. *Explorations in personality.* New York: Oxford University Press, 1938.

33. PURDY, O. M. The structure of the visual world. I. Space-perception and the perception of wholes. *Psychol. Rev.,* 1935, **42**, 399-424.

34. RAPAPORT, D. (ed.) Toward a theory of thinking. In *The organization and pathology of thought.* New York: Columbia University Press, 1951.

35. STORCH, A. The primitive archaic forms of inner experiences and thought in schizophrenia. *Nerv. ment. Dis. Monogr.,* 1924, **36**, 111.

36. THURSTONE, L. L. *A factorial study of perception.* Chicago: University of Chicago Press, 1944.

37. TOLMAN, E. C. Discussion. *J. Personal.,* 1949, **18**, 48-50.

38. VON BERTALANFFY, L. The theory of open systems. *Science,* 1950, **111**, 23-29.

39. VON HELMHOLTZ, H. *Handbuch der physiologischen Optik,* (3d ed., 1910). Translated by J. P. C. SOUTHALL. Cambridge, Mass.: Optical Society of America, 1925. Vol. III.

40. WERNER, H. Motion and motion perception: a study on vicarious functioning. *J. Psychol.,* 1945, **19,** 317-27.

41. WERNER, H. *Comparative psychology of mental development.* (rev. ed.). Chicago: Follett Publishing Co., 1948.

42. WERNER, H., & THUMA, B. D. A disturbance of the perception of apparent movement in brain-injured children. *Amer. J. Psychol.,* 1942, **55,** 58-67.

43. WERNER, H., & WAPNER, S. Sensory-tonic field theory of perception. *J. Personal.,* 1949, **18,** 88-109.

44. ZIETZ, K., & WERNER, H. Über die dynamische Struktur der Bewegung. (Werner, Stud. Strukturgesetze 8.) *Z. Psychol.,* 1927, **105,** 226-49.

CHAPTER 13

PERSONALITY THEORY AND PERCEPTION

By Else Frenkel-Brunswik, Ph.D.

The present symposium is one in an increasing number of manifestations of the convergence of personality and perception research. But instead of taking this new trend for granted, we may inquire how these two lines of research, until recently widely separated, could have come together. We may ask which developments within the field of personality, on the one hand, and within the field of perception, on the other, make such a rapprochement possible, a rapprochement which is significant for psychology as a whole. Instead of making perception the starting point, as has been the case in the introductory considerations by Blake, Ramsey, and Moran (Chapter 1) and in the symposium as a whole, the present writer will reverse the order and take the development of and changes within personality theory as the point of departure for this Chapter. The writer will then attempt to indicate how this development has served as a basis for bridging over into the field of perception. Some attention to problems of motivation, ego structure, and reality adaptation, as well as to problems of social influences upon personality, will have to precede all this, since they define the elements upon which any personality theory must draw. Previously in this symposium, especially in the papers by Blake (Chapter 1), Bruner (Chapter 5), and Cameron (Chapter 10), these elements have been traced throughout their interweavings with perception. The general plan of procedure here will be to discuss them first in relation to the clinical level and then to apply them to the empirical findings on the interrelationship of personality with perception and cognition.

The lumping together of perception with other, more general modes of cognition requires a word of justification. The argument in favor of sharper differentiation—raised in discussion by the editors of this volume—stresses that in perception one is confronted with external stimuli actually present, whereas cognition deals with inferences from such data. Granted that there is a continuum, with relatively clear-cut perception on the one end and relatively pure theoretical constructs on the other, we must not overlook the fact that there is some element of inference in every perception, and that conceptual constructs always relate to perceptual data; this is a point which has also been made by Hilgard and Dennis in their contributions to the present symposium (Chapters 4 and 6).

The absence of a fundamental difference between the more direct and the more indirect modes of cognition must especially be stressed in the personality-centered type of research in thing-perception which by its very definition deals with individual differences as elicited by vague or ambiguous rather than clear-cut stimulus configurations. Even more this is the case for self-perception and the perception of others—*Fremdwahrnehmung* in the sense of Max Scheler (56)— both topics of focal interest and widely discussed in the present symposium. Although there can be no doubt that the self or the social partner constitutes an actually present perceptual stimulus, there can likewise be no doubt that there is a substantial contribution on the part of inferential, more broadly cognitive factors, along with the obvious emotional factors, to perceptual responses as global, as vacillating, as vague, and at the same time as vital as is self-perception and the perception of others.

From Surface to Depth [1]

General Considerations.—Interest in the dynamics of human behavior in its full complexity appeared on the scene of psychology rather suddenly, and chiefly under the influence of psychiatry and psychoanalysis. The suddenness was a result of the fact that those interested in personality as a unit did not choose to wait until academic psychology, using experimental and laboratory techniques, arrived step by step at the same goal by studying the relatively simple units customarily involved in this latter approach. Unhampered by the difficulty of objectifying the tangled relationship between overt behavior and the patterns of underlying dynamics, the new and vital trend in the study of personality proceeded to an understanding of what has long been considered basic and important about human beings by physicians, philosophers, artists, and poets.

More concretely, this trend consisted in a turning away from the more segmentary approach of, let us say, the earlier form of behaviorism with its emphasis on overt responses to immediate stimuli. Mainly under the influence of psychoanalysis, a bold attempt was made in the direction of interpretation in terms of underlying dynamics,

---

[1] Many of the issues in the present and in the next section have been documented in greater detail in two previous publications (13, 14).

overt reactions being relegated to the role of mere steppingstones for inference. There is no doubt that this branch of psychology, in avoiding the errors of an overcautious and stimulus-bound approach, has often fallen into another error, that of overinterpretation and of making far-reaching conclusions on the basis of insufficient material evidence. At present a steadily improving balance between these two extremes is being attained.

Before entering into a discussion of the present status of personality research and theory, however, the writer would like to underscore once more the powerful impetus which the psychology of personality has received from psychoanalysis. The shift of emphasis from the level of external, overt manifestation to the level of motivational dynamics, stemming from psychoanalysis, has opened the way to highly fruitful explanations and predictions and thus is chiefly responsible for the establishment, within psychology, of a scientific discipline which really deals with personality. Data which looked from a phenotypical point of view like a mass of unrelated and even contradictory expressions became ordered, meaningful, and unified when the motivational approach was introduced. By conceiving of seemingly diverse behavior reactions as alternative manifestations of one and the same dynamic force, many an apparent inconsistency was successfully resolved. By this method central motivations can be established and consistent themes in a person's life uncovered.

It was psychoanalysis which first made us question the validity of the literal meaning or face value of a manifestation per se. In this manner we have come to acknowledge that exaggerated friendliness may hide destructive tendencies, that heterosexual promiscuity may be a defence against homosexual desires, or that apparent indifference may conceal a strong interest. An intense striving may thus find expression in no more than subtle and inconspicuous manifestations. On the other hand, the most conspicuous behavioral features may in certain instances have little dynamic significance or lasting effect. Dynamic concepts, as Lewin points out, "circumscribe a whole range of possibilities of manifestations" (36).

Quite aside from the question of the material correctness or incorrectness of any specific extrapolations into central dynamics as made by psychoanalysis, one must recognize that it has succeeded in conceptually integrating in a general manner an apparently chaotic variety of behavioral reactions relevant to life. These novel groupings of symbols or substitution mechanisms are sufficiently known so that we need not go into the far-reaching implications of the theory of the instincts and their modification by early interpersonal relationships. In the present symposium, much of the content of psychoanalysis relevant in this context has been discussed by Bronfenbrenner (Chapter 8). The layer of the instincts is here made accessible by analyzing materials relatively removed from the rational sectors of the personality, among them free associations, the content of dreams, and transference and symbolism in general. In all this, the interest in the adult was centered about diagnosing the persistence of infantile or archaic tendencies.

Since about 1930, the picture of psychoanalytic endeavors has somewhat departed from this original type of emphasis. Before discussing these changes, we must first come back to the importance of motivation for the psychology of personality. The influence of needs, of irrational tendencies and motives, upon perception has been stressed all through this symposium, most explicitly by Miller (Chapter 9) and Bruner (Chapter 5). In view of such agreement, it seems justified to take some time for a more detailed discussion of human motives and the methods of their ascertainment.

Our knowledge of motivation is established by means of a complex process of inference and interpretation, utilizing the most minute cues as well as gross features of behavior. Instead of grouping phenomena together on the basis of their overt similarities, we have learned from psychoanalysis to group them on the basis of genetic or symbolic similarities. Delving into depth in this manner has brought us awareness of rules and laws quite different from those found on the surface. To quote from Anna Freud (19, p. 7): "In the id the so-called 'primary process' prevails; there is no synthesis of ideas, affects are liable to displacement, opposites are not mutually exclusive and may even coincide, and condensation occurs as a matter of course."

Polarities in Psychoanalysis.—Similarly, in discussing the vicissitudes of instincts, Sigmund Freud (21) deals with such crucial mechanisms as the reversal of an instinct into its opposite. He speaks of such changes as the replacement of a passive aim (for instance, to be looked at) by an active aim (to look at), or the reversal of a content as found in the change of love into hate.

In general, Freud believes that our mental life is governed by three polarities, namely, subject-object, pleasure-pain, activity-passivity, in each of which one opposite pole may be replaced by the other.

We as psychologists may add that the closeness of opposites found by observing the vicissitudes of the instincts actually turns out to be a general personality characteristic. Let us take from one of our studies the example of a delinquent boy, Jeff, whose overdaring, aggressive masculinity is interpreted as a counteractive façade for his basically insecure and passive attitude. The assumption of his under-lying passivity may help us to understand a larger sector of his behavior. Thus, we will not be surprised to find in his Thematic Apperception Test stories gratuitous endings in which the hero is apt to get things without too much effort on his part, as well as a generally passive attitude toward his environment, perhaps especially toward other men. We may find feminine identification and interest in getting food or in being fed. As long as we assume only the existence of aggressiveness, we may understand only the criminal acts of Jeff. However, if we add the hypothesis of underlying pas-sivity, the content of other less conspicuous but not less crucial aspects of his behavior, as well as the content of his fantasy, free associations, etc., become intelligible to us.

We might also bring to bear a specific example in the opposite direction, Merle, whose exaggerated friendliness may serve, or may even be the direct result of, strong destructive tendencies. Quite often in life real motivations cannot be shown openly. The distinc-tion between manifest personality and inferred motivational person-ality seems to be especially important in our culture. In the two examples given, cultural pressures are at work in opposite directions. Merle, in reality a boy identified with middle-class values, was found to have developed defense mechanisms against his hostility. Jeff, a lower-class delinquent boy, was found to have tried exhibiting the tough and rugged façade he believes his environment expects of him. We have endeavored to indicate in both cases how a variety of behavioral features must be taken as circumstantial evidence in sizing up the subject.

An Analysis of Alternative Behavioral Manifestations of Motivation.—In trying to nail down the differences between the depth-oriented and the more conventionally psychological approaches, one must point to the fact that psychoanalysis and psychiatry usually fall short of making fully explicit the relationship between the infer-ences involved and the observational data. For concrete illustration, the writer would like to refer here briefly to a monograph (14) which she published some years ago as a part of the University of California Adolescent Growth Study (for a general description of the entire study see 31, 32). This monograph had the double aim of showing the predictive value of motivational hypotheses and of demonstrating the relationship of motivation to behavioral data.

The California Adolescent Study had collected over a number of years such data as physiological measurements, achievement test scores, ratings by adult raters of the subjects' behavior in social situations, the subjects' self-reports, and projective material. Correlations between the observed behavior of the children, on the one hand, and their self-reports and fantasy material, on the other, were found to be on the whole rather low; this is not surprising if one considers that these two sets of data reflect different aspects of personality.

The writer's assumption was that if we introduced motivational ratings, they might be found to account for apparently diverse manifestations and that an important lead for uncovering relationships might lie in comparatively few but fundamental characteristics of the subjects, as might be brought out in such ratings. The judges, who had known the children over a period of eight years, were asked to forget about the manifest behavior of the children and to group them according to assumed motivation rather than according to similarities of displayed techniques. The aim was to obtain intuitive, interpretative ratings based on wide knowledge of the children's behavior. Explicitly excluded from inspection, however, were indirect performances, such as self-reports and projective materials, in order to maintain the independent status of these for purposes of comparison. There were only nine motivational categories, most of them selected from Murray's list of needs. Since Murray's list covers different levels of personality, we selected from this list mainly drives we considered the most basic, such as "aggression," "abasement," or "succorance."

The results of our analyses show that this perception-in-depth is probably not inferior to surface perception so far as inter-rater agreements are concerned; this bears out the impression that in day-to-day living we tend to perceive not only the social techniques of those with whom we come in contact but their basic motivations and purposes as well. What is more, our results supported the original assumption that the drive ratings are of considerable advantage in organizing the previously collected data on overt behavior observed in social situations. As will be shown later in this Chapter, they also help to predict and explain the perception of self, of others, and of the thing-world.

It seemed from the outset that different classes of behavioral expressions not related among each other were often related to the same drive, apparently as "alternate manifestations" of that drive. A statistical analysis of our material, based on a total of ninety-five subjects, in terms of multiple correlation corroborated the hunch that two phenotypically unrelated, or even diverse, types of manifestations can be related to one and the same set of dynamic factors. To give an example: Overt behavioral ratings on "exuberance" and "irritability" were found to intercorrelate negatively with one another and thus to be relatively incompatible; however, both these behavioral traits showed some positive correlation with the ratings on the drive for aggression. The multiple correlation between aggression and the two diverse behavior features was found to be relatively high, thus establishing the principle of alternative manifestations of a drive. For our boy subjects, the quantitative results are shown in the following schema of alternative manifestations. The gain of the multiple

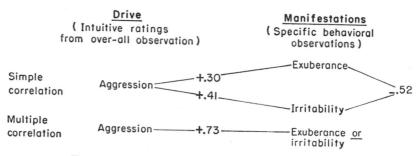

FIG. 39.—Alternative manifestations of the same drive.

over the two basic, zero-order correlations, checked in all such cases by means of the Wherry shrinkage formula, was found to be statistically significant.

Less drastically, the following patterns point in the same direction. For boys, the intercorrelations of "energy output," "social participation," and "leadership," on the one hand, with "irritability," on the other, are −.27, −.30, and −.38 respectively. The corresponding correlations of these items with ratings on the drive for aggression range from .32 to .46. Multiple correlations, however, are between .66 and .75. Leadership is here the more direct expression of the drive for aggression, whereas tenseness and anxiety are manifestations of aggression of lesser phenotypical similarity to the underlying motive.

In short, adolescents whose ratings on the aggressive drive cluster are high are likely to be either maladjusted, tense, and anxious, or else successful in their overt social activity, say, as leaders; or they may even display both manifestations.

Since in the examples mentioned thus far the relationships described involve negative intercorrelation of the two (or more) overt manifestations among one another, the simultaneous presence of both manifestations will be somewhat less likely than if the intercorrelations were zero or positive. Such patterns thus tend, to a certain extent, toward an exclusive "either-or" rather than toward what may be called an "and/or" type of alternative manifestation.

An example of the latter type is the following: In the girls of our group the behavioral traits of "altruism" and "insecurity" were found to be uncorrelated. Ratings on the drive for abasement, however, were found to correlate about .53 with both of them. The joint multiple correlation with ratings on abasement is .75. Girls tending toward abasement thus seem to have the choice between sublimating their abasement in altruism or being insecure, but there also is a good chance that they will be both altruistic and insecure.

Analogously, but in the opposite direction, certain manifest features, especialy those concerned with adjustment, seem to originate in a variety of underlying motivational conditions. For example, for the general behavioral trait "insecurity" (the opposite of "security feelings"), combinations of ratings on the need for abasement, succorance, absence of need for achievement, and presence of the need for escape in girls and for aggression in boys, yield third-order multiple coefficients of .78 for girls and .83 for boys. In girls none of the basic coefficients surpasses .53, and in boys none of them surpasses .62.

Drive ratings furthermore show good relationships to independent data such as self-reports and projective material, indicating that these ratings can contribute to predicting the behavior of the subjects in situations which do not enter as a basis for the drive inferences. Self-perceptions and self-reports do not mirror behavior directly, to be sure; but they are interlaced with some of the underlying drives and thus indirectly bear on behavior related to these drives. For example, the low correlations between maladjustment in actual behavior and in the self-reports can be accounted for by the fact that only where maladjustment stems from, or is coupled with, a strong drive for abasement will it be frankly admitted in the self-reports. There were linear correlations of about .5 between ratings on the need for abasement and self-reported maladjustment; whereas actual maladjustment as rated by clinicians tended to show curvilinear relationships to self-reported maladjustment, with both the best- and the least-adjusted children perceiving themselves as optimally adjusted.

Our analysis further revealed positive correlations between our motivational ratings and ratings on the same drives based on projective material. In contrast to this, Sanford, Adkins, et al. (54) found no relation between ratings of what they termed "manifest needs" and need ratings based on Thematic Apperception Test stories. In our opinion this is due to the fact that anything manifest represents only the unrepressed, and thus often less dynamic, aspect of the motivational tendencies. Resorting to the concept of manifest drives actually implies a return to a straight behaviorism and its endless lists of "habits" which are of little use for purposes of parsimonious reduction.

To avoid these pitfalls, we have gone so far as to advocate reserving the concept of motivation, or of underlying "drives," for the realm of inferential constructs which go beyond, or "behind," the gross features of behavior (13, 14). It is only such qualities which would seem to deserve the designation of "depth." Among the drives in our list all show alternative manifestations in the sense described above, with the exception of the need for "achievement." Although ratings on the drive for achievement probably reflect a basic personality orientation toward certain long-term effects—as may also be indicated by the existing correlations with other rated drives as well as with behavioral features—a striving for achievement may by its greater closeness to the ego with its reality-orientation lend itself less to indirect, phenotypically heterogeneous manifestations than, say, a striving for aggression, dependence, or escape.

Our results have lent support to the assumption that the concept of underlying motives supplies us with an instrument which, due to its particular level of abstraction, or depth, is helpful in uncovering relationships and consistencies in the field of personality, provided that the relation between inferred drives and behavior has been analyzed and the meanings of the former have been specified operationally. While the issue of underlying dynamics was first clearly raised by psychoanalysis, it is in the tradition of academic psychology that the necessity to relate the dynamic concepts to behavioral data is being stressed. But it is this same tradition which is apt to overemphasize the importance of behavior as such.

Referring once more to our example of the boy who was rated high on underlying need for aggression and low on overt aggressive behavior, we must stress that both types of data are relevant; he certainly would be another kind of boy if his drive for aggression were coupled with overt aggressiveness, but he would even more certainly be another kind of boy if his surface friendliness were due to a genuine lack of aggressive drive. To cite another example: Sadism and masochism may be closely related, but the effects may be as far apart as the impact of a mass murder or of a saint upon society.

In the manner described, the problems of overt behavior which make up the core of traditional psychology, such as social adjustment, or perceptual and cognitive mastery of reality, must all be brought within the scope of personality research and personality theory. Here psychology will meet with a trend which has developed within psychoanalysis proper, namely, the partial turning away from depth toward an ego-psychology.

From Depth Back to the Surface

Shifts Toward the Ego and the Mastery of Reality in Psycho-analysis and Personality Theory.—The exclusive interest in the central region of the personality as displayed by psychoanalysis in its beginnings proved to be too narrow to catch all the essentials of personality. As long as psychoanalysis concentrated its efforts upon the "id," that is, the unorganized, primitive, pleasure-seeking system of instinctual drives, the resulting reduction left too little space for further differentiation in social terms. There was relatively little interest in the question of what a person had made out of his complex, that is, whether a drive pattern had, in spite of conflict, been success-fully worked out to socially approved achievement, as in art, or whether it had led to a highly unsuccessful adjustment. Yet, as we indicated in the previous section, it is of far-reaching importance to have learned that in both cases similar drive patterns could have been at work and that underlying central forces might have differed from each other only in shades.

On the other hand, restriction of interest to the id actually means a depreciation of the functions directed toward the mastery of reality —the ego—to the role of mere diagnostic data. It also means that the environment as a stimulus enters the scope of investigation mainly in so far as it permits a repetition of childhood reactions to father, mother, and other persons in the past social environment of the child.

As we have said above, psychoanalysis has been undergoing a change in this respect, thus rendering irrelevant many of the older objections. Anna Freud (19, pp. 3, 4) herself seems to consider the early stages of psychoanalysis as limited to the central, but she emphasizes at the same time the shift toward the ego, which is defined in psychoanalysis as the agent governing the relationship of the individual to actual reality and responsible for the obtained results:

There have been periods in the development of psychoanalytical science when the theoretical study of the individual ego was distinctly unpopular. Somehow or other, many analysts had conceived the idea that, in analysis, the value of the scientific and therapeutic work done was in direct proportion to the depth of the psychic strata upon which attention was focused. Whenever interest was transferred from the deeper to the more superficial psychic strata —whenever, that is to say, research was deflected from the id to the ego—it was felt that here was a beginning of apostasy from psychoanalysis as a whole. The view held was that the term "psychoanalysis" should be reserved for the new discoveries relating to the unconscious psychic life, i.e., the study of re-pressed instinctual impulses, affects, and fantasies. With problems such as that of the adjustment of children or adults to the outside world, with concepts of value such as those of health and disease, virtue or vice, psychoanalysis was not properly concerned. It should confine its investigations exclusively to infantile fantasies carried on into adult life, imaginary gratifications and the punishments apprehended in retribution for these. . . . When the writings of Freud, beginning with *Group Psychology and the Analysis of the Ego* and *Beyond the Pleasure Principle,* took a fresh direction, the odium of analytical unorthodoxy no longer attached to the study of the ego and interest was definitely focused on the ego-institutions. Since then the term "depth-psychology" certainly does not cover the whole field of psychoanalytical research.

Other contributors to this symposium, especially Bronfenbrenner (Chapter 8), have pointed out that this shift toward the ego in psychoanalysis brings us closer to cognition and perception. As Sigmund Freud (23) writes:

It is easy to see that the ego is that part of the id which has been modified by the direct influence of the external world, acting through the perception consciousness. In a sense it is an extension of the surface differentiation. . . . Moreover, the ego has the task of bringing the influence of the external world to bear upon the id and its tendencies and endeavors to substitute the reality principle for the pleasure principle which reigns supreme in the id. In the ego, perception plays the part which in the id devolves upon instinct. The ego represents what we call reason and sanity in contrast to the id, which contains the passions.

Freud is explicit in his judgment that the function of the ego is not to be limited to external perception but includes internal perception as well. Though in his view the concept of the ego is not identical with that of perception—parts of the ego are considered to be unconscious—perception certainly is one of its main functions. (Parenthetically one may add that the animistic language of the psychoanalysts can easily be translated into a more objective and operational language.)

Parallel to the increased interest in the ego, attention in therapy is no longer being focused exclusively on transference effects of early infantile contents but is directed more and more frequently to resistance stemming from the ego; censorship operating in dreams is considered as crucial a material as their latent content, and modes of defense are as much studied as the impulses against which they are erected.

The function of the ego is seen mainly as the achieving of a compromise between the instincts, on the one hand, and reality and ethical and moral demands, on the other, as well as in the accomplishing of a synthesis of the three institutions of id, ego, and superego. Thus Anna Freud (19, pp. 8, 47) states:

No longer do we see an undistorted id impulse but an id impulse modified by some defensive measure on the part of the ego. . . . Were it not for the intervention of the ego or of those external forces which the ego represents, every instinct would know only one fate, that of gratification.

Impulses are exposed to rejection and criticisms and are modified under the pressure of the reality principle, which is considered by Sigmund Freud a basic "principle of mental functioning." The neurotic is described as "turning away from reality," as "being alienated from actuality," and as being unable to dethrone the pleasure principle in preference to a safeguarding of reality (20).

Since, with the study of the ego and the defense mechanisms, psychoanalysis moves into the field of psychology, we may turn briefly to these defense mechanisms, especially since much of the experimental work to be reported in the second part of this chapter builds upon our knowledge of defense mechanisms. Anna Freud mentions ten defense mechanisms: regression, repression, reaction formation, isolation, undoing, projection, introjection, turning against the self, and reversal; the tenth mechanism, pertaining to the study of the normal, is sublimation. The first nine defenses are considered as pathogenic and as closely related to the formation of neuroses and psychoses. However, all of them are found, at least to some degree, in the development of the normal personality.[2]

In this chapter we are interested in the defense mechanisms mainly from the cognitive angle. Denial of painful sensations and facts represents the grossest falsification of reality and is thus found more often in young children. We find, however, milder degrees of denial in adults, where a truth can be known without its full implications being apparent or where "screened memories" may substitute for original memories. All manner of compromises between one's memory and the tendency toward denial can be observed and have in part been studied experimentally.

It is internal dangers rather than external ones that are the prime source of the mechanism of projection, through which the unpleasurable is seen as outside instead of inside. Paranoid patients produce the crudest projective misinterpretation of reality. To a certain degree, however, this mechanism is called upon to explain misunderstanding of actual reality in the direction of unconscious needs.

Repression consists in an unconscious forgetting or in the failure to become aware of internal impulses or of events connected with the impulses considered to be objectionable. The sex instinct seems to

[2] The summary of defense mechanisms given here and in the following discussion is based on S. Freud (21, 22), Anna Freud (19), and Fenichel (10).

lend itself mainly to repression, whereas aggressive impulses elicit other types of defense mechanisms. The mechanism of repression is most clearly exhibited in hysteria.

What has been said so far can provide a basis for extensive personality-centered research in cognition and perception both in normals and in the pathological. Thus we would expect more omissions of reality on the part of the hysteric and more commissions of distortion on the part of the paranoid patient. More precisely, we may find distortion of reality in the paranoid combined with faithful stimulus-boundness; the latter constituting an attempt toward the restitution of a reality experienced as slipping.

Still different results would have to be expected in the case of the compulsive and obsessive patient, where we would be likely to find a series of actions one of which would be a direct reversal of the other—undoing—with frequent repetitions to make sure that the original impulse is undone and with continuing doubts that this has really been achieved. In the mechanism of isolation prevalent in the compulsive, parts are recognized as such, but they are kept apart by interjecting spatial or temporal intervals or by using other techniques, such as, for instance, the isolation of an idea from its emotional context. The so-called detached, logical thinker may often be warding off anxieties by isolation and may thus miss many important relationships and restrict his creativity. From an examination of the general dynamics of the compulsive syndrome, Fenichel proceeds to a description of the need for being systematic and for clinging to definite systems as it occurs in the compulsive character-structure. This need, often manifested in the tendency to "type" and to classify in categories, is seen as protection against surprise and fear of drive impulses. Deviations from symmetry are not tolerated; they are experienced as deviations from general norms, especially moral ones.

Perhaps we should emphasize at once that we are far from considering different forms of perception and cognition merely as a result of different ways of warding off instinctual anxiety. We shall expand on this later. Here we are more concerned with stressing the provocative angles under which the cognitive approach has been put by psychoanalysis.

We may now conclude our discussion of the mechanisms of defense by pointing to reaction formation; this mechanism involves a definite change of personality away from the feared impulse. Cleanliness, when developed in this manner, will be exaggerated, but there will be a persistent occasional breaking-through of dirtiness. The same holds true for kindliness, which often represents a true reaction formation against hatred. The origin of these types of defensive attitudes is indicated by the rigidity which they assume and by the occasional breaking-through of the original impulse. These original tendencies may be seen with exceptional clarity in the case of the disintegration of a reaction formation.

In spite of the fact that various psychoanalysts have attempted more or less explicitly to describe the clinical data which are the basis for inferences about defense mechanisms, much remains to be done in this direction. In any event, defense mechanisms seem to be among the functions which are relatively accessible to direct observation. It is as yet open to question, however, which types or aspects of defense mechanisms should be studied in the laboratory and which should be handed over to other, more clinically oriented psychological techniques or should be left to be checked in the therapeutic procedure only. We shall have more to say about this after the discussion of some experimental material.

The increasing concentration on the ego and the defense mechanisms renders partially invalid the objection, often leveled against psychoanalysis, to the effect that reduction to instincts was carried too far and that what all people have in common was stressed too much, while important differences were neglected. So long as psychoanalysis concentrated on instincts, there undoubtedly was some validity to the objection made by Allport (3) that in psychoanalysis "needs are disembodied and depersonalized to a greater degree than is justified in elements that are to serve as the radicals of personality." But we find psychoanalysis now increasingly concerned with needs as modified by the defense mechanisms. This is a step which introduces a great deal more in the way of differentiation and which connects human behavior not only to its internal sources but also to external realities. The defense mechanisms may be recruited to explain at least partially such differences as the one between a masochist who remains a sexual pervert and a well-disciplined monk, to use an example of Allport's. With the increasing study of the defense mechanisms we thus find in psychoanalysis an increasing emphasis on the study of character formation.

The definition of anxiety may serve as a good example of the change of framework in psychoanalysis. Anxiety was first seen mainly as the result of dammed-up sexual instincts. Later, however, anxiety—at least in its lesser degrees—was seen also, among other things, as a signal for the use of protective measures, as an anticipation of the future. In other words, it has come to be considered as an indicator of an increased alertness of the ego toward reality.

All this, however, meets only partially the above-mentioned objections against psychoanalysis. It may still be argued that, by and large, psychoanalysis has considered defense mechanisms and character structure mainly under the defensive aspect and relatively little under the aspect of positive adaptation. This is admitted by one of the most orthodox psychoanalysts, Fenichel (10, p. 52). Freud (24) also was aware of this fact, and this was the reason why he did not regard psychoanalysis as a closed system. Rather, he conceived of psychoanalysis as needing other types of psychology to complement it:

By itself this science is seldom able to deal with a problem completely, but it seems destined to give valuable contributory help in a large number of regions of knowledge. The sphere of application of psychoanalysis extends as far as that of psychology, to which it forms a complement of the greatest moment.

The approach merely hinted at by Freud was taken up by his students. Heinz Hartmann (29) goes far beyond the view of the ego as a mere defense against instinct. Taking intellectualization as an example, he stresses that a phenomenon of this kind cannot be completely defined by considering it only as a defense; it is also characterized by properties and laws which result from the primary orientation of the intellect toward mastery of the external world. Even in cases in which the process of intellectualization was first developed as a defense, it can become independent of the source and serve a different, exclusively constructive function. The same holds even more for perception, of course.

In general, memory, learning, and other mental capacities are no longer seen as developments in the conflict between the ego and the instincts or in the conflict with love objects; rather, they are seen primarily as adjustive mechanisms. Allport originally thought of his principle of functional autonomy as at variance with psychoanalytic theory; but now we find him in agreement with a student so faithful to Freud as Hartmann.

Hartmann and some of the other psychoanalysts are in a sense discovering many of the phenomena which for a long time have been the exclusive concern of psychology and the social sciences. We should welcome this state of affairs; we even should be grateful that psychoanalysis for a long time ignored these aspects of human behavior which are so obvious to the psychologist. It was this oversight which made it possible for psychoanalysis to concentrate upon a formerly neglected aspect of human behavior and to introduce a novel, crucial, and, in the true sense, dynamic aspect into the study of human nature.

Changes similar to those within the psychoanalytic movement may be observed within the fields of personality theory and research.

At first, the principal methods in this field were the so-called projective techniques, mainly the Rorschach and Thematic Apperception tests. They were designed to reach the deeper layers of the personality by making reality vague and unclear, thus providing an opportunity for the projection of the "private world," to use a term suggested by L. K. Frank (11). Thus, these deep and subjective tendencies replaced the reactions of the subject to the standard objective world as the focus of attention. Now a shift is taking place—as this symposium bears witness—with the personologists increasingly interested in perception and cognition. They thus return to the fold of general psychology only to find that, in the meantime, general psychology itself has faced in the new direction of an interest in personality.

Changes in the Social Sciences and in Social Psychology.— Before discussing this matter further, we must follow another trend of personality theory which, similarly to the interest in cognitive processes, leads away from the preoccupation with the deep, the private, and the subjective. We refer to the problems of social adjustment and the whole realm of topics included under the label of "personality and culture."

First, we must stress the positive contributions which psychoanalysis has made to these topics, at the same time trying not to lose sight of the limitations of these contributions. Let us emphasize that it was Freud and psychoanalysis which first pointed out the intimate interaction of biological and social factors in the individual. Thus, such processes as sucking, bowel movement, and masturbation, considered as purely biological phenomena before the advent of psychoanalysis, have been woven by the latter into the fabric of social interaction. Sucking is considered not only as a means for getting food but also as a means of experiencing and expressing affection and aggression, and the process of bowel movement is seen as being utilized by the child in his struggle with the parents and with authority in general. Dreams, which were considered as private and meaningless before Freud, are now used as a basis for a reconstruction of the most decisive and subtle aspects of interpersonal relationships. These aspects also permeate perception, as will be remembered from the discussion of the defense mechanisms.

While psychoanalysis stresses in the development of the individual his contact, or rather his clash, with society, it does not as a whole concern itself with the characteristics of society as such nor with social institutions so far as they appear as independent of the single individual. Here again psychoanalysis attacks only the most intimate aspect of the problem, namely, how social influences—mainly represented by parental figures—disturb and modify the deepest layers of our biological and instinctual lives. Social influences are seen as a series of traumata which bring to a halt and discontinue instinctual expansion. The concept of sublimation is adduced to explain how the energies of the ungratified instincts are transferred to socially constructive goals. This concept, however, remains relatively sterile and vague in the writings and teachings of psychoanalysis. We hear very little about the satisfactions which may be derived from successfully adopted social roles and identities.

In the meeting of psychoanalysis and anthropology we are able again to discern the change from depth to surface which we have sketched for the meeting of psychoanalysis and psychology. Géza Róheim, one of the first psychoanalytically oriented anthropologists, sees most cultural phenomena as deriving from early traumata in infancy (50). The handling of the child's needs and the approach to child-rearing in general are definitely not seen by Róheim as part of the broader social structure. On the contrary, the social structure is seen as the result of the ways a few individuals handled their own and their children's instinctual problems, ways which they transmitted to the other members of the tribe. The specific traumata inherent in the different methods of upbringing and enforced renunciations are said to form the basis for customs and religions. Again, this point of view, though one-sided and incomplete, has enriched anthropology and the social sciences in a decisive way. It points the way to increased emphasis on child development in different cultures, toward searching for unified themes in the private modes of experience as well as in religion and ideology. It leads to the inclusion of such materials as dreams, free associations, and projective materials in general in the study of personality and culture. This approach in combination with the original emphasis of the social sciences on historic tradition, on the ways of subsistence, on the organization of society has led to a more fruitful understanding of the individual in his society.

Further examples of this type of synthesis are the works of Fromm (25), Kardiner (33), Kluckhohn (34), Erikson (9), Margaret Mead (39), and Linton (37).

One of the special fields of the social sciences which is increasingly influenced by psychoanalysis to the benefit of both is social psychology. Changes are along lines similar to those in the social sciences in general. An increasing number of social scientists have moved away from the exclusive use of public opinion polls and are concerned with relating social attitudes to personality as well as to sociological factors. The work of Ross Stagner (59), of Hartley (28), of Gordon Allport (2), and our California studies on ethnic prejudice (1, 17) may be cited as examples. The latter combine methods and outlook of social psychology with those of clinical psychology.

For example, in the California studies we were primarily interested in a certain subject's social attitudes, say, his attitude toward Roosevelt, and not only as a basis for understanding his attitude toward, say, his own father. But we probably would never have been able to understand the range and subtlety of the subject's attitude toward Roosevelt had we not been guided by the findings on his attitude toward his father. Social attitudes and social techniques are at least as real as the underlying motivation, but often we need to speculate on the latter to understand the former.

Changes in the Psychology of Perception.—Not only the social sciences but also general psychology, as we have mentioned above, changed under the impact of psychoanalysis and the science of personality. General psychology, especially represented by the fields of learning, perception, and other aspects of cognition, seemed at first untouched by so-called dynamic psychology. More recently, however, these fields have been invaded. We find Murphy (40), Murray (41), Sanford (53), Bruner, Postman and others (5, 46), and Sherif (58) among the pioneers who have looked at perception mainly from the angle of needs. Murphy designates the fact that cognitive processes move in the direction of needs as "autism" and stresses that "all cognitive processes are apparently continually shaped in greater or lesser degree by the pressure of wants" (40, p. 365). "There is no standard objective world except through our slow yielding to a rather painful compromise process." Fear, hunger, need for conformity, and values have been explored as determining perception.

Again we find here, on a smaller scale and in a more rapid succession, steps of development parallel to those described previously for psychoanalysis and for personality research. The reality which the cognitive processes are supposed to transmit to us has in the past been interpreted by general psychologists as something reflected in perception in an absolute and universal manner. An important system of the psychology of perception which deals exclusively with the veridical functions of the cognitive processes is that of Egon Brunswik (6). This system represents a crucial progress over the classical psychophysical approach insofar as it is oriented toward the perceptual conquest of the world of physical and social objects, whereas psychophysics is arrested in mediation and stimulus-boundness without reaching the functionally important part of the stimulus world. More specifically, it is the orientation toward "thing-constancy" which reintroduces the "distal" reality lost in the traditional psychophysical approach. Another example of a functional approach to perception is represented by Hilgard in his contribution to the present symposium (Chapter 4).

The next step, the discovery of autism, shows us how subjective and shifting this conquest of reality is when exposed to changing systems of needs, with their power to select or distort many aspects of perceptual reality.

Summarizing we may say that "reality," first lost in psychophysics, was reinstated in the work on the constancy problem, but became again lost in a one-sided emphasis on motives as determinants of perception. The last step seems paradoxical in view of the fact that psychoanalysis, which had been an influence in this emphasis away from reality, had itself stressed the reality orientation of perception as soon as it had come around to deal with the matter.

Still more recent workers in the field of personality and perception have managed to balance their interest in the mastery of reality, in the perceiver's different ways of handling it effectively, with an interest in the subjective distortions. As may be seen from this symposium and the Symposium on Personality and Perception in the *Journal for Personality* (Sept. and Dec., 1949), we are now about to reach a fruitful compromise by combining the study of the veridical and subjective functions of the cognitive processes.

Another line of thought which converges into the synthesis of personality and perception research is that of such German typologists as Kretschmer (35), Jaensch (30), Goldstein (26), and Werner (66). Relatively little interested as they are in both the influence of needs on perception and in the veridical functions of perception, they have stressed over-all styles of personality as expressed in behavioral patterns as well as in the cognitive approach to the environment. Among the perceptually loaded variables that have become prominent in this course of development is the one defined by the opposition of the "synthetic" and the "analytic" approach as adopted, among others, by Kretschmer and his school and also represented by the "whole" vs. "detail" emphasis in the evaluation of the Rorschach Test; further pairs of opposites borrowed from the psychology of perception are "diffuse" vs. "articulated" (Werner), "concrete" vs. "abstract" (Goldstein), as well as such rather specific distinctions as color-dominance vs. form-dominance (Kretschmer, Schroll, and others, and again Rorschach; see also the treatment in Thurstone's factorial study of perception, 62).

Not only are most of the major theories in German academic psychology rooted in perception (see the Gestalt psychologists, and the constancy approach of Egon Brunswik and of others), but the same holds for the German psychology of individual differences as exemplified by the typologists just mentioned as well as by William Stern (60).

The work of Rorschach, the Swiss psychiatrist (52), represents a merging of psychoanalysis and the work of the German typologists. Unlike the materials used by the German typologists, Rorschach used his vague ink blots in order to get as much projection as possible and proceeded to an interpretation at least in part along the lines of his psychoanalytic orientation.

In the workshop of the clinical psychologist we find all these trends combined. Case histories are collected and combined with the results of a battery of tests, which include projective materials as well as intelligence and concept-formation tests.

We have seen that with the greater emphasis on perception and cognition, as well as on social factors, personality theory is reintroducing the manifest personality or phenotype. Perceptual and cognitive performances as well as social attitudes are being carefully and systematically observed and are used not merely for extrapolations into the deeper layers. On the contrary, speculations about the deeper layers are considered as detours necessary for the prediction of what is in the end our greatest interest, namely, the so-called surface behavior, whether this consists in a political attitude or in the solution of a cognitive task. Expanded understanding of human behavior in the sense just indicated will contribute to a dynamic ego psychology considerably beyond the contribution of psychoanalysis in this field. Precisely at which points and to what extent the dynamic ego psychology, which seems now to emerge as the major interest of psychologists, is based on the dynamic ego psychology developed by psychoanalysis and precisely how much change the topic has undergone under the impact of psychology proper may better be discussed after the presentation of some experimental and empirical material to which we now proceed.

Perception of Self and of Others

We now enter into the discussion of the empirical material by way of problems in the perception of the self and of others, using some of our California studies as examples. In the framework of this symposium the problem of the perception of the self and of others has already been introduced by Carl Rogers (Chapter 11) with an emphasis mainly on the changes that occur in the course of a successful therapy. Our emphasis, however, will be on a comparison of self-perception with actual behavior as observed by others. We will ask ourselves what factors of adjustment and motivation determine the accuracy or distortion of our self-image, and what are the cues by which we can tell whether or not self-descriptions and descriptions of others are representative of actual reality. We hope to answer some of the questions posed in this symposium by Bruner as to the conditions under which certain aspects of the self become more salient in our perception than others. In the final sections we will deal with the reality-adequacy of thing-percepts and concepts in their relation to personality factors.

A Study of Mechanisms of Self-Deception.—Our first example is a study conducted by the present writer some years ago at the Psychological Institute of the University of Vienna (12). Its aim was to compare the actual conduct of a group of students, as observed by four independent judges, with the students' own statements about their conduct. Besides asking the students to describe their own behavior, we also inquired about the "guiding principles" of their conduct in general and their "demands upon the environment," that is, the way they perceived their immediate working environment and what changes they would like to make in it. These three types of query represented three different degrees of directness in approaching the personalities of the students concerned.

The results, based on about forty subjects, showed that the functional realities of one's own behavior are distorted when they enter consciousness and are verbally reported. This holds true, above all, so far as shortcomings of the subjects are concerned, but it is also true for positively valued traits.

The most striking mechanism found here was "distortion into the opposite." For example, one of the students was characterized by all the judges as lacking in sincerity. The student himself declared he was "sincere under all conditions."

There are marked statistical correlations between the tendency to perceive oneself in an extremely favorable light on a certain personality characteristic, such as popularity or sincerity, and an opposite, unfavorable rating on the same characteristic by the judges. In general, it is social maladjustment as rated by the judges which correlates with the presence of this mechanism of self-deception. Intellectual ability as rated by the judges is relatively unrelated to the tendency of "distortion into the opposite." This may be regarded as supporting the assumption of the relative independence of intelligence and emotional adjustment. Moreover, there was no evidence of such mechanism of distortion into the opposite in regard to the trait of scientific ability.

A second mechanism of self-deception as found in our material is that of "exaggeration." In the case of the subject quoted above who declared himself to be "sincere under all conditions," one is reminded of Shakespeare's warning that "the lady doth protest too much." Indeed, exaggerated formulations—as here the denial of guilt—were found to be statistically symptomatic of the absence rather than the presence of the asserted trait.

A third, more subtle mechanism found was that of "omission." In this case the subject did not mention a positive or negative characteristic of his which the judges had especially noted as displayed by him.

There was, fourth, a kind of apologetic camouflage constituting an attempt at justification of a defect. For instance, one of the subjects, characterized by the judges as extremely aggressive, stated about herself, "I do not let myself be intimidated."

"Minimizing" is still another, fifth, mechanism. Here a trait is seen by the subject in an unconcealed way but is minimized by his regarding it as not very strong or by his shifting the emphasis away from it by mentioning it relatively late in his self-characterization. Thus, in the case of one student all the judges had noted first of all in their list of traits that he was extremely social-minded, altruistic, and self-sacrificing. The subject himself said, "I try to help others if I can," but he put down this statement only after he had listed nine other traits in the description of himself.

On the whole, we have found more self-deceptions, in the sense defined here, in the area of more generalized behavioral dispositions than in that of the more palpable particulars of conduct. Thus there is relatively little illusion about one's own behavior in concrete situations, such as the bringing back of books to the library on time. Reality-testing is easier and more obvious in such situations than it is in the case of the more generalized traits. Only in pathological cases do we find false self-perceptions concerning relatively unambiguously defined, concrete behavior. Thus, one student, diagnosed as an incipient schizophrenic, explained his lack of contact with other students by his being so seldom at the Institute, while the observers agreed that he was regularly present, although without actual participation.

By comparing the language of the self-perceptions with that of the perception and description of others, we find that, in the case of our

Viennese students, self-reports were more concerned with (often spurious) motivational aspects of behavior, while the reports of the judges were focused more upon the overt social effects. Though the two sets of descriptions may thus deal with somewhat different topics, we may still speak of self-deceptions, since our subjects were explicitly asked to talk about their overt behavior. It would seem to be very difficult for one to see his own behavior without introducing immediately the aspect of motivation with its implicit element of justification. We function as judges of the behavior of others, but rather as doctors or mothers when we are viewing the behavior of ourselves.

What has been said for the perception of one's own behavior holds even more true in the case of the guiding principles of conduct listed by our subjects. Declaration of such principles often turned out to represent a compensation for behavioral shortcomings rather than a reflection of strength. As in the case of the behavioral traits, we can make a list of the guiding principles in the order of their probability of being actualized in real behavior. Thus, we find that "sincerity" listed by a subject as a guiding principle is negatively related to real sincerity, and "to be helpful" is not at all related to being helpful in reality.

On the other hand, what may be called the principles of achievement were found to be lived up to in almost every instance in which they had been mentioned by the subjects. Achievement, like intelligence, thus seems to be more interlocked with conscious design or purpose than is emotional or social conduct.

Shortcomings in social and personal attitudes are often not directly represented by conscious guiding principles but are rather expressed or signalized there in a diametrically opposite way. The ultimate aim of this inverse signalizing is probably a modification of behavior. A compensatory function of the guiding principles is also indicated by the fact that overemphasis, e.g., use of superlatives and repetition, was found to stand more often for a shortcoming than for a strength in the area concerned. The production of a great number of explicitly formulated guiding principles for one's behavior likewise often was found to go with its opposite, that is, with lack of fortitude of character.

In the perception of the environment and the demands for changes in it as expressed in the protocols of our subjects we find different types of statements. One group may be called "matter-of-fact," indicating, say, the demand for more books in the library, a demand which, according to the judges, was undoubtedly justified.

Another group of statements demands that the environment meet the subject's own personal shortcomings without his seeming to realize his own defects. For example, a subject considered as very aggressive by the judges demanded that others should be more friendly. His wishes for reform seemed to be directed exclusively toward the environment, so that he might live in it with as little friction as possible.

Finally, a third type of statement asks help of the environment in overcoming the subject's own shortcomings, which are here less repressed than in the case mentioned previously. For instance, one of the subjects, rated as lacking in self-discipline, demanded a much stricter organization of the Psychological Institute.

In the manner described, the demands which are made upon the social environment, and the general way this environment is perceived, seem to give a better picture, in an indirect, projective way, of the real dynamic forces within the person than is contained in his own self-reports. These demands indicate a comfortable way in which these shortcomings, which as such remain unperceived, could be remedied. It would appear that we do not always see ourselves as we are but instead perceive the environment in terms of our own needs. Self-perception and perception of the environment actually merge in the service of these needs. Thus, the perceptual distortions of ourselves and the environment fulfil an important function in our psychological household.

Case Studies of Self-Deception in Adolescents.—Our second example of mechanisms of perception is based on an analysis of material on three girls which the writer carried out as a part of the University of California Adolescent Growth Study referred to in the first section of this paper. This analysis—not hitherto published—shows in somewhat greater detail some of the mechanisms in the perception of the self and of others just described and relates them to the general dynamics of the personality. As mentioned above, a schematic description and evaluation of the adolescents' overt behavior as well as of their underlying motives had been made by adult observers and by their classmates. This had been done over a period of eight years. Detailed material about the self-evaluation of these children, concerned with the way they saw themselves and described their way of behaving, their feelings, and their status, was also available. In the focus of our attention for the present purposes will be the devices which are used on the different levels of personality to secure mental balance by settling at least temporarily on a certain self-image as well as on a certain image of one's environment.

On the behavioral observation ratings done by the staff of the Adolescent Study one of our three girls, Nell, was usually rated high on "talkativeness" and "display." Nell was thus seen as a girl who was rather uninhibited in vying for the attention of others. That no doubts entered her mind concerning the appropriateness of her behavior is indicated by her marked degree of "poise," as noted by the adult observers. However, she was one sigma below average in "relaxation," and there were signs of "anxiety" which might indicate underlying insecurity, although Nell was considered to be, on the surface at least, a carefree and cheerful girl.

The observers further rated Nell as having an "unpleasing expression," as being "unattractive," and as "unpopular" except for a period in the eighth grade when she achieved some degree of popularity. Though she never really achieved popularity, she was rated consistently high on "social interest" and on "initiative." Her ratings on "good-naturedness" were also usually below average, giving further evidence of her egocentricity. She received especially low ratings, almost two sigmas below average, on "calmness," "cooperativeness," and "contentedness." Also below average were her ratings on "tolerance," "earnestness," "responsibility," "constancy of mood," and "social insight." She was more than one sigma above average in "exploitiveness." All this points to the picture of a restless, impulsive, tense girl who was highly inconsiderate toward others and, in general, lacking in responsibility. This impression is further confirmed by Nell's being above average on all the items expressing overactivity, social striving, and aggressiveness, that is, on "self-confidence," "bold behavior," and "self-assertion." She was also above average on "busyness," "initiative," "activity," "quick comeback," as well as on "drive for social contact" and "attention-getting-ness."

There were no striking developmental changes in Nell's behavior pattern during the years of the study. The only consistent trend was one of slight improvement during the end of her school career. It was in the eleventh grade that Nell was for the first and only time rated as above average in "relaxation" and "good-naturedness." Her rating on "awareness of the audience" rose at this time from one sigma below average to one above average, indicating an increasing sensitivity and concern about the impression she made. After developing this awareness, a slight improvement with respect to her adjustment could be found.

We next turn to the data indicating the way Nell was seen by her classmates. The Reputation Test (sometimes called the "Guess

Who")[3] provides a means of determining the reputation a certain child has with his fellow-students on a series of personality attributes.

Nell was rated by her classmates as very low on grown-up behavior and high on being restless, attention-getting and talkative. Again, Nell's reputation improved in the ninth and tenth grades, when she was considered as happy, enthusiastic and as having a good sense of humor.

So far we have discussed how Nell has been rated by others, both adults and classmates. Now we turn to Nell in her function as a judge of herself and of others. The Reputation Test also is a test of self-evaluation, since every child is asked to consider himself for inclusion in his list of names for each trait, aside from his being judged by his classmates.

Though Nell was not being rated by the others as popular, she herself considered that she was popular. It is important to note in this context that in her judging of others Nell used a concept of popularity which deviated from that of the group. Her unusual method of judging the popularity of others reveals, even more than do her illusory direct judgments of her own popularity, her personal liability in this area. Her way of judging becomes clear from the following facts. Although Nell agreed with the group in rating the girls whom she considered popular also as happy, enthusiastic, friendly, and daring, she differed from the group in linking popularity with talkativeness, with being assured with adults, and with attention-gettingness. Recalling her own high standing on the last three items, we find in her association of these traits with popularity, when she was judging others, an indirect revelation of—and at the same time a defense against—these weaknesses existing in herself. Furthermore, unlike most of the girls, Nell associated tidiness and good looks with lack of popularity; she herself was rated low on good looks and on tidiness, and it is obviously for this reason that she did not consider these traits as necessary for popularity. She saw the unpopular girl as tidy, not talkative, not attention-getting, and shy about making friends. Only in the last of these items did her conception coincide with that of the group. Here she could afford to have an undistorted judgment because she herself was not shy. On the whole Nell showed a marked inclination to judge her classmates unfavorably.

We have seen how Nell, in her judgments of others, revealed herself indirectly by projecting her own weaknesses onto them. In her

---

[3] Extensive use is made here of the "clusters" of traits which Caroline McC. Tryon (64) developed on the basis of the Reputation Test.

direct statements about herself all defenses were activated. She put herself down as being a popular, good-looking girl who was a leader, active in games, friendly, talkative—we remember that she evaluated talkativeness as being an attribute of popular girls—and happy, as well as assured in class and with adults. Her classmates agreed with her about herself on talkativeness, happiness, and enthusiasm, especially in the last years in school. But she was not considered as popular, nor as good-looking (average or below), nor a leader. She also considered herself as daring at a time when she got a marked rating for being afraid. She mentioned herself as being assured in class, though she usually received either no mention or a negative score on this trait from others. The one year in which she received a positive score on being assured in class she did not mention herself on that item, whereas when she was rated negatively she paradoxically put herself on the positive side. In the seventh grade, when her reputation for being attention-getting was at its height, she claimed she was not attention-getting; but in the eleventh grade, when for the first time none of her classmates mentioned her as attention-getting, she, for the first time, admitted that she liked to be the center of attention.

Nell's realization of her weaknesses when she was in the eleventh grade is especially enlightening in view of the fact that it was in this period that her external behavior showed the first signs of increasing insight and contemplation.

With the exception of such isolated instances of partial insight as the one just discussed, however, Nell may be said, on the basis of the material presented here, to reveal a number of mechanisms of self-deception. First, she displayed the crudest of the mechanisms of self-deception found in our above-mentioned Viennese study, that of distortion into the opposite. In Nell's case the distortion went in the direction of ego-inflation and maximation, implying a complete denial of an unfavorable reality.

Second, there is evidence of the mechanism of projection. She described her classmates in an unfavorable light, thus indirectly blaming the others for whatever difficulties might arise. Furthermore, by degrading the others she apparently hoped to lift herself up.

A third mechanism detected in Nell is distortion and omission in judging others. So her conception of a popular girl was found above to differ from that of the group in a way which made more possible her inclusion in this classification. As far as omission is concerned, Nell, in spite of rating herself as popular, did not make much use of this category in judging others. In spite of her overt denial, she apparently felt some uneasiness on this issue and thus preferred to by-pass it.

From the point of view of developmental stages, we find that in Nell both the mechanisms of self-deception and the aggression against others seemed most marked at the ages of thirteen and fourteen. In those years she considered herself as good-looking, having older friends, being tidy, friendly, happy, enthusiastic, and social. To others, especially to boys and to her friends, she attributed negative characteristics. But this was the year in which no one selected her as a friend. At the age of sixteen, on the other hand, her mechanisms of self-deception and projection appear to have been toned down, while at the same time her behavior improved. Of the total of 72 mentions of herself, which Nell made over a period of eight years on the Reputation Test, all but 11 were positive. Those 11 negative judgments were made during the last two years, when in fact she was about to be accepted by the group.

Another of the instruments used in the California Adolescent Study, the Adjustment Inventory,[4] was intended as a broad and systematic approach to self-evaluation. The children were asked to rate themselves on approximately 600 specific items at yearly intervals over a period of seven years beginning with the fifth grade. While the Inventory has since proved of somewhat limited value when responses are taken at face value, it gains new significance when interpreted as material on self-perception and as indirect evidence on motivation.

In line with results on the Reputation Test, Nell's score on "social adjustment" as based on self-evaluation was usually somewhat above average (about one sigma), the major exception being in the eleventh grade, when it was below average. As noted above, this was the year in which Nell's behavior actually improved. The rest of the time she grossly overestimated herself, especially her acceptance by others. As before, however, Nell's answers to the more indirect questions reveal her ardent but partially frustrated social ambition and her doubts that everything was well in her relationships with others. She thought that the other boys and girls were often mean, snobbish, and "stuck-up."

---

[4] The Inventory (65) consisted of several series of items, including a number of sections from tests reported by Rogers (49) and by Symonds and Jackson (61). Examples are the checking of three wishes or aspirations, or of any number of fears, out of prepared lists; the naming of three persons to share one's life on a desert island; there also was a checklist of self-evaluations and corresponding wishes concerning one's personality and social relations. The categorization of the material was in the hands of Caroline McC. Tryon (64).

Nell's score on "personal inferiority" was likewise most of the time well above average, demonstrating once more that Nell evaluated her personal attributes positively. There was a marked tendency toward ego-inflation as reflected, for example, in her aspirations. Every year but one, Nell wished to be a movie star, a choice which was made by only a small proportion of the children. This choice is especially conspicuous in view of the fact that Nell was consistently rated as below average in good looks. Only rarely did Nell mention vocational aspirations that were more realistic, and when she did so her aspirations became very modest. Again, however, in the last year in school Nell seemed less self-satisfied.

Her "school adjustment" as seen by herself stayed, with the exception of the fifth grade, well above average. She, herself, however, complained almost every year about being told that she was "too noisy and talks too much" and about "not having a chance to recite in class." Instead of facing her restlessness and her drive to exhibit herself, she felt herself unjustifiably restrained by her teachers. It was only in these indirect complaints that Nell indicated difficulties in her relation to the teacher. Five out of the seven times she filled out the Adjustment Inventory, she considered herself as "a girl who is very much liked by the teachers," and only twice did she consider herself as completely rejected, adding that she did not wish to be liked by them. Here is one instance in which an extreme affirmation of an alleged asset alternates with an extreme denial, showing the closeness of the two extremes to one another and indicating an insecurity in this respect. (For a general discussion of closeness of opposites, see 18.) Nell's insecurity was justified, since we know from other sources that she was not very highly regarded by the teachers.

Nell's responses in regard to the items which deal with the attitude toward family show marked ambivalence. She expressed a great deal of attachment to her family in the direct questions, e.g., in her preference to go home after school, a preference which she shared with only 10 per cent of the girls; but she usually omitted her family when asked about the three persons she would take to a desert island, while most of the girls did choose some family members.

In her as yet unpublished presentation of Nell's case, based on home interviews, Mary C. Jones describes the eager social ambition of Nell's parents, especially of her mother, and the pressure put upon Nell to fulfil this ambition. On the basis of the behavioral data, we have seen Nell identified with the attitude of her mother and displaying the same social ambition. However, in her reactions to the indirect questions concerning her attitude toward her family, such as the one about companions on a desert island mentioned above, Nell revealed her wish to escape from this pressure and her resentment about not getting enough love and affection. As will be seen later, the type of ambivalence toward parents which is not utterly conscious and accepted goes very often with an inclination toward black-white solutions and an avoidance of emotional and cognitive ambiguities in general.

We have said before that exaggeration is one of the most important signs of compensatory as contrasted with representative statements. The number of exaggerated responses in the Adjustment Inventory is measured by the category "overstatement." Nell is found to do a great deal of overstating. Her overstatements usually expressed an extreme satisfaction with herself. As mentioned above, she judged herself as very well liked, as very bright, very well dressed, having very much fun, and the like. On the few occasions when Nell thought she was lacking in a positively valued characteristic, she overdramatized this lack and denied emphatically the wish to be different.

Nell yielded extreme responses not only in judging herself but also on the corresponding questions indicating her wishes and ideals. When both self-description and aspirations are extreme, there is very little room for discrepancy between the two. The average child shows more discrepancy, yet neither his self-description nor his aspirations customarily go to such extremes as those reached by Nell. We recall here Rogers' statement in this symposium (Chapter 11) stressing the diminishing discrepancy between ideal self and real self after successful therapy; we should like to add that the absence of such a discrepancy is probably not always a sign of adjustment. It is certainly not such a sign in Nell's case.

Along the same line are some of the findings in our studies on ethnic prejudice (1, 17). Prejudiced persons, who as a group are less well adjusted than the unprejudiced, reveal less awareness of discrepancy between real and ideal self than do the latter. Here is a minor point of difference between Rogers' and our findings on self-perception. Otherwise our results are remarkably similar and mutually confirmatory.

Aside from overstatement, there is still another category in which Nell, in spite of her displayed self-satisfaction, revealed an underlying anxiety. At the time she reached the climax of her apparent satisfaction with herself, she also rose above the average on the category "fears." More specifically, her fears reflected the notion of a threatening, aggressive environment. In the eleventh grade, which will be remembered as a period of increased insight, more correct self-perception, and more effective mastery of difficulties for Nell, her "fears" decreased to one sigma below average.

A second case which we should discuss briefly is that of Joyce, a girl who, in contrast to Nell, was highly successful though somewhat egocentric and lacking in basic adjustment. Her success started about the sixth or seventh grade when she got the highest ratings on popularity, poise, and social prestige and low ratings on the tendency toward display. Later there are indications that, behind Joyce's smooth social façade (she was two sigmas above average on this trait), there were some preoccupations which interfered with her ability for good object relations. At the age of sixteen, Joyce was rated one sigma below average on "cooperativeness" and one sigma above average on "exploitiveness." These ratings indicate that, in spite of her remarkable success, her social adjustment was on a superficial level. But at first no one besides herself seemed to know much about her inner difficulties. One of her more palpable reactions was that her judgments of herself on the Reputation Test were rather distorted. In contrast to Nell, Joyce showed a total of only 41 judgments about herself, and 24 of these were negative. In spite of the fact that she received the highest possible score on "tidiness" and "good-lookingness," she gave herself a negative score on these items.

Not only does Joyce point in her judgments to liabilities where she actually possessed assets, but she realistically faced her true weaknesses. In the sixth and seventh grades she had credited herself with a sense of humor, but from the ninth grade on she indicated that she had no appreciation of jokes and no sense of humor. It was precisely at that time that her reputation on "having humor" dropped rather drastically. Since she frequently ascribed to girls she considered popular certain characteristics which she thought she lacked, such as being active in games, assured in class, happy, good-looking and having an appreciation for jokes, we can assume that she really thought she was not liked. Her way of perceiving others may be used as an indirect check on her self-judgment to the effect that she was unpopular.

We find Joyce's self-judgments shot through with understatement and self-minimization when we compare them with judgments made about her by others. We have every reason to believe that this tendency on her part was not due to a mere display of modesty but to real insecurity. The means of defense here was not verbal ego-maximation as in Nell, but a strong striving toward all kinds of actual success. This striving was successful but, at the same time, insatiable and, therefore, never really satisfied. Because of her actual success Joyce could afford to admit to herself her underlying weaknesses.

It might be interesting to speculate further about the source of Joyce's tendency to understate her assets and to dramatize her shortcomings. One source might be the lack of actual personal equipment, not so much as compared with reality, but as compared with her aspirations. These, we find, were most unrealistic. On the Adjustment Inventory she expressed, in the course of the years, the wish to be a princess, an aviator, a movie actress, a singer, and the like. In her self-perception she obviously compared herself with the aspired-to self more than with the real self. From this predicament she apparently attempted to escape into a "make-believe world"; in fact, in her self-reports during the first three years, she admitted this. Her wish, in the eighth grade, "not to grow up" points in the same direction.

In the sense that she understood her real shortcomings earlier than her classmates did, Joyce's unfavorable judgment of herself in certain respects was an anticipation of her reputation with others in later years. In the end she did lose status with the group to a certain extent, although she continued to be rated more favorably by others than by herself. According to an analysis of Joyce's case by a clinician, there seems to be more agreement between her picture of herself and the diagnostic picture presented of her than between either of these pictures and her social façade as reflected in her reputation. As seems to be quite often the case, Joyce perceived herself more with the eyes of a clinician than with the eyes of a surface-behaviorist. The latter point of view, reflected in the ratings of manifest behavior discussed earlier in this chapter, brings to the fore the "persona," that is, the social role the individual has grown into, rather than the core of personality.

Although Joyce's inner difficulties did not lead to depressions, they did find expression in "fears." It is especially interesting that the number of Joyce's fears increased sharply in the course of her last three years in school. At this time an increase in the expression of her basic difficulties was to be expected. It occurred. Perhaps the fact that she was, at least in some respects, very successful, enabled her, in contrast to Nell, to face some of her inner maladjustments. Whereas Nell's lack of awareness functioned as a defense to reduce tensions that would arise from an objectively very difficult situation, Joyce's conscious perception seems to have had an opposite function. Her acute awareness of shortcomings and her generally negative attitude toward herself seem to act as a warning rather than as a defense mechanism. She actually needed these warnings because external assets, such as her good looks and general attractiveness, made her life appear smoother—at least for a while—than it actually was.

To repeat: Both Nell's and Joyce's perception of their own behavior and of their acceptance by the group was at variance with the actual facts as stated by close acquaintances, both adult observers and classmates. Nell's exaggeratedly inflated picturing of herself—as revealed by overstatement, contradictions between answers to direct and indirect questions, and a distorted perception of others—was clearly of a defensive and compensatory character. While Joyce's distortions went in the opposite direction, that of gross understatement, the unusual number of negative statements in her self-evaluation should serve to caution us regarding the actual and direct validity of her self-perception. As was the case with some of our Viennese subjects, her statements signalize possible dangers and pitfalls which in fact toward the end of her school years started to disrupt even the external social adjustment which she at first so grossly underrated.

To conclude this section, we may highlight a few points from the material on a third case, Ann, who differed from the first two girls in being unusually free of self-deceptions. From the beginning Ann was rated, by both adults and classmates, as cooperative, good-natured, unexploitive, responsible, and even-tempered. These judgments were coupled with extremely low ratings on the tendency toward display. Here is a perfect picture of personal and emotional adjustment. Ann's social adjustment, specified under the headings of sociability, expressiveness, and effect on the group, started at about average but rose consistently as she grew up.

During the seven years of observation Ann made only 27 mentions of herself on the Reputation Test in contrast to Nell's 72 and Joyce's 41. Of these 27 judgments, 19 were positive and 8 were negative. This seems an unretouched, balanced proportion. As for the few discrepancies between self-mentions and mentions by classmates, we find Ann for the most part on the modest side.

There is only a single area in which Ann seemed to be subject to self-deception, and this is sex adjustment. At the same time, this was an area of comparative maladjustment for Ann. As noted by the adult observers, her interest in the opposite sex was below average; in a girl this is often linked with masculine identification. Support for this assumption as applied to Ann is that she showed an unusual tendency to attribute masculinity to girls whom she considered popular. Furthermore, until her last year at school Ann consistently gave the boys more favorable ratings than the girls and at the same time tended to attribute to boys rather than to other girls the same characteristics she attributed to herself.

Drives as Determiners of the Perception of Self and of Others.
—Turning back to our initial topic, the importance of motivational
considerations for the understanding of personality in general and of
perception in particular, we will conclude our discussion of the three
cases by referring to the ratings these children received on underlying
motives as introduced in the study of alternative manifestations of
drives presented above. This will throw light on the causes of the
differences among them with respect to self-perception.

Although Nell's own evaluation of her behavior and status was
found to be at odds with the evaluation of her specific overt behavior
by other observers, such a discrepancy ceases to exist when we proceed
to compare her self-perception with her drive pattern as rated intuitively by trained adult observers on the basis of prolonged close
acquaintanceship. (As has been mentioned above, the self-reports
were not included as a basis of these ratings.) It is especially her
need for an inflated ego-image that becomes evident in these over-all
ratings. Nell was rated high on the drives for aggression, for recognition, for dependence, and for escape, whereas she was rated low on
the drives for autonomy, for achievement, and for abasement. Un-
relentingly driven toward success without the ability really to work
for it, and without benefit of the dampening influence of abasement,
she escaped into a short-cut and into deceiving herself about what
she had actually reached among all the things she desired. Her high
degree of aggression had become evident primarily through her way
of judging her environment.

Joyce, on the other hand, received only an average rating in
aggression. We remember that, in accordance with this, she did not
put projective blame on the environment for her own weaknesses.
Her excessive self-blame can be understood best in terms of the relatively high rating she received on the need for abasement. This latter
rating may seem to be in contradiction to her external success; but
we must recall that she did not enjoy her success and that she seemed
headed for some sort of dramatic upheaval in her personal life. (This
actually came to pass later on, after she had left school.) Joyce also
received the highest possible rating on the drive for escape. Accordingly, we found her escaping from real obligations through all kinds
of means such as external success or the exaggerated and unrealistic
level of aspiration. This high level of aspiration was one of the few
characteristics she shared with Nell. More basically, it was the drive
for escape which she shared with Nell and which in both must be
made responsible for the lack of real adjustment. Unlike Nell, Joyce
was not rated high on the drive for dependence, and this may account
for her relative indifference toward her social success.

Our third case, Ann, received the lowest possible rating on the drives for aggression and for escape, and next to the lowest on the drive for recognition. She was markedly above average on the drive for achievement. This drive was sharply differentiated in our study from the drive for recognition and was meant to refer to the desire to do a good job rather than to receive approval. Ann was also rated above average in her drive toward affiliation with others. It was perhaps precisely the relatively weak strivings for aggression, escape, and abasement which accounted for Ann's comparatively undistorted perception of herself and of others.

Again, intuitive drives seem better able to explain self-reports than does the observed manifest behavior. However, all these types of material are needed fully to explain self-perception. Only by considering Nell's low social standing in class and her poor social techniques, together with her strong drives for escape, recognition, and aggression and her low ratings on the drive for abasement, can her particular pattern of mechanisms of self-deception be understood. The same holds in reverse for Joyce. Obviously, it is the combination of social and behavioral with motivational realities which determines the perception of the self and of others.

The data just reported support the general assumption that the perception of the self—or more specifically, the perception of the self as related to actual behavior—is a crucial index of personality adjustment. We also found that in cases where self-perception was distorted there was a tendency to project the unaccepted tendencies onto other persons. It is evident that the problem is of special importance for the therapist, the clinician, or any other person involved in making judgments of others.

The Clinician's Bias in Perceiving the Subject.—Still another aspect of the analysis carried out by the present writer at the California Adolescent Growth Study was aimed at analyzing the personal equation which enters into the judgment of the clinician (14, chap. iv). Such influences would be expected especially in interpretive judgments, of which the ratings of motivational tendencies discussed in the first section of this paper constitute an important special case.

The question is as to how the personality of the rater as well as his theoretical background is apt to influence his percepts of the children. More specifically, there are three separate problems here that demand discussion. Drive ratings may be influenced differentially by (a) the way in which the drive is conceived by the judge; (b) the degree to which the child is liked or disliked by the judge; and (c) the intensity of the drive in question in the personality of the rater.

In the study under attention there were three independent women judges, the "rating personalities" of whom could in this manner be compared with one another.

In order to investigate the implicit definitions of any of the drives rated in terms of other drives, intercorrelations of the ratings of the children on each of the drives were computed for each judge separately. As an illustration, let us consider, for each of the three judges separately, the interrelationships of the ratings she made on the drive for autonomy with those she made on other drives. In the case of one judge there was a sizable negative correlation of "autonomy" with "social ties" and also with "succorance"; that is, in the opinion of this judge, these drives are to a certain degree mutually exclusive. In the case of the second judge neither of these two correlations, nor any of the others for that matter, was significantly negative. The ratings of the third judge showed positive correlations of "autonomy" with "aggression," a pair which in the ratings of the other two judges exhibited no relationship. In other words, there was no uniform conception of the drive for autonomy; the discrepancies arose apparently from the fact that the various judges differed in their opinions as to whether this drive constituted a reaction formation or not. On the matter of the interdependency of the remaining drives under consideration, the judges differed somewhat less than on the drive for autonomy. On the whole the varying conceptions of a given drive did not seriously interfere with inter-rater agreement, which for the most part turned out to be satisfactory.

A similar examination of the explicit emotional attitudes of the raters toward the subjects seemed to indicate that these attitudes have even less effect upon inter-rater agreement than the varying conceptions of drives. After completing the ratings on drives, the judges were asked to indicate on a five-point scale their like or dislike for each of the children involved. Correlations of these preference ratings with the drive ratings given by the judges to the children were computed for the individual judges. Many of the coefficients were close to zero, indicating that in the case of several of the drives the ratings were not tied up with verbalized emotional preferences. Exceptions occurred in connection with the drives for aggression, for escape, and for succorance; here negative correlations were obtained, indicating that dislike went with high ratings on these drives.

It is interesting to note that the one judge, who showed in her ratings of the children the highest correlation between ratings of dislike and ratings of aggression and succorance, did not show any poorer judgment about the drive for aggression when agreement with the other judges is taken as a measure of accuracy. Thus, on the basis of a comparison of her ratings with those of the rater least prejudiced against the drives in question, we say that at least in this instance an extreme aversion toward a certain drive did not go with an unusual bias of judgment. It is reassuring to see that the freely admitted liking or disliking of a subject on the part of the judge did not necessarily distort perception. There are slight variations among the judges with respect to this matter, however.

This leads us to our third problem, that posed by the question as to how far the presence or absence of a drive in a judge himself influences perception of the same motivational tendency in others. Murray (42) found a slight tendency toward rating by contrast, that is, a rating of people as if they were different from oneself. Sears (57) found that persons who have insight into a trait in themselves rate by contrast and those who repress the awareness of a trait in themselves rate by projection.

In order to obtain further evidence on this matter, each of the three judges was rated by the other two on the same list of drives on which they had rated the children. They also rated themselves on the same list. Bearing out the findings of Sears, the rater who showed the best insight, as indicated in the least amount of discrepancy between her self-ratings and the ratings given to her by the others, showed a slight tendency to rate the children by contrast. Also consistent with Sears's results are the findings in the case of another of the judges who had somewhat less insight than the remaining two and who tended to rate the children by projection. The third judge, however, presented a picture differing from that to be expected according to Sears, insofar as she combined good insight with some tendency toward projection. In agreement with the results of the Vienna study on self-deception previously reported in this paper (12), there was a tendency on the part of the judges to give extreme ratings to the children on those drive variables on which they disagreed most with the other raters regarding their own status.

On the whole it seemed that within the limits of the Adolescent Study material the tendency toward rating by projection is stronger than the one toward rating by contrast, that the raters showed a stronger tendency to project when rating children of their own sex than when rating children of the opposite sex, and that the tendency to project their personality as seen by themselves was stronger than the tendency to project one's personality as seen by others. This last result, however, may hold true to a greater extent for raters with self-insight than for those without.

Similarities between judges were computed, and it was ascertained that two of the judges tended to give subjects more similar ratings on those variables in which they themselves were more similar. This trend seemed by no means consistent for the remaining two possible combinations among the judges, however.

In brief, we must acknowledge that there are various subjective factors that seem to influence the perception of others even in clinically trained observers. These factors could be averaged out by using large and representative samples of judges. An encouraging feature is the fact that the three raters showed satisfactory inter-rater agreement in making highly interpretative judgments about the children, even though a personal equation had entered into these judgments.

In the theoretical parts of this paper the question was posed whether or not defense mechanisms of the type described in this section are the same as those described in psychoanalysis. It is our opinion that at least in part we are dealing with the same mechanisms. To be sure, psychoanalysis is chiefly concerned with defenses established in early childhood against instinctual dangers. In our case the defenses are mainly against loss of self-esteem. In a formal sense, however, the two types of mechanisms are very similar. Projection, for example, is in both cases defined as the ascribing to the environment of what is internal and at the same time unpleasant. This similarity holds especially for the mechanisms discussed in the present section, which involve a mobilization of defenses against such vital issues as lack of popularity and the like. The similarity holds to a lesser degree for laboratory experiments, where success or failure is usually of little relevance.

Intolerance of Ambiguity and Distortion of Reality in Personality-Centered Studies of Perception

Rigidity and the Problem of Unity of Style.—The importance of individual differences in the tendency toward unqualified assertions was brought out in the discussion of mechanisms of self-deception. As a rule, however, the greater the definiteness, exaggeration, and lack of shading in the description of favorable traits in oneself the less often were such assertions verified in the judgments of close acquaintances. Let us now turn to cognition and object perception proper, as studied in a project on social discrimination in children (17, 18).

A certain inability, in the perceptual and cognitive approach of an individual to tolerate more complex, conflicting, or open structures might, it seemed, occur also to a certain extent in the emotional and social areas. Proceeding from the observation that some persons can tolerate the coexistence of love and hate less than others can and that these persons seem to tend toward perceiving people generally in terms of positive or negative halos and dichotomies rather than allowing for independent and continuous variability of traits, we attempted to ascertain just how pervasive this disposition might be by undertaking a number of experiments on memory, concept formation, and perception proper.

Results so far collected support the conjecture that, by and large, such tendencies as the quest for unqualified certainty, the rigid adherence [5] to anything given—be this an authority or a stimulus,—the inadequacy of reaction in terms of reality, and the like, operate in more than one area of personality. It can be demonstrated, further, that such specific forms of reaction as orientation toward concrete detail (stimulus-boundness) tend to occur again and again within an individual in contexts seemingly far removed from each other. Inclination toward mechanical repetition of faulty hypotheses, inaccessibility to new experience, satisfaction with subjective and at the same time unimaginative, overconcrete or overgeneralized solutions, all appear to be specific manifestations of a general disposition which holds sway among certain groups of individuals, such as the ethnically prejudiced, in their approach to emotional and social as well as more purely cognitive problems.

Before going into the discussion of individual cases which show different degrees and patterns of acceptance of ambiguity, let us summarize a few more general findings. We found evidence, in certain groups of our subjects, of intolerance of ambiguity in the perceptual as well as in the emotional and social areas. In these individuals there is, on the surface, a rigid, unambiguous adherence to cultural and conventional values, but this is combined with an underlying destructiveness directed toward these same values; this combination of opposites is in contrast to the establishment of a healthy "medium distance" to the culture.

In a similar manner, an underlying ambivalence toward the parents is split into a positive and a negative side and expressed through alternative media, e.g., stereotyped and exaggerated admiration in response to direct questions, combined with the conception of punitiveness and harshness in parents revealed in the indirect material. Medium distance is again lacking, and feelings are expressed in terms of the ends of a continuum rather than of a continuum proper.

---

[5] Recently Cattell and Tiner (8) have pointed at some of the confusions in the use of the term "rigidity." In the present chapter the term is used in two definitely interrelated meanings. One is the traditional usage, referring to perseveration and resistance to change (see also Rokeach, 51). The second usage is as an abbreviation for "intolerance of ambiguity" as discussed in this chapter.

Furthermore, perceptual stimuli not too familiar and lacking in firmness and definiteness seem to be more disturbing to the rigid, prejudiced group. In experimental situations involving a change of stimuli, this disturbance is expressed either in a persistent use of the name of the object originally shown or in a bout of random guessing. In either case there seems to be an effort to replace the vague by known and structured objects.

In brief, the group of which we speak here shows emotionally dramatized responses to middle-class values, parents, outgroups, and people in general as well as to perceptual and cognitive material, especially if it is vague or otherwise threatening. The choice is between total acceptance and total rejection; if the two coexist, they do so in different layers of the personality.

Rather than a conscious coexistence of acceptance and rejection, leading to qualified feelings and statements, however, we find avoidance of complexities on the surface, with chaos lurking behind and breaking through the rigidly maintained façade. With internal conflict being as disturbing as it is in the rigid group, there apparently develops a tendency toward denying external ambiguity as long as such denial can be maintained. Underlying anxiety issuing from the confusion of one's social identity and from other conflicts is apparently so great that it hampers individuals in this group in facing even the purely cognitive types of ambiguity. The mechanism discussed is somewhat related to what Postman, Bruner, and McGinnies (46) have called "perceptual defenses." A desperate effort is made to shut out uncertainties the prejudiced individual is unable to face, thus narrowing what Tolman (63) has called the "cognitive map" to rigidly defined tracks.

Persons with less severe underlying confusions, on the other hand, may be able to afford to face ambiguities openly, although this may mean at least a temporary facing of conflicts and anxieties as well. In this case the total pattern is that of a broader integration of reality, in which no parts are left out, and thus a more flexible adaptation to varying circumstances.

The lack of integration and the resultant break between the conscious and unconscious layers in the rigid person, as compared with the greater fluidity of transition and of intercommunication between the different personality strata in more flexible individuals, appear to have the greatest implications for the respective personality patterns. The shutting out of certain aspects of feelings and of inner reality in general must be seen as the root of the distorted perceptions and judgments of outer reality shown by the rigid group.

In spite of the rather consistent recurrence of elements of rigidity in various areas, there is thus no all-pervasive unity of style in this pattern of personality. In listing the attitudes which go together in the same individuals, we are in the end faced with the coexistence of rigid perseverative behavior and a haphazard, disintegrated, random approach. Another related phenomenon seemingly at odds with the principle of personal unity concerns the discrepancies from one level of personality to another. To further elaborate a point discussed above, we may say that, in our prejudiced subjects, the negative side of the feelings toward parents is repressed without losing its dynamic force, only to be transferred at least in part to other objects, such as minority groups. The clinging to definite dichotomies and demarcation lines apparently reduces the conflict on the conscious level but at the same time increases the underlying confusion. The conception of a unity of style within the personality can be restored by defining styles in a more complex manner, say, by the inclusion of opposites within the same pattern.

Paradoxically, the prejudiced person, who, by virtue of the mechanism of isolation, displays less integration of the different aspects of personality, at the same time often shows more consistency of reaction; the subjective factors eventually invade and disrupt even those forms of reaction which in the unprejudiced have largely managed from the start to remain determined by objective reality. Of course, one may interject that reality-adequacy is the consistent response of the mature person. This is, however, a kind of consistency which at the same time is inconsistent insofar as it varies to a higher degree with changing stimuli. Along the same line we may observe that normal subjects, in performing simple perceptual tasks, show but small individual differences, whereas a psychotic person may behave in a very atypical manner yet remain true to a form of his own, whether this be extreme deviation from the stimuli or a compensatory, in essence equally "unrealistic," slavish clinging to its irrelevant details.

Case Studies in Personality and Perception.—Over and beyond these general considerations which must warn us against a superficial implementation of the unity-of-style principle, consistencies as well as inconsistencies of a more specific kind can be found in individual cases. We have selected from the project on social discrimination in children mentioned above a few specific cases and will now examine their social, emotional, and cognitive reactions.

We turn first to the case of Bob, a thirteen-year-old boy high on ethnic prejudice whose outstanding characteristic is his desire to conform. His entire outlook is one of intolerance of ambiguity. His statements in response to questions covering a variety of topics reveal his rigid adherence to conventional values and his great anxiety about making the grade. His conceptions about people show that he draws clear lines of demarcation between the "right" and the "wrong" people. He has a tendency to resort to black-white solutions, achieve premature closure on a restricted basis with respect to evaluative aspects, and to arrive at unqualified over-all acceptance or rejection of other persons. Thus, he thinks that Americans are only "those born here" and he considers it would be best "if all the different races all went back to their own states."

In general, Bob's approach, in discussing social and political problems as well as values in general, consists of what we may call "poor hypotheses"; he reveals a relative lack of information and a highly stereotypical kind of thinking, and he repeats himself a great deal. Asked what a perfect boy is, he answers, "He's clean. Well, he has clean clothes, and he combs his hair, and he keeps his ears clean." Asked what the worst job would be for a man, he answers, "I wouldn't like to dig ditches. Well, it doesn't give you a very good standing." It should be added that the more rigid children tend to answer this question by referring to a fixed social hierarchy, whereas the other children think of jobs in terms of whether one likes them or not.

Bob dichotomizes sharply between weakness and strength, between the feminine and the masculine, and so forth. His preoccupation with physical strength is further revealed in the interview as well as in the Thematic Apperception Test. This preoccupation appears in a general way, as well as more specifically in admiration for his father, whom he considers as strong, and in his contempt for his mother, whom he considers weak. Bob's reactions in the perceptual and cognitive tasks are consistent, to a large extent, with the over-all clinical picture. Though there is a great deal of conformity and compliance in Bob, we also find tendencies toward explosive aggression, which are expressed in fits of rage.

The first experiment to be discussed here in relation to the case of Bob is one undertaken by Norman Livson and Florine Berkowitz-Livson in connection with our study on social discrimination in children.[6] The experiment was somewhat similar to one by the present writer that had involved transitions from the picture of one familiar

---

[6] The results of the experiment by Mr. and Mrs. Livson referred to here, as well as of one by Marvin Hyman on concept formation mentioned below, will be published in greater detail by the respective authors and are referred to here by their consent.

object—a cat—to that of another—a dog—(18, p. 128) and bore out
its tentative results. The Livsons presented the subjects with a series
of cards showing numbers slowly emerging from indistinctness; then
certain numbers presented would, on successive cards, change into
other numbers.

It was found that the unprejudiced group recognized the changes
significantly earlier than the prejudiced. Bob's response in this
experiment was very cautious, as evidenced by the fact that he
did not present any perceptual hypotheses before the fourth card,
or relatively late as compared to the group as a whole. Once he
had ventured a guess, however, he clung to it even if objective support was not forthcoming. He did not correctly recognize changing
numbers before the twelfth card, whereas correct response on the
ninth card was the average.

In another experiment, undertaken by the same investigators,
blank spaces had to be filled in with words previously memorized.
Bob was on the whole careful. His one error was that of filling in a
wrong word which was implicitly suggested by the experimenter.
Submission to the experimenter thus proved even stronger than faithful adherence to the stimulus.

Though Bob manifested a rather consistently careful, restricted,
and conservative attitude toward the stimulus on the experiments just
discussed, his behavior was different on a likewise as yet unpublished
investigation of concept formation conducted with the children of our
study by Marvin Hyman. It involved an adaptation of the well-
known Vigotsky Test in which blocks are to be ordered according to
certain abstract principles. Bob made an unusual number of mis-
takes. He began with a good hypothesis, but when he could not work
it out fully his behavior disintegrated in the direction of concreteness,
repetitiveness, and randomness. Examples are the fitting together of
only two blocks at a time, without orientation toward an over-all
principle. Bob produced seven such random arrangements. He did
not respond to the attempts at correction made by the experimenter,
since he seemed unable to grasp the principle involved and continued
to repeat his trials based on bad guesses. The number of corrections he made is third highest in the total group. He was found
never to repeat one of his rare good hypotheses, but he did so frequently with poor hypotheses. Though prejudiced children generally
tend to take a longer time to make a correction than the unprejudiced,
Bob made his corrections in a relatively speedy way. This was due,
however, to a relatively large number of undirected trials and errors.
As is the case with most children in the prejudiced group, the quality
of his hypotheses was not too high. It took Bob almost 40 minutes to

arrive at the right solutions, which is unusually long for his age.[7]

Bob generally tended to turn from a careful and restricted approach to a haphazard one when the situation became too difficult to master. We have noted above, on the basis of his clinical data, that his otherwise docile and obedient pattern was occasionally disrupted by break-throughs of explosive aggression; the same docile and restricted approach found to be dominant in his perceptual reactions is thus analogously disrupted by disintegrated behavior when the strain of coping with the task becomes too great.

In his responses to the Thematic Apperception Test, Bob showed the same cautious, unimaginative, and careful approach that he displayed in the interviews and on the other cognitive tests. He tended to be preoccupied with the details of the pictures rather than being ready to let go and tell a story. We find references to "nice, clean boys," and to "smart men who can get through life pretty easy." He says in response to a picture which shows white and Negro children playing together, "If I saw all the others playing with a nice Negro boy, I guess I would too." This quotation shows that the basis of Bob's prejudice is mainly conformity. From his other responses to the test, as well as from the interview, it seemed to be evident that a further contributing factor is his desire to overcome his weakness.

In the light of our assumption, developed elsewhere (18), to the effect that there is a correspondence between such social factors as the type of discipline used at home and the way children approach perceptual stimuli, it may be of interest to refer to a few points from the interview with Bob's mother. As far as Bob's upbringing is concerned, his mother seems to be defensive: "He rather had to be forced to do things—to eat and go to bed and go to sleep. He isn't so willing to cooperate." All kinds of measures were used to make him cooperative. "When he doesn't come home in time—if he is more than fifteen minutes late, he can't go next time with that boy when he wants to. . . . I am forever after him. Personal appearance, too. I think we do nag him for that."

Asked about her own upbringing, the mother says: "I wouldn't disobey, oh boy! I feel that way right now (*about parents*). I can't get my children to obey like that." She descibes her own mother as follows: "She was a good little German woman, busy having children. . . . She was very strict, I should say." Her father is described as follows: "He was German, too. All my grandparents were born in Germany. He was the strict one. A hard-working man, had

---

[7] The ages of the children given in this paper are those at the time of the clinical explorations. The experimental data referred to here were gathered more than one year later.

definite ideas and you couldn't change him. They were good, honest people." (Father too severe?) "Yes, I really felt so. I guess he really couldn't help it, though. Gosh! We couldn't do anything, we didn't have any privileges. . . . All our folks were for morality, didn't drink or go to night-clubs and things. My husband's parents were strict with him. He was kept in the yard until he was twelve years old."

Bob's mother verifies our description of his aggressive behavior: "He really gets mad, wild. He just stamps off, is mean, hateful in his talking, but it doesn't last long. He's just like his father that way." She further substantiates our assumption about his dependency: "I notice him. He follows the boys he is with whether they are good or bad. It's a problem of choosing friends, I think."

All this indicates that Bob may have been under great pressure during his childhood. His mother's insistence on quick obedience and his ensuing fear of punishment may well have led him to handle situations in an abbreviated and stereotyped manner. This is, as mentioned above, a frequent contributing factor in the patterns found among our rigid, prejudiced group to which Bob belonged.

It is of interest to note that Bob also shared with others of our rigid children some constitutional weakness. This may be another factor contributing to their rigidity. Bob's mother told us that he was "premature one month, so he wasn't strong and had a slow start." Phyllis Greenacre (27) has emphasized the fact that premature children lack the necessary equipment to cope to a satisfactory degree with the requirements of the initial stage of their lives. She assumes that this, along with unfavorable factors in the social environment, occasions increased tensions and inadequate mastery of life. In a similar vein, our interviewer remarked that Bob always appeared to be tired and undernourished and that a physical checkup uncovered a state of serious anemia. His mother told us, further, that he was always a "cry-baby" and that he had pneumonia when he was two years old. Physiological insufficiency together with harsh discipline at home may go a long way in explaining the oversimplified, rigid, and often panicky form of reaction found in Bob.

Now we turn to the case of Joan, a twelve-year-old child with an extremely low questionnaire-score on ethnic prejudice. Her more informal remarks about social issues revealed great flexibility, openmindedness, tolerance, permissiveness, and the attempt to weigh all aspects of the matters presented. Even her remarks about Hitler were more restrained, qualified, and less aggressive than those of most of the other children: "Well, he wasn't exactly the kind of man you would want to rule your country. I guess he wasn't the right kind of man to rule any country." Her open-mindedness and inclusiveness were expressed in her suggested remedy for conflicts between different countries: "Oh, we would visit one another's countries and study more about them." She was inclined to say positive things about everybody and everything. Asked about Negroes, she referred to a ". . . lady who has become very famous, she taught school . . . and she brought a lot of education to this country." She thought one ". . . might study them and give them a chance to prove that they are equal by giving them better schools and better places to live." She was against segregation of whites and Negroes. "I don't think it's quite right, because they are human and like us except for their color."

The pupils Joan liked were "ones that seem to get along with everyone, good in their school work." The absence of any fixed set was especially apparent in her answer to the question, "What would be the best job for a man?" She replied: "Well, that just depends on what he is fit for. The job he can do best probably. . . ." To the question, "What would be the worst job for a man?" she replied, "Well, a person that probably couldn't do a job and happened to be put in the wrong place and if it was serious it might take other people's lives." She did not mention a specific job as good or bad but gave a broader definition which provided latitude for a number of variables which had to be considered. To the question, "What do you want to be when you grow up?" she answered: "I don't know exactly now. But I think it's going to have to do with animals." Again, there is no need to give too definite an answer.

Joan had difficulty in expressing aggression against anybody except herself. To the question: "How would you change yourself if you could?" she answered with a longer list of desired traits than most of the children: "Oh, try to behave better, try to get along better with my friends, be able to play better in sports, oh, be able to get better grades; just be able to get along." In the light of available objective evidence, this self-perception was faulty only in that it minimized Joan's real assets.

In the experiment with the slowly emerging numbers she made the right guesses relatively early, close to the average of the unprejudiced and generally flexible group. She was somewhat cautious in making these early guesses, however. This caution is rather characteristic of unprejudiced children, who in general seem better able to accept ambiguity instead of having immediately to transform it into something definite, as do many of the prejudiced. (The total number of hypotheses given in response to ambiguous stimuli tends to be larger for the prejudiced than for the unprejudiced.)

In spite of her caution in the face of ambiguous figures, Joan responded very easily to changes in the stimulus configuration. This distinguished her from Bob, who lacked her flexibility and, though cautious most of the time, on occasion became extremely incautious.

Joan showed considerable aptitude in remembering a list of words without making errors. In spite of the unusual precision of her whole performance, she saw no necessity for sticking to the original order of words in her recall, however. During the entire series of experiments she was rather critical of her own performance.

In the Luchins type of experiment involving water-container problems (38) which Rokeach (51) adapted for these children, Joan very quickly found the set necessary for solving the original tasks; what is more, she was also quick in solving further tasks in this context by switching to the short-cut which becomes possible at this later stage rather than clinging rigidly to the method established at the beginning.

On the concept-formation test mentioned before, Joan's performance was very different from Bob's. She started with a good but not fully adequate hypothesis. When corrected once by the experimenter, she stopped altogether for ten minutes. This was most unusual for the group as a whole. On the basis of observations in a variety of situations, we found that such pausing and thinking was more likely to occur in unprejudiced than in prejudiced children, however. When unprejudiced children were blocked, they waited and reconsidered the problem, whereas the prejudiced rushed into random activities or gave up the problem altogether. Joan had the independence to remain in the suspense of thinking in spite of some pressure on the part of the experimenter toward action. After pausing for ten minutes, she found the right solution without any further trial and error. Whereas Bob made fifteen rather random corrections, apparently without any over-all hypothesis, Joan made only three corrections in all. Whereas Bob did not repeat his original good hypothesis but repeated a poor hypothesis four times, Joan repeated a good hypothesis only twice and never made a poor one. In all, she thus received a much higher ranking on the quality of her performance than did Bob.

Joan had in common with Bob a certain cautiousness and lack of readiness for adventure in her approach to problem solving. This was further manifested in her relatively descriptive approach on the Thematic Apperception Test. Here a comparative lack of initiative was again common to both. However, Joan's performance was much the superior of the two and showed much higher flexibility.

These similarities and partial differences recur in a somewhat analogous manner in the patterns of aggression exhibited by Joan and Bob. Their similarity lies in the fact that both Bob and Joan repressed aggression. The difference lies in the strength of aggression, which was much greater in Bob, as manifested in his fits of rage and in an extreme rejection of people. More rigid defenses were necessary to keep this aggression down. Joan's aggression was of a mellower quality, as witness a genuine love for her parents and the acceptance of other people in general. Whatever aggression might be present in Joan, she was unable to verbalize save against herself. Had her aggression been given freer expression, she might well have been more imaginative.

That Joan's aggression was in reality mild rather than just being repressed was revealed in her deep acceptance of parents and people, a fact supported by all the indirect and direct material, including the interview with the parents. There was, in fact, a very permissive and affectionate atmosphere in her family. Bob repeated his submission to, and rebellion against, stern parental authorities in his approach to perceptual stimuli, whereas Joan had a flexible relation to both parental and stimulus authorities.

Bob was on the whole an example of a more cautious and conservative type of a prejudiced boy whose approach to social and personal issues had been mainly governed by conformity. Another twelve-year-old boy, Jerry, represented the near-psychopath type of prejudiced boy whose outstanding characteristics are recklessness and aggressiveness, with conformity taking a second lead. His performance on the perceptual and cognitive experiments thus showed more consistently an adventurous and uncautious approach than that of Bob. In response to the ambiguous stimuli he immediately made a large number of guesses, many of them altogether on the wrong track, but he got the right solution earlier than Bob. In his approach to the concept-formation task he made approximately as many random arrangements and corrections as Bob, with an even larger total number of hypotheses. Four of these hypotheses were good and six were bad, but both types were repeated frequently by Jerry. Unlike Bob, he did not get any final solution. (Only nine children of the total group of forty-four who were given the test did not reach the right solution.) The over-all rating of the quality of his guessing was, however, not any better than that of Bob.

Clinically, Jerry exhibited a pattern closer to the fascistic or pre-fascistic type than did Bob. About his choice of a profession he said, "I like adventure. I intend to be a policeman when I grow up, on the homicide squad. That has been my ambition for a long time." In discussing his friends in the neighborhood, he manifested marked contempt for those he considered weak: "There is one around the corner that's a softy. There is another boy twelve years old. He's a softy too. Anybody can take him." The only time Jerry exhibited any affect during the interview was when he talked about the necessity of wearing glasses, expressing his concern that this might interfere with his being taken into the police force. He showed open rejection of people, including his parents. He rejected his parents mainly because they were old. (Actually his parents were much older than the parents of his classmates.) He showed contempt for his father because "he has to take pills all the time. He could only eat milk; he has a milk stomach. . . . I take after my dad in temper. He has a vile temper." About girls Jerry said, "They are gold-diggers," and a perfect friend was "somebody that doesn't tell things behind your back." At the same time this boy was much concerned with conventional values. For instance, he felt very defensive about his family's not having a car and said quite formally, "Circumstances forced us to sell our car." In discussing his wish to be a policeman, he stated, "People look up to you and it gives you a good feeling."

The mixture of recklessness and aggressiveness, on the one hand, and fear and anxiety, on the other, further became apparent in Jerry's Thematic Apperception Test stories. We found a number of aggressive themes. However, Jerry alternated between rushing into these themes, telling them with a high degree of confidence, and the excessive use of such words as "probably," "well," "maybe," coupled with a tendency to modify and change his plots and a readiness to take back what he had said.

A General Rigidity Scale and Its Relationship to Patterns of Perceptual Outlook.—In connection with the discussion of their approach to perceptual and cognitive tasks, it may be of interest to consider briefly the standing of Bob, Joan, and Jerry on a scale designed to measure general personality rigidity.[8]

We find both Bob and Jerry agreeing with a number of items representing a rigid, white-black approach to life. Whereas Joan disagreed, both of the boys agreed with the statement: "There are just two kinds of boys, the regular guys and the no-goods." (Of the whole group of 300, 70 per cent of the prejudiced and 45 per cent of the unprejudiced children agreed with this statement.)

Bob's perseveration and rigidity were revealed in his agreement with the following statements: (a) "A person should always stick

---

[8] This scale was developed in 1945 and 1946 as part of our project on Social Discrimination in Children. The writer is indebted to Murray E. Jarvik and Milton Rokeach for their assistance. A monograph describing in greater detail this and other scales used in the project, as well as the results obtained from three hundred to six hundred preadolescents and adolescents, is in preparation.

to a decision he makes." (Of the prejudiced children 50 per cent and of the unprejudiced children 45 per cent agreed with this statement.) (*b*) "Order and cleanliness are just about the most important things in life." (About half of all the children agreed.) (*c*) "There is only one right way to do anything." (Of the prejudiced children 73 per cent and of the unprejudiced children 56 per cent agreed.) (*d*) "Take care of the pennies and the dollars will take care of themselves." (About 60 per cent of all the children agreed.)

In the same vein, Bob disagreed with this statement: "It does a kid good to be lazy once in a while." (Only about 30 per cent of the children disagreed with this statement.)

Bob's hierarchical conception of human relations is expressed in his agreement with the following statements: (*a*) "Parents should always tell the children what they should do." (Of the prejudiced children 36 per cent and of the unprejudiced children 24 per cent agreed.) (*b*) "The world would be perfect if we could put on a desert island all the weak, crooked, and feeble-minded people." (Of the prejudiced children 45 per cent and of the unprejudiced children 22 per cent agreed.) (*c*) "Appearance usually tells us what a person is really like." (Of the prejudiced children 66 per cent and of the unprejudiced children 58 per cent agreed.)

Bob's underlying aggression is revealed in his agreement with such items as: (*a*) "Criminals should be more severely punished." (About half of the children agreed.) (*b*) "Brothers and sisters are more trouble than fun." (Of the prejudiced children 35 per cent and of the unprejudiced children 26 per cent agreed.)

Jerry checked many of the above items representing conventional values which Bob checked, and in addition he subscribed to a number of items expressing a less conventional and more fascistic ideology with which Bob disagreed. Examples of such items are: "People who are leaders are usually born to be leaders and the others are born to do what the leaders say." "It would be better if the teachers would be more strict." "A good leader should be strict with the people under him in order to gain their respect." (One third to one half of the children subscribed to these items.)

With only a small minority of the children, Jerry subscribed to items which express superstition, such as: "The position of the stars at the time of your birth tells your character and personality." (Only 12 per cent of the prejudiced and 8 per cent of the unprejudiced subscribed to this statement.)

Jerry also subscribed to statements which express a self-defensive attitude and pride: "An insult to a person's honor should always be punished," and "It is best never to admit defeat." (Of the prejudiced children 42 per cent and of the unprejudiced children 31 per cent agreed with the latter statement.)

Jerry's antifeminine attitude led him to subscribe to items like the following: "Girls play up to teachers and that is why they get better grades," and "Boys should play only with boys; only a boy can understand a boy." (Only 27 per cent of the prejudiced and 18 per cent of the unprejudiced children agreed with the latter statement.)

In many ways Jerry was even more rigid than Bob. He agreed that: "It is best to have regular hours for everything," and "It is best to do some things at the same time and in the same way each day." (Approximately half of the children agreed with these two statements.)

Jerry's readiness for adventure and quick judgment were expressed in his agreement with such items as: "It is best for a person to make up his mind quickly," and "It is usually pretty easy to judge other people." (Approximately one third of the children agreed with the first item, and predominantly the prejudiced children agreed with the second.)

With a minority of the children, Jerry further subscribed to the item: "If everything should change, things would be much better." (Only 33 per cent of the prejudiced and 23 per cent of the unprejudiced agreed.)

The last three items indicate an affinity with haphazard action and chaos, often found, as in Jerry, in combination with extreme rigidity. This combination is revealed not only in Jerry's pattern of response to the rigidity scale but also in his perceptual and cognitive problem-solving approach.

Joan's emotional and cognitive flexibility, which has been revealed in the clinical data as well as in her problem-solving approach, was also expressed in her disagreement with most of the items indicating rigidity and in her agreement with such items as: "It is interesting to be friends with someone who thinks or feels differently from the way you do," or "It feels good to stand up against a group and defend someone who has been picked on."

It is noteworthy that the frequency of agreement with the items which are designed to measure rigidity, egocentrism, externalization, and the tendency to dichotomize decreases significantly with age. The developmental argument can be called upon here to point toward the emotional and intellectual immaturity of the prejudiced child. The items which correlate with prejudice are the same as those to which the younger children subscribe more often than do the older ones. Some of the trends which are connected with ethnocentrism are thus natural stages of development which have to be overcome if maturity is to be reached. There is a surprising similarity between the tendencies found in our prejudiced children and those described by Piaget (44, 45) as the chronologically earlier stages of the moral and intellectual outlook. Since we are fortunate enough to have Piaget's views described in greater detail in this symposium by Wayne Dennis (Chapter 6), we do not need to elaborate further on this comparison.

In going back to our main line of argument, we may repeat briefly that Bob's and Jerry's rigidity in approaching perceptual and cognitive tasks was found to correspond with a high standing on a scale measuring rigidity in different spheres of life. The reverse picture holds for Joan.

Though Bob and Joan and Jerry showed some consistent differences in their social, emotional, and cognitive outlook, such clearcut separation does not hold to the same degree in all cases. Another boy, Dick, who was also high on prejudice but who differed somewhat in his personality makeup from Bob and Jerry in the direction of being more manipulative and exploitive rather than conformist and aggressive showed at the same time less rigidity in his perceptual reactions. The protocol of his responses to the emerging numbers was barren, but he recognized the final numbers not later than average. On the concept-formation task he also performed quite well, and he showed only a mild degree of rigidity on the water-container experiment. Thus, in Dick the in-group vs. out-group dichotomy does not go with an unusual degree of rigidity in the total personality makeup and in the cognitive approach.

On the other hand, we also find unprejudiced children who show relative rigidity in their perceptual approach. This may be due either to an atypical general rigidity of personality or to an increased anxiety and a blocking on the tasks concerned, these tasks being often less congenial to unprejudiced children than they are to the prejudiced.

In this group we found an unprejudiced girl, Pat, whose poor performance was probably mainly due to a lack of interest in this aspect of reality, since her orientation was mainly toward people. Personality consistency in Pat's case was clearly disrupted; the general quality of her performance in social and human tasks did not agree with the low performance level on simple cognitive tasks. In most cases of this kind, however, a more detailed phenomenological analysis of the cognitive approach, especially in tasks of higher sophistication, revealed features which go quite well with the over-all clinical picture. For examples of apparent or real disruption of personal consistency on a much broader scale, it may suffice to point to well-known examples of creative men in whom intellectual or artistic achievement has served as a compensation for a barren and restricted life lacking in emotional maturity.

Form and Content

The traditional concepts of "form" and "content" are notoriously relative and of a shifty meaning. Yet they will prove very useful in rounding out our discussion. Without attempting to make a sharp distinction between them, we will include under "content" such issues as attitude toward parents or authority in general, generalized motivational tendencies like aggression or dependence, such instinctual realities as heterosexual or homosexual development, and social adjustment. By "form," on the other hand, we shall understand the different ways in which such motivational categories are handled. Here we are thinking mainly of the defense mechanisms which determine the differential destiny of sex and aggression. Related to the defense mechanisms and also subsumed under formal categories are the general perceptual and cognitive modes or styles in the approach to the social and object world, as discussed in this chapter, and finally the linguistic or related semantic properties of statements [9]

Form Less Subject to Censorship Than Content.—It is the writer's opinion that relationships can be ascertained between the contentual and formal aspects of behavior in spite of the complexities involved. These relationships are especially important in personality studies in well-developed cultures, where it is usual for many motivational tendencies to be modified and distorted under the impact of external and internal censorship. It will be maintained here that the formal elements of personality style, since they are not as directly threatening as its content, are not subject to censorship in the same manner as is content and that they, therefore, can be used as powerful tools in diagnostic procedures. The above-mentioned study on mechanisms of self-deception, as well as some of the later evidence cited, seems to suggest that such formal style elements as exaggeration, easy generalization (as contrasted with salient specificity), intolerance of ambiguity, and the like may be of greater penetrating power within the personality, more nearly alike on the surface and at greater depth, and thus of greater generality and greater diagnostic validity than such content elements as, say, sex, aggression, the Oedipus complex, and the like.

---

[9] While in the present section linguistic properties as related to content are brought into the picture in a merely casuistic manner, a number of more precisely defined formal linguistic accompaniments of certain content elements in Thematic Apperception Test stories will be presented in a separate publication.

Whereas in our discussion the relations between form and content concerned have so far remained more or less implicit, we will now conclude with an attempt to make some of these relations explicit, thereby summarizing our findings and adding some new material. All this seems integral within the framework of our symposium. Not only has the perception of each individual a formal side all its own which is a reflection of his total personality, but by virtue of the possibility that peculiarities of perceptual style may be less subject to repression they may furnish substantial cues for the intuitive perception as well as the more explicitly cognitive diagnosis of these total personalities by others.

The theoretical introduction to this paper was concerned in a general way with the problem of how certain motivational tendencies may be camouflaged from being perceptible by others behind a façade of phenotypically opposite character. Next we discussed a number of concrete examples of formal characteristics which help us to discern whether a certain social façade or verbal statement is representative of, or else compensatory to, the social realities and the dynamics of motivation. Among the major formal cues used in the interpretation of such phenomena were, more specifically, the following: exaggeration; absoluteness of emphasis; intolerance of ambiguity; the predominant use of the extreme values of what actually are continua; such inconsistencies as are found in the comparisons of general with specific features of behavior or of verbal statement, or in the comparison of responses to direct with those to indirect questions; the occasional breaking through of a pattern of denial; deviations from the perceptions, from the concepts, and from other answers which constitute the norm for the group as a whole; stereotypy; concreteness; small range of variability in response; repetition; and all manner of rigidity. Gordon Allport (4, p. 132), in discussing the work on self-deception described above, states that, if it is extended, "it may not be too much to hope that psychologists will one day produce a 'Guide to Rationalizations and Projections' to assist users of personal documents in discovering those passages in which the narrator is, in the narrow and specific sense of the term, deceiving himself."

Closeness of Opposites.—We had found, in the work referred to, that in self-description a statement is often indicative of its opposite. Closeness of opposites emerged, on the basis of several of our studies, as one of the general formal principles in personality organization. One may trace back to psychoanalysis the original realization of the possibility that apparent opposites may be psychologically closer together and more apt to combine with each other in the same subject than any of them would with an intermediate position along the same scale. To be sure, in psychoanalysis this pattern is discovered primarily in the field of the instincts and the emotions, and mainly through the phenomenon of ambivalence. Conscious love of extreme and exaggerated intensity is viewed by the psychoanalyst with the same suspicion as are extreme feelings of hate. On the basis of more strictly psychological evidence, we must now proceed from the emotional to the perceptual-cognitive sphere and include with the dynamically interchangeable opposite extremes such pairs of formal classifications as extreme rigidity and extreme fluidity, extreme abstractness and extreme concreteness, extreme subjectivity and extreme objectivity, and so forth.

Form and Content in an Experiment on Memory.—The existing relationships between more specific motivational contents and their formal accompaniments may be illustrated by the following example. In an experiment on memory distortion (18), it was found that those of the children who recalled mainly the aggressive aspects of a story that had been told to them tended to show also a series of formal features, especially a tendency to alternate between rigid stimulus-boundness (for example, literal repetition of certain phrases) and a complete neglect of the stimulus in favor of purely subjective fantasies. A selective memory for aggressive content was here combined with poor form; the latter consisted either in an overcautious, segmentary, and rigid approach or else a disintegrated and chaotic one; sometimes one and the same child manifested both patterns in alternation or in a variety of bizarre combinations.

More research will be necessary before we may be enabled to tell what kind and degree of aggression are apt to sharpen our cognitive tools and what kind is likely to diminish or destroy our ability for cognitive mastery. On the basis of data from different contexts, the present writer is inclined to think that it is the destructive, not ego-integrated contents and forms of aggression which go with poor cognitive mastery; true to the principle of the closeness of opposites, extreme degrees of repression of aggressive tendencies may not be much better; it will likely be the milder and ego-integrated varieties of aggression that will be found most closely connected with increased cognitive capacity.

Form and Content in Projective Tests: Case Material and Statistical Results.—In proceeding to an analysis of the interrelationships between motivational content and cognitive form found in projective material, we may begin by adding a further example on the topic of aggressive preoccupation just discussed. The Thematic Apperception Test stories of an extremely prejudiced preadolescent boy, Karl, who was one of the subjects of the Adolescent Growth Study, were concerned with murder and gore to a much greater extent than is usual in stories of children of his age. More specifically, the implicit recurrent theme in his stories seemed to be that neither the role of the aggressive man nor that of the passive one is workable. The man who is passive and in possession of some fortune is usually attacked in some surprising way—from behind or while asleep—and is destroyed. The aggressive man, on the other hand, is regularly caught by the police and sentenced to life imprisonment at least, though more often he is executed in the electric chair. In one of these stories the "crooked place was turned into a big Safeway store," a clear revelation of Karl's deep-seated longing that all the dangerous men should be removed and that he should be allowed to be passive and surrounded by food, without fear of aggression and the ensuing necessity for being aggressive himself. This was also the way he imagined girls to live. Though the girls in the stories were in the more enviable position, even they were not always safe. In almost every one of his stories Karl mentioned food and money.

Of the two types of men, the passive and the aggressive, Karl really felt closer to the former. In one story he described in detail how a passive boy always was being hit by a tough boy who "had taken exercises from a guy that helps you make muscles." We thus have evidence of insecurity about masculinity and of feminine identification; the latter is also manifested in the occurrence of many phallic symbols and castration threats and in Karl's apparent embarrassment about his body build and genital organs. In a story in which he described a swimming scene, he was careful to point out that the boys had swimming suits under their clothes and thus did not have to strip naked. Karl's stories were not only exaggerated versions of the stories common among the prejudiced boys in general but were also similar in some ways to the stories of overt homosexuals.

The formal correlate to this pattern of content in Karl's stories was as follows. His narration was long and flowing, an uninhibited and uncontrolled stream of free association. We note here a kind of fluidity which goes with a low form level. The stories were neither coherent nor structured, and what seemed like imagination was really a kind of ruminative repetition of the same scenes over and over again. The repetitiveness extended even to such details as numbers. The stories were, furthermore, utterly unrealistic as far as general probability was concerned; they were full of bizarre elements and they strayed away to a marked degree from the subject matter of the picture which, after the first few sentences, was frequently lost from sight entirely.

Karl's perceptual outlook was thus upon a world which, on the one hand, was full of aggressive men and other dangers, although it offered, on the other, an abundance of food and other infantile gratifications; quite fittingly this content went with a lack of grasp of reality and of logical consistency so far as the formal level was concerned. The connecting link was a general immaturity which extended to content and form.

An as yet not fully published statistical analysis of projective material on extremely prejudiced and extremely unprejudiced adult women done in collaboration with Suzanne Reichard (15, 48) yielded findings of a similar kind. In the Thematic Apperception Test stories there were significantly more acts of destructive aggression, such as killings, rape, etc., in the stories of the prejudiced group as contrasted with milder forms of aggression, such as quarreling, in the stories of the unprejudiced group. Prejudiced women significantly more often than unprejudiced women, perceived parental figures as unloving and punitive rather than as benevolent, and they made significantly more frequent reference to supernatural forces. On the formal side it may be said that the prejudiced women made much greater use of moralistic terms, such as "bad," "good," "criminal," and the like, than did the unprejudiced. The former tended to view people from an evaluative, distal point of view rather than from a motivational, central one.

On the Rorschach Test the same prejudiced group showed some tendency toward poorer form level and more rigidity than the unprejudiced. The results have further indicated that "prejudiced subjects tend to be less productive mentally, less responsive emotionally, and less original than unprejudiced subjects. They tend to be more inhibited and more compulsively overmeticulous" (48).

The problem of the affinity of certain content and form elements in the Thematic Apperception Test stories first became fully clear to the writer some time ago in the context of a number of longitudinal case analyses undertaken at the Institute of Child Welfare of the University of California (13, 15, 16). The approach has not at present reached the quantitative stage of evaluation. Thus, the following listing of patterns is based on an inspection of case material rather than on statistically conclusive findings.

The content of the Thematic Apperception Test stories of a twelve-year-old boy, Tom, revealed an ambivalent preoccupation with the problem of male authorities. In many of his stories total submission, to the point of self-destruction, was advocated; it was not the authorities but rather the victim of coercion and deprivation who was considered the culprit.   In a few stories there was an indication that achievement—for instance, becoming a famous surgeon—would be the solution of the authority problem.   We find, furthermore, on the content side a frequent mention of money and possessions.

As to form, Tom's stories were of good quality, realistic, and of high logical consistency.   There was good intellectual penetration of the problems involved without, however, much sign of imagination or familiarity with the world of fantasy.   Further characteristics of his stories were frequent expression of doubts and suggestions of alternative stories.

The very few stories in which Tom expressed aggression against male authorities were made unreal by an introductory remark that what was to follow dealt with a picture rather than with reality; these stories were somewhat more incoherent, less logical, and less realistic than those in which no aggression of this kind occurred.   They did not, however, tend to become particularly improbable; they were, rather, real life put into the garb of fiction.

Tom not only repressed his hostility against his father but also his strong love for his mother.   In a story about a mother and her baby, the baby came too close to the railing of a balcony, fell off, and was "crippled for life. . . . Something happened to its leg."   Here is still another type of formal element than those discussed so far; it may be called the mechanism of "symbolic translation."   From the total context of Tom's stories the assumption may be ventured that the balcony stands for the mother, and coming too close to the mother implies the danger of being crippled.   The ensuing ambivalence, especially toward the father figure, seems to be connected with alternative formulations and ramifications.   Thus, in one of the stories which started with the statement, "This is the picture of a woman," we were told that the husband had been shot.   Quite in contradiction to this version—and contradictions were very rare in this boy's stories —we heard two sentences later that "The husband wasn't killed— just wounded—and unconscious."   Tom apparently did not dare to kill the husband of the woman.   On the other hand, the hostilities were there.   And he corrected himself again by saying, "He was wounded very badly, however."   Considering both content and form, a highly developed compulsive syndrome, quite unusual for this age, must be assumed in Tom.

One of the classmates of Tom also showed a great deal of hostility toward his father, although on a more immature level.   In one of his

stories he described in the following circumstantial—not to say high-
flown—style the death of a husband: "Something dear to her left
her in a very drastic way."

In a third boy in the same group the love for the mother was more
uninhibited; it was expressed directly as well as indirectly, orally as
well as genitally, with the husband left out completely most of the
time. At the same time the rich, undisciplined, yet high original
fantasy indicated the prevalence of the dream world. Though the
stories were unrealistic, they suggested the potentiality of great
creativity. Whether these creative fantasies and unconscious resources will be channeled into real achievement and a better grip on
reality or whether they will disrupt the integration of this boy's personality will depend on forces favorable or unfavorable to the development of his ego strength.

The stories of still another boy in this study, the last to be mentioned here, showed a passive sensuousness combined with a great
deal of expansion on concrete and palpable impressions such as the
enjoyment of a landscape, of the act of smoking, of resting, and of
related physical sensations. His stories neither posed nor solved big
or dramatic problems nor did they show a flight into imagination.
On the content side we find this boy passively, and seemingly without conflict, oriented toward men. It was the men in his stories who
gave affection and who took care of children. One father took care
of thirty children. On the basis of all his stories, the assumption that
this boy may become an overt homosexual does not seem too far-
fetched. Though Thematic Apperception Test stories of overt homosexuals seem to show an orientation toward sensation, they are by no
means always as well organized and lacking in bizarre elements as
are the stories of this boy.

We may conclude the discussion of form and content in the
Thematic Apperception Test stories with a reference to two contrasting girls. In one case there was an uncontrolled, undisciplined,
unimaginative flow of free associations combined with an infantile
preoccupation with the mother, especially with feeding and being fed.
The stories of the other girl showed a creative, subtle and differentiated view of human relations combined with a genuine interest in
love and heterosexuality, in spite of overtones of an undue attachment
to the father.

Form and Content in Interviews of Ethnocentric Subjects.—
Relationships between form and content similar to those just discussed
were also found on the basis of interviews (1, 17). On the content
side, in ethnically prejudiced adults and children certain attitudes such

as overt acceptance were found coupled with underlying aggression toward parents, authority, and society in general, fear of weakness, passivity, and sex impulses. Rigid forms of defenses have to be erected against many of these tendencies; one of these is the mechanism of projection, by which much that cannot be accepted as a part of one's own ego is externalized. As discussed in the previous section, a pervasive rigidity and intolerance of ambiguity, as well as a distortion of reality, are among the further formal characteristics related to the contents just mentioned.

Whether such tendencies as aggression or homosexuality are accepted or not determines the forms of their expression. Aggression which is accepted will be relatively mild, tending toward regular release and toward verbal expression, and it will be directed toward the objects which were the original targets of the aggression. Unaccepted aggressive tendencies, on the other hand, will assume a destructive and explosive character and will tend toward all-or-nothing expressions.

The inability to accept one's self will in due course interfere with an adequate perception of one's self and of others. Instead of viewing himself as a unit in continuous development, the prejudiced subject tends to offer apologetic "explanations" in terms of unscrutinized accidental, hereditary, or physical factors. The inability to accept one's self finally altogether prevents a social-psychological outlook and leads to an unscientific or pseudo-scientific outlook on man and society. Furthermore, when one's fears and wishes are not integrated and not modified by reality, in the way indicated in the first part of this chapter, autistic thinking in goal behavior and an unrealistic view of means-end relationships results.

On the preceding pages an effort was made to provide material and discussion by which the relationship between such contents as aggression or the attitude toward authority, on the one hand, and the formal elements of the perceptual and cognitive approach, on the other, would be approached in some detail. It may be emphasized, again on the basis of case studies rather than of conclusive quantitative evidence, that most of those among the prejudiced subjects who performed well on some of the relatively simple perceptual and cognitive tasks discussed in this chapter nonetheless revealed signs of rigidity in their performance. Here we are reminded of the frequently noted technological abilities of the German Nazis. Those in this group who performed poorly often were found to slide into overfluidity and disintegration. The unprejudiced subjects, on the other hand, tended more toward creative flexibility, although they sometimes displayed utter blocking in the solving of the tasks concerned.

Many other findings and topics could, and perhaps should, be discussed under the heading "form and content." The writer is thinking primarily of such findings in clinical psychology as those by Rapaport (47) Schafer (55), and others concerning the relationships between Rorschach and intelligence test results, on the one hand, and life histories and patterns of emotional and cognitive disturbances, on the other; also of some of the developmental problems discussed by Heinz Werner (66), Piaget (44, 45), Charlotte Bühler (7), and others involving the establishment of developmental stages from the point of view of both content and form. Unfortunately, a comprehensive discussion of all this cannot be attempted in the present framework.

This Chapter may conclude with a few remarks on possible trends in future research. The study of personality in its relation to perception must certainly be considered a going concern. We shall probably have a period in which every imaginable perceptual experiment will be related to every imaginable personality variable. Often these two types of variables will not be clearly differentiated from each other, either theoretically or experimentally; the fact that sometimes the same term is used for both will give the a priori illusion that real relationships are involved.

In spite of such pitfalls—pitfalls which endanger undertakings in every field of research which becomes fashionable—we can look forward with confidence to important discoveries along these lines. Probably they will come especially from those who attempt to formulate and clarify their problems thoroughly before rushing into the computing of correlations. All this will necessitate the increasing use of identical sets of subjects for a variety of assessments, as was first attempted at the Harvard Clinic (42) and the OSS Assessment Center during the war (43). The choice of the subjects will have to be carefully determined both from the sociological and the psychological point of view, since now we are less concerned with normative and more concerned with differential problems.

A great need, and one which the writer hopes will be filled in the future, is that of research on children. On the motivational side, the original drives are most openly accessible and least modified by cultural pressures in the child. Considering that children present such excellent opportunities for direct verification of the basic assumptions of psychoanalysis, it is surprising that so few of the psychoanalytically oriented psychologists have worked with them. Furthermore, an analysis of the more complex perceptual and cognitive approaches to reality can be achieved with the least interference in children. The ready accessibility of different developmental stages leads most naturally to an analysis of the forms of cognition; this has been attempted with particular penetration by Werner (66) and Piaget (44).

Thus it would seem that the most promising avenue of approach should be the one which combines emphasis on general personality variables, both motivational and cognitive, with an emphasis on developmental aspects. In any event there can be little doubt that this is a most challenging period in psychology, a fact to which this symposium has given eloquent testimony.

BIBLIOGRAPHY

1. ADORNO, T. W., FRENKEL-BRUNSWIK, ELSE, LEVINSON, D. J., & SANFORD, R. N. *The authoritarian personality.* New York: Harper & Bros., 1950.
2. ALLPORT, G. W. Attitudes. In C. Murchison (ed.), *A handbook of social psychology.* Worcester, Mass.: Clark University Press, 1935.
3. ALLPORT, G. W. *Personality.* New York: Henry Holt & Co., Inc., 1937.
4. ALLPORT, G. W. *The use of personal documents in psychological science.* New York: Social Science Research Council, 1942.
5. BRUNER, J. S., & GOODMAN, C. C. Value and need as organizing factors in perception. *J. abnorm. soc. Psychol.*, 1947, **42**, 33-44.
6. BRUNSWIK, E. *Wahrnehmung und Gegenstandswelt.* Vienna: Deuticke, 1934.
7. BÜHLER, CHARLOTTE. *From birth to maturity.* London: George Routledge & Sons, Ltd., and Kegan Paul, Trench, Trubner & Co., Ltd., 1935.
8. CATTELL, R. B., & TINER, L. G. The varieties of structural rigidity. *J. Personal.*, 1949, **17**, 321-41.
9. ERIKSON, E. H. Childhood and tradition in two American Indian tribes: with some reflections on the contemporary American scene. In C. Kluckhohn & H. A. Murray (eds.), *Personality.* New York: Alfred A. Knopf, Inc., 1948.
10. FENICHEL, O. *The psychoanalytic theory of neurosis.* New York: W. W. Norton & Co., Inc., 1945.
11. FRANK, L. K. Projective methods for the study of personality. *J. Psychol.*, 1939, **8**, 389-413.
12. FRENKEL-BRUNSWIK, ELSE. Mechanisms of self-deception. *J. soc. Psychol.* (*SPSSI Bulletin*), 1939, **10**, 409-20.
13. FRENKEL-BRUNSWIK, ELSE. Psychoanalysis and personality research. In G. W. Allport (ed.), Symposium on psychoanalysis as seen by analyzed psychologists. *J. abnorm. soc. Psychol.*, 1940, **35**, 176-97.
14. FRENKEL-BRUNSWIK, ELSE. Motivation and behavior. *Genet. Psychol. Monogr.*, 1942, **26**, 121-265.
15. FRENKEL-BRUNSWIK, ELSE. Dynamic and cognitive categorization of qualitative material. I. General problems and the thematic apperception test. *J. Psychol.*, 1948, **25**, 253-60.
16. FRENKEL-BRUNSWIK, ELSE. Dynamic and cognitive categorization of qualitative material. II. Interviews of the ethnically prejudiced. *J. Psychol.*, 1948, **25**, 261-77.
17. FRENKEL-BRUNSWIK, ELSE. A study of prejudice in children. *Human relations*, 1948, **1**, 295-306.
18. FRENKEL-BRUNSWIK, ELSE. Intolerance of ambiguity as an emotional and perceptual personality variable. *J. Personal.*, 1949, **18**, 108-43.
19. FREUD, ANNA. *The ego and the mechanisms of defence.* London: Hogarth Press, Ltd., 1937.
20. FREUD, S. Formulations regarding the two principles in mental functioning (1911). In *Collected papers.* ("The International Psychoanalytical Library," No. 10.) London: Hogarth Press, Ltd., 1925. Vol. IV.

21. FREUD, S. Instincts and their vicissitudes (1915). In *Collected papers*. ("The International Psychoanalytical Library," No. 10.) London: Hogarth Press, Ltd., 1925. Vol. IV.

22. FREUD, S. Repression (1915). In *Collected papers*. ("The International Psychoanalytical Library," No. 10.) London: Hogarth Press, Ltd., 1925. Vol. IV.

23. FREUD, S. The ego and the id (1923). In *Collected papers*. ("The International Psychoanalytical Library," No. 12.) London: Hogarth Press, Ltd., 1927. Vol. XII.

24. FREUD, S. An autobiographical study (1924). In *Collected papers*. ("The International Psychoanalytical Library," No. 26.) London: Hogarth Press, Ltd., 1935. Vol. XXXVI.

25. FROMM, E. *Escape from freedom*. New York: Rinehart & Co., Inc., 1941.

26. GOLDSTEIN, K. The problem of the meaning of words based upon observation of aphasic patients. *J. Psychol.*, 1936, **2**, 301-16.

27. GREENACRE, PHYLLIS. The predisposition to anxiety. In S. S. Tomkins (ed.), *Contemporary psychopathology*. Cambridge, Mass.: Harvard University Press, 1943.

28. HARTLEY, E. L. *Problems in prejudice*. New York: King's Crown Press, 1946.

29. HARTMANN, H. Ichpsychologie und Anpassungsproblem. *Internat. Zeitschrift für Psychoanalyse und Imago*, 1939, **24**, 62-135.

30. JAENSCH, E. R. *Der Gegentypus*. Leipzig: Barth, 1938.

31. JONES, H. E. The adolescent growth study. *J. consult. Psychol.*, 1939, **3**, 157-80.

32. JONES, H. E. *Development in adolescence: approaches to the study of the individual*. New York: Appleton-Century-Crofts, Inc., 1943.

33. KARDINER, A. *The individual and his society*. New York: Columbia University Press, 1939.

34. KLUCKHOHN, C. *Mirror for man*. New York: McGraw-Hill Book Co., Inc., 1949.

35. KRETSCHMER, E. *Körperbau und Charakter* (15th & 16th ed.). Berlin: Springer, 1942. Chap. xiii.

36. LEWIN, K. *Vorsatz, Wille, und Bedürfnis*. Berlin: Springer, 1926.

37. LINTON, R. *The cultural background of personality*. New York: Appleton-Century-Crofts, Inc., 1945.

38. LUCHINS, A. S. Mechanization in problem solving: the effect of *Einstellung*. *Psychol. Monogr.*, 1942, **54**, No. 6, 1-95.

39. MEAD, MARGARET. *Male and female*. New York: William Morrow & Co., Inc., 1949.

40. MURPHY, G. *Personality: a biosocial approach to origins and structure*. New York: Harper & Bros., 1947.

41. MURRAY, H. A. The effect of fear upon estimates of the maliciousness of other personalities. *J. soc. Psychol.*, 1933, **4**, 310-29.

42. MURRAY, H. A. *Explorations in personality*. New York: Oxford University Press, 1938.

43. OSS Assessment Staff. *Assessment of Men*. New York: Rinehart & Co., Inc., 1948.

44. PIAGET, J. *The child's conception of the world*. New York: Harcourt, Brace & Co., Inc., 1929.

45. PIAGET, J. *The moral judgment of the child*. London: Kegan Paul, Trench, Trubner & Co., Ltd., 1932.

46. POSTMAN, L., BRUNER, J. S., & McGINNIES, E. Personal values as selective factors in perception. *J. abnorm. soc. Psychol.*, 1948, **43**, 142-54.

47. RAPAPORT, D., SCHAFER, R., & GILL, M. *Manual of diagnostic psychological testing: personality and ideational content*. New York: Macy Foundation, 1946. Vol. II.

48. REICHARD, SUZANNE. An analysis of Rorschach data of prejudiced and unprejudiced subjects. *J. Orthopsychiatry*, 1947, **18**, 280-86.

49. ROGERS, C. R. *Measuring personality adjustment in children nine to thirteen
years of age.* Teach. Coll. Contr. Educ. No. 458. New York, 1931.

50. RÓHEIM, G. *The origin and function of culture.* Nerv. ment. Dis. Monogr.
Series No. 63. New York, 1943.

51. ROKEACH, M. Generalized mental rigidity as a factor in ethnocentrism. *J.
abnorm. soc. Psychol.*, 1943, **48**, 259-78.

52. RORSCHACH, H. *Psychodiagnostics.* Berne: Hans Huber, 1942.

53. SANFORD, R. N. The effects of abstinence from food upon imaginal processes:
a further experiment. *J. Psychol.*, 1937, **3**, 145-59.

54. SANFORD, R. N., ADKINS, M. M., et al. *Physique, personality, and scholarship.
Monogr. Soc. Res. Child Develpm.*, 1943, **8**, No. 1.

55. SCHAFER, R. *The clinical application of psychological tests.* New York: International Universities Press, Inc., 1948.

56. SCHELER, M. *Wesen und Formen der Sympathie* (2d ed.). Bonn: F. Cohen,
1923.

57. SEARS, R. R. Experimental studies on projection. *J. soc. Psychol.*, 1936, **7**,
151-65.

58. SHERIF, M. *The psychology of social norms.* New York: Harper & Bros.,
1936.

59. STAGNER, R. Fascist attitudes: their determining conditions. *J. soc. Psychol.*,
1928, **1**, 405-25.

60. STERN, W. *General psychology from the personalistic standpoint.* New York:
The Macmillan Co., 1938.

61. SYMONDS, P. M., & JACKSON, C. E. An adjustment survey. *J. educ. Res.*, 1930,
21, 321-30.

62. THURSTONE, L. L. *A factorial study of perception.* Chicago: University of
Chicago Press, 1944.

63. TOLMAN, E. C. Cognitive maps in rats and men. *Psychol. Rev.*, 1948, **55**, 189-
208.

64. TRYON, CAROLINE McC. Evaluation of adolescent personality by adolescents.
Monogr. Soc. Res. Child Develpm., 1939, **4**, No. 4, 85-114.

65. TRYON, CAROLINE McC. *California adjustment inventory.* Berkeley, Calif.:
University of California, 1939.

66. WERNER, H. *Comparative psychology of mental development* (rev. ed.). Chicago: Follett Publishing Co., 1948.

INDEX OF NAMES

(A page number in boldface indicates a bibliography reference; "n" indicates a footnote reference.)

INDEX OF SUBJECTS